Getting Started With EEG Neurofeedback

A NORTON PROFESSIONAL BOOK

Getting Started With EEG Neurofeedback

SECOND EDITION

John N. Demos

W. W. Norton & Company
Independent Publishers Since 1923
New York • London

Note to Readers: Standards of clinical practice and protocol change over time, and no technique or recommendation is guaranteed to be safe or effective in all circumstances. This volume is intended as a general information resource for professionals practicing in the field of psychotherapy and mental health; it is not a substitute for appropriate training, peer review, and/or clinical supervision. Neither the publisher nor the author(s) can guarantee the complete accuracy, efficacy, or appropriateness of any particular recommendation in every respect.

Previous edition published as GETTING STARTED WITH NEUROFEEDBACK

Cover images were created with BrainAvatar Software by BrainMaster Technologies, Inc.

For information about special discounts for bulk purchases, please contact W. W. Norton Special Sales at specialsales@wwnorton.com or 800-233-4830

Manufacturing by Versa Press
Book design by Vicki Fischman
Production manager: Katelyn MacKenzie

Library of Congress Cataloging-in-Publication Data

Names: Demos, John N., author.
Title: Getting started with EEG neurofeedback / John N. Demos.
Other titles: Getting started with neurofeedback
Description: Second edition. | New York : W.W. Norton & Company, [2019] | Revision of: Getting started with neurofeedback. c2005. 1st. ed. | "A Norton Professional Book." | Includes bibliographical references and index.
Identifiers: LCCN 2018024792 | ISBN 9780393712537 (hardcover)
Subjects: LCSH: Biofeedback training. | Neurofeedback.
Classification: LCC RC489.B53 D45 2019 | DDC 615.8/514—dc23 LC record available at https://lccn.loc.gov/2018024792

W. W. Norton & Company, Inc., 500 Fifth Avenue, New York, N.Y. 10110
www.wwnorton.com

W. W. Norton & Company Ltd., 15 Carlisle Street, London W1D 3BS

1 2 3 4 5 6 7 8 9 0

Contents

Acknowledgments

I HAVE LEARNED SO MUCH from those I have taught and consulted with over the past 12 years. So many questions that need to be answered have been raised by my students and those seeking mentoring or consultation. Their needs have driven me to know and learn more—for that I thank them all.

I wish to thank Judy Crawford of the BCIA. Her listening ear has been invaluable over the years—I always look forward to our discussions on professional ethics and changes in the field.

Tom and Terri Collura have been supporters of my research. Terri seems to network with everyone in the entire field of neurofeedback and Tom manages to keep up with the exploding science behind neurofeedback. They have helped me and many others to stay afloat when things get tough.

There are others I would like to thank including Jeffrey Reich, Jeff Tarrant, Penijean Gracefire, Mark Smith, Donna Creasy, Robert Milicia, Nicholas Dogris, Derk Mulder, Andre Keizer, Dave Siever, Robert Thatcher, Joel Lubar, and Richard Soutar for their teachings, writings, practical help, and words of wisdom.

I had special help in creating the second edition. I would like to thank my secretary, Ada Brown, for handling much of the paperwork for the second edition that was required by W. W. Norton. Her help reminds me that I just cannot do it all. Kathy Gelineau was my editorial support agent who worked with me closely during the final review of the text.

I had two professional reviewers: Tom Collura offered me the encouragement I needed at the right time. Donna Creasy provided editorial advice and suggestions that were very important during the final editing. She has a long history of teaching and promoting neurofeedback in the field and in her community.

Last, I would like to thank my wife, Marge, for being patient with me when I was under pressure to finish the second edition.

Preface

GETTING STARTED WITH EEG NEUROFEEDBACK, second edition, is a major update to the first edition.The field of neurofeedback has exploded with new modalities such as Z-score training, 3-D standardized low-resolution electromagnetic tomography (sLORETA) imaging, and brain networks such as the default mode network (DMN) and training and brain networks. There is a growing interest in functional and structural neurology. There is a need to understand terms such as diffusion tensor imaging (DTI) and cross-frequency coupling (CFC). More and more licensed practitioners are reading articles published in peer-reviewed journals inside and outside the field of biofeedback. This edition includes well over 150 color images, many of which have been enhanced by the graphic artist Franco Guaglianone. Color images appear throughout the book and are not confined to a color insert.

Since the first edition was published in 2005, my clinic, Neurofeedback of Southern Vermont, LLC, has been accredited by the Biofeedback Certification International Alliance (BCIA) to teach their blueprint of knowledge. Consequently, the second edition reflects key topics from the BCIA curriculum. Additionally, I have been mentoring and consulting with countless practitioners and clinics that want to institute EEG neurofeedback training and become certified by BCIA as neurofeedback clinicians or technicians.

The goal of this book is not to prove that EEG neurofeedback is an effective treatment. The past 12 years have presented me with overwhelming evidence of the power of this modality. The history of biofeedback has been omitted from this edition as other books and many articles have thoroughly explored this topic. The second edition was written to help professionals get started by providing them with an overview of basic assessment methods and training interventions.

Getting started now in 2018 is much easier than it was for me nearly 20 years ago. For example, excellent books have been written, Z-score training has been completed, and automated symptom checklists based on brain maps are available. Newcomers to the field can become successful after a few short months of training, mentoring, and practice. Always keep in mind the importance of keeping up with the ever-expanding field of neurofeedback. There will be books and journals to read and workshops to attend. Becoming an expert requires more knowledge of the brain and the EEG than it did when the first edition was published in 2005. Consequently, the earlier chapters of this book simplify the entire process of doing EEG neurofeedback, whereas the later chapters explore topics that will be needed as one progresses in the field.

There are so many approaches and modalities within the field of neurofeedback and so much we can learn from the many experts in our field. It is my hope that in the future all licensed neurofeedback professionals will respect the work of others even if it is outside their own area of expertise.

Illustrations

FIGURES

Part III

Appendixes

CHARTS

Part I

Part II

Part IV

Part V

Part VI

Abbreviations

AC	alternating current
ADHD	attention-deficit/hyperactivity disorder
ANS	autonomic nervous system
A/T	alpha/theta
BA	Brodmann area
BASK	behavior affect sensation and knowledge
BCIA	Biofeedback Certification International Alliance
BDI	Beck Depression Inventory
BORTT	burst of rhythmic temporal theta
BWE	brain wave entrainment
CBF	cerebral blood flow
CC	corpus callosum
CEN	central executive network
CFC	cross-frequency coupling
CNS	central nervous system
CPS	cycles per second
CPT	continuous performance test
Cz	central position
DAN	dorsal attention network
DC	direct current
DMN	default mode network
DTI	diffusion tensor imaging

EDF	European Data Format
EEG	electroencephalograph
EKG	electrocardiogram
EMDR	eye movement desensitization and reprocessing
EOA	electro-ocular
fMRI	functional magnetic resonance imaging
GABA	gamma-aminobutyric acid
HEG	hemoencephalography
HPA	hypothalamic-pituitary-adrenal
HRV	heart rate variability
Hz	hertz
ILF	infra-low-frequency
Int'l	International
ISF	infra-slow fluctuation
ISO	infra-slow oscillation
LED	light-emitting diode
LH	left hemisphere
LORETA	low-resolution electromagnetic tomography
MRI	magnetic resonance imaging
mTBI	minor traumatic brain injury
μV	microvolt
NIR	near infrared
OCD	obsessive-compulsive disorder
PDR	posterior dominant rhythm
pEMF	pulsing electromagnetic field
PET	positron-emission tomography
PIR	passive infrared
PNS	peripheral nervous system
PTSD	post-traumatic stress disorder

qEEG	quantitative EEG
rCBF	regional cerebral blood flow
RH	right hemisphere
RIA	relaxation-induced anxiety
ROI	region of interest
SD	standard deviation
sEMG	surface electromyography
SMR	sensorimotor rhythm
SN	salience network
SPECT	single-positron-emission computerized tomography
SSRI	selective serotonin reuptake inhibitor
ST	skin temperature
SUDS	subjective units of distress
TBI	traumatic brain injury
TMJ	temporomandibular joint
VAN	ventral attention network

Getting Started With EEG Neurofeedback

Introduction

NEUROFEEDBACK ADDS A CLINICAL EDGE to traditional talk therapies and is rapidly becoming a state-of-the-art treatment for mental health issues. Modern computers and neurofeedback equipment have made it possible to view cerebral activity (electroencephalograph, EEG) and see how clinical symptoms are reflected in that activity. Because problematic activity can be targeted in specific brain areas, training the EEG (brain training) often results in symptom reduction—usually with no negative side effects. Fortunately, since the writing of the first edition of this book advancements in training and assessment software have simplified the process of learning neurofeedback.

Terms

EEG: A graphic display of the electrical activity of neurons in the form of brain waves with unique patterns.

qEEG: A quantitative statistical evaluation of amplified and filtered EEG data acquired from multiple electrodes placed on the scalp. The data are used to create brain maps. They can also be used for assessment and treatment planning, especially protocol development.

EEG neurofeedback/EEG biofeedback: Learning that uses special devices to provide instant feedback when the desired mental state is achieved. The computer-driven feedback may be auditory, visual, or tactile.

This book is written for:

1. Newbies: licensed professionals who are searching for information about neurofeedback and thinking about adding it to their practice.
2. Experienced providers: neurofeedback clinicians and technicians seeking to enhance their skills and learn more about the brain.

Common questions professionals have:

- How long will it take to learn enough to provide neurofeedback?
- How complicated is it?
- Can I use unlicensed staff to provide neurofeedback?
- Can it be used for all mental disorders?
- Does it work for everyone?

And here are the answers:
Neurofeedback . . .

- Cannot be learned in a weekend workshop: a four-day introductory workshop is the typical starting place.
- Cannot be handed over, 100%, to an unlicensed staff member. BCIA now has technician certification programs available for individuals working under licensed and certified professionals.
- Does not work with every client or patient, but it usually does improve symptoms and cognitive functioning.
- Should not be used by mental health professionals to treat physical conditions and diseases because it is outside the scope of practice for most of us. Neurofeedback has been useful in treating migraines, some seizure disorders, and other physical issues—but these should only be treated by experienced professionals acting with a medical doctor.

But neurofeedback . . .

- Is much easier to learn than when I wrote the first edition of *Getting Started With Neurofeedback* in 2005 because of significant advances in assessment and training software.
- Improves brain functioning and reduces symptoms in most clients. (An initial clinical assessment will help you document treatment efficacy and client readiness.)
- Can improve your health care practice in many ways:

- More is known now about successfully treating a wider scope of mental disorders using neurofeedback as an adjunctive therapy.
- Clients usually get faster symptom relief than with drugs or talk therapy alone.
- Many individuals become more available for talk therapy after their brains feel calmer.
- Using trained technicians can expand your clinical services.

ADVANCES IN ASSESSMENT

Brain imaging or mapping with quantitative EEG software often reveals how brain activity reflects clinical disorders. Brain mapping software works with assessment software.

Data acquisition for qEEG is usually accomplished with EEG recording caps or sometimes with individual electrodes. However, newer EEG caps and other recording devices have been designed that do not require gels or pastes. This time-saving development is a growing trend in the field of neurofeedback—and more alternatives are in the works.

MAJOR ADVANCES IN NEUROFEEDBACK TRAINING

Z-score neurofeedback training emerged over 10 years ago and rapidly became very popular among many professionals. In Z-score training, the individual's data are compared to statistical data from normative databases, matched by age and training condition (e.g., eyes open or closed). The clinician can easily read what's happening in terms of standard deviations from the norms and focus training on problematic issues. Before this, most training focused on amplitudes of the various bandwidths, but Z-score training allowed us to also look more easily at relationships between and among training sites. LORETA or sLORETA training is an expansion of Z-score work, allowing us to use cortical sites to affect what's going on beyond the cortex, in the deeper parts of the brain. Z-score training protocols are easy to set up and adjust—yet they perform hundreds of complex calculations instantly. Some clinics do almost all training with Z-score training protocols.

Protocol-generating software is a more recent development. Based on qEEG data and symptom information, this helpful software selects training locations and protocol designs. Although many of the protocol decisions are made by the software, its value also depends on clinician input about symptoms and diagnosis. Many clinicians appreciate the simplicity of this software, which allows very sophisticated neurofeedback training with relative ease.

THREE CRITICAL PRINCIPLES BEFORE YOU START

1. Licensed health care professionals bear the responsibility for clinical evaluations and guiding neurofeedback training. While BCIA certification is not a requirement (at least at this time, nor is a license to practice) it reflects a level of professional preparation and commitment.
2. Good EEG data are essential for both assessment (qEEG evaluations) and training. The clinician should inspect the data to ensure that they are free of artifacts (interference from factors such as muscle movement or electrical activity in the room). Accurate data provide the foundation for positive results.
3. Good clinical evaluation is critical before neurofeedback training begins, and monitoring changes in symptoms is a necessary element in the process. Symptoms can be tracked by clinical software (computer) or paper-and-pencil assessments. Quick assessments such as SUDS (subjective units of distress, rated 1–10) scaling questions can be helpful, but neurofeedback training is not guided by moods that wax and wane. Over the course of training, good standard assessments are important to track actual progress.

Here's an example of how easy it can be to set up a training protocol using the Z-score approach and my Jewel software:

1. Data (19 channels of EEG) are acquired and processed. Figure 1 shows a good sample of a clean recording.
2. A brain map is generated by the software, and symptoms are selected by the clinician, resulting in training sites being identified or highlighted as shown in Figure 2. (Auditory processing is selected in this example.) All of this is automatically uploaded into the software for training. The Jewel software also creates a treatment plan for clients to help them understand the neurofeedback training process.
3. An sLORETA Z-score training screen (Figure 3) shows live

Z-scores as they change during training (top part of screen). The lower part of the training screen shows 3-D images of the brain and 2-D flat brain maps for a visual review of what's going on electrically in the brain.

Figure 1. Good or Clean EEG Data

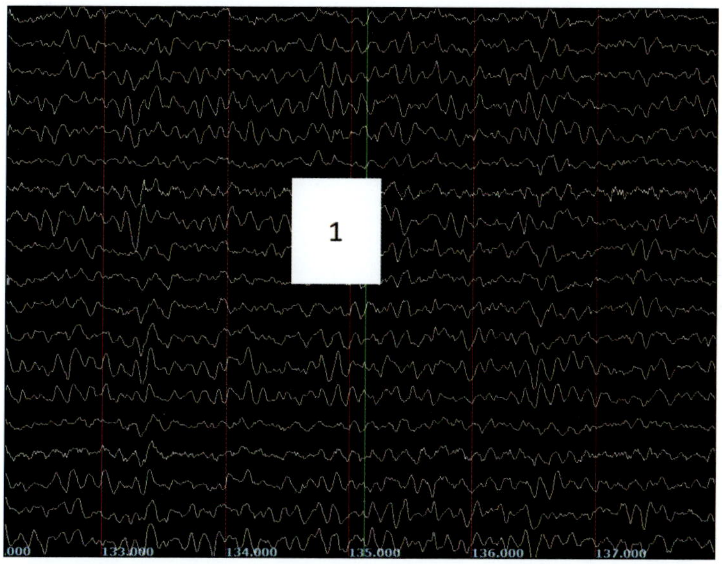

Figure 1 adapted from BrainAvatar software by BrainMaster Technologies, Inc.

Figure 2. Highlighted Sites

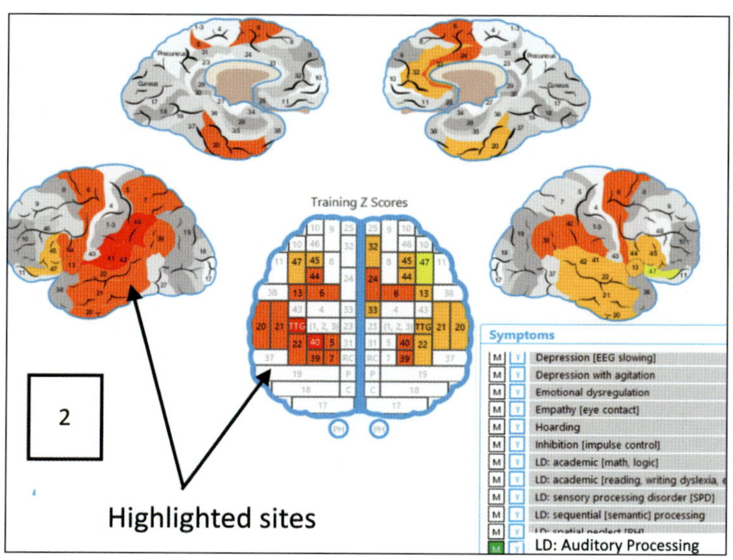

Figure 2 produced by Jewel database and Report Writer software

Figure 3. sLORETA Z-Score Training

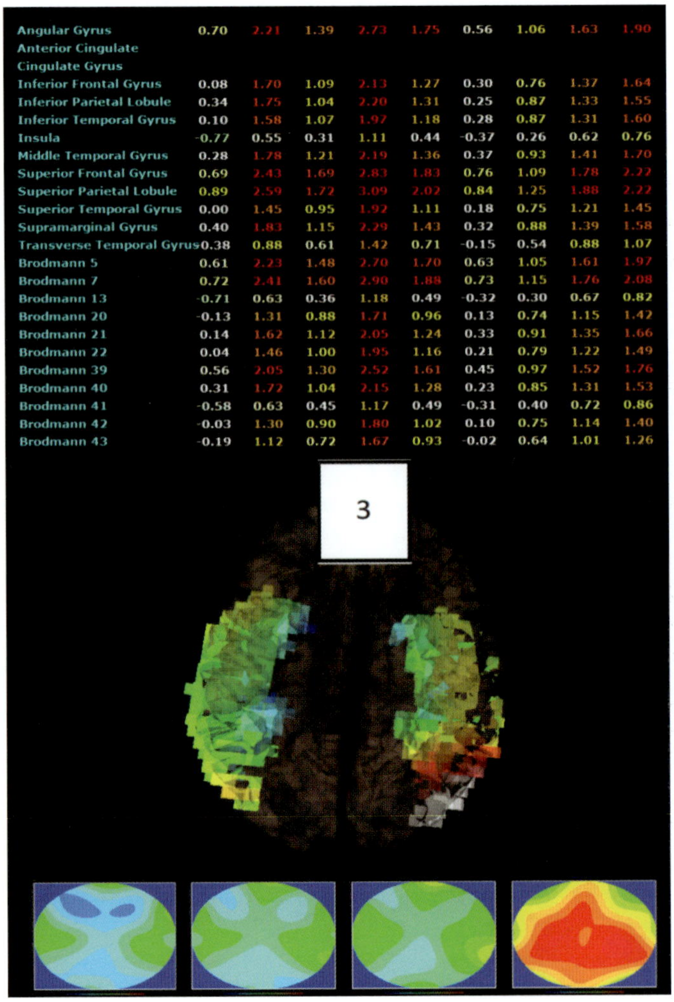

Angular Gyrus	0.70	2.21	1.39	2.73	1.75	0.56	1.06	1.63	1.90
Anterior Cingulate									
Cingulate Gyrus									
Inferior Frontal Gyrus	0.08	1.70	1.09	2.13	1.27	0.30	0.76	1.37	1.64
Inferior Parietal Lobule	0.34	1.75	1.04	2.20	1.31	0.25	0.87	1.33	1.55
Inferior Temporal Gyrus	0.10	1.58	1.07	1.97	1.18	0.28	0.87	1.31	1.60
Insula	-0.77	0.55	0.31	1.11	0.44	-0.37	0.26	0.62	0.76
Middle Temporal Gyrus	0.28	1.78	1.21	2.19	1.36	0.37	0.93	1.41	1.70
Superior Frontal Gyrus	0.69	2.43	1.69	2.83	1.83	0.76	1.09	1.78	2.22
Superior Parietal Lobule	0.89	2.59	1.72	3.09	2.02	0.84	1.25	1.88	2.22
Superior Temporal Gyrus	0.00	1.45	0.95	1.92	1.11	0.18	0.75	1.21	1.45
Supramarginal Gyrus	0.40	1.83	1.15	2.29	1.43	0.32	0.88	1.39	1.58
Transverse Temporal Gyrus	0.38	0.88	0.61	1.42	0.71	-0.15	0.54	0.88	1.07
Brodmann 5	0.61	2.23	1.48	2.70	1.70	0.63	1.05	1.61	1.97
Brodmann 7	0.72	2.41	1.60	2.90	1.88	0.73	1.15	1.76	2.08
Brodmann 13	-0.71	0.63	0.36	1.18	0.49	-0.32	0.30	0.67	0.82
Brodmann 20	-0.13	1.31	0.88	1.71	0.96	0.13	0.74	1.15	1.42
Brodmann 21	0.14	1.62	1.12	2.05	1.24	0.33	0.91	1.35	1.66
Brodmann 22	0.04	1.46	1.00	1.95	1.16	0.21	0.79	1.22	1.49
Brodmann 39	0.56	2.05	1.30	2.52	1.61	0.45	0.97	1.52	1.76
Brodmann 40	0.31	1.72	1.04	2.15	1.28	0.23	0.85	1.31	1.53
Brodmann 41	-0.58	0.63	0.45	1.17	0.49	-0.31	0.40	0.72	0.86
Brodmann 42	-0.03	1.30	0.90	1.80	1.02	0.10	0.75	1.14	1.40
Brodmann 43	-0.19	1.12	0.72	1.67	0.93	-0.02	0.64	1.01	1.26

Figure 3 adapted from BrainAvatar software by BrainMaster Technologies, Inc.
Z-Scores are derived from qEEG-Pro database

GETTING STARTED

1. Find a good four- or five-day comprehensive workshop authorized to teach the BCIA blueprint. The workshop should involve practicing with equipment.
2. Identify a mentor. Most newbies benefit from having an experienced mentor (either in person or over the internet), and 25 hours of mentoring are a requirement for certification.

3. Practice, practice, practice! Feeling competent takes practice. Colleagues who are also learning neurofeedback can be a great asset and professional support.

Adding neurofeedback to your practice requires a commitment to continue learning—through conferences, additional training workshops, webinars online, and reading. The rewards to you, the clinician, will quickly become apparent. Neurofeedback can be used to expedite change and to create transformations that are unlikely to occur through traditional talk therapies. Health care professionals who have added neurofeedback to their practices have usually found that it quickly became an indispensable part of their therapeutic toolbox.

The first part of this book provides an overview of the basic information needed to get started. After that, the content becomes more complex with additional information about the brain and the mechanics of protocols.

You can start with very simple Z-score-generated protocols that are easy to set up and run. Later on you can advance to other training modalities—the important thing is to get started. Neurofeedback is on the cutting edge of mental health treatment.

Part I: Getting Started With the Basics

Chapters

1

What Is EEG Neurofeedback?

ALMOST 60 YEARS AGO, scientists discovered the amazing plasticity of the brain—its lifelong capacity for growth and change. Our brains were designed to learn and master new challenges. Neurofeedback challenges the brain to greater efficiency and effectiveness.

Neurofeedback provides information to the trainee about the brain's rhythms and functioning in real time, as it is happening. It instantly relays information (feedback) about minute changes—informing the individual by sounds, graphics, or even vibrations. The brain seeks more of that stimulation and gradually changes its activity, providing the opportunity for change and growth. Neurofeedback training promotes efficiency in using the brain's energy resources and promotes self-awareness. EEG Neurofeedback is a form of biofeedback and is sometimes called EEG biofeedback.

Biofeedback is not a drug. Drugs work—or don't work—when they are taken. They work with or without conscious client cooperation. For example, if someone on the verge of a panic attack takes a benzodiazepine (e.g., Xanax, Valium, or Ativan), it will likely calm the individual within minutes. The change from panic to calm comes automatically. But the change is not permanent because no learning occurred—the brain did not learn how to behave differently on its own.

Biofeedback requires compliance: the trainee needs to sit, pay attention to the feedback (usually tones), and allow changes to happen—it is both active and passive learning. One cannot force the brain to change. Change begins with awareness. Neurofeedback is a form of experiential learning similar to playing music or driving lessons and not a single event. Also, trainees may be assigned homework that supports biofeedback learning.

EEG neurofeedback is a form of computer-guided learning; powerful instruments detect and then feed back timely information about the brain's electrical or metabolic fluctuations to the trainee. The goal of the feedback is to promote awareness that leads to functional changes. Neurofeedback is a *self-regulation* skill because trainees are empowered to regulate their own specific cerebral functions including EEG, event-related potentials, and slow cortical potentials, infra-slow frequencies and regional cerebral blood flow (rCBF).

Biofeedback training promotes a stronger sense of self because clients change themselves. It is theoretically intertwined with principles of behaviorism, including Ivan Pavlov's classical conditioning and especially B. F. Skinner's operant conditioning. Biofeedback always rewards the trainee—it never punishes.

In classical conditioning, Pavlov's dogs learned to salivate at the sound of a bell because meat and bell were introduced together. The meat was the unconditioned response (natural dog response) and the bell ringing was the newly learned conditioned response. How is biofeedback similar to classical conditioning? Biofeedback learning shares at least three important concepts with classical conditioning: generalization, extinction, and discrimination.

- *Generalization* means that the newly conditioned stimulus may be activated in more than one venue; for example, the dogs also salivated when hearing a church bell. Hence learning is not limited to strict experimental conditions. In biofeedback, the relaxation that is learned through instrumental learning in the office continues in real-life situations, and many other examples demonstrating generalization could be found.

- *Extinction* refers to the gradual loss of the experimental effect. In biofeedback, training is continued after goals have been met to ensure learning solidification. Hence extra training sessions are needed to prevent or limit extinction, similar to long-term depression.

- *Discrimination* means that the stimuli are customized to fit each subject's biological responses. Hence, experimenters did not salivate at the sight of meat, just the dogs. It is the same with EEG neurofeedback; reinforcement graphics and tones are in sync with the rhythmicity of the trainee's brain and not the clinician's brain.

Operant conditioning is a subconscious process that depends on a regular flow of naturally occurring events that can be reinforced the moment they occur. It is the foundation of all forms of biofeedback learning.

Consider the story of the professor whose students trained him with operant conditioning. The professor had the habit of pacing back and forth (right to left) while delivering his lecture. Each time he moved toward the right side of the room, the students paid rapt attention. Each time he moved to the left side of the room, they gradually paid less attention. By the end of the lecture hour, his shoulder was pressed against the right wall. What can we learn from the experiment?

1. The professor was unaware of the ruse (subconscious process).
2. Pacing back and forth was a naturally occurring event that could be reinforced.
3. Reinforcement occurred whenever the professor moved in the desired direction.
4. The professor wanted classroom attention, so he was engaged in the process.

How does this example relate to EEG neurofeedback? In Figure 1.1, EEG neurofeedback equipment tracks the rise and fall of brain waves. Brain waves are naturally occurring events; they fluctuate (rise and fall) outside of conscious awareness. Without instrumentation, changes to the brain's rhythmic patterns come indirectly or gradually through life experience, counseling, or education. With EEG neurofeedback instrumentation, changes follow a direct route. Reinforcing desired brain wave patterns,

Figure 1.1. Brain Rhythms and EEG Neurofeedback

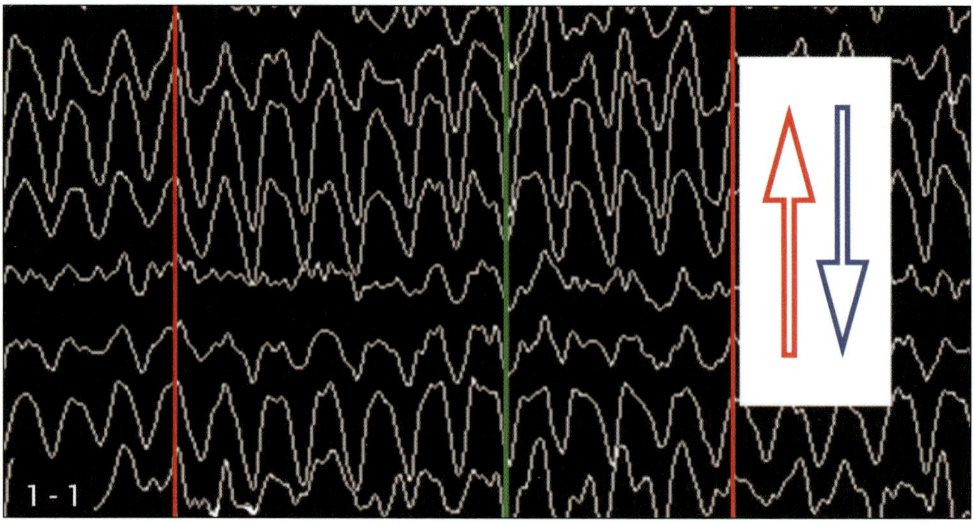

Figure 1.1 adapted from BrainAvatar software by BrainMaster Technologies, Inc.

in the exact moment they happen, is the fundamental principle behind EEG neurofeedback, a.k.a. operant conditioning. Feedback tones are recognized by the brain because they are in sync with the rhythmicity of the brain. In the same way, the rhythmic beat of an orchestra is detected by dancers, who move their bodies in sync with the music.

2

The EEG: The Brain's Electrical Signals

THE HUMAN BRAIN is the most complex known system in the universe, with a vast network of nerve cells that communicate. Messages flow from the brain to the body and back again in a mind-body connection (Pert, 1997). The brain communicates within itself and then interfaces with the outside world in many ways, including electricity. The goal of EEG neurofeedback is to tap into that electrical activity with the goal of enhancing learning, thinking, emotions, and behavior. The brain's electrical activity creates brain waves. An EEG can view those brain waves in action.

Figure 2.1 EEG

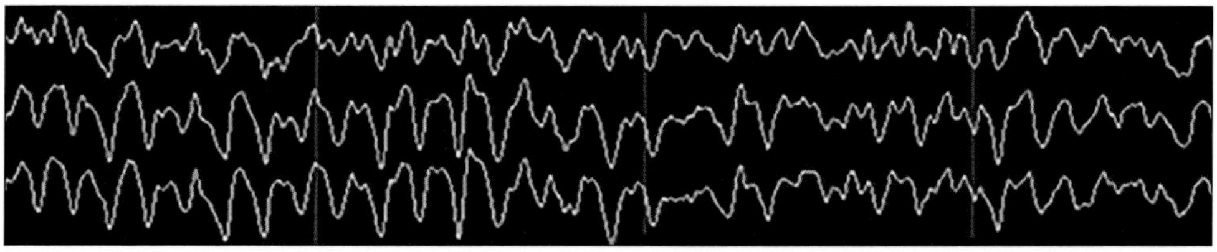

Two critical functions are directly related to the EEG:

1. Thalamic-reticular interactions
2. Pyramidal cells or neurons: the synapse

THALAMUS–TO–BRAIN STEM INTERACTION

The *thalamus* is a subcortical brain structure that processes all incoming sensory data, except for sense of smell. It reaches out to many brain structures, including visual, auditory, sensory, and motor areas. In tandem with the *reticular formation,* it keeps us alert and awake. Thalamic pacemakers regulate EEG rhythmic activity. Signals move upward toward the cerebral cortex, then back downward to the thalamus, over and over again (Figure 2.2).

Figure 2.2. Thalamic-Reticular Role in Generating EEG

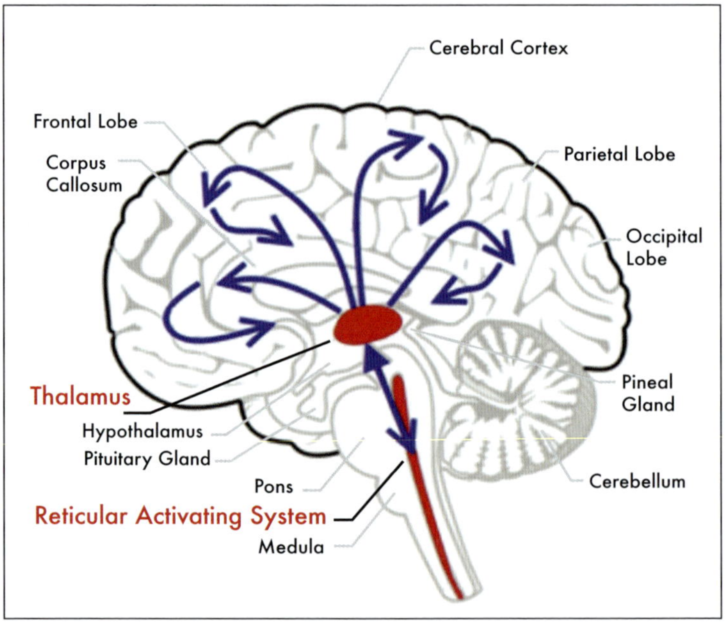

The EEG comes from the total rhythm caused by a large assembly of neurons. One sensor placed on the scalp can pick up a portion of this rhythmic activity at the cortical level. The information is then sent to an EEG amplifier that displays brain waves

MACROCOLUMN RESONANCE

But there's more: the signals that move upward and downward form columns of neuronal transmission. Columns of neurons resonate with each other. Columns that are closer to each other promote faster waves known as beta, whereas the columns that are farther apart from each other promote slower waves, such as delta and theta. The macrocolumn theory shows some of the complexity behind the EEG. The whole picture (Edmonds, 2015):

1. Brain waves start at the thalamus, when thalamic relay neurons repeatedly excite and then inhibit cortical interneurons, causing a cycle of communication between the thalamus and the cortex.
2. The rhythmicity of the EEG is regulated by thalamic pacemakers.
3. Neuronal pathways form columns that resonate with each other and influence EEG frequency.
4. Meanwhile, in the brain stem, the reticular formation may inhibit the thalamic cycle, which results in EEG desynchronization or lower amplitudes. If no inhibition takes place, then brain wave synchronization-desynchronization cycles occur according to thalamic control (Figure 2.3).

The reticular formation sends a continuous flow of impulses toward the cerebral cortex. It keeps the brain alert, awake, and ready to receive more information. "The outstanding feature of the reticular neurons is their far-flung axonal connections. . . . Such wide spread connections make reticular neurons ideal for governing the arousal of the brain as a whole." The reticular activating system is an "arm of the reticular formation." It filters out sensory data. For example, it can shut out sensory data in noisy and crowded environments to prevent sensory overload. The hypothalamus and other neuronal circuitry shut down the reticular activating system when it's time for sleep (Marieb, 1995, p. 402).

Damage to the brain stem (reticular formation) such as whiplash can result in symptoms such as difficulty focusing in crowded environments, poorly regulated sleep-wake cycles, and weak alpha-wave amplitude. Remember that thalamus and brain stem interactions are responsible for rhythmic EEG activity including, alpha (8–12 Hz). Consequently, training alpha in the occipital lobes with EEG neurofeedback equipment can help to restore healthy communication between the thalamus and the brain stem.

Figure 2.3. Synchronization of Cortical Columns

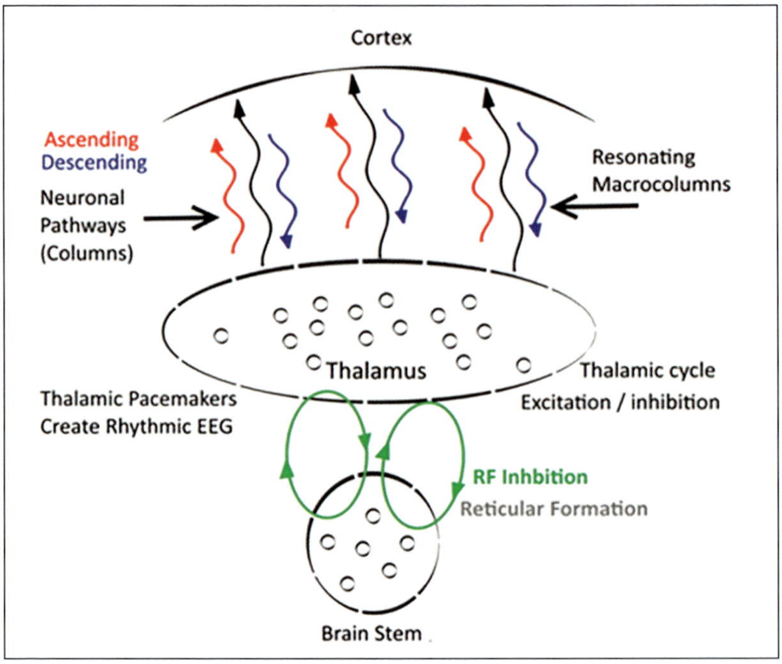

PYRAMIDAL CELLS AND THE SYNAPSE

The basic unit of the nervous system is the nerve cell, otherwise known as the neuron. The brain has billions of neurons with trillions of connections. Neurons are arranged in a complex yet well-defined circuitry that is only partially understood by modern science. Neuronal communication occurs throughout the nervous system. Many neurons in the central nervous system (CNS) are multipolar in design. For the purposes of our discussion, imagine a multipolar neuron on its side, stretched out from right to left (Figure 2.4). On the far right are the dendrites, which receive information and transfer it to the cell body, or soma. Next in line comes the axon: some axons are gray, whereas others are white. White axons are coated with myelin—hence the white matter of the brain. Myelinated axons transfer signals faster than unmyelinated (gray) axons. Myelination increases with maturation.

Most of the cell bodies are found within the CNS. The “little gray cells” that help detective Hercule Poirot solve the case are the cell bodies (soma)

Figure 2.4. Neuron or Nerve Cell Parts

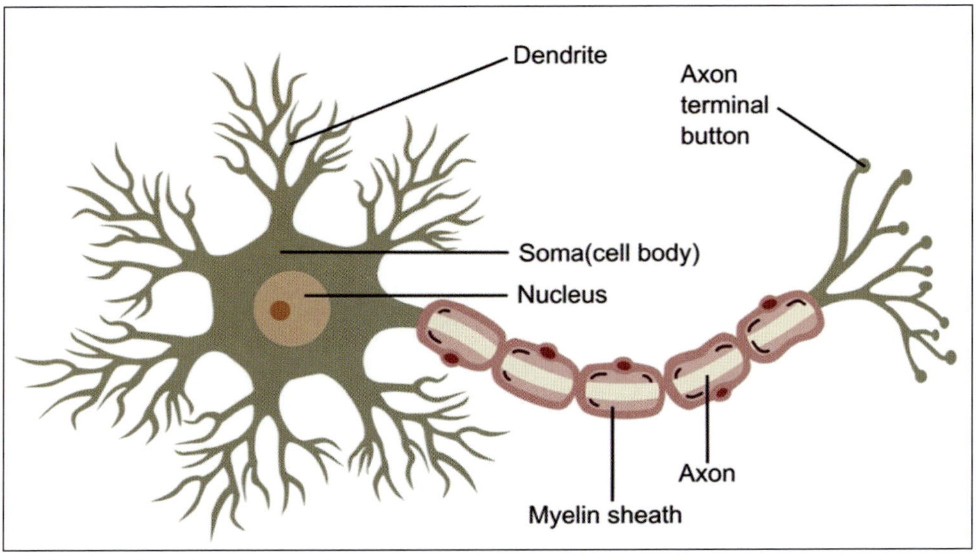

covering the outer cerebral cortex; these cell bodies have white myelinated axons extending beneath the surface. At the end of each axon branch is a terminal button (Figure 2.5) that is filled with neurotransmitters ready to be released for the purpose of activating or inhibiting adjacent neurons. The spaces (gaps) that separate axon terminal buttons from adjacent receptor dendrites are called synapses. Communication is one-directional.

Brain communication includes sensory, motor, and interneurons that build associations between neurons. Neurons in the brain operate like a complex subway system that makes both local and express stops. Nonpyramidal neurons make local stops, whereas pyramidal neurons (cells) carry the information over longer distances like an express train. This long-distance route starts at the hub or thalamus and travels up to the cortex and then returns. Nonpyramidal neurons may have an influence on pyramidal cell communication. Neurofeedback providers are mainly interested in pyramidal cells because they produce the electrical activity of the brain that creates the EEG.

Communication between neurons is an electrochemical event. A nerve impulse, also called an action potential, is an electrical charge that travels from the cell body toward the terminal buttons at the ends of the axons. A stimulated cell body sends a signal toward the terminal buttons. The

Figure 2.5. The Synapse

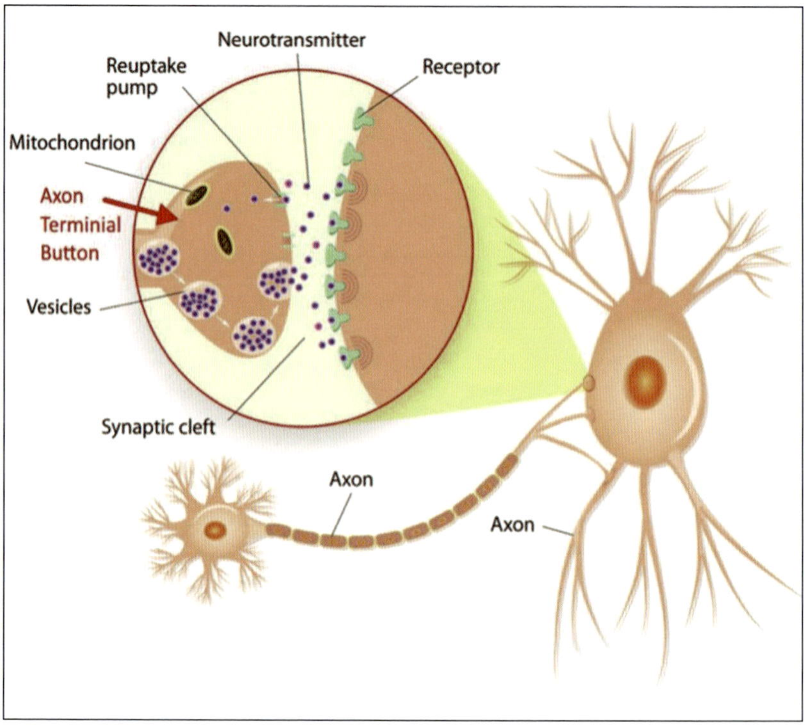

impulse travels along the axon in bucket-brigade fashion; each membrane has the job of stimulating the next membrane down the line. The whole process, known as depolarization, resembles a chain reaction. At this point the terminal buttons release neurotransmitters into the synapse, which are sent into the synaptic gap from the axon terminal button in order to excite dendrites located in adjacent neurons.

Dendrites from adjacent neurons pick up the message and try to keep the ball rolling, from neuron to neuron, until the reason for the initial impulse is accomplished. Sometimes an action potential starts and then quickly stops due to a weak signal. Consequently, it never reaches a threshold of power. Action potentials happen in an all-or-none fashion. Once an individual neuron has completed an action potential, it begins to repolarize in order to rejuvenate itself. The time period needed to do this is called a refractory period, in which no further communication can take place.

Brain waves are formed by a dual action—a push-pull process. A cycle starts when a terminal button releases the neurotransmitter from the vesicle sac into the synaptic cleft in order to excite the receptor in the adjacent neuron (see Figure 2.5). It ends when the process reverses due to an inhibitory response. Two terms define the process of making brain waves:

- *Excitatory* postsynaptic potential
- *Inhibitory* postsynaptic potential

Each dendrite of the adjacent neuron can be excited or inhibited by the release of a neurotransmitter. The inhibitory process is invoked by the release of an inhibitory neurotransmitter. Electrodes placed on the scalp measure electrical potentials in nearby cellular membranes. When the information coming from pyramidal cells is caused by synchronous excitation or inhibition, it results in large EEG amplitudes. Synchronization occurs when columnar pyramidal cells all have the same valence or charge. Note that brain waves are by-products of excitatory and inhibitory postsynaptic potentials and not measurements of action potentials.

Of course, the process of making brain waves as shown in Figure 2.5 above relies on both electrical and chemical actions. Neurotransmitters are the chemicals, including serotonin, dopamine, gamma-aminobutyric acid (GABA), epinephrine, and others. They are stored in numerous individual sacs, called vesicles, within axonal terminal buttons—ready to be released into the synapse. Once the neurotransmitter has done its job, it returns to the axon terminal button. Each button has channels that allow for the entry and exit of neurotransmitters. Prozac, Paxil, and Zoloft likely plug some of the channels in order to keep more serotonin in the synapse. Those drugs are known as selective serotonin reuptake inhibitors (SSRIs).

3

Bandwidths Measured by Frequency and Amplitude

THE ELECTROENCEPHALOGRAM (EEG) is a graphic representation of the electrical activity produced by the brain's pyramidal cells. Neurologists carefully observe the EEG (or brainwave morphology) for abnormalities that reflect clinical disorders. The raw EEG (Figure 3.1) is simple amplification of the brain's electrical activity.

Brain wave morphology refers to the unique shape or appearance that distinguishes one banded frequency from another in the raw EEG. Hans Berger named the first brain wave he identified "alpha" based on its shape. Normal and abnormal brain waves have a shape or morphology; Figure 3.2 shows additional raw wave morphologies.

Figure 3.1. Frequency (Hz) and Amplitude (μVs)

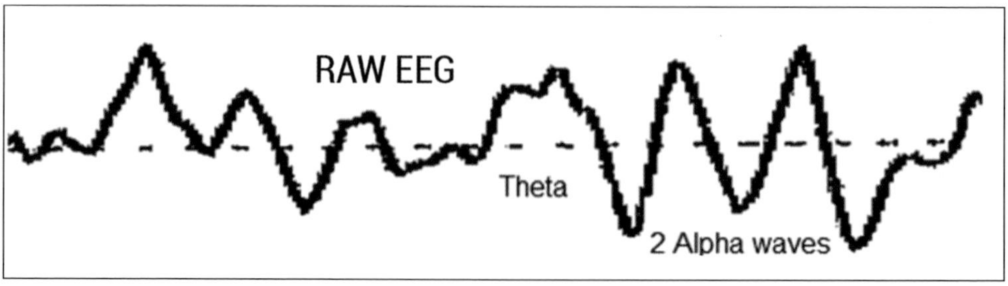

Figure 3.2. Normal Adult Brain Waves

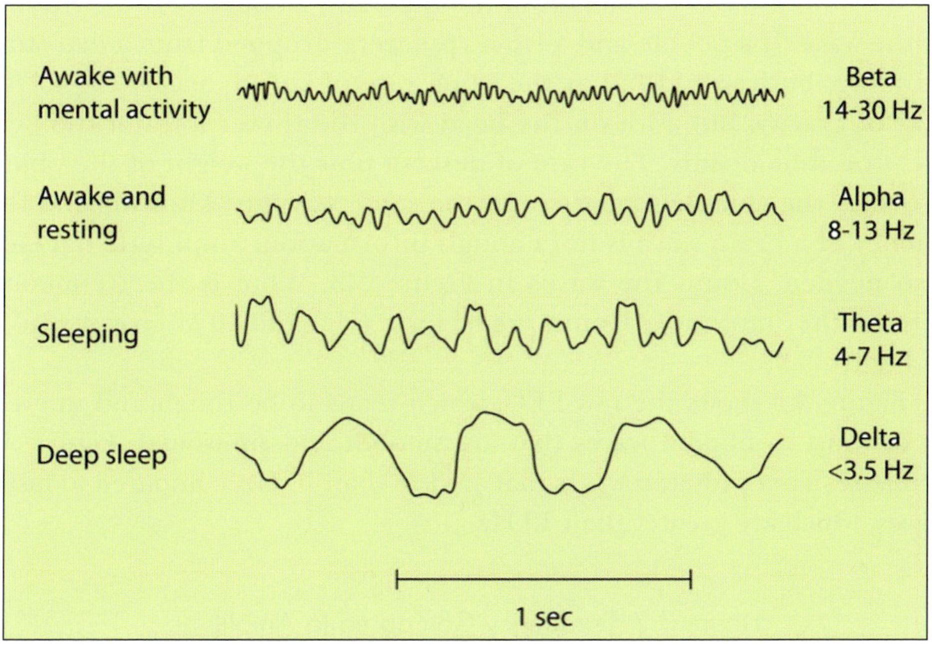

FILTERED EEG

Neurologists focus on brain wave morphology; neurofeedback practitioners focus on filtered or processed EEG after they have carefully reviewed brain wave morphology. EEG processing is accomplished by filters that define the EEG using frequency ranges such as Alpha (8-12 Hz) or Theta (4-8 Hz). Each filtered frequency range has an intensity, or amplitude, that is measured in microvolts.

Filtered—not raw—EEG is trained. Filters are needed to assess the EEG. To illustrate, before buying a steak it is inspected for quality and price. Each component part is examined: How much bone? How much fat? How much gristle? How red is it? The visual inspection looks at the whole and then the parts. Looking at the parts is similar to filtering. After the amplifier gathers the raw EEG, software separates it into filtered bandwidth ranges. Two basic metrics begin the filtering process:

- Frequency = speed, rhythm, hertz (Hz), or cycles per second (CPS)
- Amplitude = weight, force, the height of the wave, or microvolts (μVs)

Amplitude (*μV*) measures size and frequency (Hz) measures rate of speed; amplitude is the height of the wave and frequency is the rhythm of the wave. If a pebble and a flowerpot were dropped from a two-story building, both would fall at the same rate of speed, according to the laws of gravity. But a hit on the head with the flowerpot, not the pebble, would be deadly. The rate of descent plus the weight of the object provides the complete picture. In the same way, just knowing the frequency of a brain wave is not enough information; amplitude data are also needed. Count the waves in Figure 3.3. What is the frequency? What is the amplitude? Count the 6 Hertz (Hz) and 10 Microvolts (μVs) in Figure 3.3:

Figure 3.3 shows the raw EEG, which tends to be rough and uneven, in contrast to filtered waves that are smooth and sinusoidal. Figure 3.4 compares slower filtered waves that are less than 10 Hz, compared to faster waves, which are greater than 13 Hz.

Figure 3.3. Frequency Compared to Amplitude

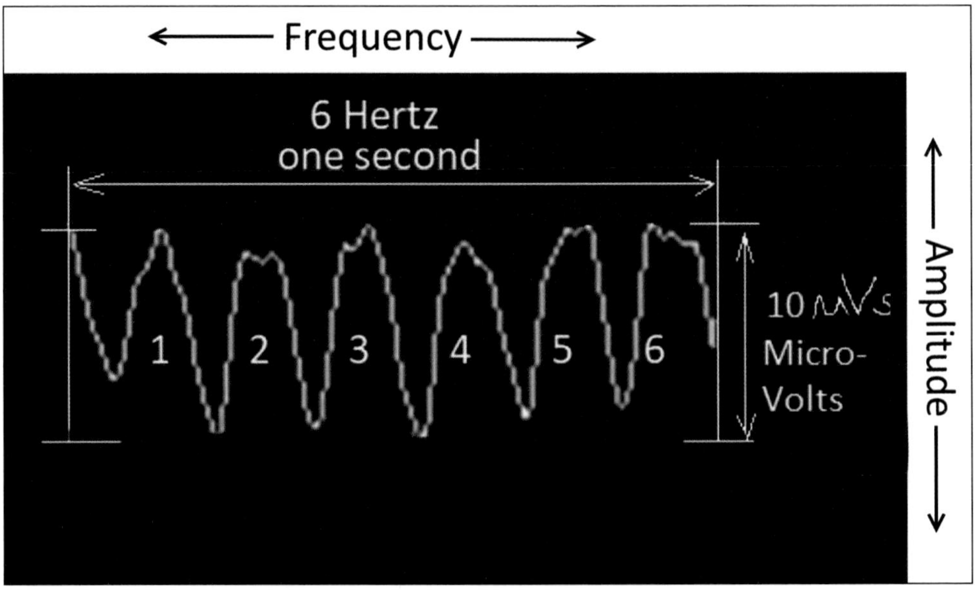

Figure 3.4. Faster Waves Compared to Slower Waves

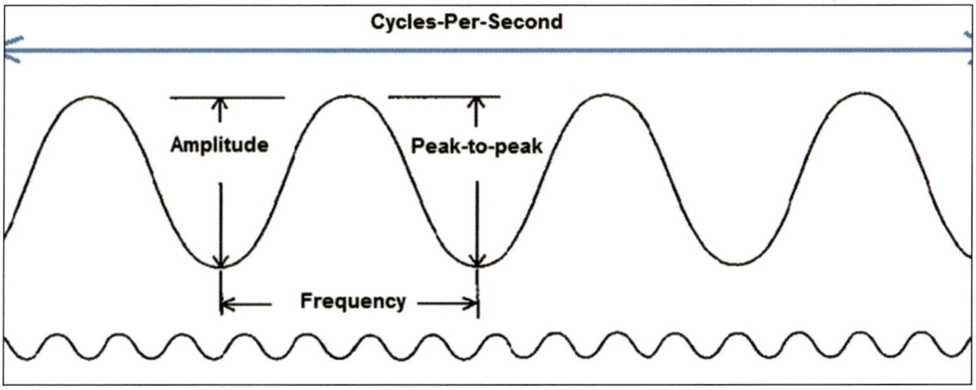

3.4: Count the 4 slow waves and compare them to the 16 fast waves

Chart 3.1. Bandwidth Names and Characteristics

Range name	Frequency range	Positive reflections	Negative reflections
Delta	1-4 Hz	Sleep, abstract Mental Processing	Brain injury: brain lesions, Sleep deprivation
Theta	4-8 Hz	Creativity	ADHD, depression, poor judgment or navigation
Alpha	8-12 Hz	Internal reflection, brain synchrony, peak performance	Depression, ADHD
Alpha 1 Alpha 2	8-10 Hz 10-12 Hz	Relaxation, calmness Alertness, fast processing	Mental Fog, slow processing Anxiety, insomnia
SMR	12-15 Hz	External reflection motor control	Sleep disorders, tactile sensitivity, hyperactivity
Beta	12-25 Hz	Alertness, focus	Anxiety, Insomnia, Migraine, OCD, perfectionism
HiBeta	25-30 Hz	Hyper focus, peak performance	Anxiety, Insomnia, Migraine, OCD, worry
Gamma	35-45 Hz (28-80 Hz)	Higher mental processing peak performance	Poor abstract thinking and memory consolidation

COMMON BANDED FREQUENCIES

Hans Berger first identified two frequency bands, alpha and beta. Additional brain wave morphologies were also discovered such as delta, theta, sensorimotor rhythm (SMR), and gamma. Each bandwidth has unique shape or morphology when it is raw, but filtered waves have a smooth sinusoidal pattern. Chart 3.1 is a quick review of bandwidth names, frequency ranges, and general functions.

4

Electrode Placements

THE INTERNATIONAL 10–20 SYSTEM

The International (Int'l) 10–20 System designates each region of the cerebral cortex by a letter and/or number. Sensors are placed on the head according to these designations (Figure 4.1). Odd numbers are on the left side of the brain; even numbers are on the right. The letter before the number usually refers to a lobe or a division of the cortex.

Figure 4.1. International 10–20 System

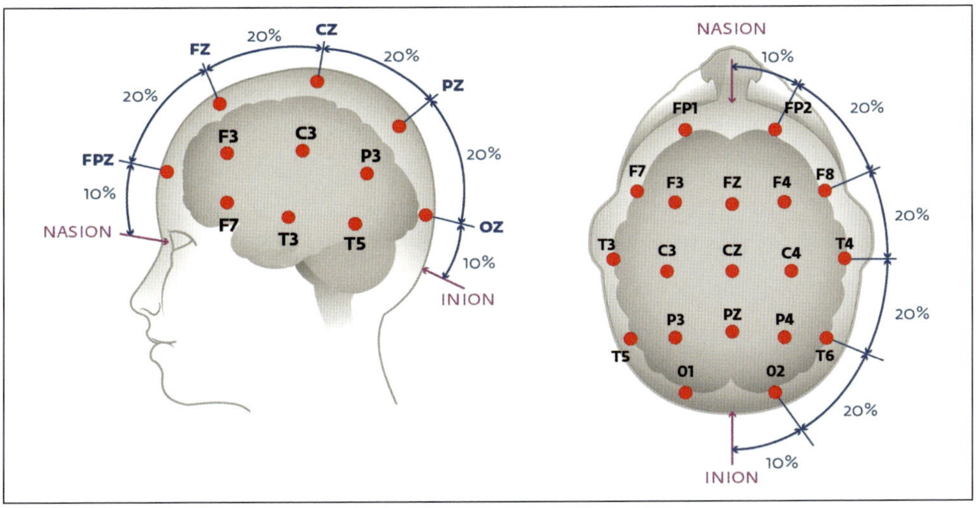

- *F*, frontal lobes
- *Fp*, frontal poles
- *T*, temporal lobes
- *O*, occipital lobes
- *P*, parietal lobes
- *C*, central and sensorimotor cortex
- *Z*, the center line that separates left and right hemispheres

Figure 4.2.
EEG Placement Cap

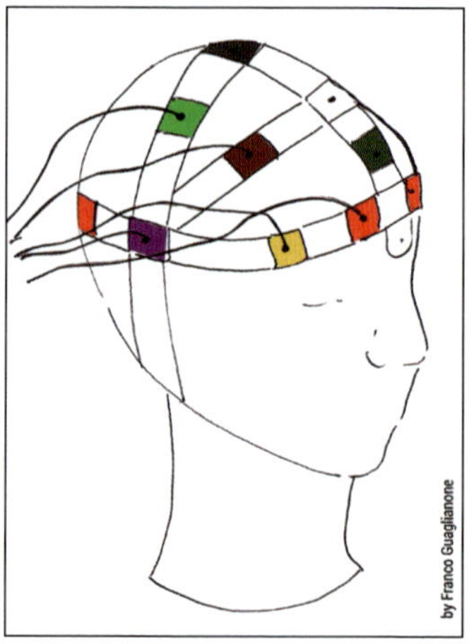

Finding correct placement for each of the Int'l 10–20 positions can be a daunting task. Before seeing clients, practice finding brain locations; it may be useful to have a dummy head in the office that has each of the Int'l 10–20 positions marked on it. Hairdressers have Styrofoam heads that can be used for this purpose. Or, to assist placing individual electrodes on the scalp for the first time, a placement cap may be purchased (Figure 4.2; sold by Jordan NeuroScience). Once you have mastered the Int'l 10–20 placement system, such a template cap may or may not be necessary.

Anatomical directions and terminology (see Figure 4.3):

- *Posterior*, toward the rear of the head
- *Anterior*, toward the front of the head
- *Vertex*, central position (Cz; also Pz and Fz)
- *Dorsal*, toward the top of the head
- *Ventral*, toward the bottom of the head
- *Medial*, midline of the brain
- *Lateral*, to the left or the right of the midline
- *Superior*, closer to the top (dorsal)
- *Inferior*, closer to the bottom (ventral)

Figure 4.3. Anatomical Terminology

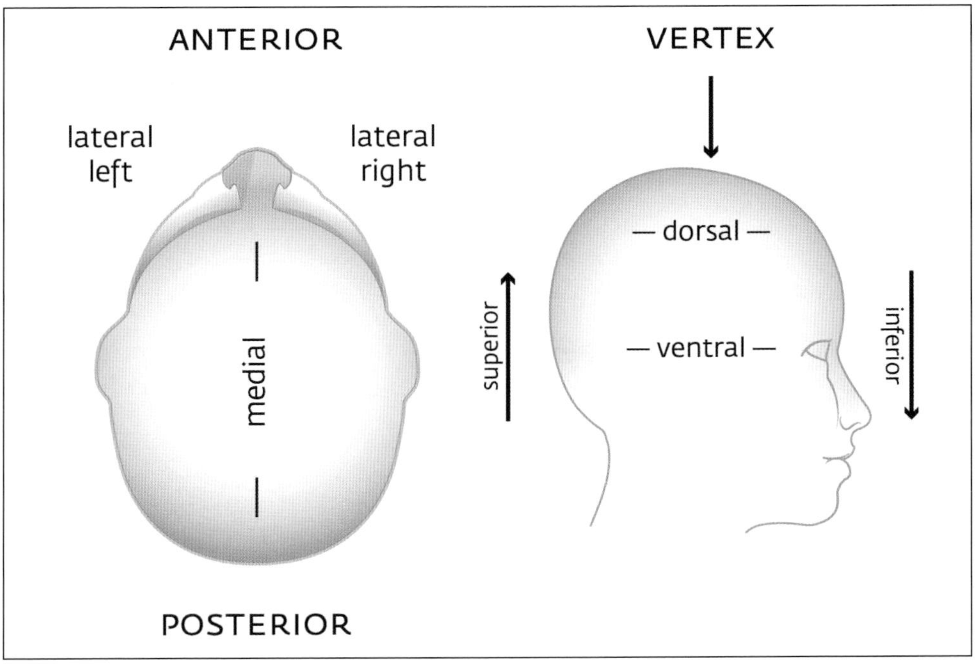

Hemispheric designations (Figure 4.4):

1. *Contralateral:* Locations that are on opposite sides; for example, the left arm is contralateral to the right arm.
2. *Homologous:* Int'l 10–20 sites that complement each other in both hemispheres. For example: F3 and F4, C3 and C4, or T5 and T6. Note that contralateral and homologous are often used interchangeably.
3. *Ipsilateral:* Limited to just one hemisphere, for example, ipsilateral left hemisphere (LH) or ipsilateral right hemisphere (RH).

Figure 4.4. Orienting Right and Left Hemispheres

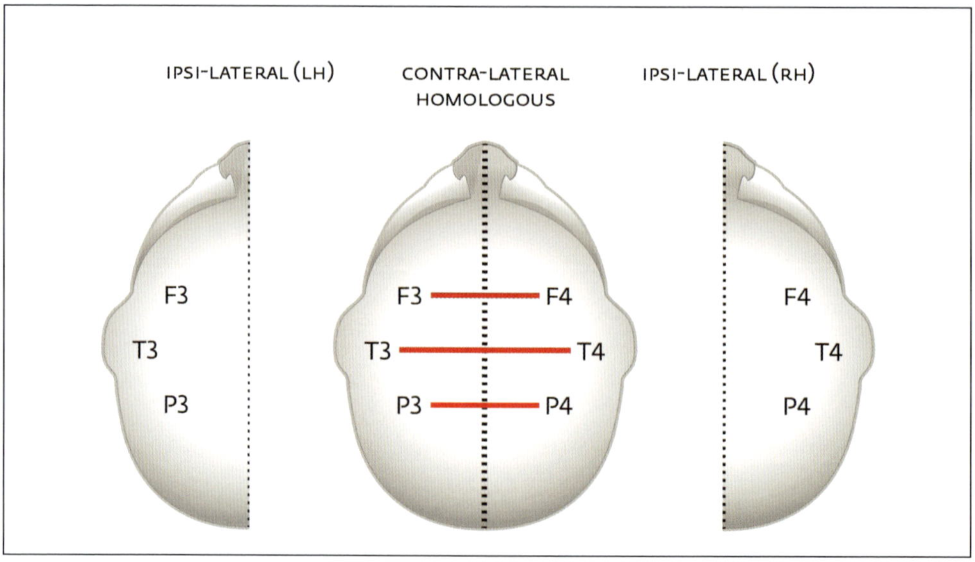

Figure 4.5. Asymmetry and Symptoms

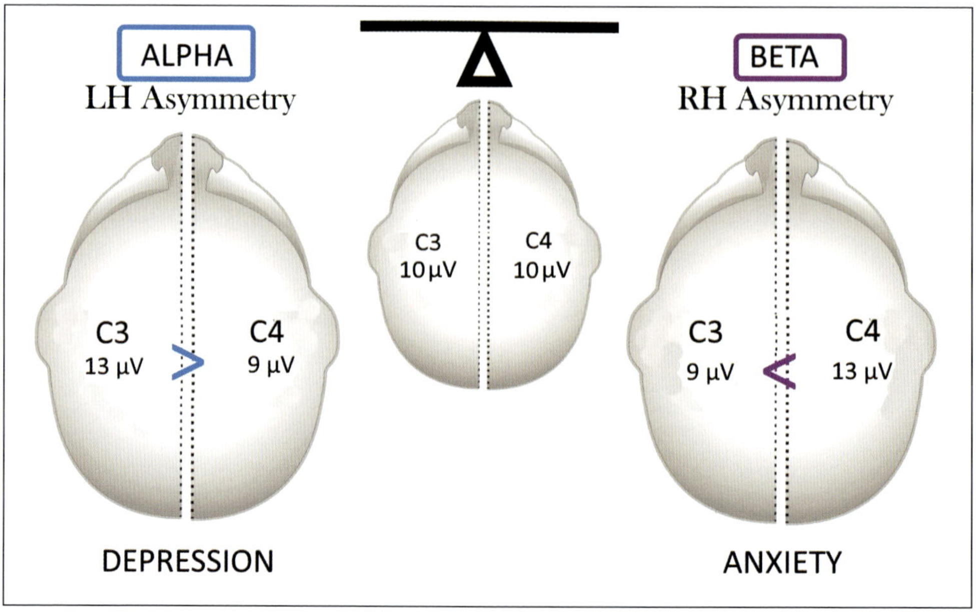

4. *Asymmetry:* An amplitude (or power) imbalance between any two sites as determined by statistics. For example, the alpha amplitude at C3 could be greater than the alpha amplitude at C4. Asymmetry can be an imbalance between two homologous sites or any two sites on the Int'l 10-20 System. Note that significant LH alpha asymmetries may reflect depression whereas significant RH beta asymmetries may reflect anxiety (Figure 4.5).

Figure 4.5 indicates when C3 and C4 alpha or beta are in balance, amplitudes are nearly equal. However, when there is a significant imbalance between two homologous sites, the following symptoms are suspected:

- LH alpha > RH alpha (suspect depression or a learning disorder)
- RH beta > LH beta (suspect anxiety, phobia, or sensory integration challenges)

It is always best to rely on standard deviations (SDs) when assessing asymmetry. Asymmetry SDs or Z-scores are output for each bandwidth and between every pair of Int'l 10–20 locations and not just homologous sites.

5

Introduction to 2-D Brain Maps

QUANTITATIVE EEG

In general, maps, when they are interpreted correctly, are directional guides that keep the traveler on course. Getting lost in the clinical arena can lead to ineffective training or even treatment failure. Efficient traveling requires advance knowledge of the main route and possible alternatives. In the same way, a brain map can be used to guide EEG neurofeedback protocol decisions. Of course, a map in itself is rarely enough to ensure clinical success. It must be supported by cognitive testing, questionnaires, and psychiatric interviewing. Indeed, symptoms are like guideposts that can direct the neurofeedback practitioner to look toward specific regions of the brain. Of course, more than one region may be responsible for any given cognitive, spatial, or emotional disturbance. Brain maps do more than locate problems; they also translate them into the language of the EEG.

Quantitative EEG (qEEG) is a comprehensive analysis of the filtered EEG into power (μV^2) and other metrics such as coherence, phase, and asymmetry, which will be considered in chapter 10. Nineteen-channel qEEG amplifiers and assessments are now common to many neurofeedback clinics. Brain-mapping software with qEEG continues to be the industry standard for clients with a history of traumatic brain injury (TBI) because cortical damage may create complex problems and multiple abnormal EEG patterns. Non-qEEG assessments may be inadequate and sometimes misleading. To make matters worse, it's not always clear who has TBI, because the impact to the brain may have happened in childhood or the distant past. Hyperactive children are prone to accidents and head injuries; domestic violence, sports-related head injuries, and car accidents happen every day; life puts all of us in harm's way. Consequently, obtaining a brain map is usually the first order of clinical business. Typically, qEEG data come from the 19 scalp locations designated by the International 10–20 System. After data are acquired, a qEEG technician removes artifacts from the data that come from muscle movements, eye blinks, electrocardiogram (EKG), and other misleading factors. Finally, the refined data are processed by normative database software. Color-coded maps and data in digital format are often printed. The nose is at the top of each circle, so that the LH is to the left and the right hemisphere RH is to the right. (This is the opposite of other brain-imaging techniques such as PET and MRI scans). Some have thought that a different normative database would be needed for each ethnicity, tribe, or culture; however, research has not supported that viewpoint:

> Normative QEEG descriptors were found to be independent from cultural and ethnic factors. High reliability was found in studies from Barbados, China, Cuba, Germany, Holland, Japan, Korea, Mexico, Netherlands, Sweden, the United States and Venezuela. . . . The independence of the EEG spectrum from cultural and ethnic factors is a remarkable characteristic of the EEG. It has been suggested that it reflects the common genetic heritage of mankind. (Congedo & Lubar, 2003, p. 4)

Getting Started With EEG Neurofeedback employs the following databases:

- NeuroGuide (lifespan normative database) for brain maps
- Jewel clinical database for BrainAvatar for brain maps, treatment plans, and protocol generation
- qEEG-Pro database for Z-score training applications

EEG neurofeedback providers also process brain maps with the following databases (not all databases are on the list):

- qEEG-Pro (comprehensive brain maps and training suggestions: internet service)
- New Mind (comprehensive brain maps and training suggestions: internet service)

- BrainDx
- SKIL
- Win EEG

In many ways, color-coded brain maps are self-explanatory. They identify areas of the brain that are outside of normal limits and would likely benefit from training. However, an accurate interpretation of maps requires an understanding of map terminology and potential pitfalls.

Brain maps rely upon databases arranged by age groups. To create a normative life-span database that ranges from 3 to 80 years of age requires hundreds of subjects. Statistics demand an *N* of 30 or at least 30 subjects for each age group. The goal is to calculate the mean as well as one standard deviation for each age group. Plus or minus one standard deviation is 68% of any given population (Figure 5.1). When considering what locations to train, EEG neurofeedback providers are usually more interested in Z-scores greater than or less than (+/–) 2.0.

Figure 5.1. Gaussian Curve for EEG Neurofeedback

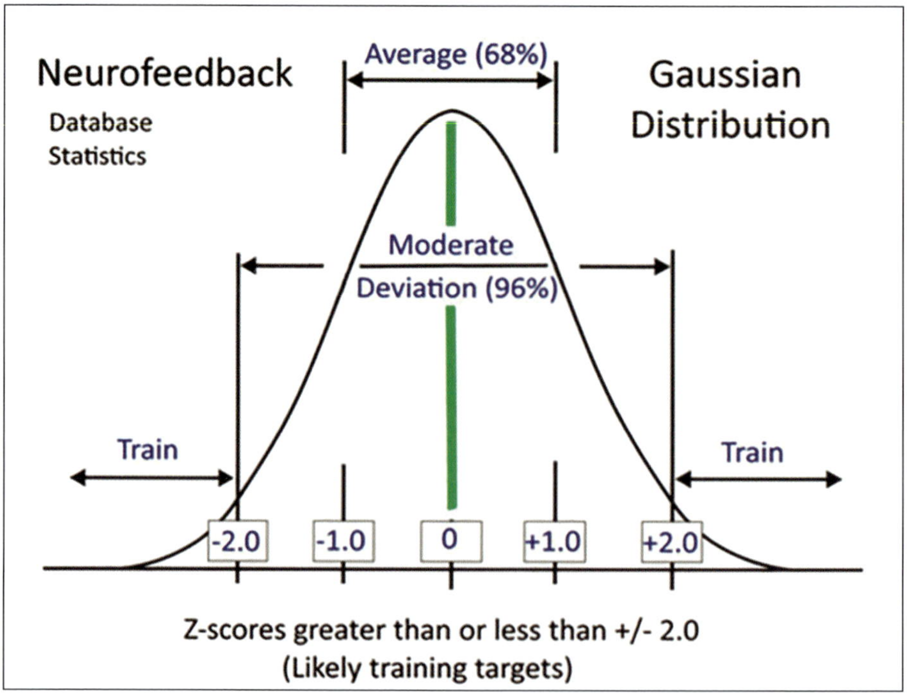

What is the difference between Z-scores and SDs? “A z-score is a number that indicates how far above or below the mean a given score in the distribution is in standard deviation units.” (Urdan, 2010)

Clinical symptoms are reflected by statistically significant results that are greater than 2 SDs from the mean or (+/–) 2.0 Z-scores. There is a match when a functional neurologically significant region corresponds to a high Z-score finding. Note that a significant region is one that governs brain functions related to diagnosed symptoms. In the brain map presentations in Figure 5.2, high Z-scores are in red and low Z-scores are in dark blue.

Figure 5.2. Z-Score Color Chart

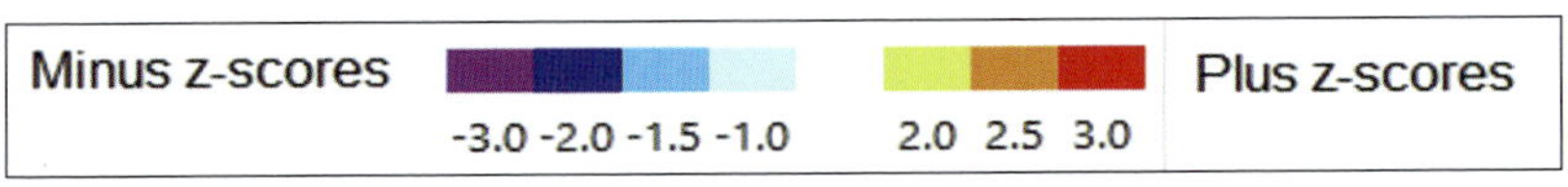

Figure 5.3. Four Most Common Frequency Bands

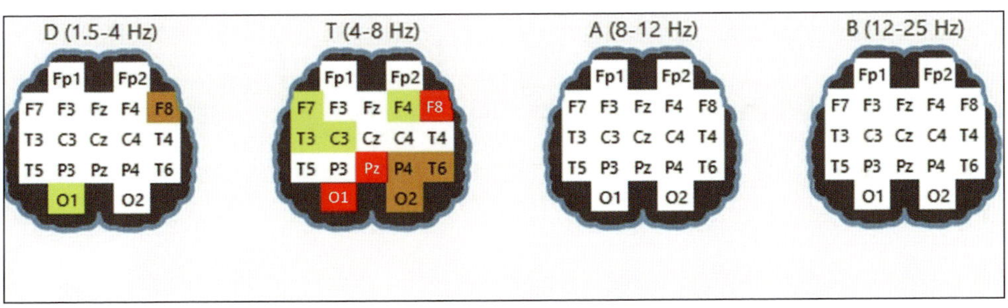

Brain Map derived from Jewel database software

Figure 5.3 shows the four most common bands: delta, theta, alpha and beta. It isolates three areas of concern: elevated theta Z-scores at F8, Pz, and O1. Neurofeedback practitioners would pay special attention to these elevated Z-scores (as shown in red). The goal is to match the clinical symptoms with neurological locations. In this case, F8 relates to poor sustained attention, and Pz and O1 relate to poor visual processing, hence poor visual attention. However, brain maps may provide more detailed information than just four bandwidths. This example is an introduction to brain map reading and interpretation. Clinical symptoms were matched to elevated standard deviations at three locations.

Figure 5.4. Jewel Report

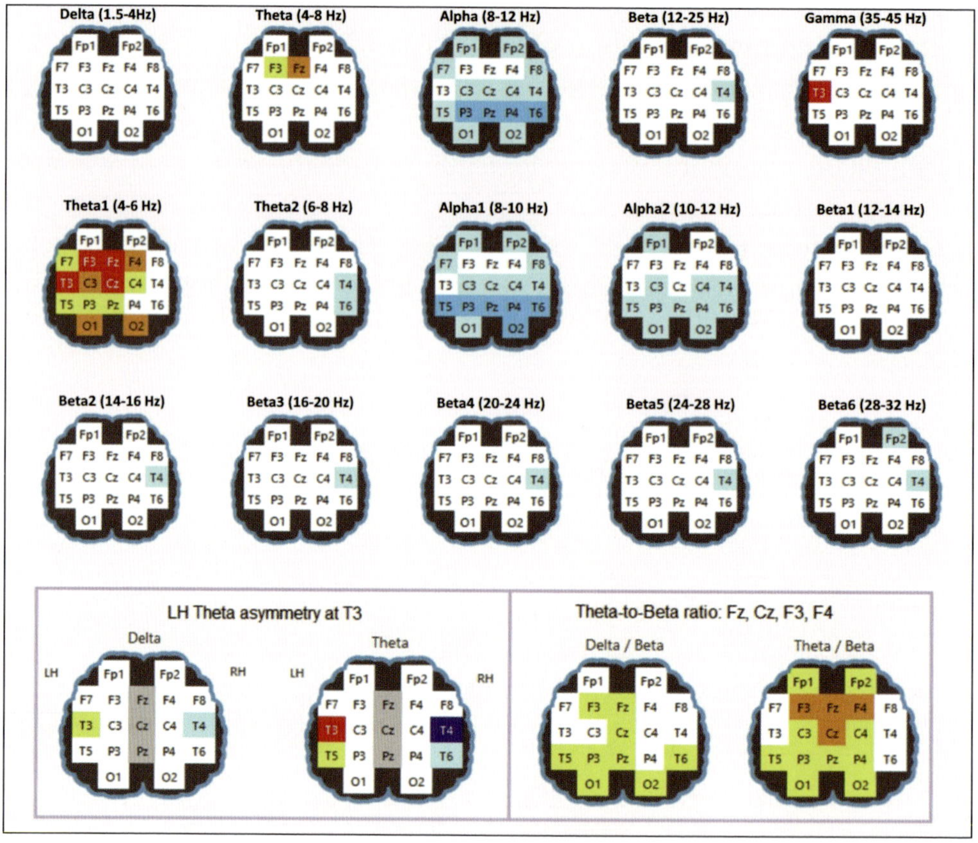

Brain Map derived from Jewel database software

Figure 5.4, Jewel database software, has 15 bandwidths: delta, theta, alpha, beta, and gamma, as well as theta 1 (4–6 Hz), theta 2 (6–8 Hz), alpha 1 (8–10 Hz), Alpha 2 (10–12 Hz), Beta 1 (12–14 Hz), Beta 2 (14–16 Hz), Beta 3 (16–20 Hz), Beta 4 (20–24 Hz), Beta 5 (24–28 Hz), and Beta 6 (28–32 Hz). The Jewel brain map matches the clinical evaluation of attention-deficit/hyperactivity disorder (ADHD), poor memory, and anxiety. See Chart 5.1 for an explanation.

High and low Z-scores in Figure 5.4 indicate areas of interest that reflect the client's distress. Chart 5.1 matches symptoms to locations and bandwidths.

Keep this in mind: high theta at T3 does not always mean a memory issue, and high frontal-lobe theta at F3, F4, and/or Fz does not always mean

Chart 5.1. Symptom-to-Site Matching

Symptom	Location(s)	Bandwidth
ADHD	F3, Fz, Cz	(+) Theta (4-6) Hz
Poor memory	T3	(+) Theta (4-6) Hz
Anxiety	T5, T6, P3, P4, Pz, O1, O2	(-) Alpha (8-10) Hz

ADHD, and weak posterior alpha does not always mean anxiety. The clinician employs a step-by-step process:

1. Diagnosis (determined during the clinical evaluation with baseline tests); thereafter, we look to the EEG to support clinical conclusions.
2. Review EEG characteristics, neurology, and EEG symptom markers. Note that an EEG marker is also called an EEG signature; it refers to an EEG pattern that is known to reflect a discrete disorder. For example, excessive beta in the recording is an EEG marker for anxiety.
3. Match 1 and 2 to sites with high or low Z-scores.
4. Train those sites.

Once symptom-related locations and bandwidths are identified, an appropriate training modality must be chosen. The two basic choices are either Z-score training or power training. Note that power training is also called amplitude training. Chapter 6 is a simplified introduction to both training methods.

6

Introduction to Power and Z-Score Training

HOW EEG TRAINING WORKS

Treatment with EEG neurofeedback is a comprehensive system that works directly with the brain. Each of us has a countless number of neurons in our cerebrum. Brain waves are associated with the electrical activation and deactivation of pyramidal neurons. They cycle up and down, over and over again. The trainee is given feedback precisely at the time when the cycle of brain waves moves into a desirable pattern. For example, if someone is training to become more alert, then the feedback would be set in the following manner.

Each time the cycle of brain waves moves into an alert state, tones are heard and computer graphics are activated. Each time the cycle of brain waves moves into a distracted state, tones and graphics cease. Amazingly, the brain cooperates; simple reinforcement teaches the brain how to prolong healthy brain wave patterns. Within a few sessions, trainees often gain a heightened awareness of mental drifting. Gradually, most trainees learn to pay attention for longer periods of time—even during boring tasks in the classroom or at work.

Amplifier: Single Channel

A single-channel EEG amplifier has three outlet holes: one ground and two actives. Data are acquired by placing electrodes on the scalp according to the Int'l 10–20 system. There are two basic methods (montages) to mount electrodes on the scalp: monopolar and bipolar. Single-channel EEG recordings require three electrodes (Figure 6.1).

Figure 6.1. One-Channel Amplifier

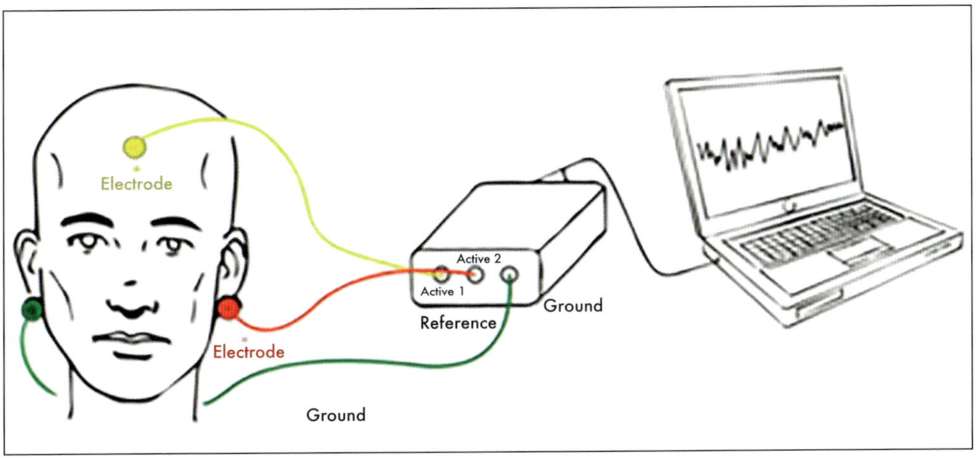

Sometimes electrodes are placed on the earlobes. However, if the trainee has numerous earlobe piercings, the mastoid bone (behind the ear) serves as a good replacement. Also, mastoid placements help to limit EKG artifacts and lower impedance.

One electrode is the *ground* and may be mounted on the earlobe or any convenient place on the scalp (Figure 6.1). The other two electrodes acquire EEG data and are called the *actives*.

Electrodes

Figure 6.2 shows a 9 mm flat electrode connected to a 1.5 mm Din connector by a wire; electrodes may be called lead wires. Electrodes can be cupped or flat and are often made of gold, silver, or tin. An electrode connected to the earlobe has an attaching spring clip.

Figure 6.2. Electrode With Lead Wire

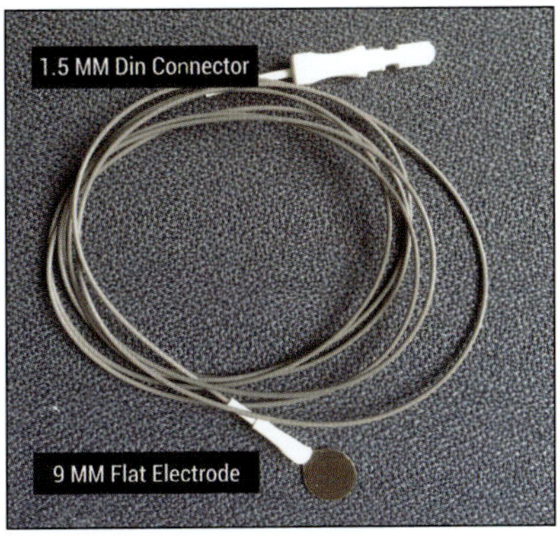

Montages

If the active electrode is clipped to an earlobe (or mastoid bone) it is called a reference active. This can also be called a *monopolar* montage. However, if the reference active is mounted on the scalp, it creates a *bipolar* montage (Figure 6.3).

Monopolar montages have one active scalp-mounted lead. The primary training is directed at the single scalp-active electrode. No training takes place at the earlobe reference active.

Bipolar montages have two active scalp-mounted leads. The primary training is directed at the difference between the two scalp electrodes. That is, the value of the signal coming from one active electrode is subtracted from the value of the other active electrode.

Figure 6.3. Montages: Monopolar and Bipolar

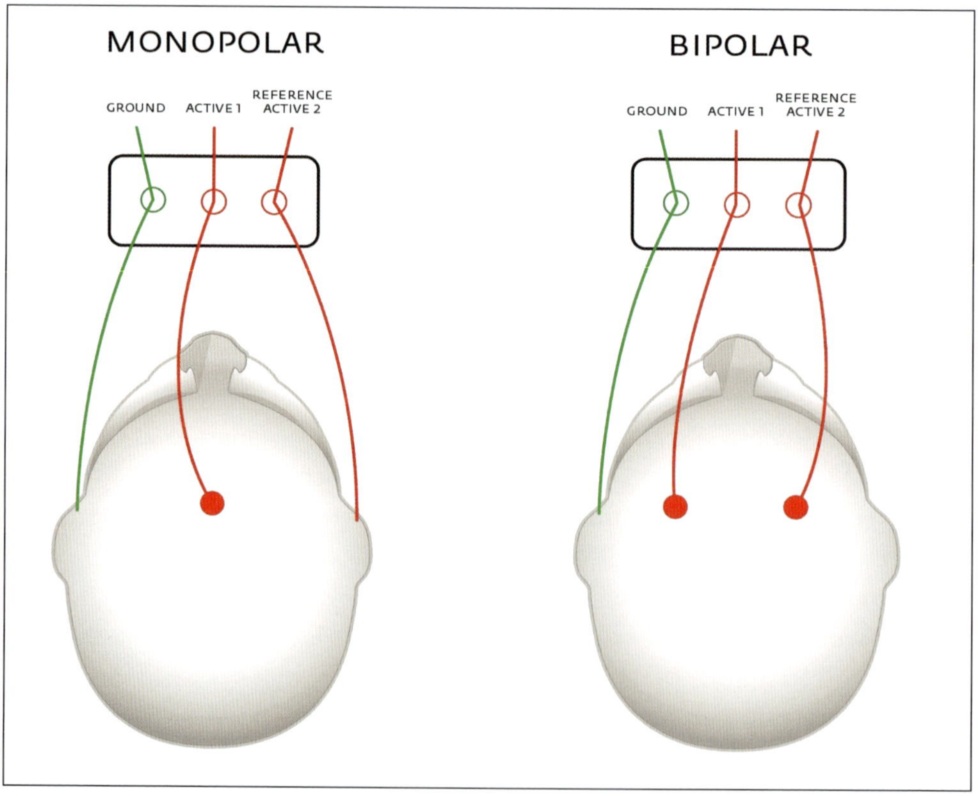

THRESHOLDS: REWARD AND INHIBIT

Figure 6.4 is an example of how to increase alpha amplitudes (in microvolts) by means of a reward threshold. Each time alpha amplitude goes above the threshold, the trainee receives feedback.

Figure 6.4. Simple Alpha Reward Threshold

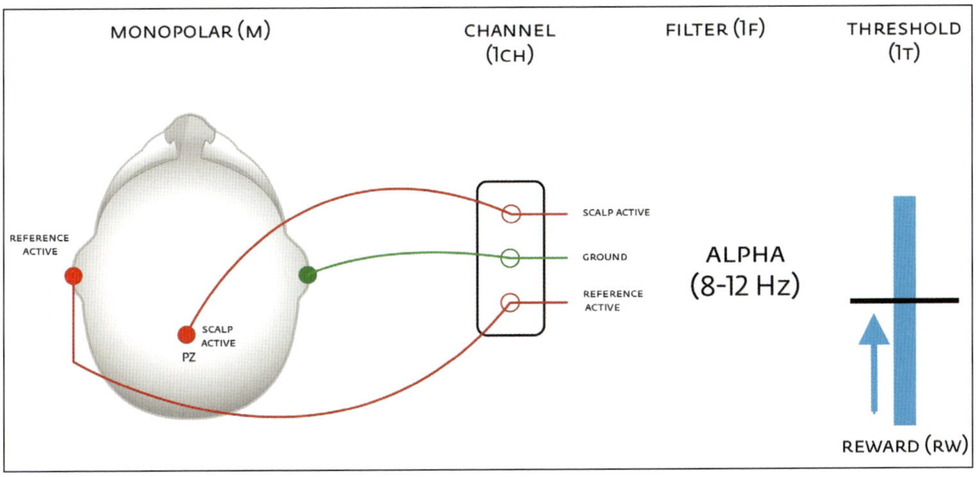

When the amplitude (µV) of Alpha at Pz is above the threshold then feedback occurs.

Inhibit feedback results in decreased theta amplitude (in microvolts) as shown in Figure 6.5). Each time theta amplitude goes below the threshold, the trainee receives feedback.

Figure 6.5. Simple Theta Inhibit Threshold

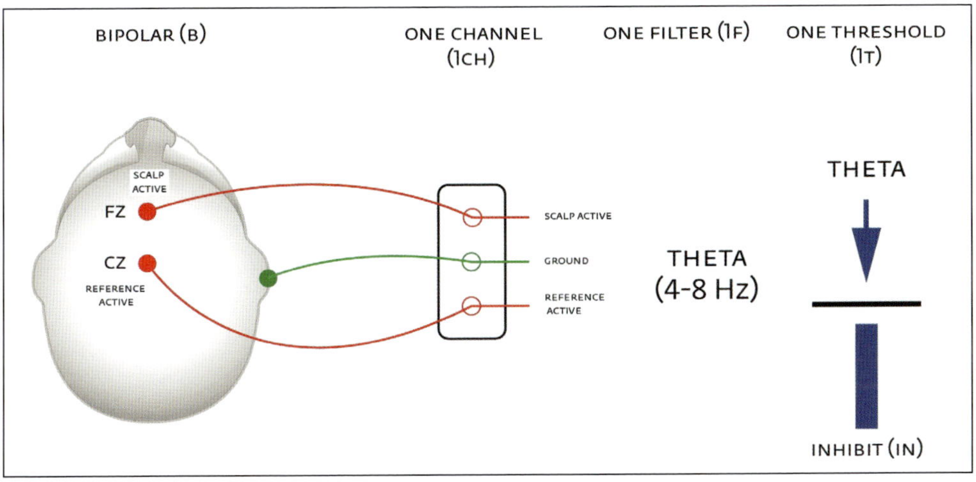

When the amplitude (µV) of Theta at Fz-Cz is below the threshold then feedback occurs.

To recap:

- Reward thresholds are like hurdles: success means going over the bar.
- Inhibit thresholds are like limbo bars: success means going under the bar.

Power (amplitude) training terminology:

- Ground (G)
- Inhibit (IN), feedback when below the threshold
- Reward (RW), feedback when above the threshold
- One channel (1CH)
- Single filter (1F)
- Single threshold (1Thr)
- Monopolar (M)
- Bipolar (B)

Each threshold is defined by a filter. For example, to train alpha, the threshold filter setting ranges from 8 to 12 Hz. To train theta, the threshold filter setting ranges from 4 to 8 Hz. The goal is to reduce or increase amplitudes (in microvolts) within the designated filter range.

Training in EEG neurofeedback can transform unhealthy EEG patterns into healthy ones. The trainee's symptoms often relate to unhealthy bandwidth distributions at specific brain locations, for example:

- Too high: the brain map shows an elevated Z-score of theta (>2.0). Consequently, theta is inhibited in order to lower its amplitude and Z-score.
- Too low: the brain map shows a depressed Z-score of alpha (<2.0). Consequently, alpha is rewarded in order to increase its amplitude and Z-score.

Note that for alpha waves (but not other bandwidths), Z-scores less than 1.0 (<1.0) may be considered for training, especially when accompanied by higher Z-scores in beta.

Two Threshold Types: Manual and Auto

Manual thresholds are fixed by the clinician and based upon trainee performance. For example, if a manual inhibit threshold is set to 10 μV, then each time the bandwidth amplitude is less than 10 μV, feedback is delivered. The reverse is true for a manual reward threshold. Each time the bandwidth amplitude is greater than 10 μV, feedback is delivered.

Auto thresholds are set by percentage of feedback success. Once the percentage is set, no further adjustment is required. Typically, auto thresholds adjust themselves every minute based on the previous minute's training performance.

To set a reward threshold for 50% success means that the threshold bar auto-adjusts so that the trainee is reinforced about half of the time. Feedback tones are emitted when the amplitude is above the threshold.

To set an inhibit threshold for 50% success means that the threshold bar auto-adjusts so that the trainee is reinforced about half of the time. Feedback tones are emitted when the amplitude is below the threshold.

Thresholds are set in such a way that the trainee feels successful. The trainee must always feel successful—I cannot overstate this principle.

Setting up single-channel, single-filter training involves site and bandwidth selection. The brain map is consulted to assist in the selection process. The decision must be made to reward or inhibit a specific bandwidth at a specific location. Many clinicians employ Z-score training because it simplifies the decision-making process.

Z-SCORE THRESHOLDS

When Z-score training is chosen, the clinician need only select training locations. Locations are based upon comparison of the brain map with the evaluated clinical symptoms. Symptom checklist software such as Jewel offers training suggestions.

Z-score training thresholds work differently than reward and inhibit thresholds; they are like windows with upper and lower limits. If the Z-score threshold is set to plus or minus 1.0 (+/–1.0), then feedback is delivered when all trained EEG values are within tolerance. The upper limit of the window is plus 1.0 Z-score and the lower limit of the window is minus 1.0 Z-score. Figure 6.6 shows the connection between Z-scores, amplitudes, and SDs.

Figure 6.6. Calculating Standard Deviations

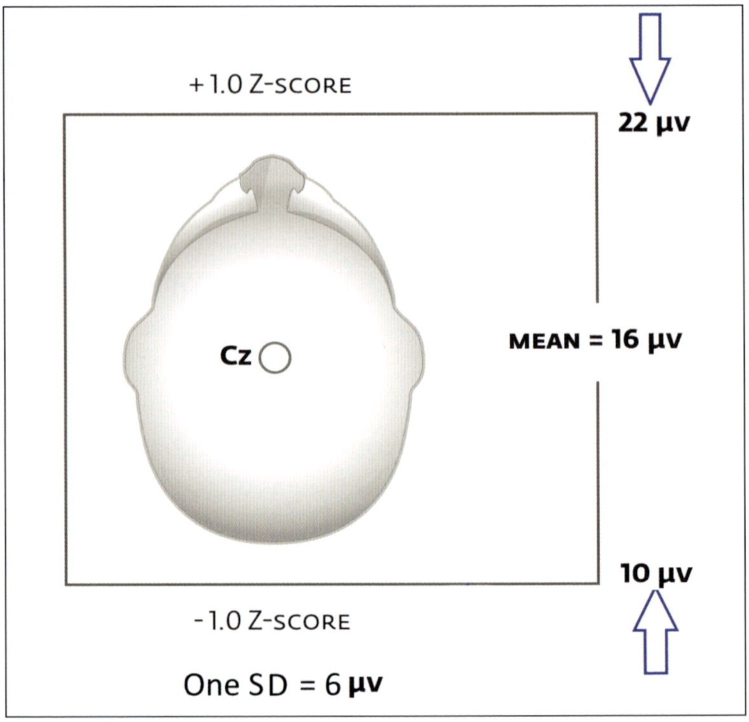

Transforming amplitudes (µV) into Z-Scores

In Figure 6.6, the amplitude in microvolts of alpha was measured at Cz for 30 subjects with eyes closed. The average or mean value of all scores was 16 µV, with one SD of 6 µV. Therefore, 16 + 6 and 16 – 6 equals +1 SD and –1 SD, respectively. When alpha amplitude measures between 10 and 22 µV, feedback starts; when it is less than 10 µV or greater than 22 µV, feedback stops. Z-scores are gleaned from normative database download libraries. During Z-score training, EEG filtered components are expressed on the training screen as Z-scores and not amplitudes.

How to Adjust Z-Score Thresholds to Increase Power

Threshold limits for Z-scores can be set to a balanced (+/-1.0) Z-scores or they can be customized to enhance training goals. In Figure 6.7, four channels are being trained: F3, F4, P3, and P4. The upper limit was set to (+)1.5 and the lower limit to (–).5. The Z-score threshold limits were

Figure 6.7. Adjusting Z-Score Thresholds

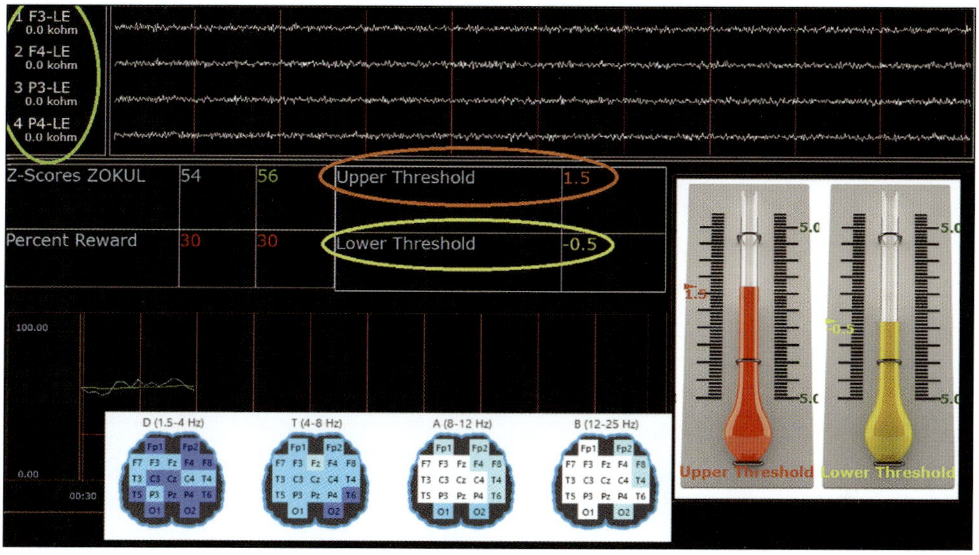

Adapted from BrainAvatar software by BrainMaster Technologies, Inc.
Brain Maps are derived from Jewel database software
Z-Scores are derived from qEEG-Pro database

biased to increase power because the brain maps show diffuse weak power (reflected by maps that are mostly blue, indicating low or negative SDs).

When setting a bias to Z-scores, not all trained components (e.g. phase, coherence, asymmetry) will be negative, as shown in Figure 6.8. If that is the case, do not train components with a positive valence. For example, this may result in training only negative power and negative coherence and avoiding other components that may have elevated SDs. Do those instructions seem confusing or difficult? Then stick to a non-biased, balanced threshold of +/−1.0 or +/−1.25 (the most typical settings).*

Figure 6.8.
Adjusting Thresholds During Training

Figure 6.8 shows the clinician observing the raw EEG, training graphs, and Z-score data; adjustments to training parameters may be made during a training

session (on the fly). Graphics have been extended from the laptop to a secondary display screen for the trainee. The graphics and tones provide feedback. Movies are sometimes used for graphics.

CASE STUDY

Figure 6.9 shows a Jewel brain map. The symptom of memory retrieval was selected from the symptom checklist. The Jewel protocol generator output four training sites that matched the symptom: T3, T4, F7, and T5. Four-

Figure 6.9. Memory Deficits

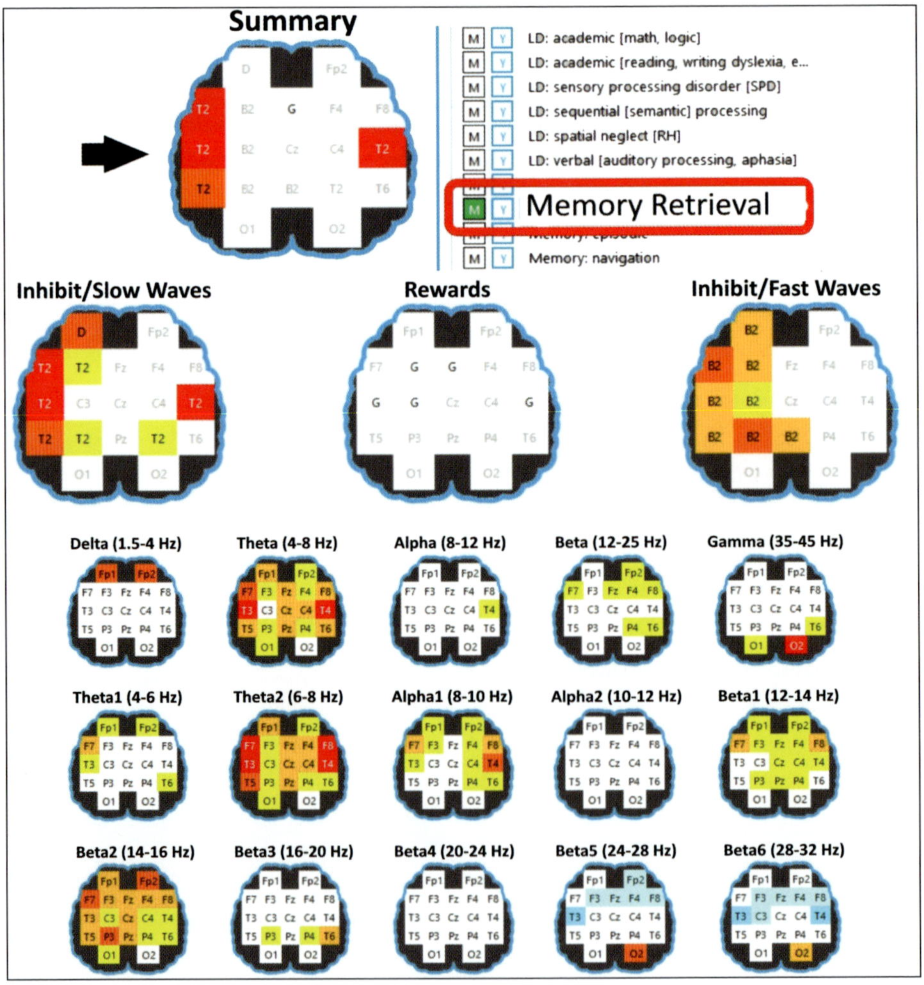

Maps created by Jewel database software

channel Z-score training was chosen. Note that some clinicians always do 19-channel Z-score training regardless of the symptom.

All four locations contributed to the lack of efficient working memory and memory retrieval in this trainee. Theta and beta bandwidths had elevated Z-scores at the same locations. Protocols were created with two different approaches: (1) four-channel Z-score training and (2) single-channel power (μV^2) training. The training goal was to improve working or retrieval memory.

(1) Z-score Training:

The four training locations were chosen by Jewel software because they match the client's symptoms with significant neurological functions. The electrodes were placed on the corresponding scalp locations (Figure 6.10).

Figure 6.10. Electrode Placement for Z-Score Training

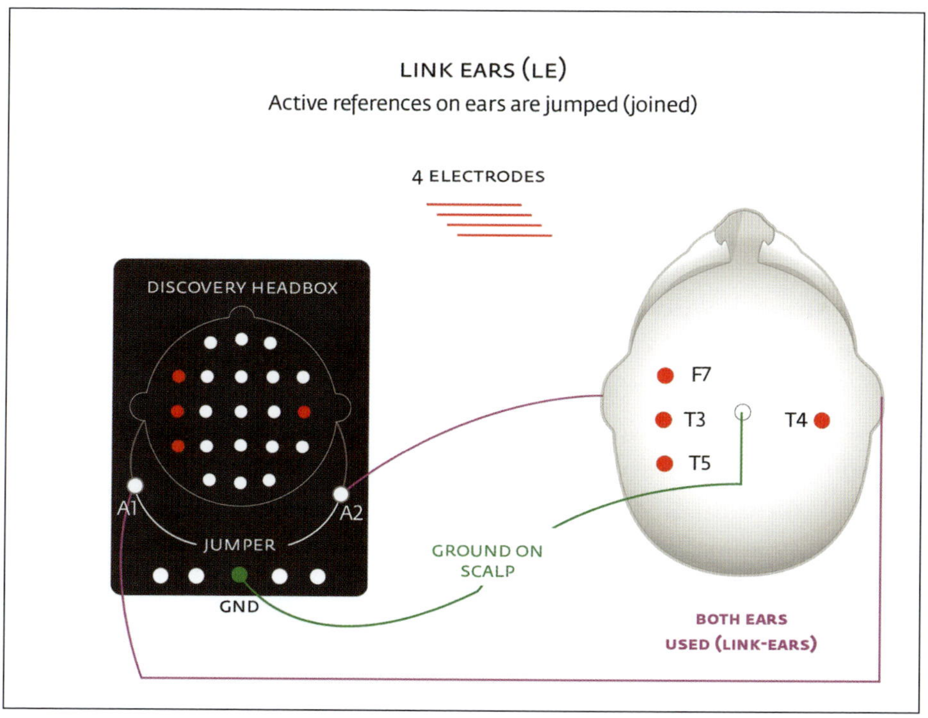

Reference (Link) ears & Ground (Cz) as well as scalp mounted sites.

Figure 6.11. Four-Channel Z-Score Training Display

SITES: F7 T3 (EO)	Abs	Rel	Rat/T	Rat/A	Rat/B	Rat/G
Delta (1.0-3.0)	-0.7	-1.0	-0.0	-0.0	-0.0	-0.0
Theta (4.0-8.0)	0.8	-0.6		0.0	0.0	-0.0
Alpha (8.0-12.0)	0.9	0.1			-0.0	0.0
Lobeta (12.0-15.0)	1.6	0.6				0.0
Beta (15.0-20.0)	1.8	0.7				
Gamma (35.0-45.0)	1.5	1.3				
Alpha1 (8.0-10.0)	0.7	-0.0				
Alpha2 (10.0-12.0)	1.0	0.1				
Delta (1.0-3.0)	0.1	-1.5	-0.0	-0.0	-0.0	-0.0
Theta (4.0-8.0)	[illegible]	2.2		0.0	1.6	-0.0
Alpha (8.0-12.0)	0.6	-0.2			-0.0	0.0
Lobeta (12.0-15.0)	1.3	0.1				0.0
Beta (15.0-20.0)	1.2	0.1				
Gamma (35.0-45.0)	0.9	0.7				
Alpha1 (8.0-10.0)	0.5	-0.4				
Alpha2 (10.0-12.0)	0.7	-0.3				

SITES: T5 T4 (EO)	Abs	Rel	Rat/T	Rat/A	Rat/B	Rat/G
Delta (1.0-3.0)	0.3	-1.1	-0.0	0.0	-0.0	-0.0
Theta (4.0-8.0)	3.0	2.2		0.0	1.6	-0.0
Alpha (8.0-12.0)	0.2	-0.6			-0.0	0.0
Lobeta (12.0-15.0)	0.9	-0.2				0.0
Beta (15.0-20.0)	1.3	0.4				
Gamma (35.0-45.0)	1.4	1.0				
Alpha1 (8.0-10.0)	0.2	-0.6				
Alpha2 (10.0-12.0)	0.3	-0.6				
Delta (1.0-3.0)	0.2	-1.5	-0.0	0.0	-0.0	-0.0
Theta (4.0-8.0)	[illegible]	[illegible]		0.0	1.6	-0.0
Alpha (8.0-12.0)	0.5	-0.4			-0.0	0.0
Lobeta (12.0-15.0)	1.0	-0.4				0.0
Beta (15.0-20.0)	1.3	0.2				
Gamma (35.0-45.0)	1.0	0.9				
Alpha1 (8.0-10.0)	0.5	-0.3				
Alpha2 (10.0-12.0)	0.5	-0.6				

Figure 6.11 adapted from BrainAvatar software by BrainMaster Technologies, Inc.
Z-Scores derived from qEEG-Pro database

In Figure 6.11, notice the elevated (in red) theta Z-scores at T3, T4, and T5. Those areas reflect the trainee's memory issue. Z-score training targeted bandwidths at those locations which were the furthest from the mean of the database.

(2) Power Training Setup:

In Figure 6.12, power training is limited to just one bandwidth. In the upper example, T5 is the monopolar montage. In the lower example, T3-T4 is the bipolar montage. In both cases theta (4–8 Hz) is inhibited. The goal of both protocols is to reduce elevated theta, which is the most likely source of the trainee's symptoms. The thermometer represents the threshold. Auto-thresholds govern threshold settings; therefore no manual threshold adjustments are required.

Four-channel Z-score training has definite advantages over power training, especially since several EEG components can be trained at the same time, including relative power, power ratio, asymmetry, coherence, and phase. When Z-score training does not bring symptom relief, it may be prudent to switch to basic power training. Note that some EEG neurofeedback clinics only use power training.

Figure 6.12. Montages (Left) and Power Training Screens (Right)

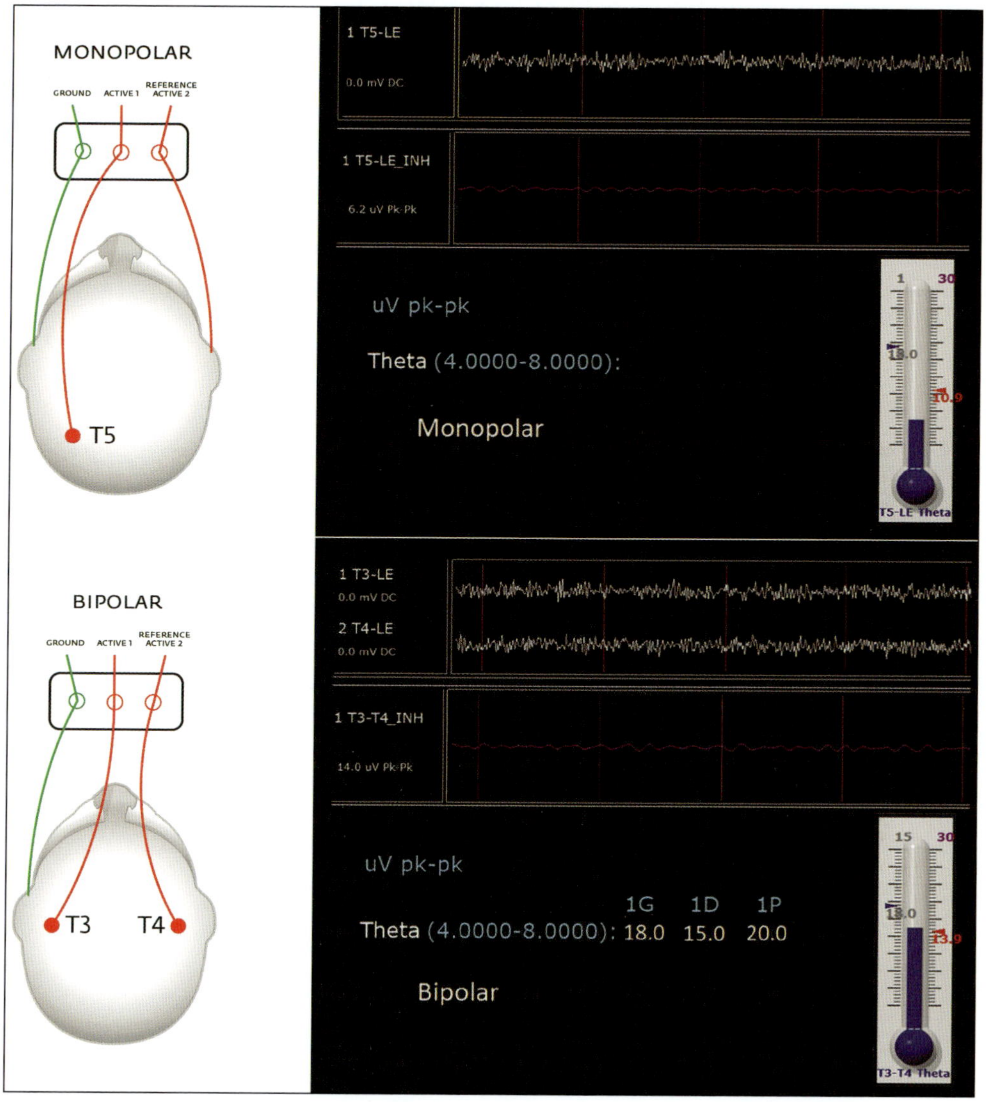

Graphics on right adapted from BrainAvatar software by BrainMaster Technologies, Inc.

CONCLUSION TO PART I

Part I (chapters 1–6) provided the basics in order to show newcomers to the field the process of creating protocols in an EEG neurofeedback practice, from brain maps to assessments to training. The remaining chapters of the book build on the core knowledge presented here. They provide added information about power training and Z-score training in 2-D (up to 19 channels) as well as 3-D (sLORETA) applications. Connectivity between locations will be explained. The structure and functions of various brain regions will be explored for the purpose of enhancing interventions. Characteristics and operations of EEG amplifiers will be explored in depth. Raw EEG examples will help the reader identify the difference between clean EEG and artifact-ridden data. Additional examples of unique EEG morphology will also be included. Non-biofeedback ancillary interventions such as photic stimulation are included in later chapters.

* The example in Figure 6.7 applies to Z-score training with simple tones. The feedback tone is either on or off. When on it means the trainee is within threshold requirements; when off the trainee is outside upper and lower threshold limits and no feedback occurs. However, when training with complex pitch variable sounds (see Chapter 18) auditory reinforcement works in a somewhat different manner. When the trainee hears the highest note it means they are moving closer to the mean of the database. Consequently, Z-score upper and lower thresholds are set to achieve an auditory experience of flowing tones that rise and fall. Upper and lower threshold limits may have a greater range such as (+) 2.4 and (-) 1.5. Mentoring or a live workshop experience is the best way to learning how to set upper and lower threshold limits for pitch variable sounds.

Part II
Amplifying and Filtering to Match EEG Signatures to Common Symptoms

Chapters

7

Amplifying the EEG

ALL EEG AMPLIFIERS

Amplifiers acquire an EEG signal with three electrodes per channel: two active leads and one ground. Two active leads, not just one, are needed because EEG amplifiers use differential electronic circuitry. Even though two measurements are taken per channel, there is only one result, as shown in Figure 7.1.

The final output by the differential amplifier is what is measured or trained; it is the difference between two actives with reference to the ground. Figure 7.1A shows how a differential amplifier accepts the difference and rejects that which is the same.

Common mode rejection comes from the use of differential amplifiers that measure the difference between the two active (scalp and reference) electrodes with reference to the ground. Look at our two cartoon characters in Figure 7.1A. They have different heights as measured from the ground. The tall guy is 7 feet tall and the short guy is 3 feet tall. Differential amplifiers would calculate the difference, that is, 7 feet minus 3 feet, which equals 4 feet (7′ – 3′ = 4′). So, the first 3 feet of height are rejected while the remaining 4 feet are accepted because that's the difference in height. The calculation for the bipolar montage is 7 μV – 3μV = 4 μV as the output.

Figure 7.1. Calculating the Output of a Differential Amplifier

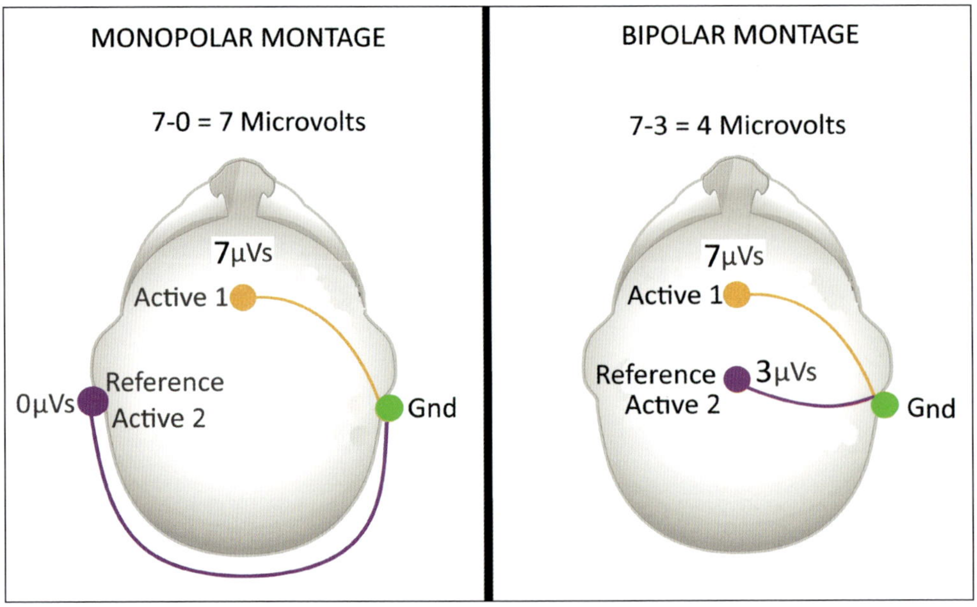

Figure 7.1A. Common Mode Rejection

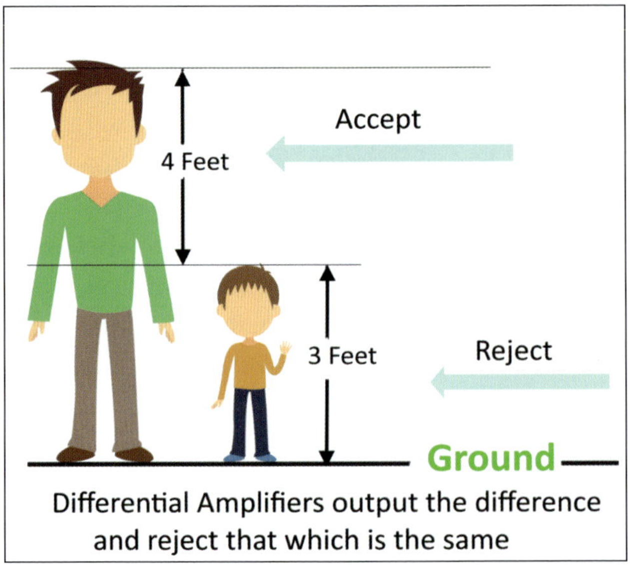

ARTIFACTS AND DIFFERENTIAL AMPLIFIERS

Amplifiers amplify both good and bad electrical data. Think of hearing aids that amplify both unwanted background noises along with clearly spoken words. Unwanted, or bad, data are often called artifacts. One type of artifact is muscle artifact or surface electromyography (sEMG), which comes from body movements or muscle tension from the jaw, neck, and forehead. High amplitudes of sEMG can drown out EEG signals. The saying "garbage in, garbage out" is true. If there is excessive artifact, the training session will be sabotaged. The training environment, locations, and montage decisions can be orchestrated to reduce or minimize artifact.

First, consider ways to limit EEG artifact in the training arena:

- Trainees need a comfortable chair with neck support.
- Young children need a chair that limits movements.
    - A low-profile footstool may be needed.
    - Do not allow eating or gum chewing.
- Limit background noises that can raise tension.
- The jaw muscles (temporomandibular joint, TMJ) are powerful; therefore, avoid carrying on a conversation with the trainee. Instead, limit comments to just a few words of coaching or gentle reminders to relax: this is not a counseling session.
- Tightly fitting clothes, tightly crossed legs, and raised (tense) shoulders contribute to muscle tension. For example, say to the trainee, "Drop your shoulders and relax."

Second, capitalize on common mode rejection. Before training, see if the raw EEG shows excessive sEMG (muscle) artifacts. If so, there may be a way around this problem. Instead of using a referential (monopolar) montage, consider using a bipolar montage that can reduce sEMG artifact. Common mode rejection tends to limit the effect of muscle tension between the two scalp electrodes that make up a bipolar montage. The way this works is shown in Figure 7.2.

Differential technology amplifies the data beneath the electrode and nearby surrounding areas.

Figure 7.2. Artifact: Monopolar Compared to Bipolar Montages

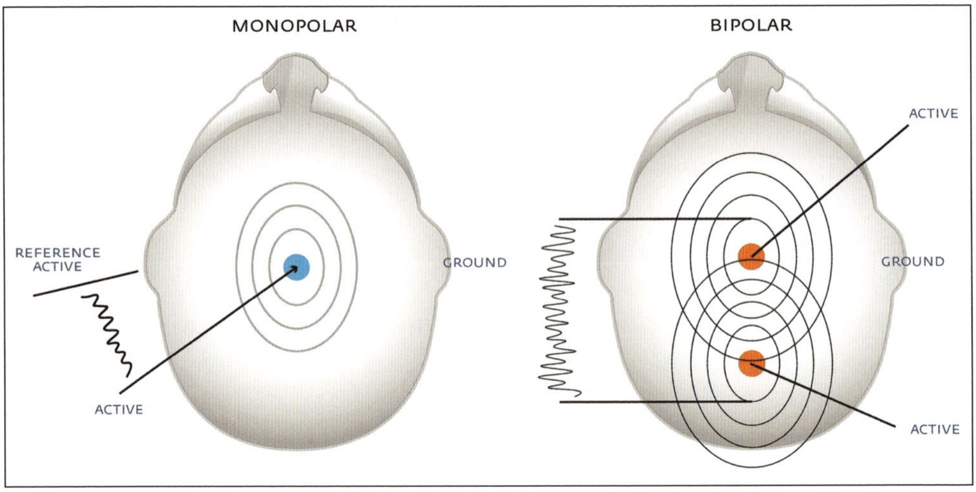

1. Monopolar montages amplify all of the surrounding data beneath the electrode with little regard for the reference active. Hence, if there is excessive sEMG near the electrode, training may be compromised.
2. Bipolar montages train the difference between the two scalp electrodes. Overlapping sEMG data common to both electrodes are rejected. Bipolar montages may be valuable when training little children who have trouble sitting still or for the adult with significant sEMG at or near optimum training locations. The TMJ is one of the greatest sources of sEMG: T3, T4, F7, and F8 are the first places to look.

Clinical experience has indicated that at times it may be more effective to inhibit beta with a bipolar montage—especially when training with a monopolar montage yields poor results. When using bipolar montages, make sure scalp-mounted electrodes are far enough apart. If they are too close, the difference between the two scalp-mounted electrodes will be very small. The closer the two electrodes are to each other, the lower the amplitude yield. Actually, if two electrodes were right next to each other, the yield would be zero.

qEEG Amplifiers

QEEG amplifiers need (Figure 7.3):

1. One shared ground for all 19 channels
2. One shared reference LinkEars (summed ears) and active electrodes for all 19 channels
3. Nineteen individual scalp electrodes for each of the key 19 Int'l 10–20 locations

For each channel, there is one scalp active and two reference actives that are jumped in order to link both ears. A LinkEar montage is shown in Figure 7.3. Also, each channel has its own amplifier. Therefore, a 24-channel amplifier has 24 amplifiers. At least 19 channels of EEG acquisition make up a qEEG recording.

Figure 7.3. qEEG: Electrode Requirements

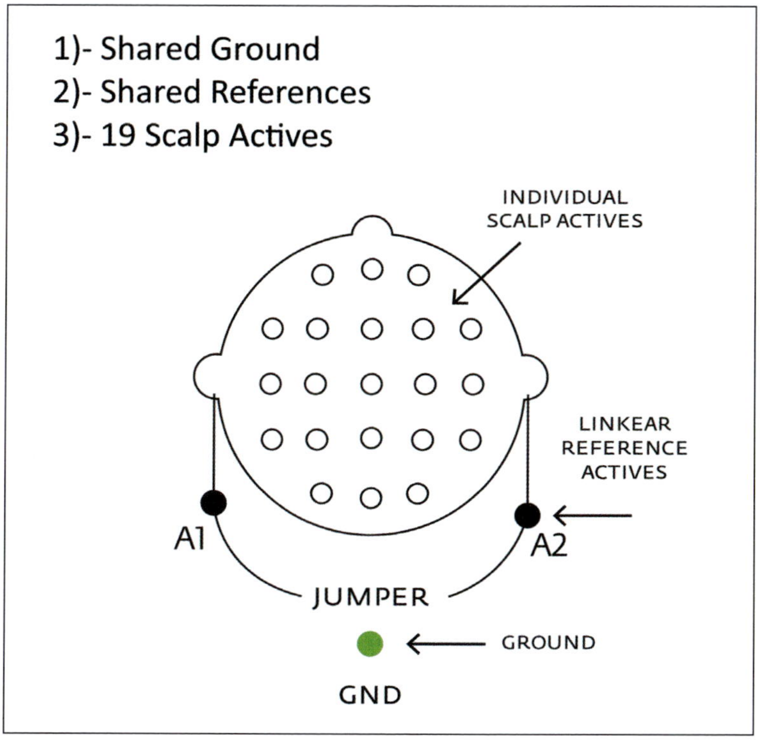

WHAT IS THE ENCEPHALOGRAM?

The EEG is a graphic display of the brain's electrical activity that can be detected from the scalp. It was first seen by the German psychiatrist Hans Berger in 1929. A quantitative EEG is a comprehensive analysis of brain wave activity. Nineteen channels are displayed in Figure 7.4. The raw EEG is referred to by neurologists as the background rhythm of the brain.

7.4. Quantitative EEG (qEEG)

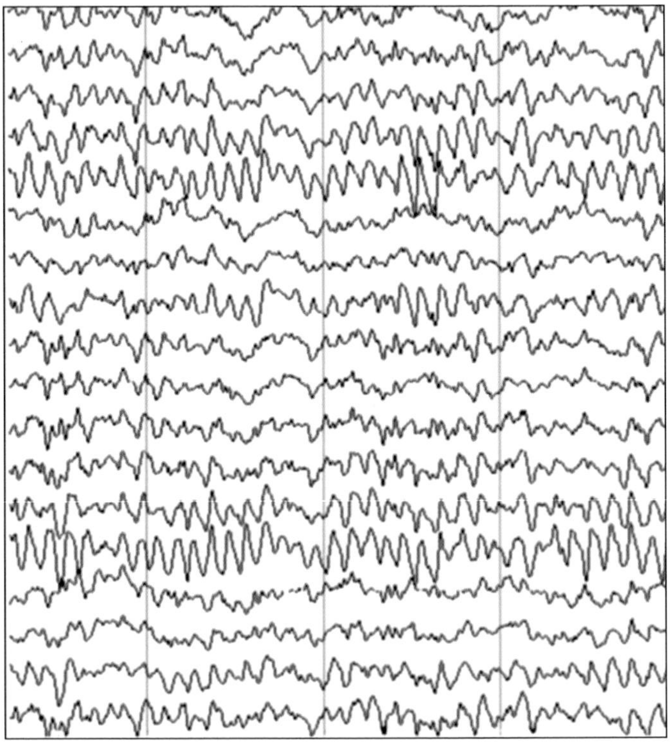

QEEG graphics adapted from BrainMaster Technologies, Inc. Software

The EEG is an epiphenomenon: it does not cause symptoms but rather reflects the electrical operation of the brain, just as the sound and vibration of an idling engine reflect the timing and smoothness of motor functions.

Epoch typically refers to a one-second length of time used to calculate the EEG, which is measured in cycles per second. Figure 7.4 displays about four epochs or 4 seconds of data, with a one-second epoch highlighted.

Most neurofeedback practitioners review and process the raw EEG signal before assessments or training. Figure 7.4 is an example of 19 channels of acceptable data.

The following is a short list of EEG amplifier manufacturers:

- BrainMaster Technologies, Inc.
- Deymed Diagnostic
- Freedom 24 (dry sensors)
- Mitsar Brain Diagnostic Solutions
- Nexus-32 MindMedia Neuro and Biofeedback Systems
- Q20 EEG by Neurofield, Inc.
- Thought Technology, Ltd.

Acquiring EEG Data for qEEG Recordings

When acquiring qEEG data, most practitioners use an EEG recording cap that locates all 19 Int'l 10–20 scalp positions. The caps are made of material that stretches; they come in sizes such as child, small, medium, large, and so on. Viscous electroconductive gels are injected into each electrode hole with a blunt syringe. The electrodes within the cap merge into a multicolored ribbon that terminates as a 25-pin D-subminiature (DB) connector. A connector port is available on most qEEG amplifier housings. Ear clips connect directly to lead wires extending from the cap. Figure 7.5 shows a typical EEG recording cap.

Figure 7.5. EEG Recording Cap

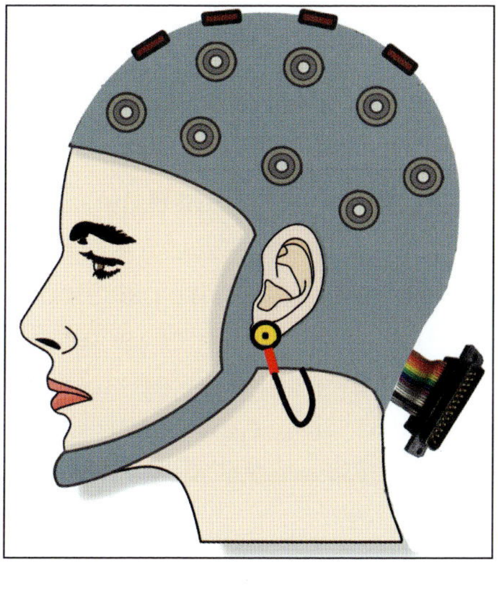

Some EEG practitioners prefer to mount individual electrodes on the scalp rather than using an EEG recording cap. Please investigate current trends in EEG recording cap products and manufacturers before you invest. The holes in EEG recording caps (Figure 7.5) allow for electroconductive gel to be injected to create an electrical connection between the scalp and the electrodes in the EEG recording cap.

Also, there are EEG recording caps that use saline solutions instead of messy gels. Last, there are costly dry electrode caps.

ADDITIONAL TERMINOLOGY

- *Electricity* is the force that causes electrons to move from one location to another: voltage travels from negative (–) to positive (+). Electricity comes from generators, batteries, lightning, and so on.
- *Volt* refers to one unit of electricity. The EEG is measured in microvolts, or 1/1,000th of a volt.
- *Direct current* (DC) means that electrons flow in one direction only. Batteries operate with DC current that flows from negative to positive.
- *Alternating current* (AC) means that electrons move back and forth in two directions. In the United States, household electricity is AC measured at 120 volts and 60 Hertz, or 60 cycles per second.
- *Gain* is the measure of the power (or ability) of the amplifier to acquire an EEG signal from the scalp.
- *Resistance* (R) is the opposition to the flow of electrons, measured in ohms (Ω). Metals such as gold, silver, tin, and copper are good conductors of electricity. Poor conductors of electricity include wood, stone, and plastic, which have a very high resistance to electrical flow. Electrodes for EEGs are often made of gold, silver, and tin.
- *Impedance* is the resistance to the flow of electrons in AC circuits. It is also measured in ohms (Ω). Impedance meters are used to check the quality of scalp-mounted electrode connections. Impedance measurements less than 5,000 Ω are excellent. Some amplifier manufacturers offer a built-in impedance meter. Stand-alone devices are also available. Impedance meters can accept individual electrodes or an entire EEG recording cap that has a port that can accept a 25-pin DB connector. Figure 7.6 shows one popular brand of stand-alone impedance meter.

Figure 7.6. UFI Impedance Meter

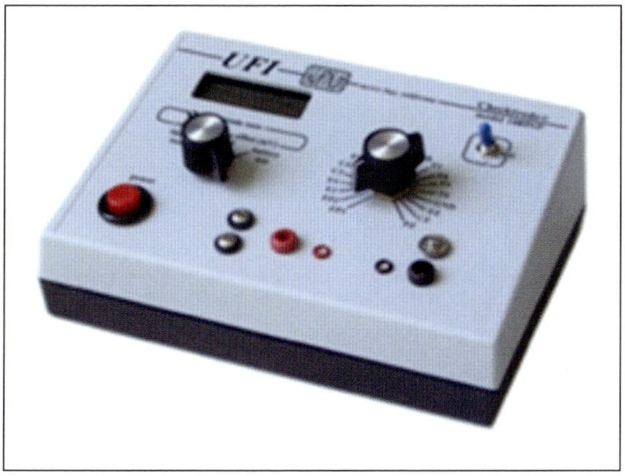

- *Notch filters* are set to match and suppress the amplitude that accompanies line voltage. For example, 60 Hz is the line voltage in the United States and 50 Hz is common in Europe. The EEG may be distorted by intrusive line-voltage activity.
- *High/low-pass filters* smooth out the appearance of the EEG. For example, even though the EEG is measured at 0–64 Hz, a high/low-pass filter can be set to view just 1–40 Hz. Artifacts less than 1 Hz and greater than 40 Hz are dampened. True EEG morphology can only be witnessed when high/low-pass filters are turned off.
- The *Nyquist principle* is a ratio that compares samples per second (SPS) with cycles per second (CPS). The minimum ratio is 2:1. For example, 20 SPS are needed to accurately measure 10 CPS (or 10 Hz), or 128 SPS are needed to accurately measure 64 CPS (or 64 Hz). Commercial EEG amplifiers offer sampling rates that exceed the Nyquist principle to ensure accuracy. Most calculate frequency with a minimum of 256 SPS, which equates to a ratio of 4:1 when measuring 64 CPS (or 64 Hz; 256 SPS/64 CPS = 4:1).
- *Power* refers to amplitude squared (μV^2) divided by frequency. Often the two terms *power* and *amplitude* are used interchangeably. For example, "power training" usually means "amplitude training." Almost all normative qEEG databases are derived from power and converted into SDs. However, the Jewel clinical database is derived from amplitudes and then converted into SDs or Z-scores.

8

Filtering the EEG Into Bins

FILTERS

RAW EEG WAVES are filtered into bins. There are single-hertz bins such as 1 Hz, 4 Hz, 20 Hz, and so on. There are filtered bandwidth ranges such as 4–8 Hz or 8–12 Hz, and so on. Filtered signals are used for assessment and training. Filtered EEG ranges have a sinusoidal morphology (Figure 8.1).

Figure 8.1. Sine Waves

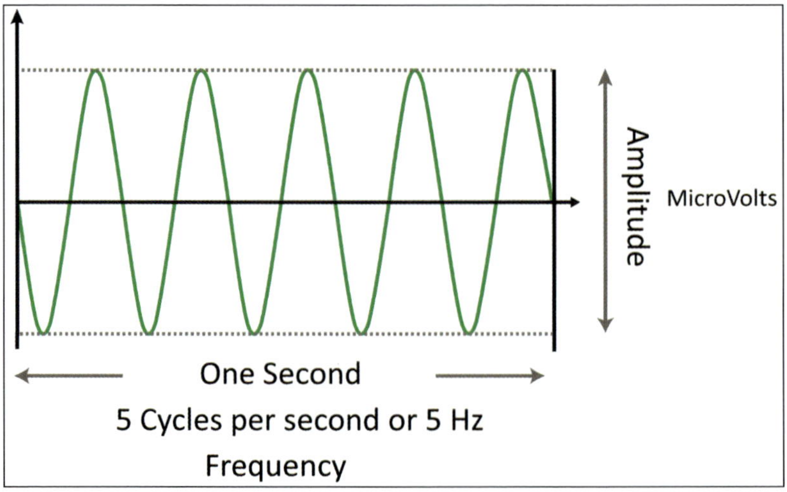

Digital bandpass filters can be compared to a glass prism that breaks down white light into many colors, which is similar to separating the raw EEG into frequency bins. Single-hertz bins (e.g., 8 Hz) are used for assessments, whereas frequency ranges (e.g., 6–10 Hz) are used for training. There are two basic methods of filtering:

- Fast Fourier Transform (FFT) filters gather the whole signal first and then divide it into frequency bins. It can be compared to baking an apple pie and then cutting it into slices.
- Infinite Impulse Response (IIR) filters do not gather the whole signal first. They measure the signal as it is being amplified and divide it into frequency bins. These filters can be compared to pouring liquid through a sieve in order to allow in what is needed and ignore what will not be trained or quantified.
- Digital bandpass filters distribute the raw EEG into its component parts. Single-hertz bins isolate problem areas in the Int'l 10–20 System. Figure 8.2 is an example of isolating an elevated SD of 8 Hz at T5.

Figure 8.2. Single-Hertz Bins From 6 to 8 Hz

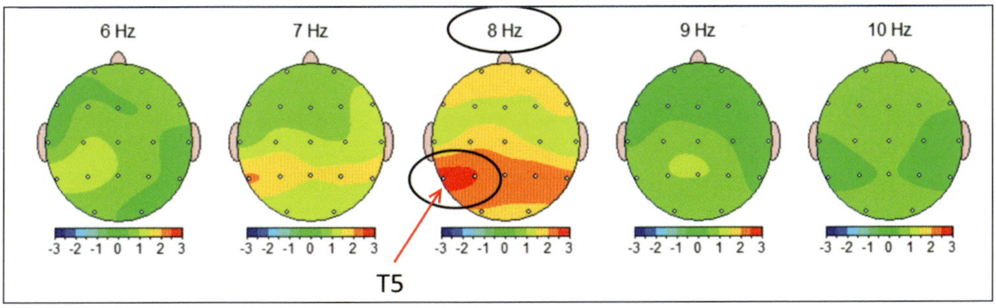

Brain Map derived from NeuroGuide LifeSpan database

Single-hertz bins help to define training ranges; if 8 Hz is the target frequency, then 6–10 Hz could be the ideal training range, with 8 Hz in the middle. When choosing a training range with single-hertz bins,

1. Find the bin with the highest Z-score.
2. Create a range that centers on that bin. For example, if 8 Hz were in the middle, then choose 7–9 Hz or 6–10 Hz as a training range.

The wider the bandwidth range, the less specific it becomes. Remember the story of the man who drowned in a lake that was only 4 feet deep on average: he drowned because the middle of the lake was 20 feet deep even though the rest was just 3 feet deep. The posted average depth obscured the danger. In the same way, a narrow range of 6–10 Hz trains with greater precision than a wider range of 2–14 Hz. Typically, the minimum training range spans 3 Hz, for example, 7–9 Hz or 10–12 Hz. Sometimes, wider ranges may be needed.

Single-hertz bins also help identify the posterior dominant rhythm (PDR) of the brain.

POSTERIOR DOMINANT RHYTHM

Posterior dominant rhythm refers to the frequency with the greatest amplitude as measured in the back of the scalp (Figure 8.3). Measurements are best done with eyes closed. Standards for PDR are based on age. The normal adult PDR is 10 Hz, in harmony with Hans Berger's research (1929). Processing speed is not the same as intelligence. For example, an adult with a PDR of 10.5 is not necessarily smarter than an adult with a PDR of 9.5. However, an adult PDR can be too low (<9.0) or too high (>11.0). The following list shows the increase in PDR with age:

- 1 year old = 6 Hz
- 8 years old = 8 Hz
- 10–12 years old = 9 Hz
- 13–14 years old = 10 Hz

Figure 8.3. Posterior Dominant Rhythm

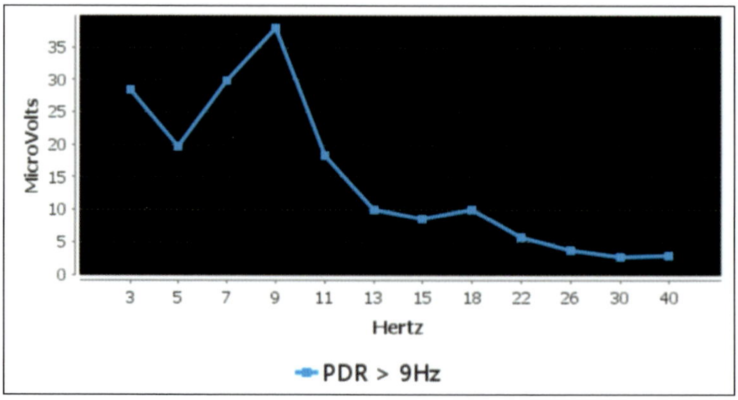

Graphics generated by Jewel database software

Figure 8.4. Calculating the PDR

5 Hz	1 µv	
6 Hz	1.2 µv	
7 Hz	1.3 µv	
8 Hz	1.6 µv	
9 Hz	1.9 µv	
10 Hz	2.0 µv	
11 Hz	2.5 µv	X
12 Hz	2.3 µv	

CALCULATING THE PDR

The Frequency with the highest microvolt reading is the dominant frequency. In this case it is 11 Hz.

Frequencies greater than 11 Hz often reflect anxiety, rumination, insomnia or perhaps nicotine use.

Figure 8.4 demonstrates how to determine PDR with calculations rather than graphics; the goal is to find the greatest amplitude by comparing consecutive single-hertz bins. The normal PDR for a young adult is about 10 Hz, but in Figure 8.5, cannabis use has reduced it to 8 Hz, which is the typical PDR of an 8-year-old child or an adult with dementia. An adult with an 8-Hz processing speed has a slower reaction time than an adult with a 10-Hz processing speed. Adults with PDRs or processing speeds that are less than 9 Hz may well have age-related cognitive decline.

Effect of common psychoactive drugs on the EEG:

1. Neuroleptics (e.g., thorazine) significantly lower PDR, which slows down the brain in order to reduce psychotic symptoms, while adding many unwanted side effects; cognitive performance is compromised.
2. Benzodiazepines (e.g., Ativan) increase beta while decreasing PDR. The combination of increasing beta and reducing PDR results in less anxiety while maintaining cognitive performance. Daily usage for anxiety creates dependency and in the long run may result in greater anxiety. It makes more sense to take benzodiazepines when necessary (PRN). Also, benzodiazepines may generate diffuse beta morphology in the raw EEG.
3. Cocaine speeds up the brain while putting users at risk for self-harm.
4. Stimulants (e.g., Ritalin) mildly increase beta while decreasing theta to improve attention and focus. Caffeine (e.g., coffee), although somewhat milder than Ritalin, is also a stimulant. Of course, too

Figure 8.5. PDR of Recreational Cannabis or Marijuana User

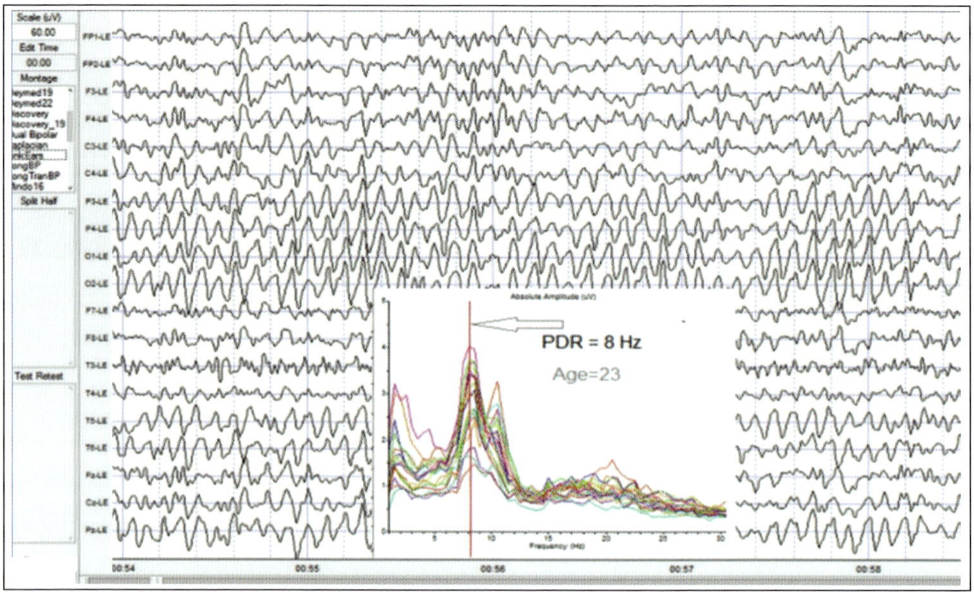

QEEG and PDR chart created by NeuroGuide LifeSpan database

much coffee or caffeinated tea is contraindicated for those who have anxiety or suffer from insomnia.

5. Nicotine (tobacco) increases alpha 2 (10–12 Hz), thereby improving cognitive performance while promoting calm without raising levels of anxiety. Of course, nicotine users do experience anxiety during withdrawal or when lung cancer is detected.

EEG neurofeedback protocol selection may be influenced by drug management therapy. The rule is to train with the drug and not against it. For example, if the client takes a stimulant medication, it may be acceptable to inhibit theta, because the drug also reduces theta. On the other hand, if the client takes a benzodiazepine, it is not acceptable to inhibit beta, because the drug increases beta amplitudes—consider rewarding alpha instead.

9

Common Filtered Bandwidths

DELTA (1–4 HZ)

Delta waves (Figure 9.1) are associated with sleep and thus predominates in infants. Thatcher commented on the presence of delta:

> At birth approximately 40% of the amplitude is in the Delta frequency band and only approximately 10% of the EEG amplitude in the Alpha frequency band. In a normal adult, the percent of amplitude in the Delta frequency band is typically less than 5%, whereas the percent amplitude in the Alpha band is approximately 70% in occipital areas. . . . Thus, EEG amplitude in the Delta frequency range is not necessarily a sign of pathology or abnormal thalamic hyperpolarization, rather it may be a normal part of the EEG. (1999, p. 47)

High-amplitude rhythmic delta in adults is an indication of traumatic brain injury and other disorders, whereas arrhythmic delta has been observed in college students during problem-solving tasks (Lubar, Angelakis, Frederick, & Stathopoulou, 2001). Some children with ADHD or learning disorders may have widespread or diffuse delta as well as theta. Inhibiting 2–7 Hz instead of 4–7 Hz may be advantageous. High delta amplitudes may also indicate sleep deprivation. Delta amplitudes may be inhibited but never rewarded with power training. Z-score training is the safest way to increase low amplitudes of delta.

Figure 9.1. Delta (1–4 Hz)

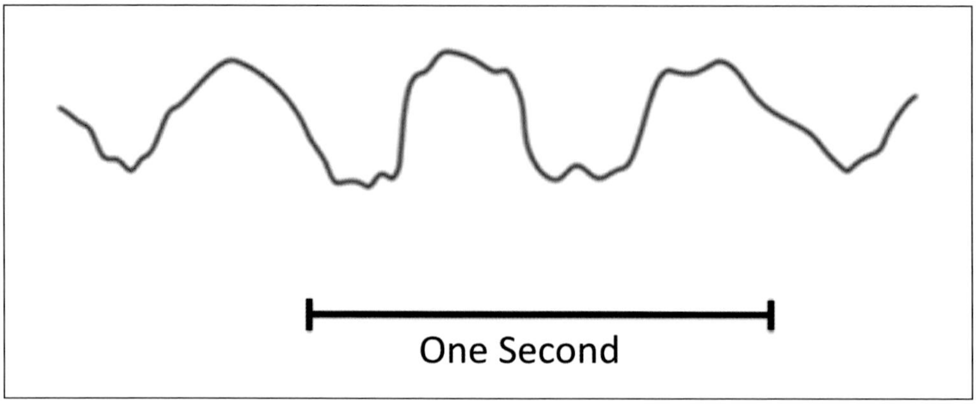

Low delta amplitudes or Z-scores are also of concern. They may relate to TBI, sleep disturbances, ADHD, anxiety, and other symptoms. What kind of training is needed to increase delta amplitudes? While it may be ill-advised to reward weak delta with power training, it is beneficial to raise delta amplitudes with Z-score training as needed. Another way to influence delta amplitudes is to employ pulsing therapies, as discussed in Part V.

THETA (4–8 HZ)

Theta waves may be rhythmic or arrhythmic. Their morphology is shown in Figure 9.2. Theta is associated with creativity and spontaneity, but also with distractibility and inattention, daydreaming, depression, minor TBI (mTBI), and anxiety. Theta that is excessive or laterally asymmetrical may reflect depression (LH), anxiety (RH), and other emotional disorders. Children have higher theta amplitudes than adults (Blume & Kaibara, 1995, p. 40). In adults, the peak theta amplitude is found at Fz.

Providers of EEG neurofeedback often inhibit theta activity when ADHD is present. Training to inhibit slow waves works well with many children. Lubar and colleagues proposed that EEG neurofeedback training could accelerate brain maturation:

> Slow activity (4–7 Hz) in children may be equivalent to higher rhythms, between 7 and 9 Hz in adults. It has been shown, for example, that the posterior dominant frequency follows such a developmental pattern of

Figure 9.2. Theta Morphology

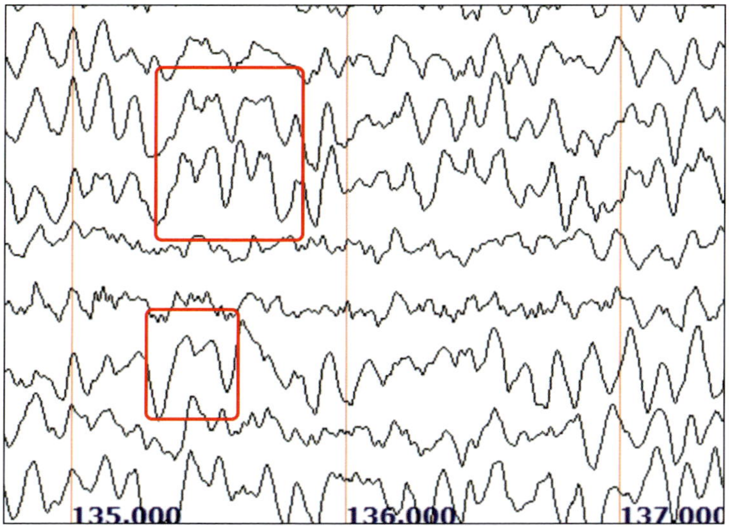

EEG data from software by BrainMaster Technologies, Inc.

> frequency increase, starting from 6–9 Hz at preschool ages and reaching the adult level of 8–12 Hz around the age of 13. In this case, children with attention deficit disorder may be developmentally delayed, and what EEG Neurofeedback suppresses is the dominant oscillating rhythm. (2001, p. 21)

Inhibiting high theta amplitudes in children is common; another approach is theta-to-beta ratio training. The trainee is reinforced each time the ratio between slow waves and fast waves decreases (Rossiter, 2002, pp. 9–35). Ratio training protocols are often included in EEG neurofeedback training menus.

Inhibiting high theta may be appropriate at any scalp location. Rewarding theta is a standard feature of alpha/theta training that is discussed in Part V. Avoid rewarding theta:

1. when there is a history of seizure disorder (Striefel, 1999);
2. in the frontal lobes, because it could result in compromised judgment or inattention; or
3. if the client suffers from post-traumatic stress disorder (PTSD), because it may trigger unwanted flashbacks.

Theta and Age-Related Cognitive Decline

During the aging process, some individuals experience senior moments, which are temporary lapses in memory. Bursts of rhythmic temporal theta (BORTTs) are seen when memory lapses occur. These BORTTs occur primarily in the left hemisphere and must be seen dynamically or as they happen (Figure 9.3). According to Maynard and Hughes (1984), BORTTs may simply reflect drowsiness or poor circulation in the hippocampal region.

Figure 9.3. Bursts of Rhythmic Temporal Theta

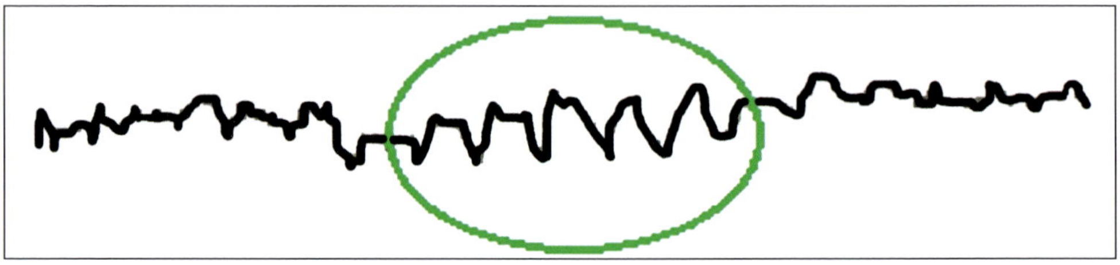

When BORTTs are observed in the EEG morphology, it makes sense to train under task using memory challenges, such as the card-matching game Concentration. Apps are available online for PCs or tablets. Train to inhibit theta on or near the left temporal lobe, especially at T3. If a prospective client is a senior or one who complains of age-related cognitive decline, then assessing the raw EEG for BORTTs while under task is a must. Note: neurofeedback training is done either with eyes closed, eyes open while watching graphics, or eyes open while performing a cognitive task such as reading.

On the other hand, if BORTTs are from drowsiness, then the training goal would be to promote restful sleep.

ALPHA (8–12 HZ)

Alpha is associated with meditation, inner calm, and peacefulness. Alpha is higher in posterior regions and lower in anterior regions of the brain (Blume & Kaibara, 1995, p. 39). Alpha may be called the adult PDR (Rowan & Tolunsky, 2003, p. 25). When it comes to the elderly, some

> maintain a steady 10 Hz frequency throughout life. . . . The usual progression however is a gradual decline in the frequency of the posterior dominant rhythm. A specific disease may not be evident, but the slower PDR probably reflects a degree of cerebral dysfunction. (p. 32)

Alpha may be divided into slow and fast frequency ranges:

- (Slow) alpha 1 = 8–10 Hz
- (Fast) alpha 2 = 10–12 Hz

High or low alpha amplitudes may be symptom markers.

- Diffuse (both hemispheres) alpha (8–12 Hz) is evidence of slow processing.
- Elevated LH alpha is a marker for depression or learning disorders.
- Elevated anterior alpha is a marker for depression, ADHD, TBI, and mental fog.
- Weak alpha with strong beta is a marker for anxiety or migraines.
- Elevated posterior alpha 2 (10–12 Hz) is a marker for anxiety, insomnia, or frequent worry.

Alpha Blocking

When your eyes close, alpha amplitudes increase unless you are concentrating. When your eyes open, alpha amplitudes decrease. Closing the eyes causes the visual system to idle, whereas opening the eyes causes the visual system to be activated (Figure 9.4).

Pyramidal neurons synchronize when the eyes close, which results in higher amplitudes of alpha. The opposite is also true; pyramidal neurons desynchronize when eyes are open, which results in lower amplitudes of alpha. This phenomenon is called alpha blocking.

Alpha and qEEG Recordings

Eyes-closed qEEG recordings are usually not started unless alpha is visible in the raw EEG. Of course, if the test subject has had a TBI or suffers from anxiety, do not expect to see much alpha in the recording. Always instruct the test subject to stop concentrating or even thinking because it interferes with alpha production.

Figure 9.4. Alpha Blocking: Eyes Closed, Eyes Open

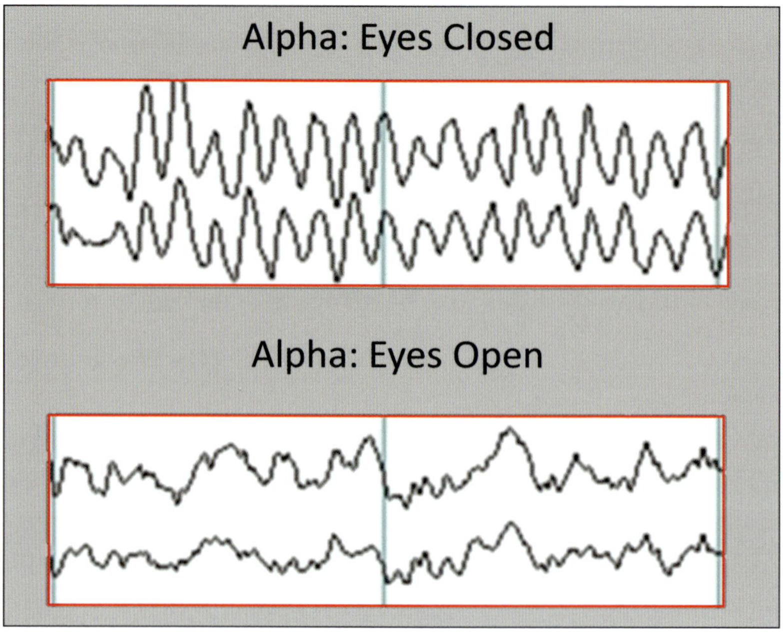

EEG data from software by BrainMaster Technologies, Inc.

If eyes-closed alpha amplitudes decrease, it usually means drowsiness (Stampi, Stone, & Michirnori, 1995, pp. 368–376). If eyes-open alpha amplitudes increase during a cognitive task, it is called inversion (Siever, 2004, p. 24). The problem of inversion can be exposed by doing qEEG assessments under task. Alpha and theta amplitudes should not increase steeply while reading or doing math problems. If they do increase, then train the client under task instead of using movies or games for visual feedback.

Keep these three things in mind for qEEG data acquisition:

1. Encourage the test subject to be mentally relaxed: perhaps say, "Imagine you are getting a massage or you are at the beach tanning."
2. Avoid qEEG recordings when the subject is drowsy.
3. qEEG assessments while under task reveal the problem of inversion.

Alpha Spindles

Alpha spindles are normal repetitious alpha-wave cycles that can be observed in the raw EEG (Figure 9.5). Also, they may be seen during meditation, drowsiness, or fatigue (Simon et al., 2011), or when there is an idling of cortical responses.

Figure 9.5. Alpha Spindles

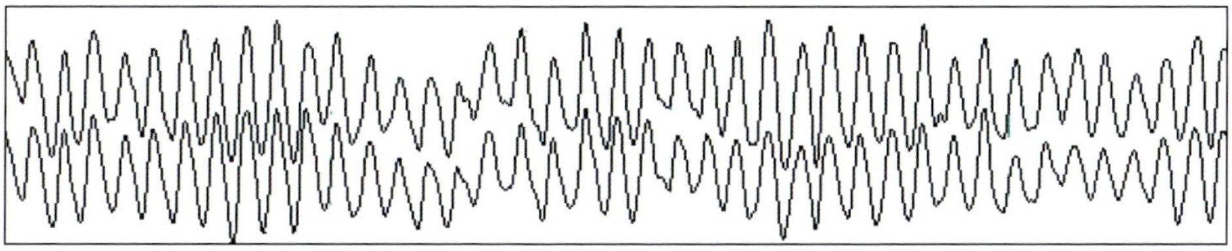

Mu (Mμ) Waves

Mu waves appear within the alpha range of 8–12 Hz. They have a wicket pattern, whereas alpha waves have a sinusoidal pattern (compare Figure 9.5 with Figure 9.6).

Mu rhythms are found in the sensorimotor cortex, or occasionally in the parietal lobes (Blume & Kaibara, 1995, p. 39). Brain maps do not differentiate between mu and alpha. The best way to discern the presence of mu rhythms is by observing raw EEG waveforms at C3 and C4. Mu waves are idling rhythms that increase when the motor system is idle; they are associated with mirror neurons and may be seen in the EEGs of children or adults diagnosed with autistic spectrum disorders. Inhibit (when training) but do not reward mu rhythms (Lubar & Lubar, 2002).

Figure 9.6. Mu Waves

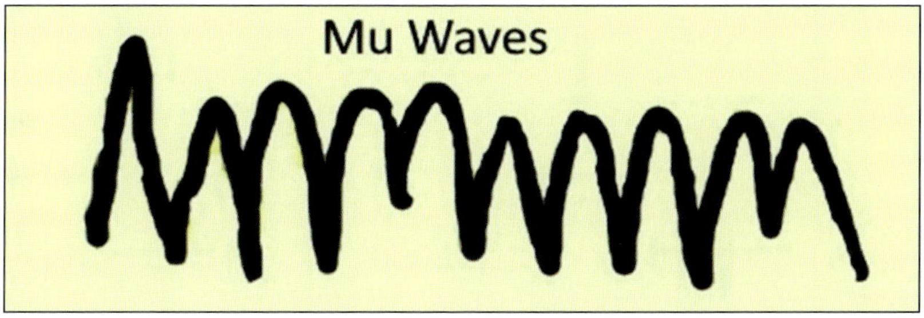

SENSORIMOTOR RHYTHM (12–15 OR 12–16 HZ)

Sensorimotor rhythm (SMR) may reflect a state of being internally oriented. Alpha and SMR are idling rhythms; SMR waves increase when the motor system is idle (or still). Barry Sterman and colleagues pioneered SMR training, first with cats and then with humans suffering from epilepsy. He rewarded 12–15 Hz at C3 or at T3 with stand-alone (noncomputerized) equipment (Robbins, 2000, p. 44). Eventually, his protocol was later combined with theta inhibition for both epilepsy and hyperactivity (Budzynski, 1999, p. 72). Note that 12–15 Hz is called lo-beta when it is measured or trained away from the sensorimotor strip.

Today, SMR training is just as important as it was over 50 years ago. Classic single-channel SMR training at C4 includes three active bandwidths, as shown in Chart 9.1 and Figure 9.7. All three bandwidths must meet threshold requirements before feedback is emitted. Next, see Figure 9.7 for a visual or graphic presentation of single-channel SMR training.

Chart 9.1: C4 SMR Training Protocol

Site	Reward Band	Inhibit Band	Inhibit Band
C4	(SMR) 12-15 Hz	4-7 Hz	20-30 Hz

Figure 9.7. Classic C4 SMR Training: Three-Threshold Design

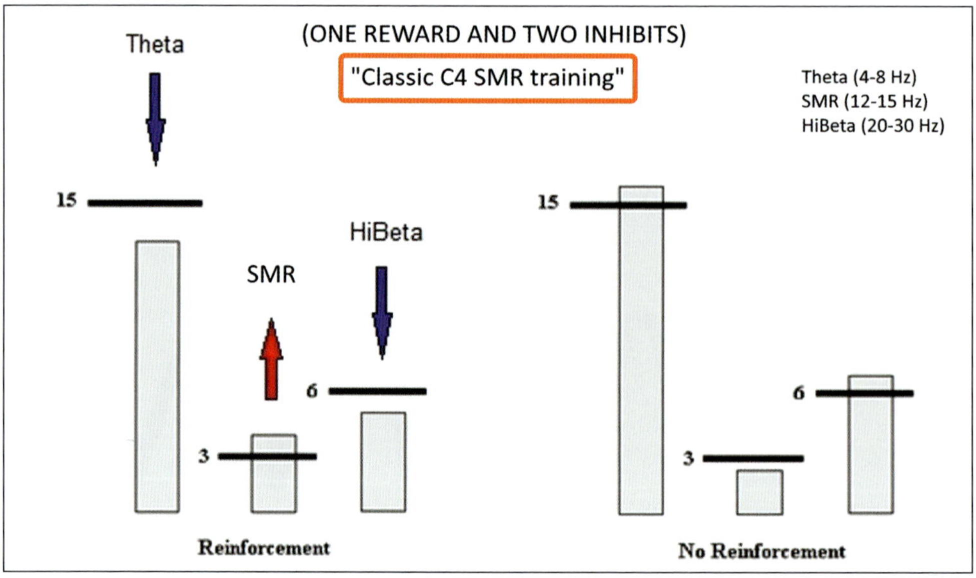

Younger children benefit more when 11–14 Hz, rather than 12–15 Hz, is rewarded. SMR training at C4 is effective for a wide range of disorders because two critical brain regions are nearby: the sensorimotor cortex and the insular cortex. The sensorimotor cortex is associated with sleep disorders, seizure, gross and fine motor skills, and sensory integration. The RH insular cortex is associated with anxiety, social integration, and pain.

In review, use C4 SMR training for:

- Anxiety disorders and panic
- Hyperactivity
- Phobia and social anxiety
- Seizure
- Pain
- Sleep disorders
- Sensory integration dysfunction

Note that classic SMR training is not used when SMR has elevated amplitudes or high SDs.

Client-Centered SMR Training at C3–C4

Single-channel bipolar montages are often used at C3–C4 to relieve anxiety or migraine (Figure 9.7A). The training approach is subjective or client-centered. Theta and hi-beta are fixed inhibits, whereas the reward band

Figure 9.7A. Tweaking the Reward Range on the Fly at C3-C4

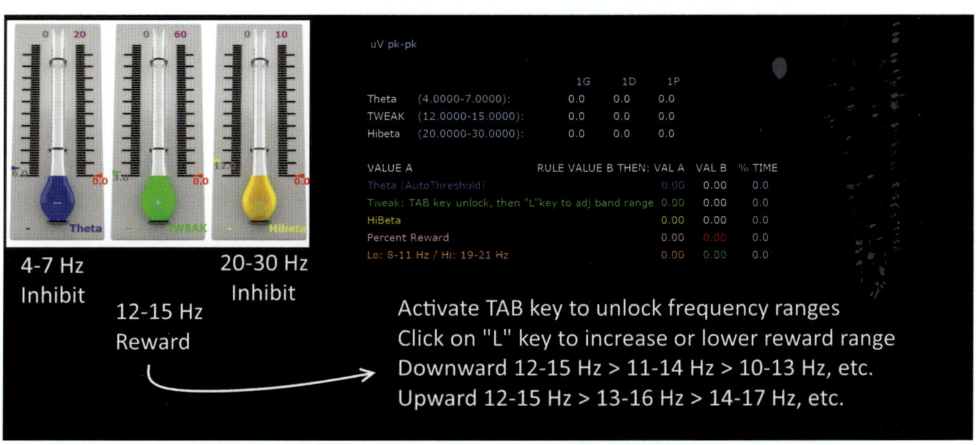

Training screen adapted from BrainAvatar software by BrainMaster Technologies, Inc.

of 12–15 Hz is flexible and may be changed or tweaked during training. Tweaking is also called an on-the-fly adjustment. The method for using this protocol is as follows.

Start the program and train for two minutes with a reward range of 12–15 Hz. Next, ask the trainee—using a scale from 1 to 10—"How relaxed are you, and do you think you could be more relaxed?" If the trainee indicates he or she could be more relaxed, then the reward range is decreased downward to 11–14 Hz. The question is repeated every two minutes. The process continues until the trainee is satisfied. The lowest tweaked range is usually 8–11 Hz. If the trainee feels foggy, then the reward band is tweaked upward. Of course, in some cases the baseline reward of 12–15 Hz is just fine and no changes are needed. In other cases, the reward band is increased to promote mental clarity rather than relaxation. The tweaking process finds the optimum reward range that will be used in future training sessions. Therefore, there is no need to repeat this process each time the client trains.

The above protocol has proved to be a very effective way to teach state awareness. Trainees are amazed when they become relaxed. Do not use this protocol with eyes closed when the trainee is at risk for panic attacks or spontaneous abreactions. Avoid relaxation-induced anxiety or RIA (Kerson, C., 2002). This protocol is not all that is needed; it will be good for no more than 10 sessions of about 15 minutes each.

SLEEP

During stage 2 sleep, "the EEG pattern becomes more irregular; *sleep spindles*—sudden, short high-voltage wave bursts occurring at 12–14 Hz appear, and arousal is more difficult" (Marieb, 1995, p. 492; Figure 9.8). If the client has insomnia, it may help to inhibit or reward 12–14 Hz to promote restful sleep. If SMR SDs are high, then inhibit; if low, then reward. One article indicated that as many as 56% of ADHD clients have excessive SMR (Gurnee, 2003).

The symptoms of sleep deprivation mimic many disorders (Nir, 2017). Therefore, before beginning any neurofeedback training program rule out sleep deprivation as the cause of the client's symptoms. Quality sleep is primary to mental and physical health. What happens when sleep is lacking?

Figure 9.8. Sleep and SMR Sleep Spindles

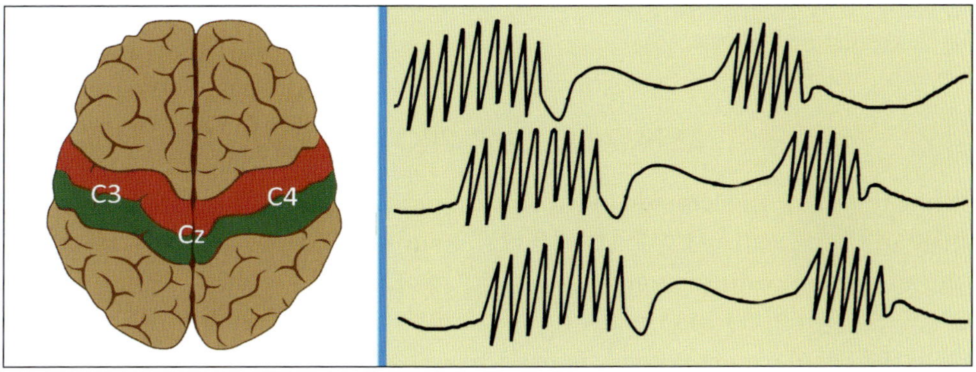

Sensorimotor Cortex; Sleep Spindles (12-14 Hz)

> Amazingly, certain regions of the brain also seemed to be taking mini-naps, while the patient was awake. "Slow, sleep-like waves disrupted the patients' brain activity and performance of tasks. . . . This phenomenon suggests that select regions of the patients' brains were dozing, causing mental lapses, while the rest of the brain was awake and running as usual." This finding agrees with earlier evidence of similar "cat-naps" in rats who were sleep deprived and having cognition problems as a result.
>
> It's well known that sleep deprivation has negative effects on a myriad of psychological parameters: cognition, attention, mood, memory, reaction time, and decision-making. Even partial sleep deprivation can have significant effects. Chronic lack of sleep also affects us physically, as it's linked to weight gain, inflammation, diabetes, and heart disease. (Walton, 2017)

If a client is sleep deprived, then inhibiting high amplitudes of delta, theta, or alpha may be in vain. The first order of business is sleep regulation. For example, I had one client who reported depression but who also chose to limit his sleep to 4 hours per night. Rather than doing EEG neurofeedback for depression, I instructed him to go to bed earlier. In just a few weeks his depression remitted.

Clinical assessments need to include questions about sleep habits and insomnia as well as the sleeping environment--a darkened and cooler bedroom may help to promote restful sleep. Of course, make sure the sleep-deprived or anxious client's diet or lifestyle is not the real culprit with questions such as, "How many cups of coffee do you drink each day?" Quality sleep is the first order of business when it comes to EEG neurofeedback treatment plans.

BETA AND SMR PROTOCOLS

What about C3, the left side of the sensorimotor cortex? How is that trained? Instead of rewarding SMR (12–15 Hz), beta is rewarded at 15–18 Hz. (Any one of the following ranges may work: 14–17 Hz, 15–18 Hz, 15–20 Hz, or 16–19 Hz, etc.) C3 beta training is used to limit depression because it is near the insular cortex, or it is used to enhance fine motor skills because it is on the sensorimotor cortex.

Further, C3 (beta) and C4 (SMR) may be trained simultaneously. Two-channel beta-SMR training has two rewards and four inhibits, as shown in Chart 9.2.

Chart 9.2: Two Channel Beta/SMR Training

Site	Reward Band	Inhibit Band	Inhibit Band
C4	12-15 Hz	4-7 Hz	20-30 Hz
C3	15-18 Hz	4-7 Hz	20-30 Hz

All six bands must meet threshold requirements before feedback is emitted. Auto-thresholds are a must. Note that in younger children, it's common to inhibit 2–7 Hz instead of 4–7 Hz and to reward 11–14 Hz instead of 12–15 Hz for SMR and 14–17 Hz instead of 15–18 Hz for beta.

Midline Training at Cz, Fz, or Pz

When doing single channel training at Cz, Fz or Pz, the clinician chooses to reward either Beta or SMR. Beta is chosen to improve alertness whereas SMR is chosen to limit hyperactivity or impulsivity. The training inhibits are Theta and HiBeta. Single channel bipolar montages are common at Fz-Cz, FCz-CPz and Cz-Pz. Often younger children are trained at Cz-Pz because the brain develops from posterior to anterior.

Beta (12–25 Hz)

Beta is defined as fast wave activity, or "any rhythmic activity >13 Hz" (Blume & Kaibara, 1995, p. 39; see Figure 9.9). It has been associated with being focused, analytical, externally oriented, or in a state of relaxed thinking. Dominant beta frequencies are higher in adults than children (Lubar & Lubar, 1999). "Maximal Beta amplitude is usually in the fronto-central regions, but it may be widespread. It does not respond to eye opening and closing, as does the Alpha. During drowsiness, Beta may seem to increase in amplitude" (Rowan & Tolunsky, 2003, p. 27). Beta bandwidths are defined in several different ranges. When communicating with other clinicians about beta, provide the frequency range of interest.

Figure 9.9. Rhythmic Beta Waves (12–25 Hz)

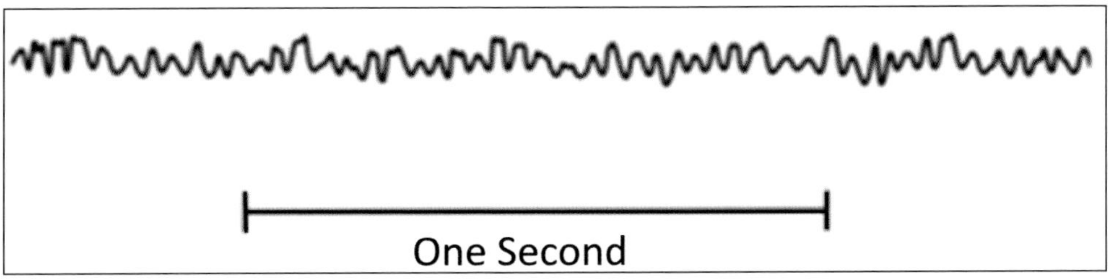

In 1999, Davidson proposed that hypoactivation of the left frontal cortex is a marker for depression, whereas hyperactivation of the right frontal cortex is a marker for anxiety (Davidson, R. J., & Irwin, W., 1999). Thus, hypoactivation in the LH means too much theta and alpha, whereas hyperactivation in the RH means too much beta. Therefore,

- Inhibit alpha or theta in the LH to relieve depression.
- Inhibit beta in the RH to relieve anxiety.

Excessive beta is commonly found in many disorders, such as ADHD, obsessive-compulsive disorder (OCD), sleep disorders, bruxism, learning disorders, anxiety disorders, depression, and many other psychiatric problems. It is common to find that anterior RH beta exceeds LH beta in this population. Beta amplitudes may be equal to or greater than theta amplitudes (beta ≥ theta). Clients with excessive beta may be anxious, on edge, or uneasy. Help clients to become active participants in the process outside of the office. Homework assignments include 15–20 minutes each day of skin temperature training, breath work, or heart rate variability (HRV) training.

Weak beta power may also be an EEG marker (signature) for poor cognitive performance or difficulty concentrating.

Surface Electromyography and Beta

Caution must be observed when rewarding beta, because the beta range overlaps with the surface electromyography (sEMG) range of electrical activity. "Never train an artifact!" warns Adam Crane (1998), a biofeedback trainer. This potential problem can be minimized if trainees are encouraged to drop their shoulders, do a body scan, and avoid poor posture. If legs must be crossed, then use a half lotus position or cross the legs at ankle level only. Make sure that fast waves are truly beta waves and not muscle tension or sEMG waves in disguise. Watch clients' body language, their forehead, shoulders, and posture. Ask them to relax or stretch. Looking at the raw EEG signal helps to identify muscle tension (Figure 9.10).

In Figure 9.10, the sEMG circled on the left is sharp and nonrhythmic, whereas the beta on the right is flowing and rhythmic. To create this effect, the subject clenched his jaw and then relaxed. I show all new qEEG test subjects how this works. It helps them to avoid clenching their own jaws during the assessment.

Figure 9.10. sEMG Sharp Waves Compared to Beta Rhythmic Waves

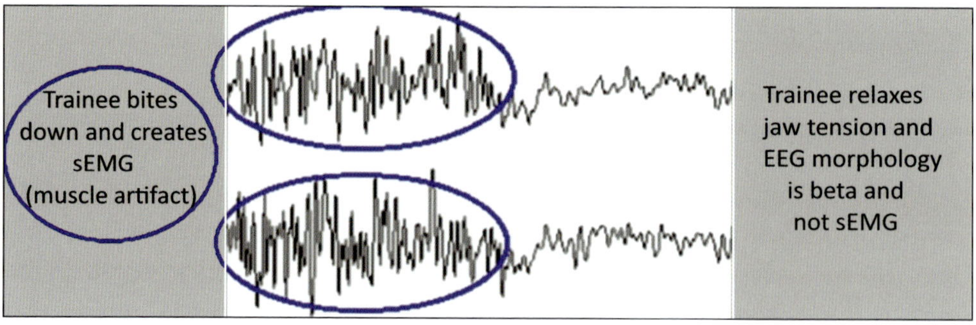

Beta Spindles

The untrained eye has difficulty differentiating between sEMG and Beta spindles. Figure 9.11 includes examples of rhythmic beta spindles that look quite different than the sharp morphology of nonrhythmic sEMG. Beta spindles are greater than 20 Hz. They typically range from 22 to 25 Hz.

Beta spindles can be an EEG marker, or signature, for a number of conditions including, but not limited to, ADHD (often with temper tantrums), epilepsy, anxiety, autistic spectrum disorders, and insomnia (Arns, Swatzyna, Gunkelman, & Olbrich, 2015).

Figure 9.11. Beta Spindles Circled

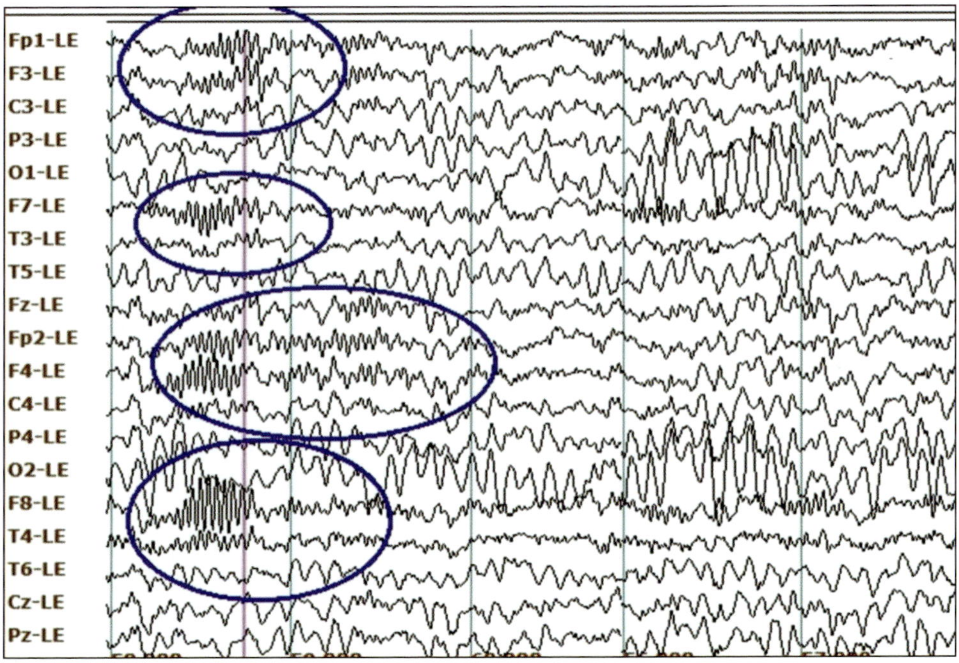

QEEG adapted from BrainMaster Technologies, Inc, software

Hi-Beta (20–35 Hz)

Hi-beta is associated with peak performance, cognitive processing, worry, anxiety, overthinking, ruminating, migraine, and OCD. Hi-beta is often inhibited during training but rarely rewarded. Elevated hi-beta ranging from 20 to 32 Hz could be a marker for any one of a number of disorders, or it could imply that the brain is compensating for excessive theta. Therefore, inhibiting theta may be just as important as inhibiting hi-beta (20–32 Hz). Note that beta/SMR protocols inhibit theta and hi-beta while rewarding either SMR (12–15 Hz) or beta (15–18 Hz).

Diffuse (widespread) or elevated hi-beta ranging from 20 to 32 Hz may respond slowly or not at all to training. Consider the following options:

1. Use a bipolar montage rather than a monopolar montage.
2. Reward beta (15–18 Hz) or SMR (12–15 Hz). The brain is a system; rewarding the amplitude of lower beta frequencies may result in the reduction of amplitudes in higher beta frequencies (hi-beta).
3. Rewarding alpha at Pz is commonly used for anxiety disorders.
4. Z-score training may also be effective, especially when elevated beta is accompanied by coherence problems.

GAMMA (40 HZ)

Gamma waves range anywhere from 28 to 80 Hz; they are often trained at 35–45 Hz, with 40 Hz being the frequency of greatest interest. Synchronous bursts of 40-Hz activity have been found during problem-solving tasks for adults and children. Gamma is often lacking when learning disorders or mental deficits are present. A 40-Hz rhythm is found throughout the scalp rather than at one discrete location. It seems to help organize the brain, promote learning, and allow for mental sharpness. It is activated when the brain needs to be active and idle when no specialized task is at hand (Hammond, 2000, pp. 95–100). In order to activate gamma, trainees need to be under task and presented with a series of cognitive challenges.

> Gamma-band coherence increases between regions of the brain that receive the two classes of stimuli involved in an associative-learning procedure in humans. An increase in coherence could fulfill the criteria required for the formation of hebbian cell assemblies, binding together parts of the brain that must communicate with one another in order for associative learning to take place. (Miltner, Braun, Arnold, Witte, & Taub, 1999, p. 434)

Gamma activity is associated with peak brain performance and meditation:

> Long-distance synchrony is thought to reflect large-scale neural coordination and can occur when two neural populations recorded by two distant electrodes oscillate with a precise phase relationship that remains constant during a certain number of oscillation cycles. . . .

Gamma training is a likely choice for most peak performance training programs because it promotes learning and memory via long distance brain connections; it has already proven its effectiveness when non-neurofeedback brain-based treatments such as photic stimulation, pulsed electromagnetic field therapy, and Vie light therapy are set to enhance gamma.

Caution: since gamma ranges (28–80 Hz) overlap sEMG ranges (13–200 Hz), please observe the raw EEG carefully to make sure that gamma and not sEMG (muscle tension) is being rewarded. This caution applies to EEG neurofeedback rather than pulsing therapies.

10

Filtered EEG Components: Asymmetry, Power Ratio, Coherence, and Phase

ASYMMETRY

Simple asymmetry assessments are performed at homologous or contralateral sites. Simple asymmetry is based on a comparison by bandwidth of the LH and RH EEG. In general, the amplitudes of the EEG at homologous or contralateral sites are fairly equal (Chart 10.1). Power tends to be some-

Chart 10.1: Contralateral Sites

LH site	RH site
Fp1	Fp2
F3	F4
C3	C4
P3	P4
O1	O2
F7	F8
T3	T4
T5	T6

Figure 10.1. Alpha Asymmetry Common in Depression

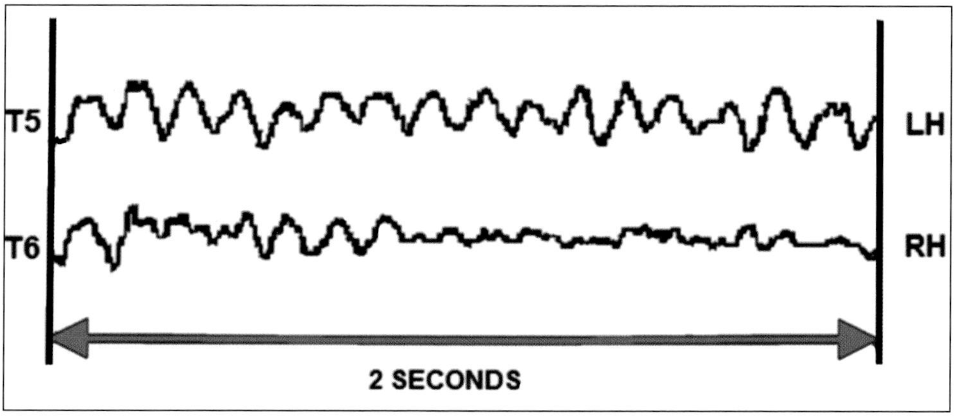

what higher in the RH posterior than the LH posterior, especially in the alpha band: P4 alpha is greater than P3 alpha by 10–15%.

Asymmetry comparisons are conducted in the same frequency range. Z-score training measures and trains more than homologous RH to LH sites. Asymmetries can be calculated between any two Int'l 10–20 sites.

Simple alpha and beta lateral asymmetries are explored in this section.

Alpha Asymmetry

Figure 10.1 shows that T5 (LH) alpha amplitude is greater than T6 (RH) alpha, which is an EEG marker for depression or a learning disorder. Since there are 16 cycles in 2 seconds at T5, the frequency is 16/2 = 8 Hz.

The asymmetry map (Figure 10.2) shows alpha at T5 to be higher than T6. Red reflects higher Z-score and blue reflects the corresponding lower Z-score. In this case, the red-blue combination is a reciprocal or opposite: red = (+)3 SD and blue = (–)3 SD. The EEG in Figure 10.1 and the asymmetry head in Figure 10.2 agree. The client suffered from clinical depression. But the same alpha asymmetry could have reflected a learning disorder, because T5 is one of the key processing sites in the brain for academic performance. Depression or learning disorders are possible when either LH alpha or theta is at least 20% greater than RH alpha or theta at homologous or contralateral sites.

Figure 10.2. T5 Alpha > T6 Alpha

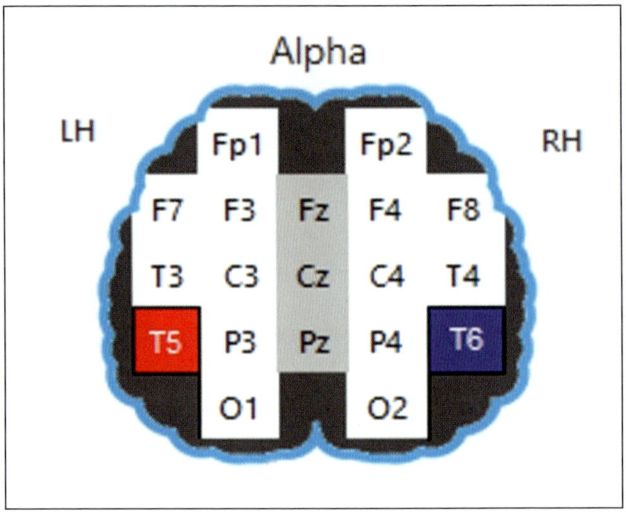

Jewel database Asymmetry head

Alpha Asymmetry Protocol

Peter Rosenfeld developed an alpha asymmetry protocol that is designed to rectify abnormal anterior (frontal) lobe alpha asymmetries. In order to execute this protocol, two separate EEG channels are set up with a bipolar montage: channel 1 and channel 2 both use Cz for the location of the reference electrode. The channel 1 active electrode is at F3, whereas the channel 2 active electrode is at F4. The ground is placed at any convenient place on the scalp or ears. The client receives reinforcement whenever RH alpha exceeds LH alpha: hence, whenever F4 is greater than F3. Clinical trials have shown the efficacy of this approach (Baehr, Rosenfeld, Baehr, & Earnest, 1999).

Asymmetry issues are also resolved with single-channel EEG. Alpha (8–12 Hz) is inhibited while beta (15–18 Hz) may be rewarded at F3. Two-channel Z-score training could be considered. Whether the clinician decides to use a two-channel or a one-channel approach, the goal is the same: facilitate a normative EEG pattern.

It is wise to consult the brain map to find out where the suspected contralateral asymmetry lies. F3 to F4 is just one of many possibilities. Others include T3 to T4, C3 to C4, T5 to T6, and P3 to P4.

Beta Asymmetry

In Figure 10.3, F8 (RH) beta is greater than F7 (LH) beta, which is an EEG marker for anxiety and agitation. Since the issue is at F8, poor sustained attention is also possible.

Figure 10.3. RH Beta Asymmetry: Agitation, Anxiety

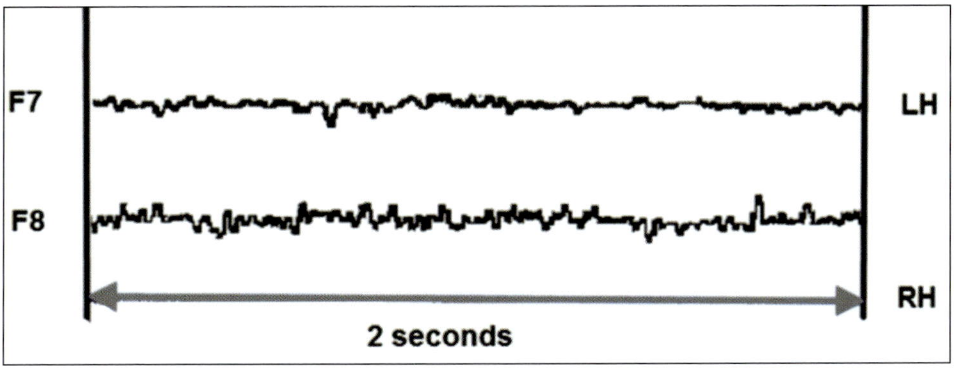

In Figure 10.4, RH beta is greater than LH beta, common to disorders such as anxiety, agitated depression, phobia, and panic as well as poor sustained attention, inadequate attachment, and poor social skills. There are two factors: (1) location and (2) bandwidth.

Figure 10.4. F8 Beta > F7 Beta

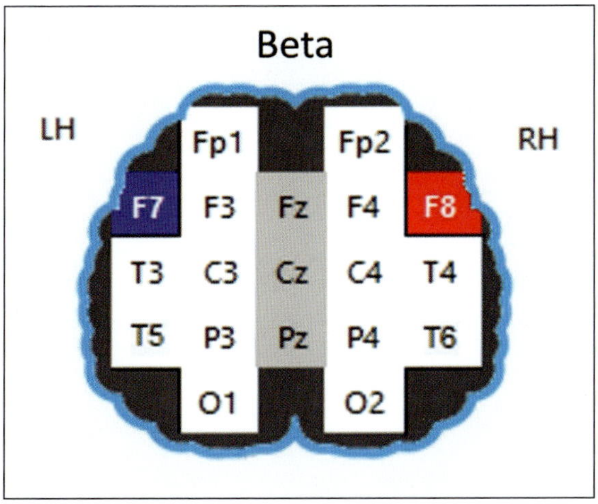

Jewel database Asymmetry head

Note that it is not possible to count beta wave cycles at F8, but it is possible to discern that F8 is greater than F7. Training options include (1) inhibiting beta at F8 with a monopolar montage, (2) inhibiting beta at F8-T4 with a bipolar montage, and (3) two-channel Z-score training at F7 and F8.

POWER RATIO

Power ratios at a single Int'l 10–20 location may be used as EEG markers or signatures to support clinical diagnoses or symptoms. Consequently, learning to differentiate between normal and abnormal EEG distributions will guide assessment and training decisions. The key is that statistics are often needed to judge power ratio problems.

Three general descriptions are used for power ratio:

1. Balanced (normative)—Figure 10.5
2. Overaroused—Figure 10.6
3. Underaroused—Figure 10.7

Balanced Ratio

Figure 10.5 shows a single-channel two-dimensional graph depicting an eyes closed balanced, or normative, adult recording at Cz.

- Alpha has the highest amplitude.
- Theta and delta are lower than alpha.
- Beta amplitudes steadily decrease as the frequency increases.

Figure 10.5. Balanced Adult Power Ratio at Cz (EC)

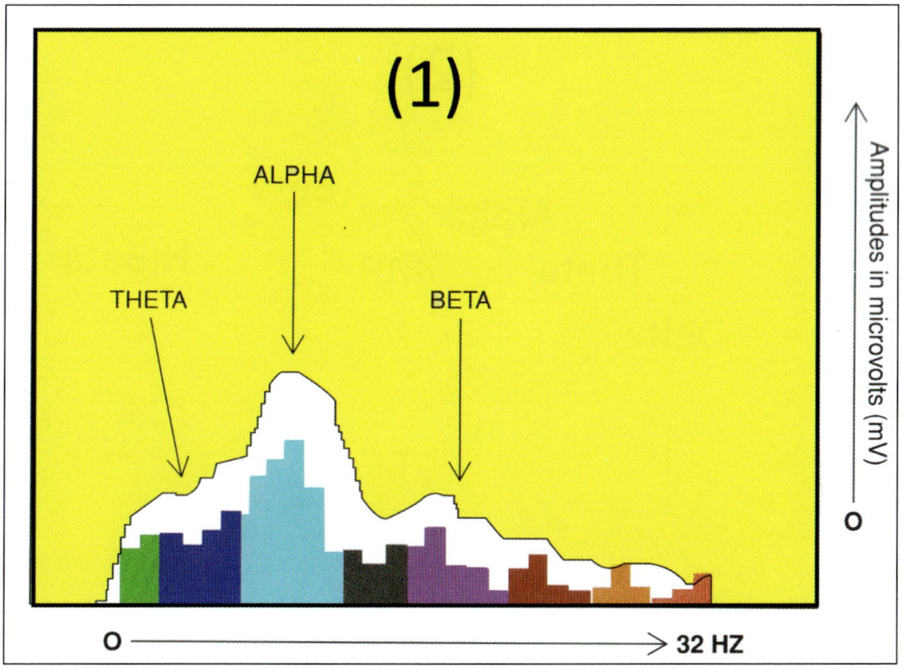

Two-dimensional chart adapted from BrainMaster Technologies, Inc. software

Overaroused Ratio

Figure 10.6 shows an overaroused power ratio because fast waves are far greater than slow waves.

- Fast waves (beta) are greater than slow waves (alpha and theta).
- As the frequency increases, the amplitude increases.

Figure 10.6 depicts an overaroused EEG presentation. The typical overaroused subject has symptoms such as anxiety, OCD, worry, obsessions, perfectionism, insomnia, or migraines. It's difficult for overaroused clients to relax and let go. The power ratio is beta greater than theta or beta greater than alpha. Often, increases in fast-wave beta are accompanied by decreases in slow-wave alpha or theta. Sometimes children with an overaroused pattern are hyperactive or inattentive; they may be misdiagnosed with ADHD, but the real problem is anxiety.

Figure 10.6. Power Ratio Is Overaroused

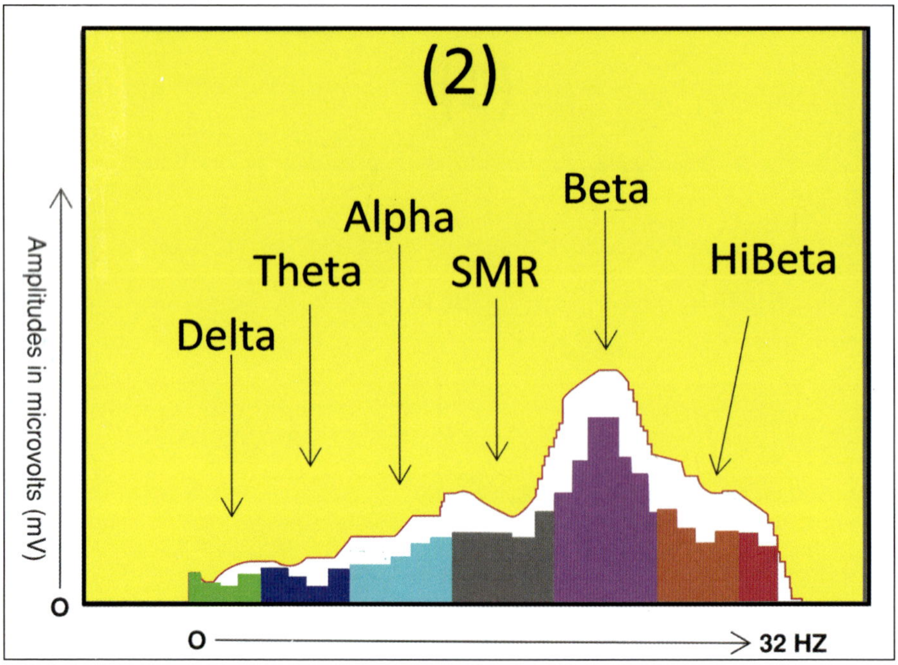

Two-dimensional chart adapted from BrainMaster Technologies, Inc. software

Underaroused Ratio

Figure 10.7 shows an underaroused power ratio because slow waves are far greater than fast waves.

- Slow waves (especially theta) are greater than fast waves (beta).
- As the frequency decreases, the amplitude increases.

What is reflected by an underaroused EEG presentation? The typical underaroused subject may have difficulty concentrating or processing information, possibly be depressed or unmotivated, or have poor executive skills. Such a subject may be diagnosed with learning disorders, ADHD, or other slow-wave disorders. The power ratio is theta greater than beta or alpha greater than beta. Joel Lubar was the first researcher to associate ADHD (in children) with high theta-to-beta ratios. He also associated inattention with elevated 6–10 Hz, which he called Thalpha. Chart 10.2 provides a developmental perspective of theta-to-beta ratios.

Figure 10.7. Power Ratio Is Underaroused

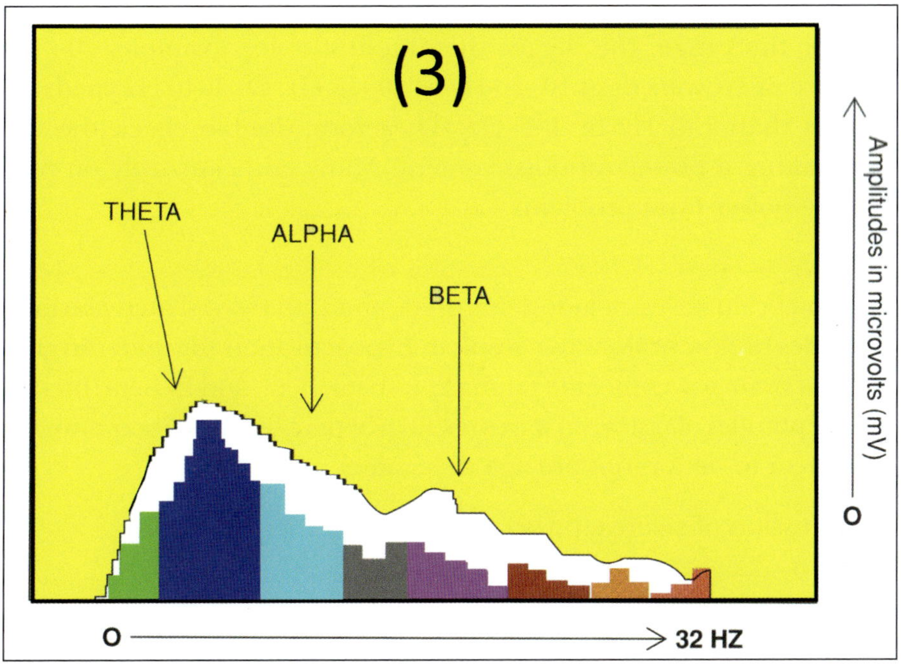

Two-dimensional chart adapted from BrainMaster Technologies, Inc. software

Chart 10.2: Average Theta-to-Beta Ratios at Cz

Age	Theta/Beta RATIO
6	3:1
8	2.4:1
10	2:1
14-to-Adult	1.5:1

The theta range is 4–8 Hz and the beta range is 13–21 Hz. Chart 10.2 indicates that a 3:1 theta-to-beta range may be quite normal for a 6-year-old but very high for an adult. Ratio-training protocols reduce elevated power ratios (Rossiter, T., 2002). They are often used along the cingulate gyrus (Fz, Cz, and Pz).

Range

The wider the range, the bigger the amplitude; for example, 10–30 Hz yields more microvolts than 10–20 Hz or 10–15 Hz. Or 1–10 Hz yields more microvolts than 1–5 Hz or 1–3 Hz. Therefore, double check the range before making a power ratio assessment. Many clinicians rely on SDs to determine power ratio problems.

Recap:

- Slow brain waves include delta, theta, and alpha waves. Increased amplitudes of slow brain waves result in hypoactivation (or underarousal).
- Fast brain waves include (alpha 2) lo-beta, beta, and hi-beta. Increased amplitudes of fast brain waves result in hyperactivation (or overarousal).
- Theta-to-beta ratios are age dependent.

For a discussion of relative power, see Appendix 1.

COHERENCE

Coherence is a measurement of the similarity between two sites on the scalp; it is a comparison of waveforms within the same frequency range and time domain. Coherence is also a measurement of information sharing between two distinct brain regions. It "can directly reflect neural network connectivity and neural network dynamics" (Thatcher, 1999, p. 49). Consider the waveform comparison between two channels in Figure 10.8:

Look carefully at the two filtered waves in Figure 10.8. They do not rise and fall in unison and yet they are not completely different. Coherence is a measurement of percentage of similarity between two waves of identical frequency: that is, the higher the percentage, the greater the similarity. Coherence between each pair of sites varies. For example, the normal or average alpha coherence between C3 and C4 is about 60%.

Coherence percentages decrease as distance increases. For example, the distance from T3 to T4 is greater than the distance from C3 to C4. Therefore, the coherence percentage between T3 and T4 should be lower than the coherence percentage between C3 and C4. For example, the average alpha coherence between T3 and T4 is about 25% and the average alpha coherence between C3 and C4 is about 60%. Figure 10.9 presents the coherence-to-distance percentage concept.

Coherence percentages can be compared to the communication between two friends. If one friend moves to a different city, then communication

Figure 10.8. Comparing Alpha (8–12 Hz) Coherence Between Two Scalp Locations

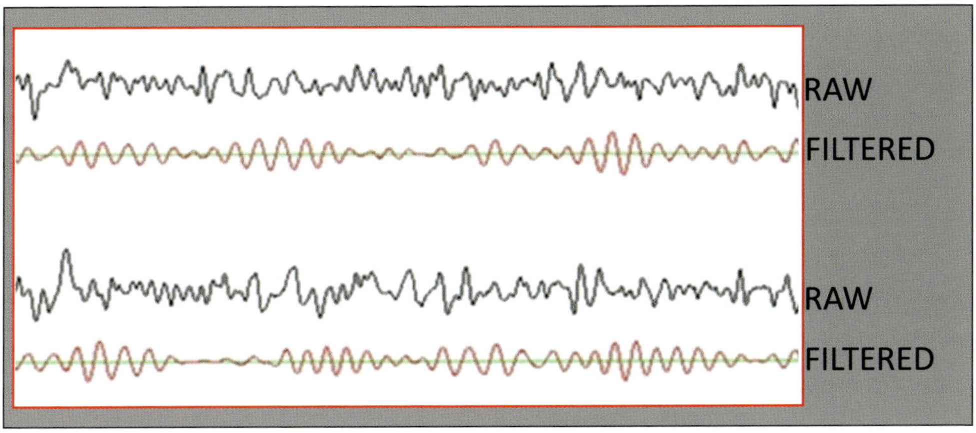

Graphics adapted from BrainMaster Technologies, Inc. software

Figure 10.9. Coherence and Distance

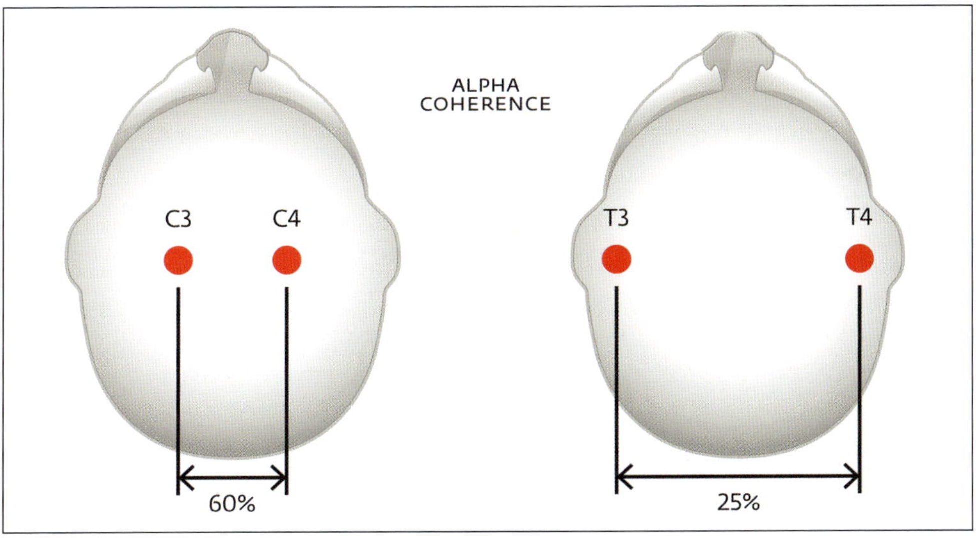

decreases. Coherence percentages vary by two factors: (1) location, and (2) bandwidth. Delta, theta, alpha, and beta all have different normative coherence percentages between paired sites. Note that most EEG neurofeedback providers rely on live Z-score values or SDs rather than percentages when assessing coherence. Two terms are used when evaluating coherence:

- Hypercoherence means that the coherence is high, for example, 90%.
- Hypocoherence means that the coherence is low, for example, 10%.

Coherence values can be compared to family therapy. A family that is enmeshed has hypercoherence, whereas a family that is detached has hypocoherence. Healthy families allow for individual freedom combined with loving care and attention. Healthy families spend time together but not every waking minute.

When assessing coherence, keep locations in mind:

1. Hypocoherence between P3 and P4 could reflect a learning disorder because the parietal lobes are involved in academic processing. The angular gyrus and Wernicke's area are key information-processing regions within the parietal lobes.
2. Hypocoherence between T3 and T4 could reflect poor memory because the temporal lobes assist in memory processing and are close to the hippocampus.
3. Hypercoherence in the frontal lobes could reflect OCD, depression, or migraines because the frontal lobes include the orbital gyrus and the cingulate gyrus as well as other regions that could contribute to excessive error detection, negative moods, and excessive focus.

Hence, when assessing via coherence, keep in mind the rule: location, location, location.

Coherence Training

Single-channel referential training can facilitate positive changes in coherence (Soutar, 2004). However, when a brain map shows hypercoherence (high SDs) or hypocoherence (low SDs), most providers choose one of the following training methods:

- Bipolar montages (indirect)
- Z-score training (direct)

Bipolar Montages and Differential Amplifiers

Coherence training with bipolar montages is ideal when both of the following two conditions are present in the same bandwidth and location:

1. High-power Z-scores
2. Low or hypocoherence

It's much easier to see this with a brain map (Figure 10.10), which shows:

Figure 10.10. Ideal Combination for F7-F8 to Inhibit Beta

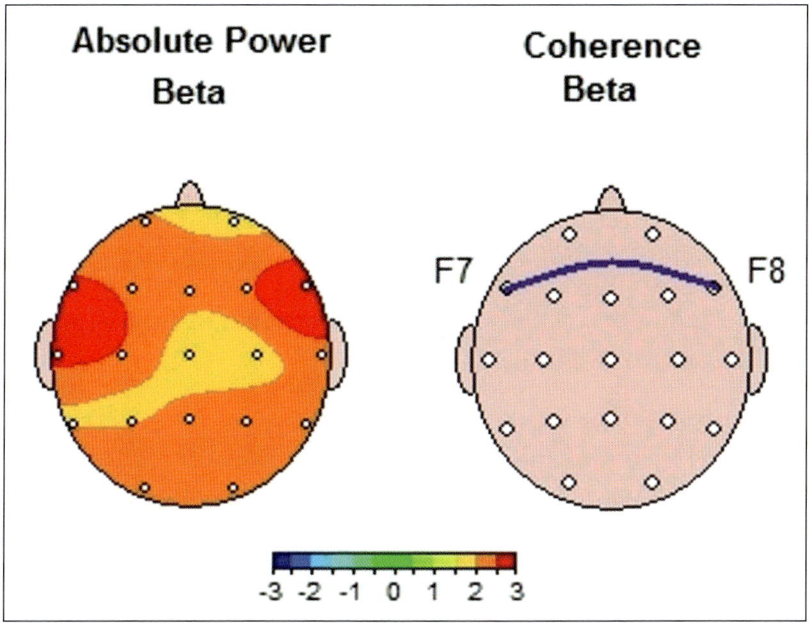

Maps adapted from NeuroGuide LifeSpan database

- Elevated beta power Z-scores at both F7 and F8 (red areas)
- Low (hypo)coherence between F7 and F8 (blue connecting line)

Inhibiting a single band with a bipolar montage increases coherence, because EEG amplifiers employ differential technology. Inhibiting a bandwidth decreases the (differential) amplitude between two sites. When you decrease the difference between two sites, they become more alike: the more similar the sites, the higher the coherence. The reverse is somewhat true; that is, rewarding a single bandwidth between two sites will likely lower coherence.

Thus, the expression "kill two birds with one stone" applies. Inhibiting beta with a bipolar montage will result in decreased beta amplitudes and increased coherence percentages. That's exactly what is accomplished in the sample case (Figure 10.10). Actually, many presentations of anxiety disorders have elevated beta power combined with hypocoherence between sites.

Two-Channel Coherence Training

Z-score coherence training requires a minimum of two channels. The trainee is reinforced each time coherence Z-scores move closer to the mean of the database. For many, Z-score training to correct coherence issues is the intervention of choice.

Depression and Coherence

Leuchter, Cook, Hunter, Cai, and Horvath (2012) "used weighted network analysis to examine resting state functional connectivity as measured by quantitative electroencephalographic (qEEG) coherence in 121 unmedicated subjects with major depressive disorder (MDD) and 37 healthy controls." Depressed subjects showed hypercoherence in one or more of the 4 bandwidths shown in Figure 10.11:

Figure 10.11. Frontal Pole Hypercoherence: Marker for Depression

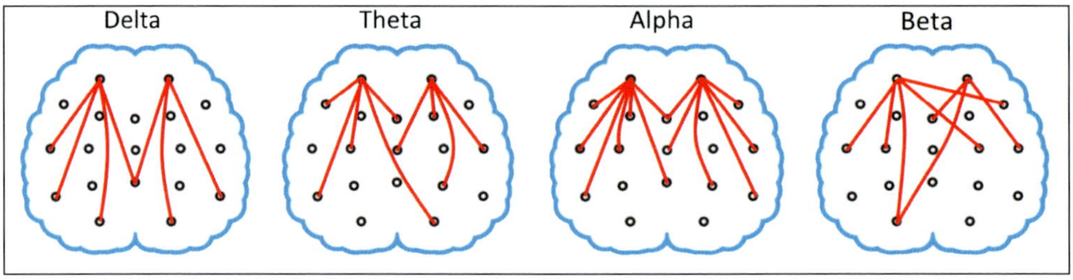

Image created by Jewel database software

Hypercoherence (Figure 10.11) from the frontal poles outward is one of several EEG markers for depression and other disorders. Each red line shows hyperconnectivity between a frontal pole area and other scalp locations. Other clinical disorders with similar EEG markers include OCD, migraine, ADHD, and executive control deficits. Z-score training and hemoencephalography passive infrared (HEG-PIR) are both used to correct frontal pole hypercoherence problems.

Comodulation

Comodulation is similar to coherence; both are measurements of connectivity. Most of the training and diagnostic principles relating to coherence apply to comodulation. In 2008, Kaiser differentiated between coherence and comodulation in the article *Functional Connectivity and Aging*: "Coherence and Comodulation are complementary spectral properties. Coherence is a normalized measure of similarity between two signals in terms

Figure 10.12. Comodulation: Learning Disorder

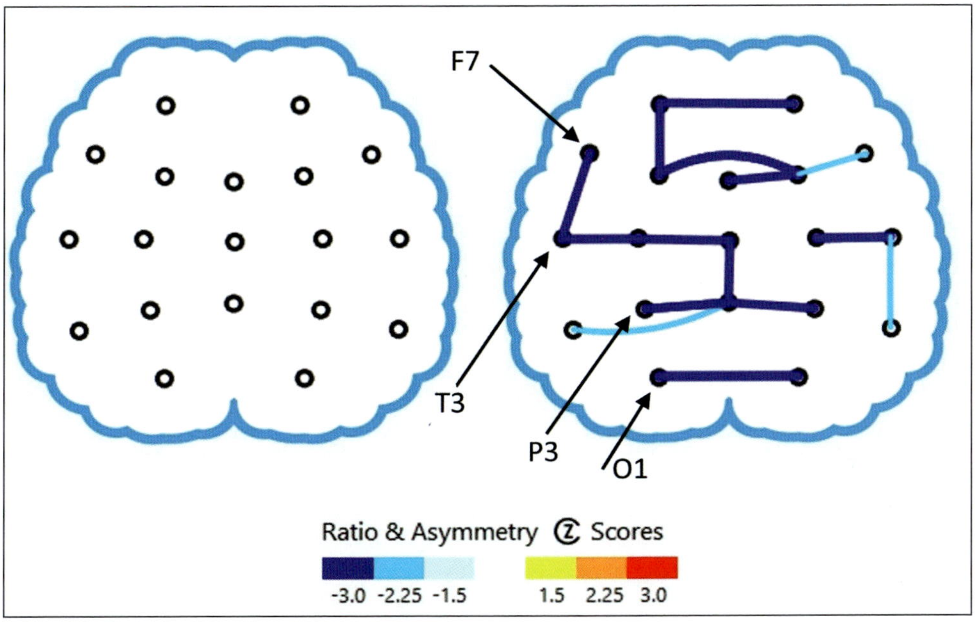

Brain Maps adapted from Jewel Clinical Database software

of phase difference. Comodulation is a normalized measure of similarity between two signals in terms of magnitude difference."

Location, location, location is still the guiding principle when using coherence or comodulation to assess clients. Always ask, what is the neurological function where the hyper- or hypoconnectivity is found; furthermore, how does it relate to the client's presenting symptom? In Figure 10.12, the locations of interest indicate a learning disorder. Hypoconnectivity at F7, T3, P3, and O1 suggests difficulty with verbal skills, reading, calculating, and memory, because those areas are all associated with academic performance. Symptoms are rooted in locations that have power and/or coherence (comodulation) issues.

PHASE

Phase is a second way to measure communication or information sharing between two sites within the same frequency range. Phase measurements tend to be the polar opposite of coherence measurements (Figure 10.13). For example, if phase Z-scores are mostly negative, then coherence Z-scores are mostly positive. Phase SDs vary so much that most clinicians rely upon coherence when making assessments. Coherence is sometimes referred to as phase stability. Phase measurements by EEG compare two frequency signals on the basis of timing and phase angles. Phase computations have been useful in diagnosing TBI (Thatcher, 1999, p. 52). Phase training is an important component in live Z-score training. In Figure 10.13, phase and coherence are displayed as red and blue lines (red for positive SDs and blue for negative SDs).

Alpha Synchrony

Figure 10.13. Comparing Coherence With Phase Lag

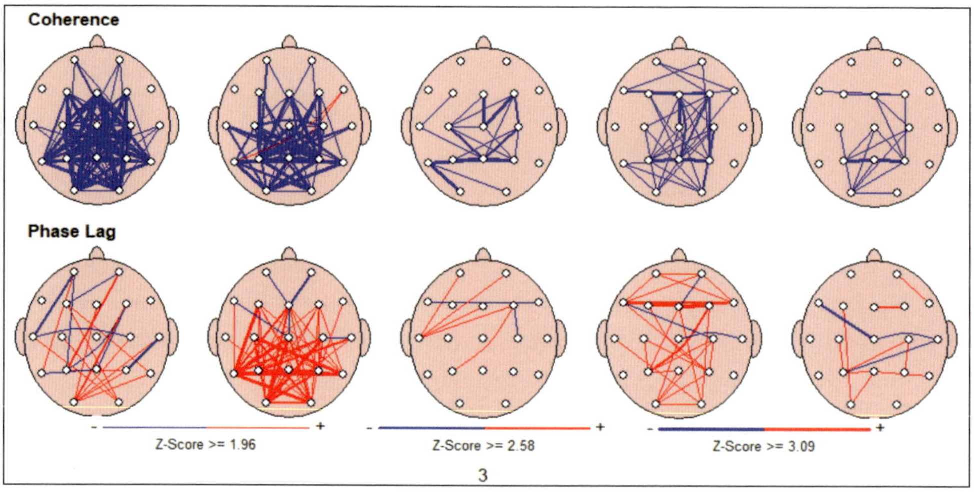

Brain Map adapted from NeuroGuide LifeSpan database

If two or more regions of the brain have increased activity at the same time, they are in sync because they approach a zero-phase relationship. For more information, see Appendix 3. Hence, amplitudes rise and fall in unison. Synchrony is a comparison of simultaneous action at two or more different scalp locations. Alpha synchrony training requires at least two EEG channel connections. Sensors are mounted in pairs in both the RH and LH, such as O1 and O2. This training is commonly used for peak performance and deep-states training (Norris & Currieri, 1999) as well as psychological depth work (McKnight & Fehmi, 2001). However, advanced practitioners utilize several channels at multiple sites. Note that cross-frequency coupling (CFC) training is considered in Part V.

11

Matching EEG Signatures to Common Symptoms and Disorders

AN EEG SIGNATURE (or marker) is an irregular EEG pattern that reflects one or more symptoms. Chapter 11 depicts common EEG markers, first with brain maps and then with a comprehensive list of symptoms.

Figure 11.1: Plus (+) three SDs of theta in the LH reflects clinical depression, which was verified by a Beck Depression Inventory (BDI) score of 28. The map nicely corresponds to the symptom because LH theta is greater than RH theta.

- Target: Inhibit T5 and P3 Theta.

Figure 11.1. Depression in Left Hemisphere

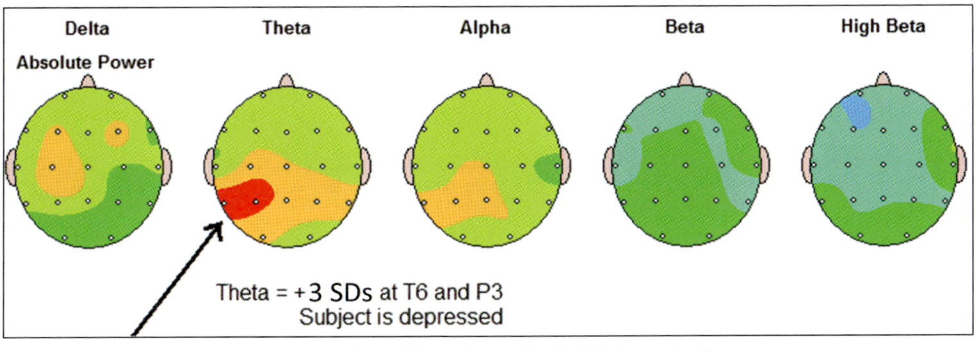

Brain Map adapted from NeuroGuide LifeSpan database

Figure 11.2. Poor Executive Functioning: ADHD, Unmotivated

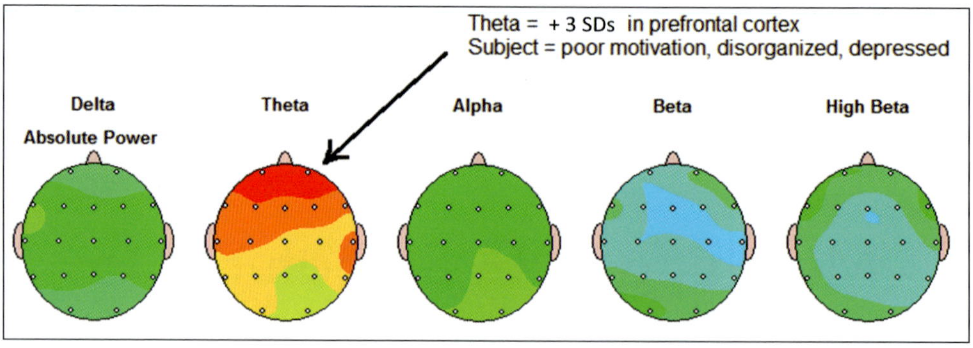

Brain Map adapted from NeuroGuide LifeSpan database

Figure 11.2: Plus (+) three SDs of theta in the prefrontal lobes (executive cortex) reflects poor motivation, disorganization, and depression. The map nicely corresponds to the subject's reason for visiting: poor motivation.

- Target: Inhibit Fp1, Fp2 theta (electrode placement near Fz).
- Consider HEG (NIR) neurofeedback (see Part V, Chapter 23).

Figure 11.3. ADHD: Elevated Dorsal and Frontal Lobe Theta

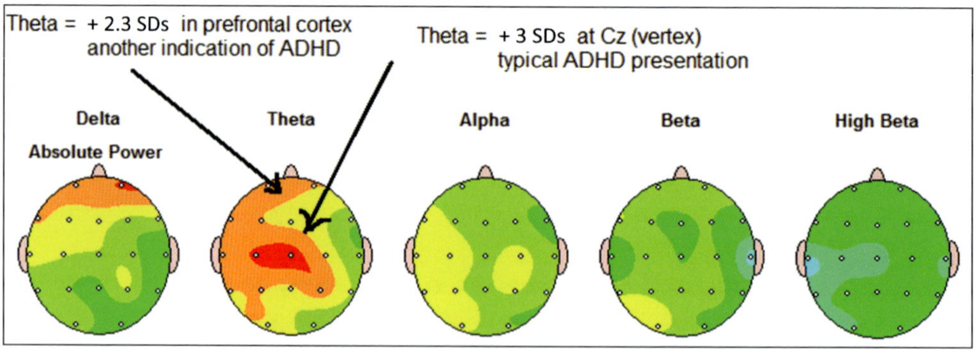

Brain Map adapted from NeuroGuide LifeSpan database

Figure 11.3: Plus (+) three SDs of theta at Cz (vertex), commonly seen in ADHD. Frontal-lobe theta slowing is also a factor with poor attention and impulse control.

- Target: Inhibit Cz and C3 theta.
- Consider HEG (NIR) neurofeedback (see Part V).

Figure 11.4. Cingulate Beta: Perfectionism, Anxiety, Worry

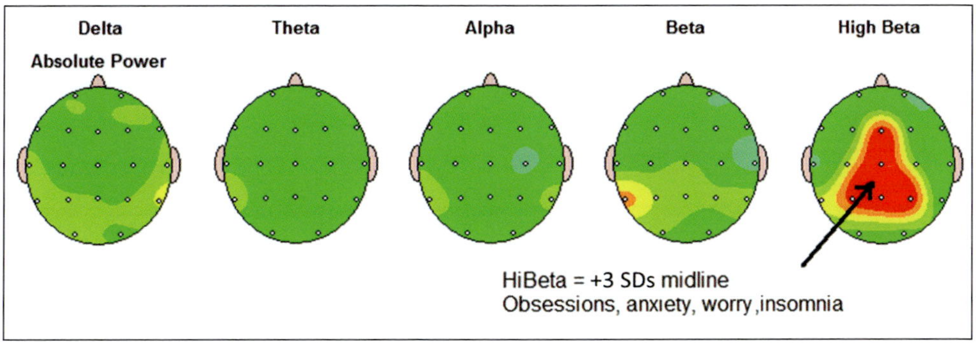

Brain Map adapted from NeuroGuide LifeSpan database

Figure 11.4: Midline beta presentations are often seen in subjects who worry, obsess, and have minds that won't shut off, insomnia, and anxiety. In addition to alpha training at Pz:

- Target: Inhibit hi-beta at Fz, Cz, and Pz.
- Consider bipolar montages to reduce hi-beta.

Figure 11.5. Weak Delta Power: mTBI, Anxiety, ADHD

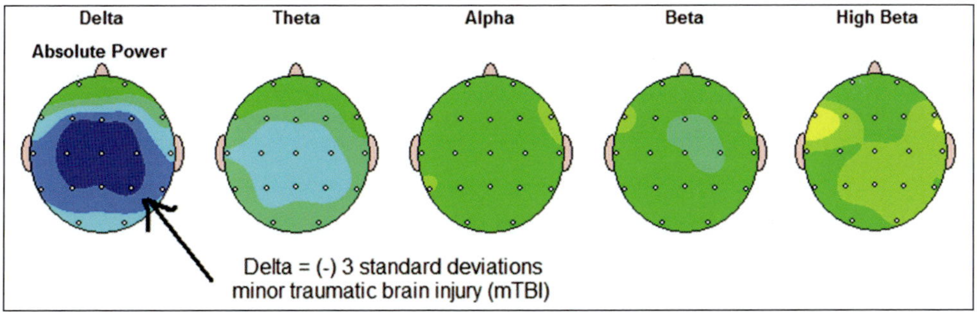

Brain Map adapted from NeuroGuide LifeSpan database

Figure 11.5: Diffuse weak delta often seen in acquired brain injury or mTBI. A similar EEG marker or signature may also reflect sleep disturbances, anxiety, depression, and ADHD.

- Target: Increase delta amplitudes—no simple standard protocol is available.
- Consider Z-score training and pulsing therapies (see Part V).

Figure 11.6. Elevated Alpha 2 (11 and 12 Hz): Anxiety, Insomnia

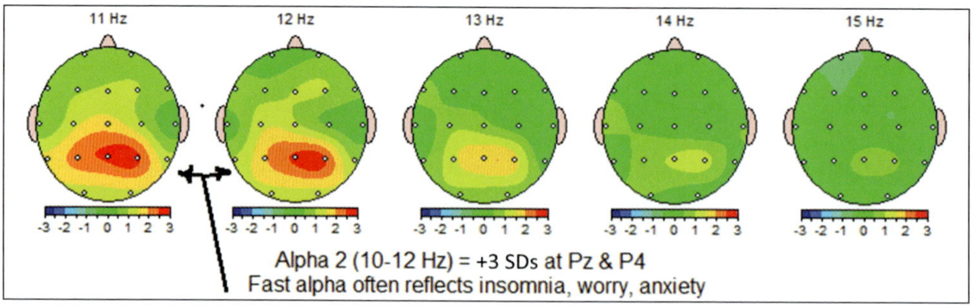

Brain Map adapted from NeuroGuide LifeSpan database

Figure 11.6: An adolescent who was misdiagnosed with ADHD. The issue was anxiety and insomnia. Also, a possible learning disorder is reflected in elevated alpha 2 SDs in parietal lobes.

- Target: Inhibit fast alpha (alpha 2) at Pz and P4.
- Consider two-channel sum squash (see Part V).

Figure 11.7. Z-Score Scale (Jewel Database Software)

Figure 11.7: Brain maps from Jewel database software (Z-score scale).

Figure 11.8. Temporal Lobe Theta: Memory Challenges

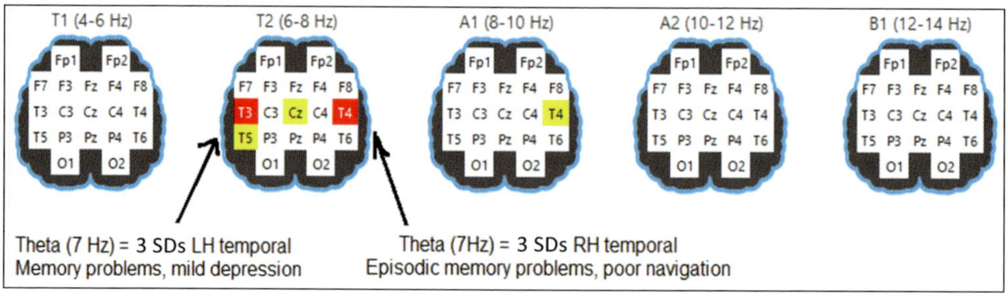

Brain Maps adapted from Jewel database software

Figure 11.8: Memory problems are often associated with the temporal lobes because they are located near the hippocampus (see Part IV).

- Target: Inhibit T3 and T4 theta.
- Consider two-channel sum squash (see Part V).

Figure 11.9. Anxiety, Insomnia, and Poor Fine Motor Skills

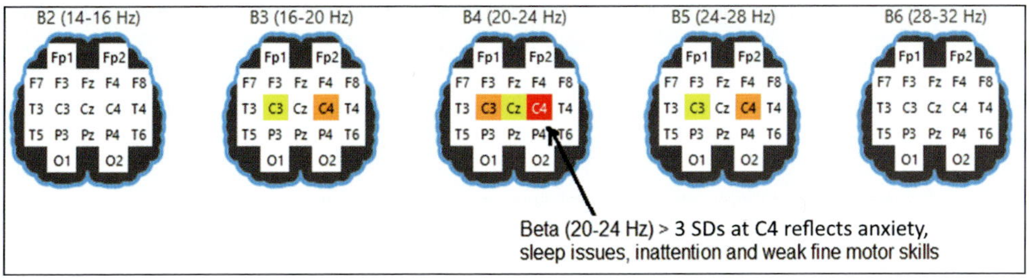

Brain Maps adapted from Jewel database software

Figure 11.9: C4 is in the sensorimotor cortex, so there may be symptoms relating to insomnia, sensory dysregulation, or poor fine motor skills. C4 is also near the RH insular cortex, so there may be other symptoms relating to anxiety, pain, or social deficits.

- Target: Inhibit C4 Beta (20–24 Hz)
- Consider C4 SMR training, which includes a hi-beta inhibit.

Figure 11.10. Learning Disorder

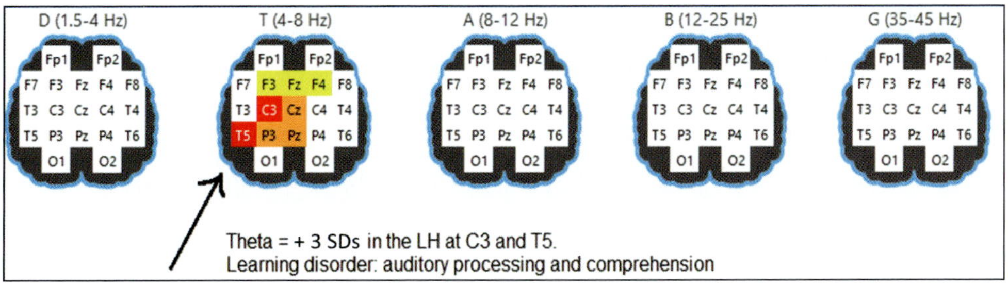

Brain Maps adapted from Jewel database software

Figure 11.10: LH slowing is a marker for learning disorders (auditory processing and reading comprehension were issues).

- Target: Inhibit theta C3 and T5.
- Consider two-channel sum squash (see Part V).

Figure 11.11. O1, Poor Visual Processing; F8, Poor Sustained Attention

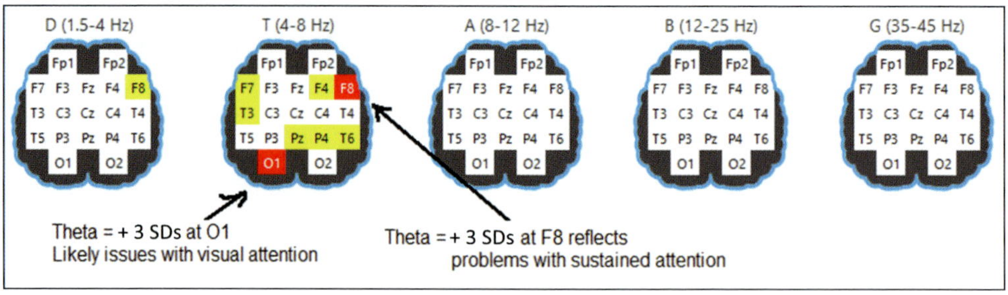

Brain Maps adapted from Jewel database software

Figure 11.11: Parents of a 16-year-old reported issues at school relating to inattention and cognitive processing. F8 reflects problems with sustained attention and O1 reflects visual inattention and reading difficulties.

- Target: Inhibit theta at F8 and O1.
- Consider two-channel sum squash (see Part V).

EEG SIGNATURES FOR 14 COMMON SYMPTOMS AND DISORDERS

The following list of definitions will clarify the descriptions that accompany each of the 14 symptoms:

- High or low microvolts also means
  - Weak or strong power (amplitude)
  - High or low Z-score power
- High or low Z-scores detect and train all EEG components:
  - Power, power ratio, asymmetry, coherence, and phase
- Beta means any range that falls within 13–28 Hz
- Beta spindles (must be observed in raw EEG)
- Frontal lobes (Fp1, Fp2, F7, F8, F3, F4, and Fz)
- Prefrontal (Fp1, Fp2, F7, F8, and Fz)
- Cingulate gyrus (Fz, Cz, and Pz)
- Sensorimotor cortex (C3, C4, and Cz)
- Dorsal (Fz, F3, F4, Cz, C3, C4, Pz, P3, and P4)
- Ventral (Fp1, Fp2, F7, F8, T3, T4, T5, T6, O1, and O2)
- Diffuse (widespread)

1. ADHD (also consult visual inattention)
    - High anterior theta microvolts
    - High theta-to-beta ratios, especially in frontal lobes and cingulate gyrus
    - High dorsal beta microvolts, with possible comorbid anxiety
    - Beta spindles
    - High Z-scores that include frontal lobes and may include parietal lobes

2. Anxiety
    - RH beta microvolts greater than LH beta microvolts
    - Diffuse hi-beta microvolts
    - Beta spindles
    - Diffuse weak alpha (microvolts) combined with strong beta (microvolts)
    - High beta microvolts or sometimes theta (microvolts) in cingulate gyrus or near T4
    - High posterior alpha 2 (microvolts)

3. Depression
    - LH alpha (microvolts) greater than RH alpha (microvolts)
    - LH theta (microvolts) greater than RH theta (microvolts)
    - High anterior theta microvolts or high alpha microvolts
    - High dorsal beta microvolts, with possible comorbid anxiety
    - Hypercoherence that includes the frontal poles (Fp1 and Fp2)
    - Seldom: RH prefrontal high theta microvolts

4. Learning disorders: math or reading
    - Hyper- and especially hypocoherence that includes P3, P4, O1, T5, and T6
    - High/low power in LH, especially P3, P4, O1, T5, and T6

5. Learning disorders: verbal
    - Hyper- and especially hypocoherence within F7, F3, T3, C3, P3, and T5
    - High/low power in LH within F7, F3, T3, C3, P3, and T5

6. Memory problems
   - Weak power (delta, theta, alpha) that almost always includes temporal lobes (especially T3 or T4) and sometimes the frontal and parietal lobes
     - LH for sequential (semantic)
     - RH for episodic
   - Coherence issues that usually includes the temporal lobes
     - LH coherence issues for sequential (semantic) memory issues
     - RH coherence issues for episodic memory issues

7. Migraines
   - High beta microvolts at most locations and sometimes high alpha 2 microvolts
   - Hypercoherence that includes the prefrontal cortex
   - High alpha variability (elevated brain wave SDs)
   - Diffuse low alpha microvolts, especially when combined with high beta microvolts
   - High/low Z-scores in occipital lobes (especially for visual aura)

8. Motivation (poor)
   - High/low Z-scores in frontal lobes
   - High theta microvolts in prefrontal lobes, especially Fp1 and Fp2

9. OCD: Obsessions and compulsions (not just obsessions)
   - Especially hyper- (seldom hypo-) coherence that includes the prefrontal cortex
   - Prefrontal high beta microvolts
   - High beta microvolts, especially on or near the cingulate gyrus (Fz, Cz, Pz)
   - High Z-scores near the cingulate gyrus (Fz, Cz, Pz) or the prefrontal cortex
   - A few OCD presentations include hi-theta power

10. Perfectionism: obsessions and rigid thinking
    - High beta microvolts, especially on or near the cingulate gyrus (Fz, Cz, Pz)

11. Poor empathy, eye contact, or codependence
    - RH posterior high/low microvolts or coherence issues
    - High Z-scores in prefrontal cortex, especially for codependence

12. Sensory integration dysfunction
    - High/low SMR microvolts in sensorimotor cortex, especially C4

13. Sleep disorders
    - High/low SMR microvolts in sensorimotor cortex, especially C4
    - High posterior alpha 2 microvolts or beta microvolts
    - Diffuse high beta microvolts
    - Beta spindles

14. Visual (poor) processing and/or inattention
    - High/low Z-scores or power in visual cortex and nearby sites
    - Especially O1, also O2, P3, P4, Pz, T5, and T6

Part III
Editing the Raw EEG

Chapters

12

The Importance of Examining the Raw EEG

THE RAW EEG and brain wave morphology are the foundation; brain maps are the structure resting upon it. In 2003, I attended a discussion panel at a neurofeedback conference that included Joel F. Lubar. A case study was presented and color-coded brain maps were projected on the screen. The moderator requested each expert on the panel to comment on the maps. To the moderators' surprise, Lubar said he needed to see the raw EEG first, and since it was unavailable he refused to participate in the discussion. He understood the value of examining the EEG first and the brain maps second. No one purchases a house without first checking the foundation. Professional EEG neurofeedback practitioners are not neurologists, but they do have a working knowledge of brain wave morphology. There are many reasons why the raw EEG needs to be inspected before reviewing the color-coded brain maps, including the following list of basic issues:

- Drowsiness artifacts reflecting lack of attention, sleep deprivation, or sleep apnea.
- EKG or pulse artifacts.
- Spike and wave formation—occasional occurrences are common in ADHD. Frequent occurrences raise a flag. When is it time to refer to a neurologist? Obtain supervision if you are unsure.

- Channels with no recorded data. A defective electrode cannot be repaired but must be thrown away. A defective EEG recording cap may be repaired unless the elasticity of the fabric is compromised.
- Bursts of rhythmic temporal theta are common in age-related cognitive decline. BORTTs are most common when the subject is under task (see chapter 9).
- Beta spindles (see chapters 9 and 13).
- Observable high-amplitude mu waves are manifestations of mirror neurons. Mu waves can be seen in the recordings of some test subjects with autistic spectrum disorders. Increased amplitude signals decreased activation. Or difficulty learning how to imitate the social behavior of others.
- Excessive beta as a result of prescribed drugs, especially benzodiazepines.
- Excessive EEG slowing as a result of marijuana (cannabis) usage.
- Excessive EEG slowing as a result of age-related cognitive decline.
- Dominant beta with weak alpha, especially in eyes-closed recordings, reflects anxiety or migraine.
- Artifacts such as:

    - Eye movements or blinks: electro-ocular (EOA).
    - Muscle tension or movement: electromyography (sEMG)—especially found near the temporomandibular joint or any ventral location.
    - sEMG is also present when the EEG recording cap is too tight.
    - Electrode pop may come from several sources, including a cap that is too loose.
    - Cable sway.
    - Electrical noise from defective electrodes, high impedance, or faulty EEG recording caps. Noise can be exacerbated by excessive electromagnetic interference from the environment such as commercial motors or pumps, high-output circuit panels, transformer stations, or faulty ballasts in fluorescent lights.

Experienced professionals find that it is occasionally possible to predict symptoms and training from the raw EEG alone, especially when there is weak alpha and strong beta (anxiety, insomnia, migraine) or obvious slow-wave LH asymmetries (depression, learning disorder) or an adult PDR less than 9 Hz (slow processing or cognitive decline) or greater than 11 Hz (anxiety, insomnia, mind won't shut off). Of course drowsiness artifacts, BORTTs, mu waves, and beta spindles are also discrete EEG markers. Most of the time, filtered and processed brain maps are needed to clarify training goals and to support symptom identification.

WHAT IS EEG EDITING?

Editing is also called artifacting or artifact removal. Brain maps are generated from clean, artifact-free data. Most recordings have some artifact, but the goal is to keep it to a minimum. Some EEG recordings are so poor they must be rejected. Brain maps that are based on artifact have no value: garbage in, garbage out. However, what if only a few locations have excessive artifact? For example, a raw EEG shows excessive sEMG at T3 and T4, which is common. In this case, when the brain map is reviewed, the clinician knows in advance that T3 beta standard deviations are skewed. Consequently, beta power and coherence leading to T3 and T4 are not valid, but the rest of the brain may be just fine.

CONSIDERATIONS BEFORE STARTING A QEEG RECORDING

Note that eyes-open recordings tend to have more TMJ artifact than eyes-closed recordings. Eyes-closed recordings may reflect eye flutter, which can be controlled by limiting eyelid movement with cotton balls secured by a jersey sweatband or medical tape.

Basic rules of qEEG data acquisition:

1. Always make the test subject aware of artifact. Demonstrate how biting down, eye movements and blinks, gulps, and body movements can compromise a recording. Show what artifact looks like on the screen.
2. Make sure the cap is the right size for the test subject. Slightly too loose is better than slightly too tight.
3. Subjects do best in reclining chairs with minimum neck support to prevent sEMG from neck muscles. Do not use chairs that push the head forward.
4. Always make sure the impedance values for every Int'l 10–20 location are acceptable. The standard for research papers is 5,000 ohms or less. However, powerful amplifiers may acquire a good

signal with somewhat higher impedance. Check with the amplifier manufacturer.

5. Never start a qEEG recording until the EEG data look good. If eyes are closed, wait until alpha morphology can be seen in the recording. Of course, anxious clients and those with TBI may have limited alpha. (Alpha reward training for TBI helps to restore the normal balance between the thalamus and brain stem.)

13

Editing Examples and EEG Signatures

EDITING

In order to process a trustworthy brain map from the raw EEG, 45 seconds of relatively clean (minimum artifact) edited data are needed. Before editing, turn off the low-pass and high-pass filters, which tend to mask sEMG and EOA. When editing with BrainAvatar, selections must exceed 1 second; avoid overlapping sections.

Note that the minimum recording time is 3 minutes, and up to 10 minutes when there is frequent artifact. Be careful with long recordings, because the test subject may fall asleep or drowsiness artifacts may increase near the end of the recording. Before recording, we instruct the test subject to let go, relax, don't ponder, don't think, just chill out. Consequently, when the brain has nothing to do, it just might decide to go off-line and zone out or fall asleep.

Entire qEEG recordings have been rejected due to widespread artifact. Some small children simply cannot sit still, and acquiring good data may be extremely difficult. Some adults have an undue amount of muscle tension on the scalp and may also have trouble sitting still. But most of the time, acceptable qEEG recordings are possible. Staff members or clinicians who acquire qEEG data must be familiar with all of the examples presented in this chapter. If the data are unacceptable from the outset, qEEG acquisition recordings should not be started.

After the recording is finished, editing begins; epochs with artifact are rejected, and epochs with little or no artifact are accepted. The selection process should not be biased; that is, beta is just as important as alpha, theta, and delta. The aim is to select data that best represent the test subject's overall brain wave morphology. The human qEEG editor should not swayed by the likely diagnosis or the client's presenting symptoms. In the following figures, green-highlighted epochs are accepted and white epochs are rejected (exceptions are noted).

Figure 13.1. Editing: Reject All

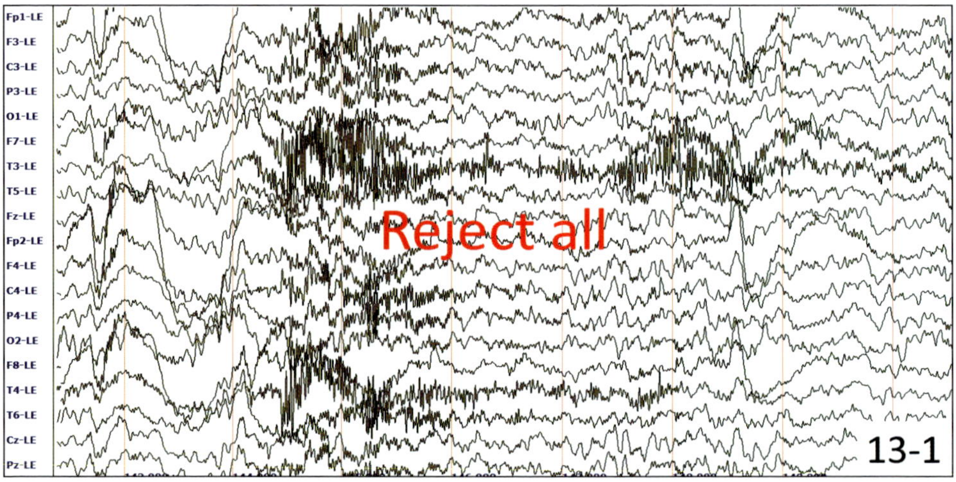

Figure 13.1 has been adapted from BrainAvatar software by BrainMaster Technologies, Inc.

Figure 13.1 is replete with body and eye movement as well as muscle tension. Electro-ocular artifact (EOA) and sEMG artifacts demand the rejection of these epochs.

Figure 13.2. Editing: Reject All

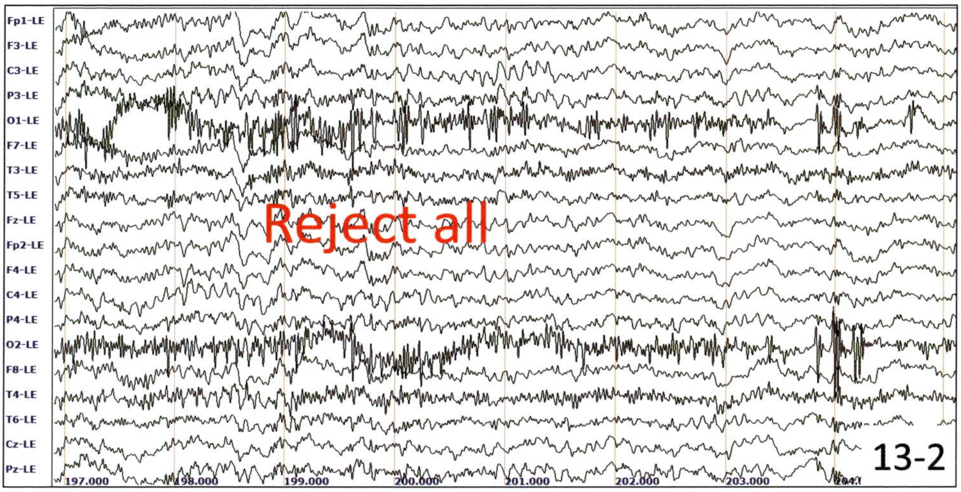

Figure 13.2 has been adapted from BrainAvatar software by BrainMaster Technologies, Inc.

Figure 13.2 is replete with body and eye movement as well as muscle tension. EOA and sEMG artifacts demand the rejection of these epochs.

Figure 13.3. Editing: Reject All

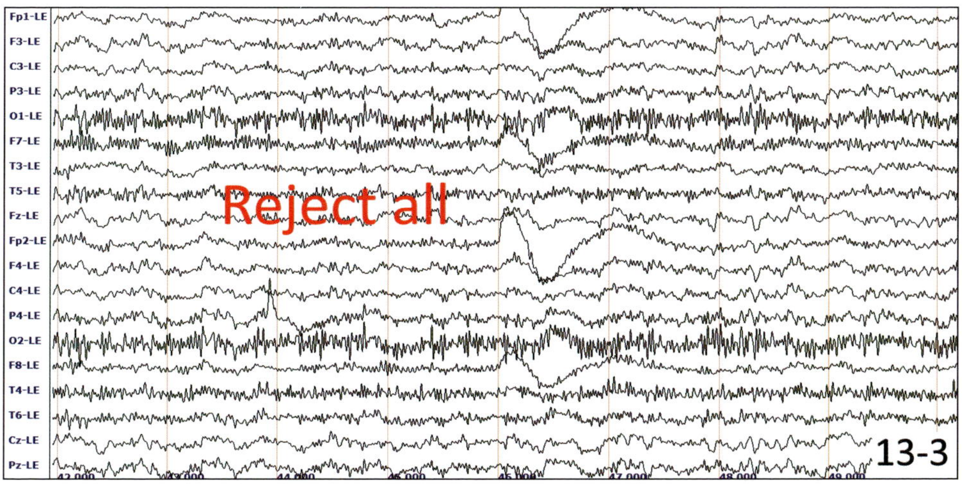

Figure 13.3 has been adapted from BrainAvatar software by BrainMaster Technologies, Inc.

Figure 13.3 is replete with eye movement as well as muscle tension. EOA and sEMG artifacts demand the rejection of these epochs. Note that sEMG is especially prominent in posterior areas such as O1, O2, T5, and T6. Likely, adequate neck support was lacking.

Figure 13.4. Editing: Accept All

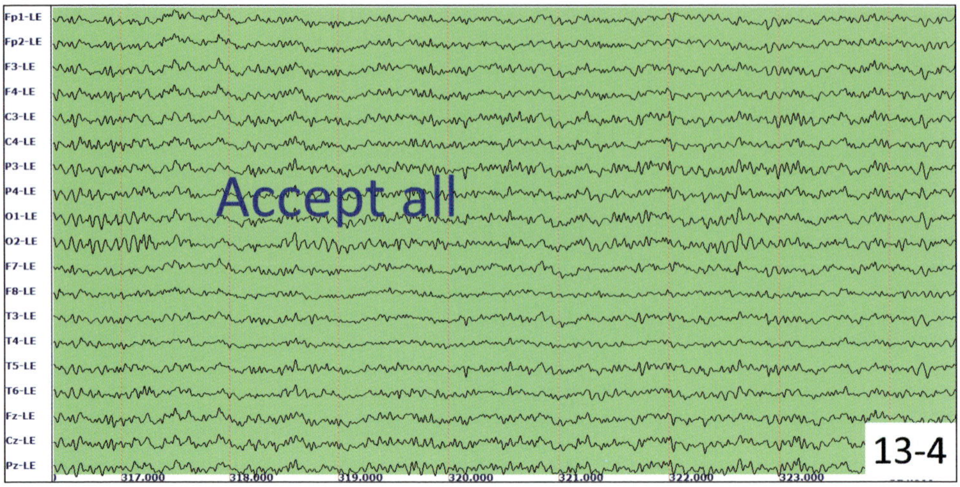

Figure 13.4 has been adapted from BrainAvatar software by BrainMaster Technologies, Inc.

Figure 13.4 is an eyes-closed recording with some alpha and beta morphology. It shows minor amounts of eye movements and muscle tension: accept all epochs.

Figure 13.5. Editing: Accept All

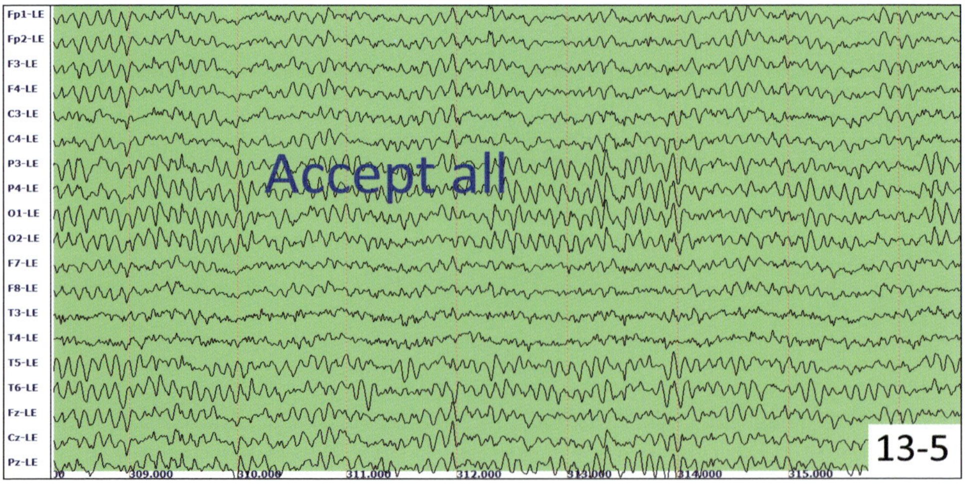

Figure 13.5 has been adapted from BrainAvatar software by BrainMaster Technologies, Inc.

Figure 13.5 is an eyes-closed recording with robust alpha. There are some eye movements but almost no muscle tension. Overall, these epochs well represent the subject's EEG presentation: accept all epochs.

Figure 13.6. Editing: Accept/Reject

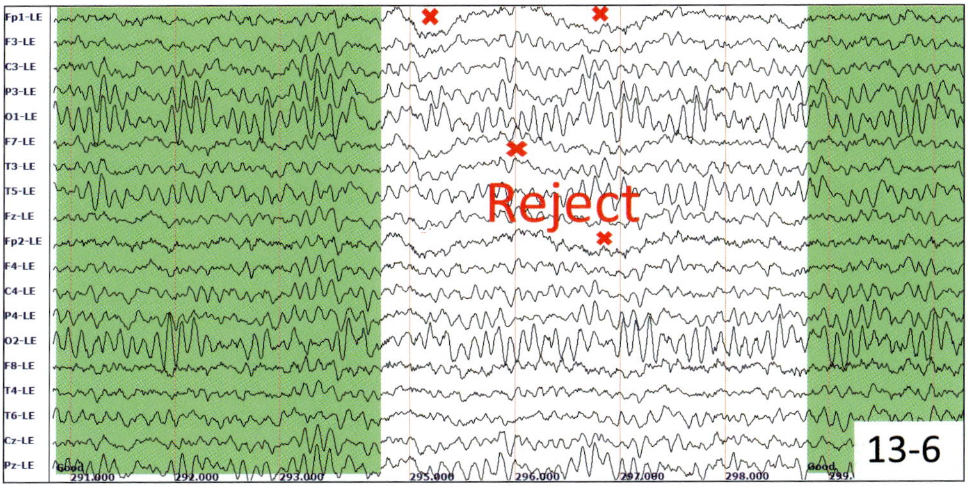

Figure 13.6 has been adapted from BrainAvatar software by BrainMaster Technologies, Inc.

Figure 13.7. Editing: Accept/Reject

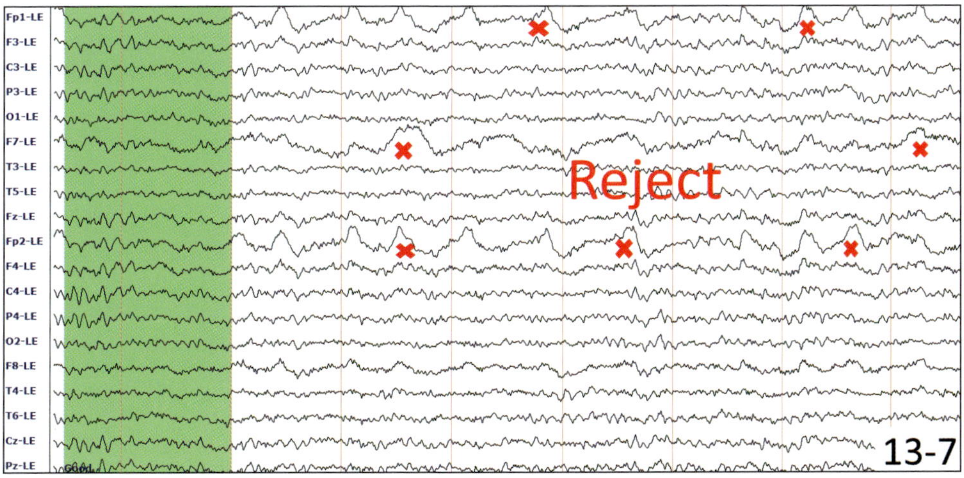

Figure 13.7 has been adapted from BrainAvatar software by BrainMaster Technologies, Inc.

Figure 13.6 includes accepted (green) epochs and rejected (white) epochs. Rejected epochs have eye movements that range from 1 to 2 Hz, which will inflate delta Z-scores.

Figure 13.7 has several rejected epochs. Frequent eye blinks will inflate delta Z-scores. EOA artifact ranges from 2 to 3 Hz. Do not be surprised that so little can be gleaned in these epochs. More artifact may require longer recordings.

Figure 13.8. Editing: Accept/Reject

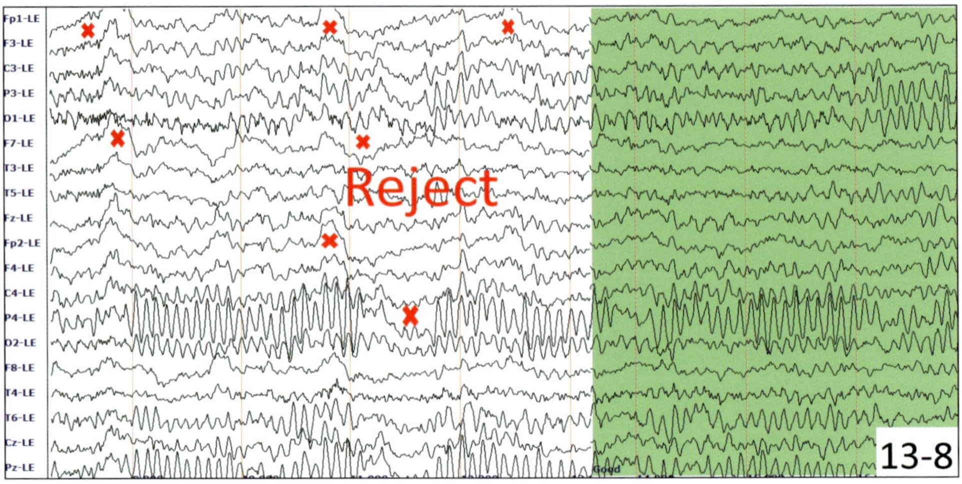

13.8 has been adapted from BrainAvatar software by BrainMaster Technologies, Inc.

Figure 13.8 has noticeable eye movements, which should be rejected. The accepted area in green has minor eye movements that are less than 1.0 Hz (<1.0). Do not expect perfection; rather, take into account the areas that have persistent problems. Do not base assessments on artifact-driven high delta.

Figure 13.9. Editing: Accept/Reject

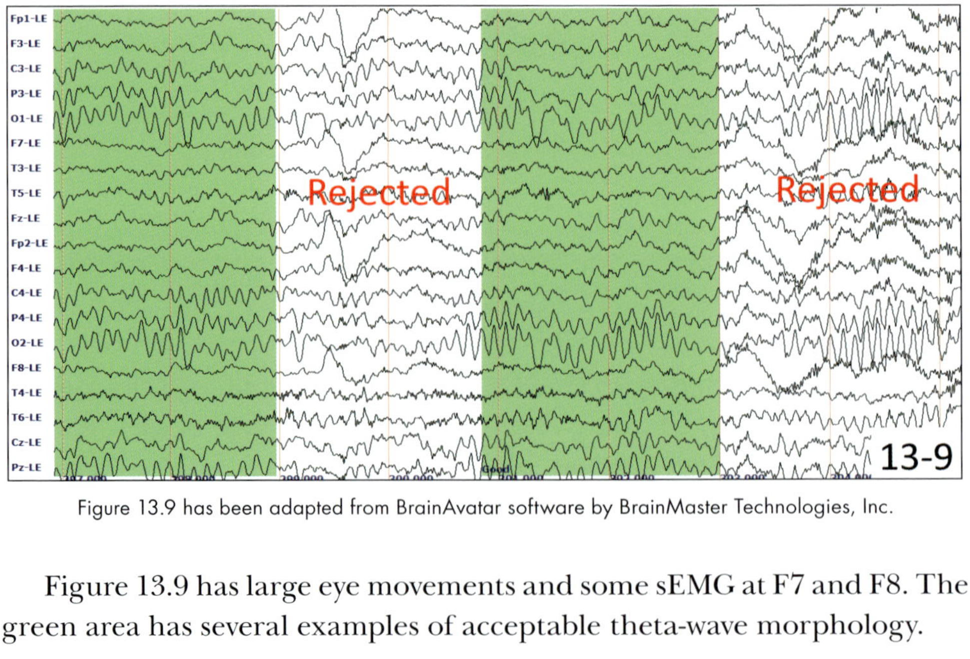

Figure 13.9 has been adapted from BrainAvatar software by BrainMaster Technologies, Inc.

Figure 13.9 has large eye movements and some sEMG at F7 and F8. The green area has several examples of acceptable theta-wave morphology.

Electrode pops are seen in many recordings. Usually they can be damped or limited. Figure 13.10 is an example of a persistent pop, which may just be EKG because it has a 1.0-Hz rhythm, which is the same as 60 beats per minute (pulse rate).

Figure 13.10. Electrode Pop or EKG?

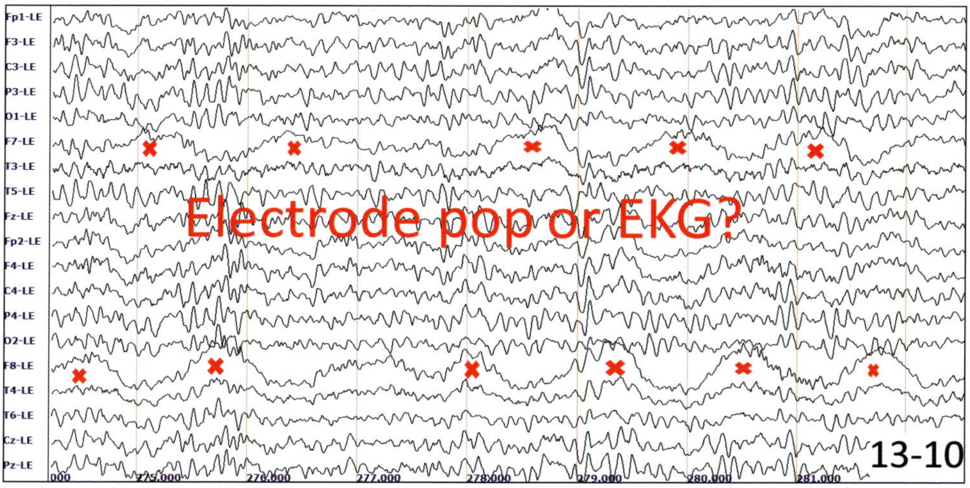

Figure 13.10 has been adapted from BrainAvatar software by BrainMaster Technologies, Inc.

Figure 13.10 has noticeable electrode pops at F7 and F8; there may be more than one reason for this artifact. Needless to say, if this recording was processed it would create a false impression that the test subject has high-amplitude delta as a result of TBI or significant sleep deprivation. What is the difference between real electrode pops and pseudo electrode pops at F7 and F8?

- Real electrode pops at F7 and F8 are related to the dip in the scalp known as the temples. Stretch caps tend to span over the temple area; consequently, the electrode pulls away from the scalp and contact is momentarily lost. Of course, any area of the scalp may be subject to an electrode pop when the electrode gel has not made good contact with the scalp. The solution for real pops is to add more electrode gel and reabrade.
- Pseudo electrode pops (EKG) at F7 and F8 are an interaction between the temples and the earlobes. Look carefully at Figure 13.10, and notice that the pop occurs about once each epoch or 1 Hz, which mirrors a typical heartbeat rhythm. Yes, this pop may

come from the pulses at the earlobes combined with pulses at the temples. But there are other factors. If there is a strong pulse at the earlobes, it may cause the ear-clip leads to sway (i.e., cable sway). In this case, the cable sway is witnessed in the recording as 1.0 Hz delta. To solve this problem, tape down and secure the ear-clip lead wire to prevent sway. Or use a mastoid montage instead of an ear clip—the mastoid bone is relatively free of EKG artifact.

Figure 13.11. Eye Blinks

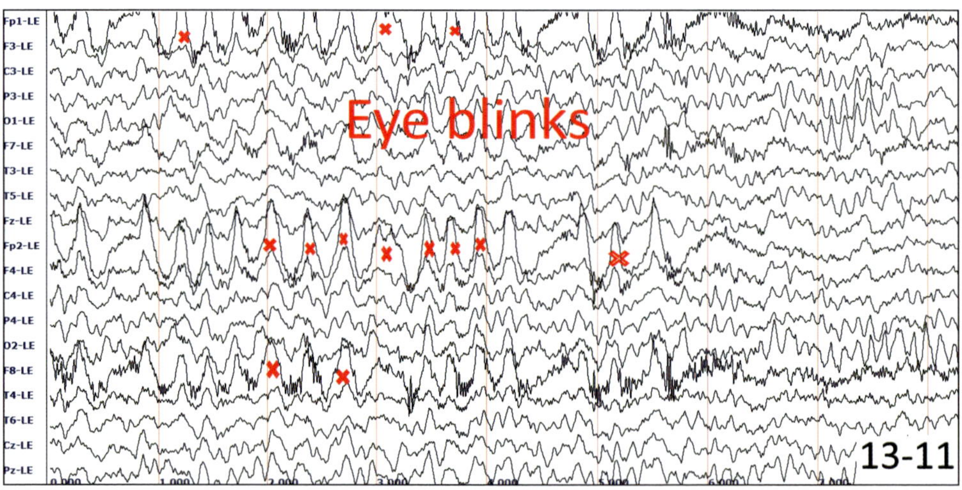

Figure 13.11 has been adapted from BrainAvatar software by BrainMaster Technologies, Inc.

Figure 13.11 demonstrates the power of eye-blink EOA. What can cause eye blinks?

- Contact lenses: remove for training as needed and always remove for qEEG assessments.
- Dry eyes—very low humidity in the clinic: get a humidifier.
- Anxiety—homework: diaphragmatic breathing or HRV training.
- Hyperactive children: distract with movie while the recording cap is being mounted—encourage them (gently) to keep their hands down and away from their face during the recording.

Figure 13.12 is an example of rhythmic beta spindles, not sharp nonrhythmic sEMG morphology. Although no epochs are selected in Figure 13.12, it does not mean that beta spindles are artifact that must be rejected. At least three or

Figure 13.12. Beta Spindles

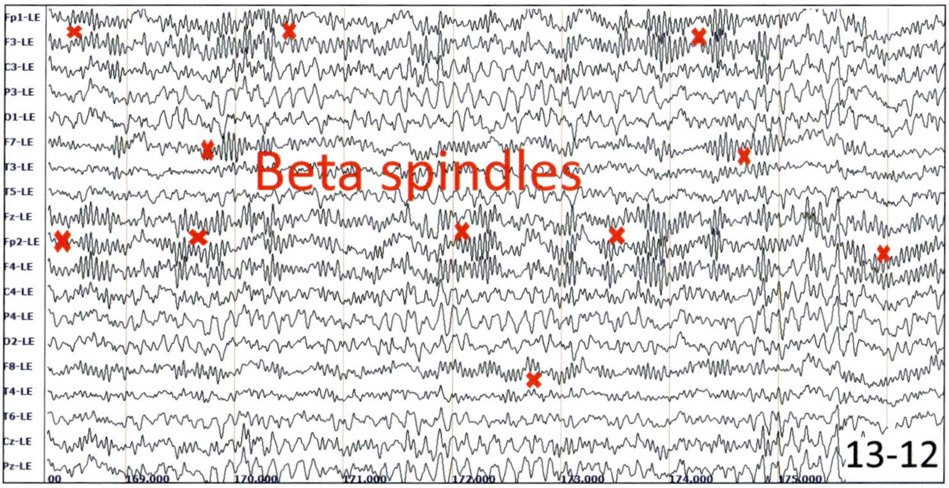

Figure 13.12 has been adapted from BrainAvatar software by BrainMaster Technologies, Inc.

four epochs are acceptable with minimum EOA. Beta spindles are reflections of several disorders. Robert Gurnee of the Scottsdale Neurofeedback Clinic offers the following observations based on decades of experience: "Spindling Beta generally reflects increased cortical irritability and is most likely seen in clinical conditions such as ADHD, Epilepsy, Psychoses including during hallucinations & Anxiety disorders." Gurnee, R. (2013). *Beta Waves.* Retrieved from http://scottsdaleneurofeedback.com.

Note that before concluding that the test subject has beta spindling, rule out the benzodiazepines and barbiturates, which may generate beta spindles. Arns and associates (2015) made it clear that beta spindling can be drug-induced or a phenotype which may reflect several disorders including ADHD, depression, addictions, impulse control, and insomnia. EEG phenotypes are clusters of commonly occurring EEG patterns found in the general population that are believed to be the result of underlying genetics. These phenotypes are purported to play an intermediate role between genetics and behavior (Gunkelman, 2006).

Figure 13.13. Low Power

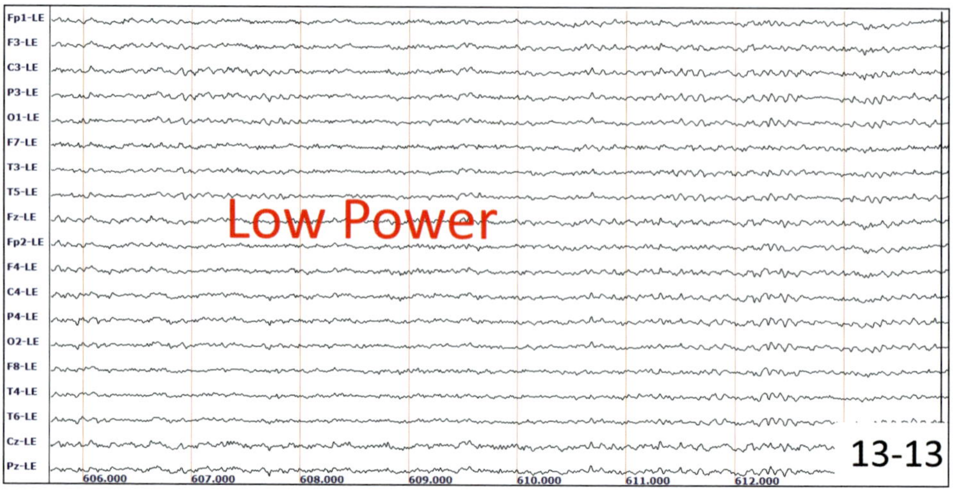

Figure 13.13 has been adapted from BrainAvatar software by BrainMaster Technologies, Inc.

Figure 13.13 is an example of weak or low power that may be associated with mTBI, anxiety, or alcoholism (rule out drowsiness). Some consider it to be a phenotype (Johnstone, Gunkelman, & Lunt, 2005; Enoch, Schuckit, Johnson, & Goldman, 2003).

Figure 13.14. Spike and Wave

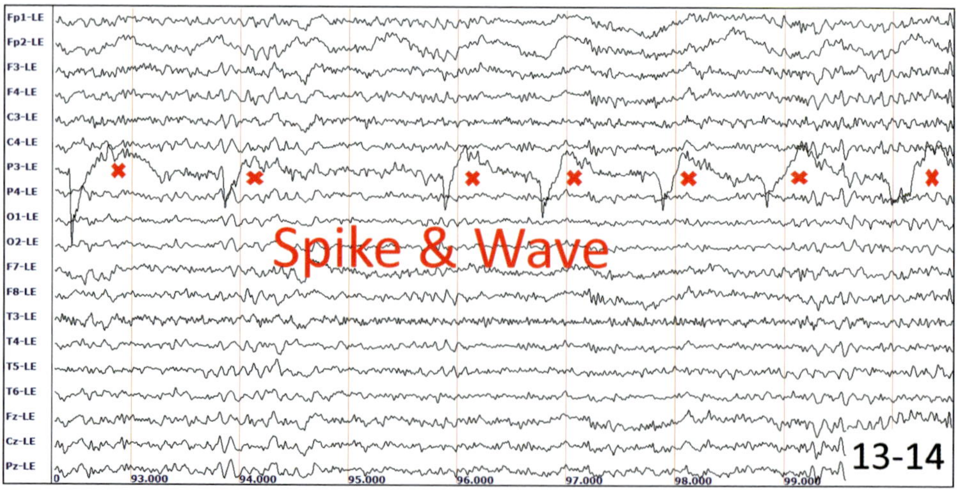

Figure 13.14 has been adapted from BrainAvatar software by BrainMaster Technologies, Inc.

Figure 13.14 is an example of a repetitive spike and wave morphology. If it continues, then consulting with a neurologist may be necessary.

Figure 13.15. Spike and Wave Epochs

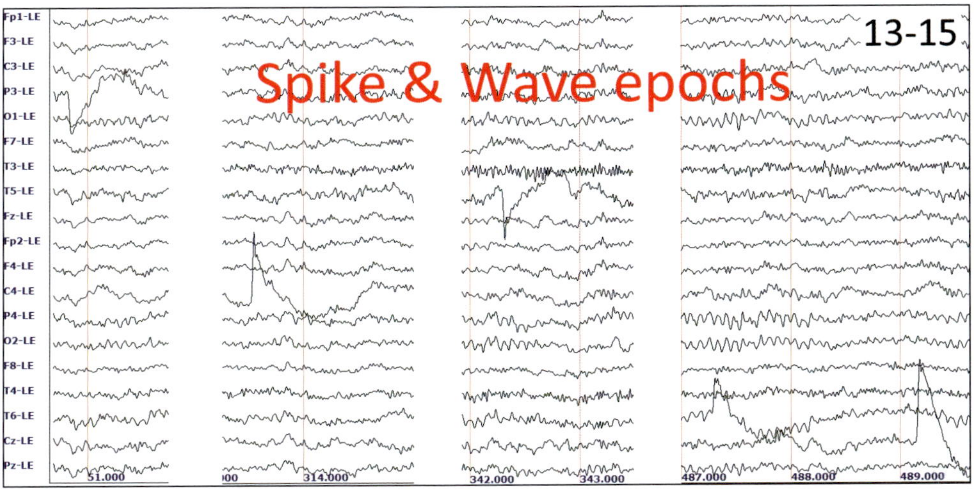

Figure 13.15 has been adapted from BrainAvatar software by BrainMaster Technologies, Inc.

Figure 13.15 shows five distinct spikes and waves over a period of 5 minutes. Spike and wave activity is not always a cause for alarm in children with ADHD. Research by Boutros, Galderisi, Pogarell, and Riggio (2011) indicates the following: "[We] found an overall rate of abnormalities (both slowing and epileptiform) of 9.1% of 49 children with ADHD diagnosis. Three children had focal or multifocal spikes (6.1%) and three had slow wave abnormalities."

Figure 13.16 is an excellent example of an absence seizure in progress. This is a rare event in most clinics. Diagnosing seizures, epilepsy, and other disorders from the raw EEG is in the purview of trained neurologists. It is important to make this distinction. Providers of EEG neurofeedback focus on statistics and the normal distribution of the EEG (regions of interest that are greater than or less than 2.0 SDs). When the EEG looks abnormal, it may or may not be time to refer to a neurologist. If you are new to the field, consult with your mentor or supervisor to determine the importance of an unusual EEG pattern. Do not diagnose a disorder based on an EEG abnormality unless it is within the scope of your practice. Figure 13.16 is part of an EEG recording of a 12-year-old boy in the midst of an absence sei-

Figure 13.16. Absence Seizure

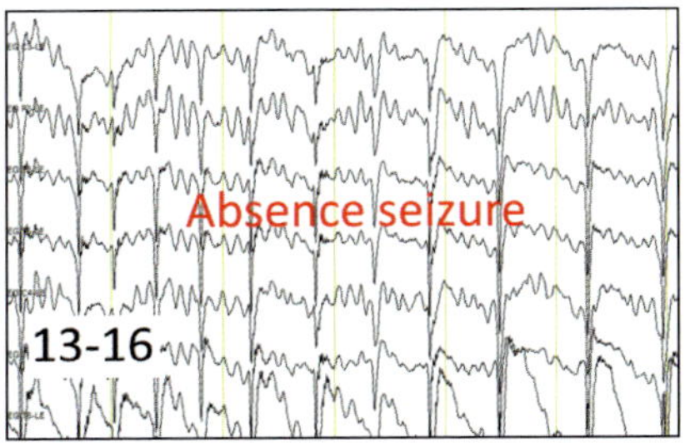

zure. He was formerly misdiagnosed with ADHD. But the symptom of inattention was due to lapses in mental presence or absence seizures. Spike and wave morphology was not seen in his first qEEG.

Figure 13.17. Adult With 7-Hz PDR

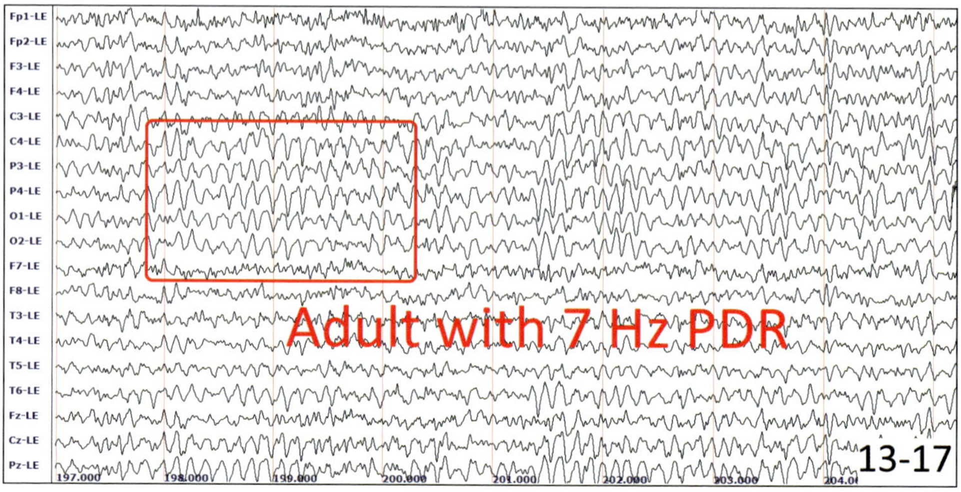

Figure 13.17 has been adapted from BrainAvatar software by BrainMaster Technologies, Inc.

Figure 13.17 is an interesting case of an adult with Asperger's syndrome with a 7-Hz PDR. The morphology in sensory regions (C3, C4, P3, and P4) may or may not be mu waves. Regardless, the qEEG shows an overall low PDR, which reflects his clinical distress due to slow processing.

Figure 13.18 shows a PDR of 11 Hz or greater. Symptoms include mild anxiety, insomnia, and a busy mind that has trouble shutting down at night.

Figure 13.19 shows the EEG of a high-functioning executive who struggles to stay focused. She is a heavy coffee drinker, which helps her to stay alert. The recording shows frequent drowsiness epochs—drowsiness artifact or zone-outs can relate to sleep apnea, sleep deprivation, and at times TBI. Remove all drowsiness artifact when sleep deprivation is the cause. The EEG morphology in Figure 13.19 is classic. (The hallmark of drowsiness artifact is the increase in EEG slow-wave activity that springs up in the frontal lobes, especially Fp1 and Fp2, and looks as if it is spreading out to most Int'l 10–20 sites.)

Figure 13.18. Adult With >11-Hz PDR

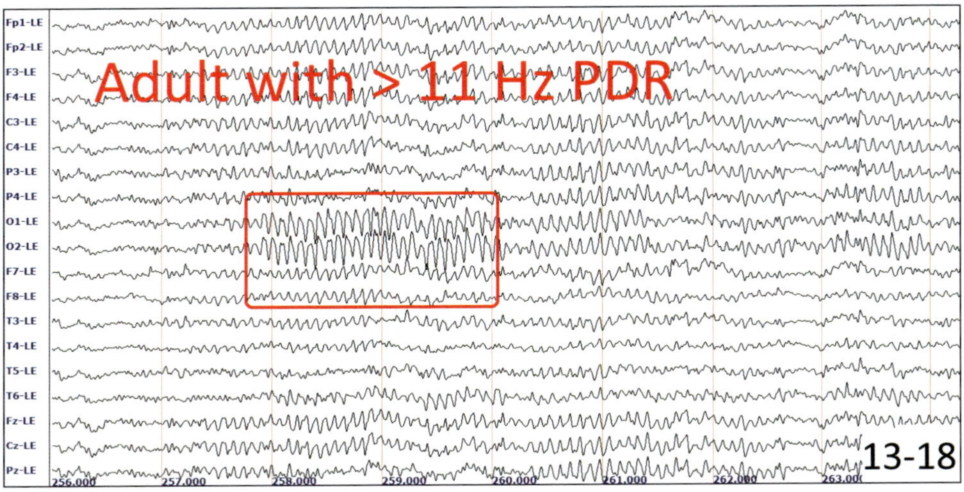

Figure 13.18 has been adapted from BrainAvatar software by BrainMaster Technologies, Inc.

Figure 13.19. Drowsiness Epochs

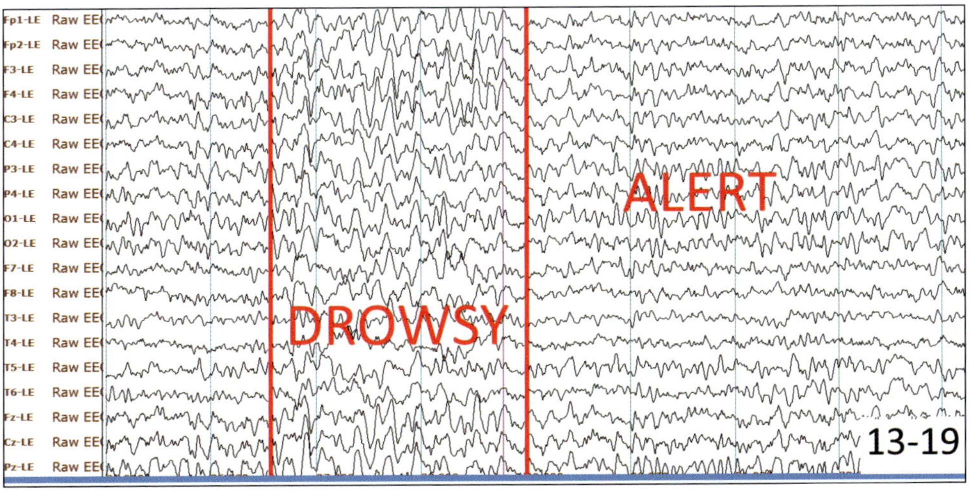

Figure 13.19 has been adapted from BrainAvatar software by BrainMaster Technologies, Inc.

Note that obstructive sleep apnea is not treatable with EEG neurofeedback. It is a structural problem that is treated with surgery, dental interventions, or the use of a CPAP breathing machine while sleeping.

Figure 13.20. Noise

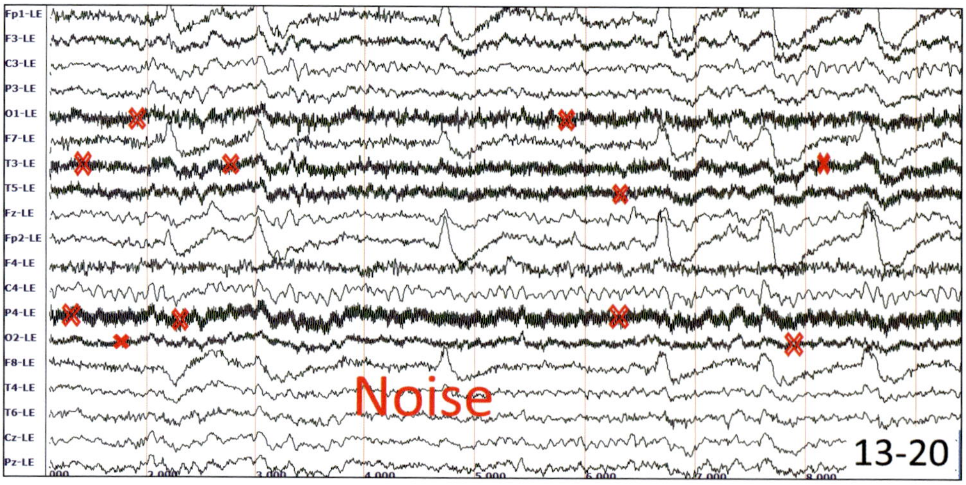

Figure 13.20 has been adapted from BrainAvatar software by BrainMaster Technologies, Inc.

Figure 13.20 has many bad connections because insufficient gel was injected into several electrode holes of the EEG recording cap and because there was no impedance test. Electrical noise creates waves that look fuzzy.

Figure 13.21. Pulse (EKG)

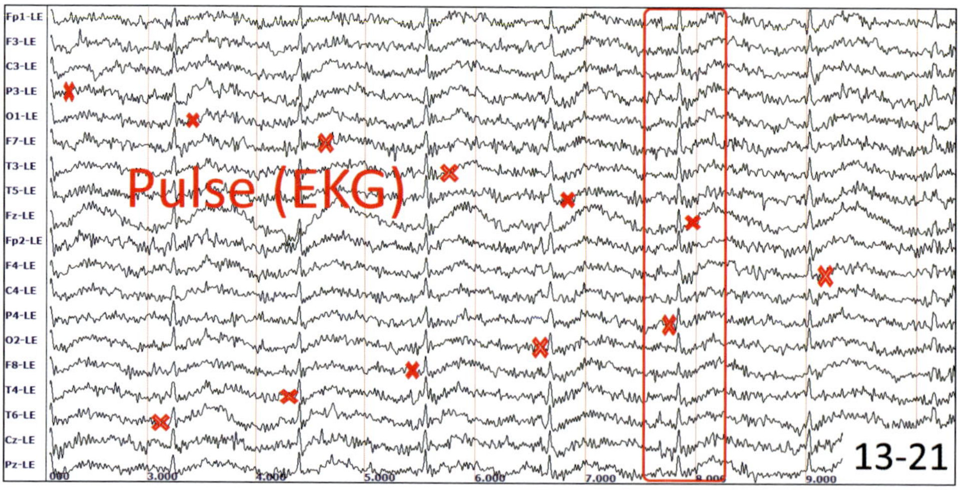

Figure 13.21 has been adapted from BrainAvatar software by BrainMaster Technologies, Inc.

Figure 13.21 shows a 1-Hz EKG. It can come from any subject. However, it happens more often with subjects with increased body mass coming from muscularity or obesity. Subjects with neck diameters exceeding 17 inches (43.25 centimeters) often have EKG visible in the EEG. This phenomenon may arise from volume conduction, or electrical pulses traveling through the tissues of the body to scalp electrodes (Wolters & Munck, 2007). It may be reduced by means of a mastoid reference montage rather than reference ear clips. The EKG is present in the earlobes of many subjects but in the thin skin above the mastoid bones.

Figure 13.22. No EEG Data

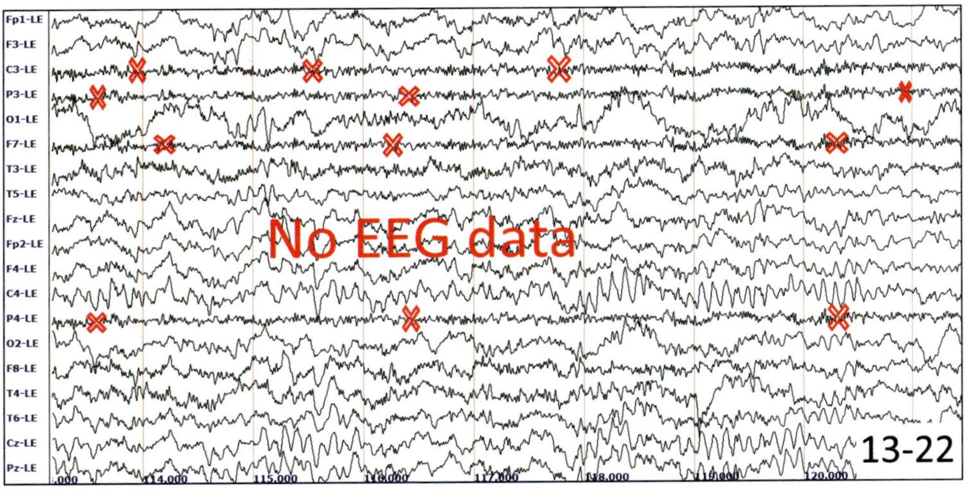

Figure 13.22 has been adapted from BrainAvatar software by BrainMaster Technologies, Inc.

Figure 13.22 shows what happens when qEEG data are acquired without an impedance check. The straightness of four lines of data means no EEG data. Straight-line EEGs come from flat-liners or deceased persons. If your clinic employs EEG technicians, the purchase of a stand-alone impedance meter is a must; it can be used for qEEG recordings and EEG training protocols. However, some clinics prefer qEEG amplifiers with built-in impedance meters.

Figure 13.22B Wet Hair/Salt Bridge

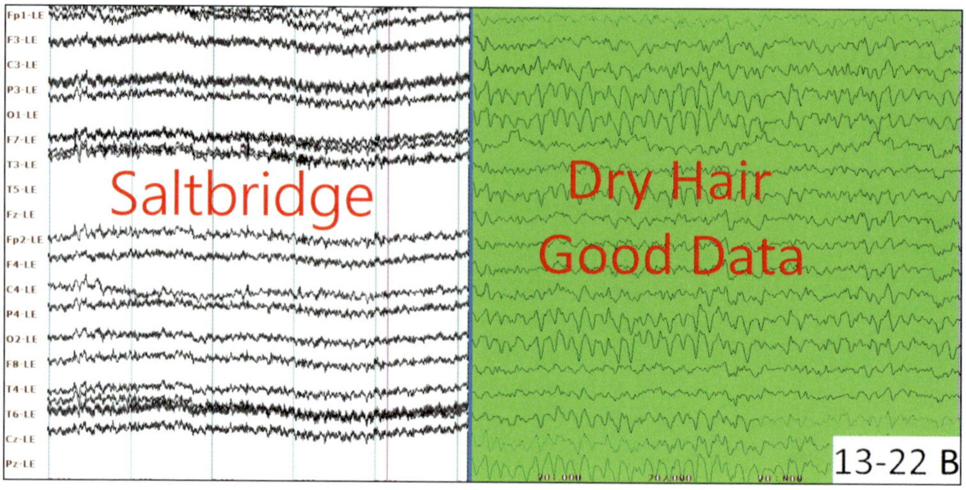

Figure 13.22B has been adapted from BrainAvatar software by BrainMaster Technologies, Inc.

Figure 13.22B shows what happens when the subjects hair is wet (left side of Figure 13.22B) which will result in a salt bridge. Notice all EEG data looks the same because all sites are connected due to electrical conductivity of the wet hair which often contains salt. On the other hand, once the subject's hair is dry we see the true EEG. Note: all clinics should have a hair dryer on hand to prevent salt bridges.

EEG SIGNATURES

Figure 13.23 shows qEEG data from a 10-year-old with ADHD. Classic elevated Z-scores and amplitudes are present in the frontal lobes. The recording shows EEG slowing in frontal lobe sites. In this recording of 5 minutes there is a lone spike and wave, which is not clinically significant. Most of the epochs shown can be accepted.

Figure 13.24 is an eyes-closed recording with minimal alpha morphology and, as predicted, this client has anxiety and insomnia. Elevated beta Z-scores verify the diagnosis. In this recording of 5 minutes there is a lone spike and wave, which is not clinically significant. Most of the epochs shown can be accepted.

Figure 13.23. Ten-Year-Old With ADHD

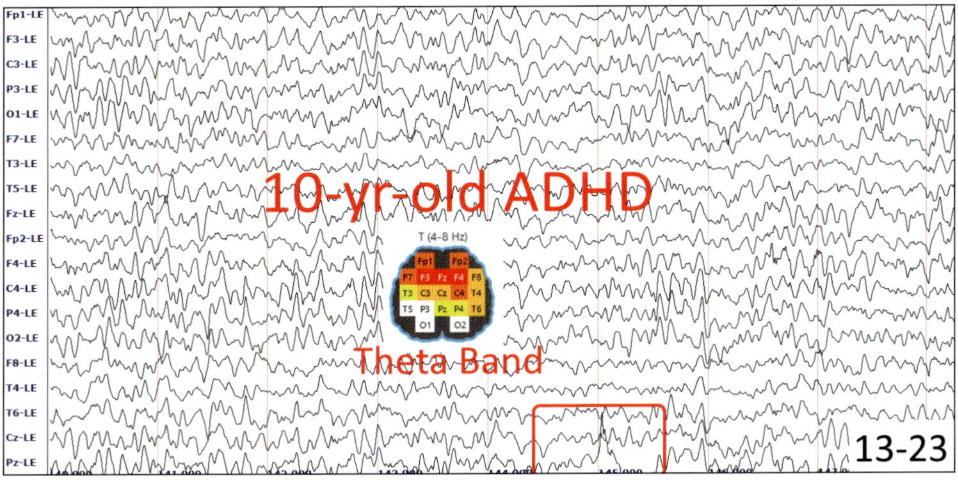

Figure 13.23 has been adapted from BrainAvatar software by BrainMaster Technologies, Inc.

Figure 13.24. Adult With Anxiety

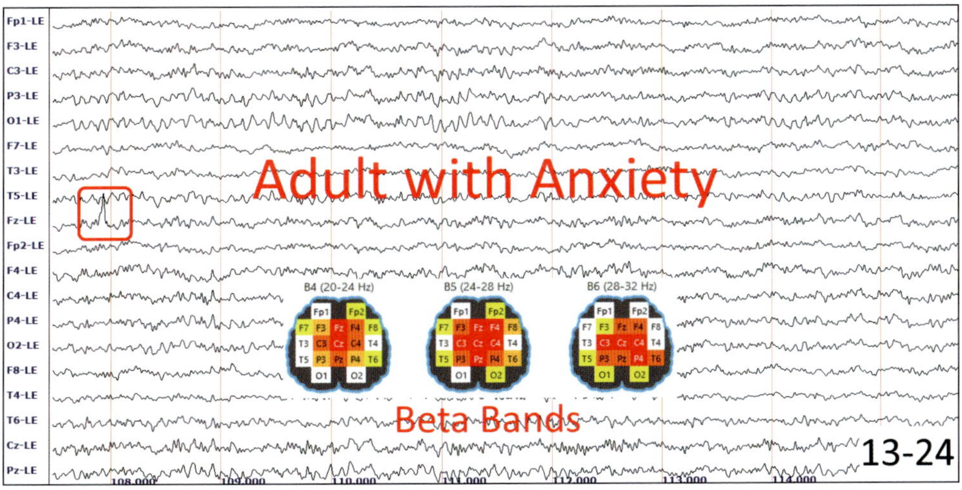

Figure 13.24 has been adapted from BrainAvatar software by BrainMaster Technologies, Inc.

Figure 13.25. Depression T5 > T6

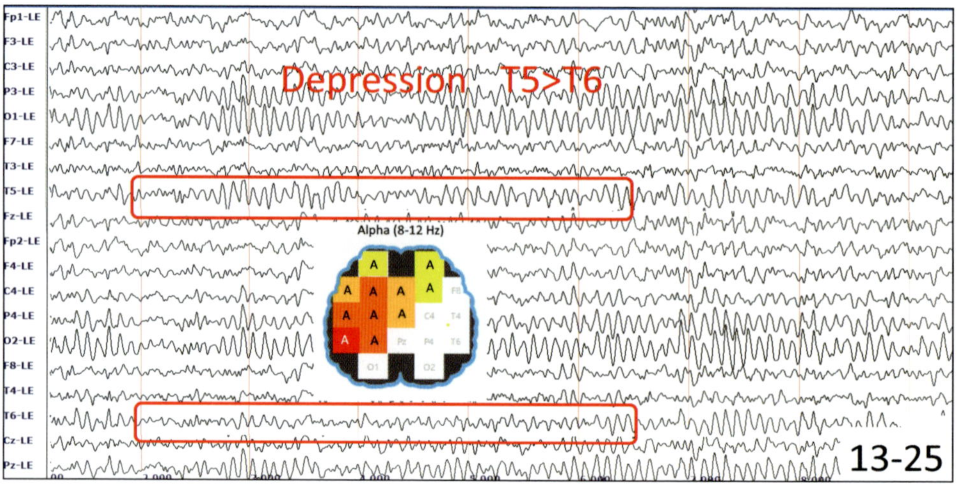

Figure 13.25 has been adapted from BrainAvatar software by BrainMaster Technologies, Inc.

Figure 13.25 reflects LH alpha asymmetry. There is also some frontal lobe slowing. This client is depressed. In some cases, LH asymmetries reflect learning disorders and not depression. Most of the epochs can be accepted during editing.

Figure 13.26. Age-Related Cognitive Decline (Age 80)

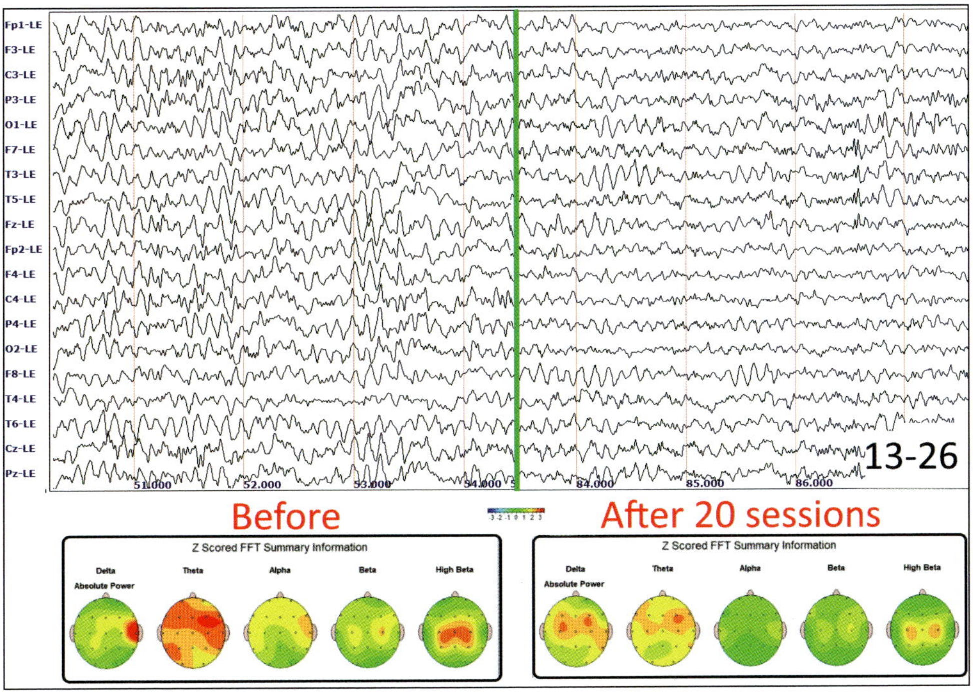

Figure 13.26 has been adapted from BrainAvatar software by BrainMaster Technologies, Inc.

Figure 13.26 is an example of training response for a subject with age-related cognitive decline. The left side of the qEEG recording is the baseline morphology. The right side shows the change in morphology after 20 training sessions. Before-and-after brain maps also reflect the change in this 80-year-old woman: "You're never too old to learn."

Part III was written to help the reader become familiar with the raw EEG. Professionals always consult brain wave morphology before brain map processing, protocol development, or assessment.

Part IV
The Dynamic Brain: Regions of Interest

Chapters

14

The Nervous System

RESEARCH AND DEVELOPMENT IN EEG neurofeedback are on the move. The advent of 3-D imaging has opened up a new door for assessment and training. Software and amplifiers can now detect cortical and subcortical brain regions, or regions of interest (ROIs). Training locations are no longer limited to the Int'l 10–20 system. For example, in the past, training the cingulate gyrus was limited to Fz, Cz, or Pz sites, but now the anterior or posterior cingulate gyrus can be trained directly (LORETA current source density); Z-score and power training can target many named cortical and subcortical areas such as the parahippocampal, subcallosal, orbital, and rectal gyrus as well as the insular cortex and the retrosplenial cortex. Part IV also introduces the reader to the Brodmann classification system, which uses numbers to define ROIs.

Neuroscience research employs ROI designations rather than the Int'l 10–20 system. For example, articles found on PubMed (www.ncbi.nlm.nih.gov/pubmed/), PLOS (www.plos.org), and PNAS (www.pnas.org/) employ ROI terminology. Furthermore, presenters at neurofeedback conferences such as those held by the International Society of Neurofeedback Research (www.isnr.org) now weave ROI terminology into lectures and workshops. In this book, Parts I, II, and III have presented fundamental EEG neurofeedback concepts. Parts IV and V provide a glimpse into what may become the future of EEG neurofeedback.

However, I assert that regardless of advancements to the field of EEG neurofeedback, interventions based upon the Int'l 10–20 System will continue to prove their worth.

THE NERVOUS SYSTEM

Many neurofeedback practitioners strive to understand how the brain communicates with itself and the body. They seek to uncover the relationship between regional brain functioning and symptoms. While it is not necessary to be a neurologist, it is necessary to have a working knowledge of the brain, including the nervous system and the endocrine system's role in the fight-or-flight response. To gain credibility with other medical professionals, it is necessary to be familiar with up-to-date neurological terms. Moreover, our clients will benefit the most if we understand how the functional brain is contributing to their distress.

The central nervous system (CNS) is the command center of the body (Figure 14.1). It sends and receives signals every second of the day. It is one of the most intricate communication systems in the physical universe. The nervous system has two parts: the CNS and the peripheral nervous sys-

Figure 14.1. Two Branches of Nervous System

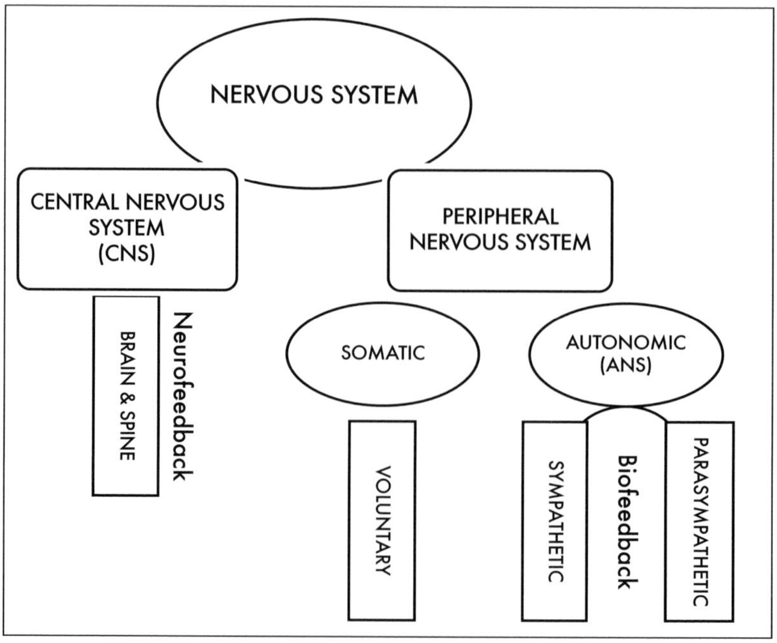

tem (PNS), as shown in Figure 14.1. Information travels within and among these two divisions via neural tissue. The PNS has two divisions: somatic (voluntary) and autonomic (involuntary). The autonomic nervous system (ANS) has two divisions: sympathetic (activating) and parasympathetic (deactivating). For example, the sympathetic nervous system accelerates the beating of the heart, whereas the parasympathetic nervous system slows it down.

The nervous system communication network includes 12 pairs of cranial nerves and 31 pairs of spinal nerves. The PNS picks up much of its information from the spinal cord and makes connections with the rest of the body. Note that outside the vertebral column, spinal nerves divide into branches and cross over each other. Consequently, the left hemisphere of the brain controls the right side of the body and vice versa. That's why an LH stroke may cause paralysis in the right side of the body (Figure 14.2). However, an LH stroke compromises LH cerebral functions such as speech and language (Broca's and Wernicke's areas as well as the auditory cortex).

Figure 14.2. Spinal Nerves Cross at the Vertebral Column

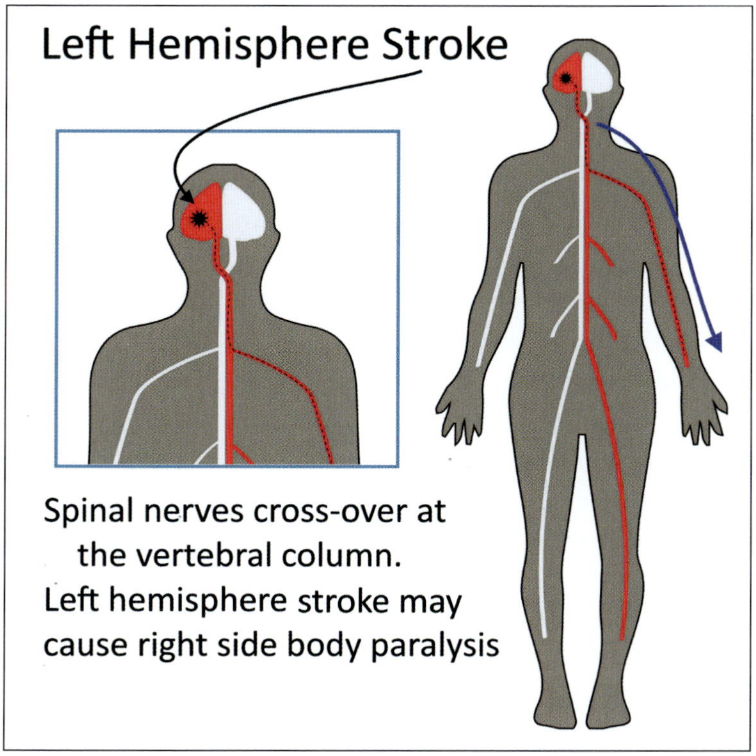

THE NERVOUS SYSTEM AND STRESS

The most prominent part of the brain is the cerebrum, which is divided into left and right hemispheres. Almost every brain structure comes in pairs. The outer layer of the cerebrum, the cerebral cortex, is responsible for higher mental functions. It is about 1/8 inch (3 mm) thick. It is divided into four corresponding lobes in each hemisphere. Each lobe is named in conjunction with the cranial bones above it and is associated with specialized tasks. Beneath the lobes of the cerebral cortex is a complex network of connections and structures. One of these structures is the limbic system, which is key to understanding emotions, memory, and the fight-or-flight response.

The hypothalamus, just below the thalamus, is a control center for the ANS and survival functions. The cerebellum, or little brain (located in the hindbrain), is responsible for coordination of motor movements and equilibrium. The brain stem holds up the brain like a stem holds a head of broccoli. It contains the reticular activating system, which helps to regulate the cycle of sleep and wakefulness.

The endocrine system works with the nervous system. It sends messages by secreting hormones that activate glands in various locations, whereas the nervous system sends messages from one neuron to another in a chain-link fashion. The endocrine system glands located in the body are the adrenal, thyroid, parathyroid, pancreas, testes, and ovaries. The endocrine glands located in the brain are the pituitary and the pineal glands. The endocrine system and the CNS talk to each other. The pituitary, dubbed the "master gland," relies on messages and direction from the nearby hypothalamus (Marieb, 2015). The pituitary functions to activate other members of the endocrine system. Neuroendocrine exchanges happen all the time. However, only the fight-or-flight response is discussed here because of its great interest to EEG neurofeedback practitioners.

The fight-or-flight response is a neuroendocrine event that happens after a real or imagined threat occurs. Two messages are sent. First, a signal is sent for instant analysis by the limbic system. Lightning-fast messages go between the amygdala and hippocampus, climaxing at the hypothalamus. Second (Figure 14.3), the hypothalamic-pituitary-adrenal (HPA) axis prepares the body for the perceived emergency, which triggers an activation of the endocrine and the sympathetic nervous systems (Sills, 2001, p. 348).

Figure 14.3. HPA Axis and Cortisol

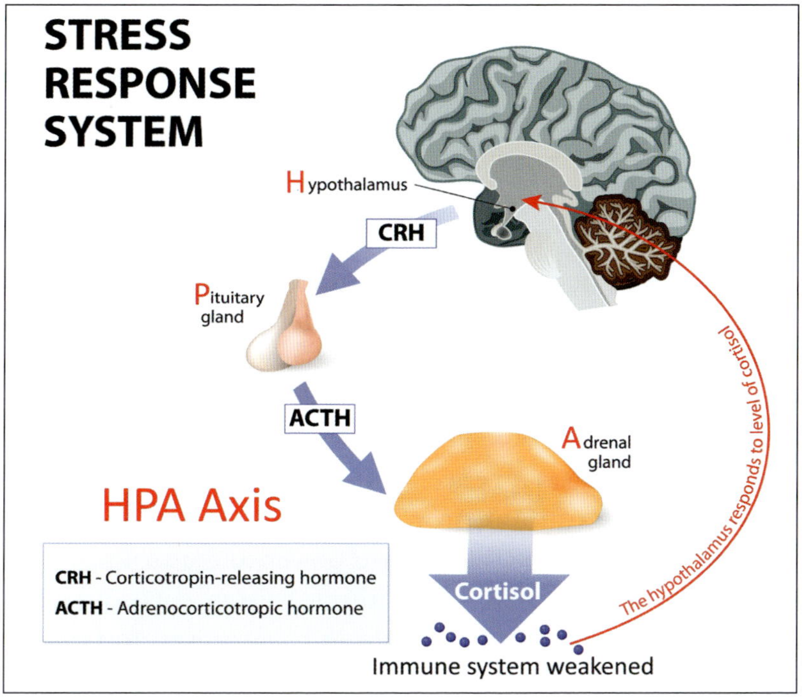

An avalanche of physiological changes begins, including increased muscle tension, breathing, brain wave frequency, blood pressure, and heart rate, and decreased skin temperature. Adrenal (medulla) glands begin secreting the corticoids (adrenaline, epinephrine, and norepinephrine), which inhibit basic bodily functions such as digestion, tissue repair, and the immune system. Meanwhile, back in the cerebrum, a second signal from the thalamus reaches the frontal lobes (the executive part of the cerebral cortex) for rational assessment (after the fight-or-flight response has already begun).

Now, if the frontal lobes make the decision to shut down (due to the fight-or-flight response) it may take as long as 3 minutes to reverse the process. However, if the frontal lobes are in agreement, the process continues. If neither fight nor flight can affect a solution—for example, a serious auto accident—then the next stage begins. Once completely overwhelmed, the energy created by the stress response is abruptly halted. The result is a shock to the system. Immediately preceding this shock, emotions (fear and rage) can become so strong that dissociation from normal conscious awareness sets in, along with numbness; the victim is frozen or immobilized. The PNS goes into action and releases neurohormones. Pain may no longer be experienced as adrenaline, and endorphins are flooding the system (Sills, 2001, pp. 349–356).

In response to stress, cortisol is released for several hours after a stressful event. That's normal, but what if there is continuous exposure to stressful events? If so, the HPA axis repeatedly exposes the body to cortisol, which leaves one at risk for a host of mental and physical health problems such as anxiety, depression, digestive problems, hypertension, sleep disruption, memory problems, and weight gain. Yes, trying to lose weight when under stress means that the dieter has to fight against emotional food cravings exacerbated by the cortisol effect. The negative feedback loop is shown in Figure 14.3.

Biofeedback training is an excellent way to cope with cortisol habituation. For example, this training promotes greater control over the cerebral cortex and the ANS. It gives the trainee power to control unconscious or involuntary physiological processes without raising cortisol levels. That's why biofeedback and alpha/theta training have proved to be effective in the treatment of addiction—because chronic alcoholics are prone to having high levels of cortisol (see Part V). For example, a therapeutic intervention by a drug addiction counselor may be deemed stressful. If so, it could result in a relapse due to elevated levels of cortisol which increase the urge to use. Elevated levels of cortisol impair thinking, reasoning, and decision making, necessary features of successful therapy.

NEURONS: THE BASIC UNIT OF COMMUNICATION WITHIN THE NERVOUS SYSTEM

The basic unit of the nervous system is the neuron. Billions of neuronal cells form intricate networks of connections throughout the body. Neuronal transmission is an electrochemical event. It can be detected and measured from the brain and from various muscle systems throughout the body. Neurons in the body are often called nerve cells. Neurofeedback amplifiers and software detect the electrical activity of muscles coming from the scalp and neuronal activity from within the brain. Electromyography is a graphic recording of nerve cells coming from muscle activity. The EEG is a graphic representation of neuronal cells coming from cerebral activity. Electrical measurements are recorded in microvolts (amplitude) and cycles per second (frequency) for both the body and the brain.

How Neurons Interact With Glial Cells

When neurons were first discovered, scientists assumed they were directing brain growth and change. However, that original supposition has been challenged (Fields, 2009).

The old theory is that all information and managerial direction in the nervous system comes from and is transmitted by electrical impulses over networks of neurons linked through synaptic connections. However, neurons make up a mere 15% of the brain. The other 85% was named neuroglia or brain glue. Glial cells were ignored for decades because scientists lacked the technology to see them in action.

Under the new theories, glial cells manage, repair, and support neurons. They are critical to the brain's information highway. Neurons and glial cells differ in operational methods:

- Neurons communicate serially across chains of synapses (e.g., like a relay race or bucket brigade). The electrical communication is rapid, occurring in microseconds.
- Glial cells broadcast their signals widely, like a cell phone network. The chemical communications generated by glial cells are slow compared to neurons. Information may take several seconds to reach its destination. (See Appendix 2 for possible training applications.)

For example, humans recoil with rapid reflexive action when exposed to pain. Only neurons (nerve cells) could transmit information that quickly. On the other hand, humans learn to play music, read, or juggle slowly and gradually. Structural changes are needed in the brain to learn these new tasks. Glial cells reinforce and direct neurons in several ways so that the new skill can be acquired (see Figure 14.4).

- Oligodendrocytes (one type of glial cell) increase the number of myelin sheath layers on axons. The more layers you have, the faster the communication. When starting to learn a new skill, performance is slow, but gradually the learner picks up speed because axonal myelin sheaths have picked up additional layers.

- Astrocytes are star-shaped glial cells that maintain the homeostasis of neuronal function. They provide nutrients to brain tissue and work to repair cells after brain trauma.
- Microglia fight infection, respond to injury, and prevent neuronal damage. They assist by doing housekeeping—the removing of unwanted waste products.

Figure 14.4. Neurons and Neuroglial Cells

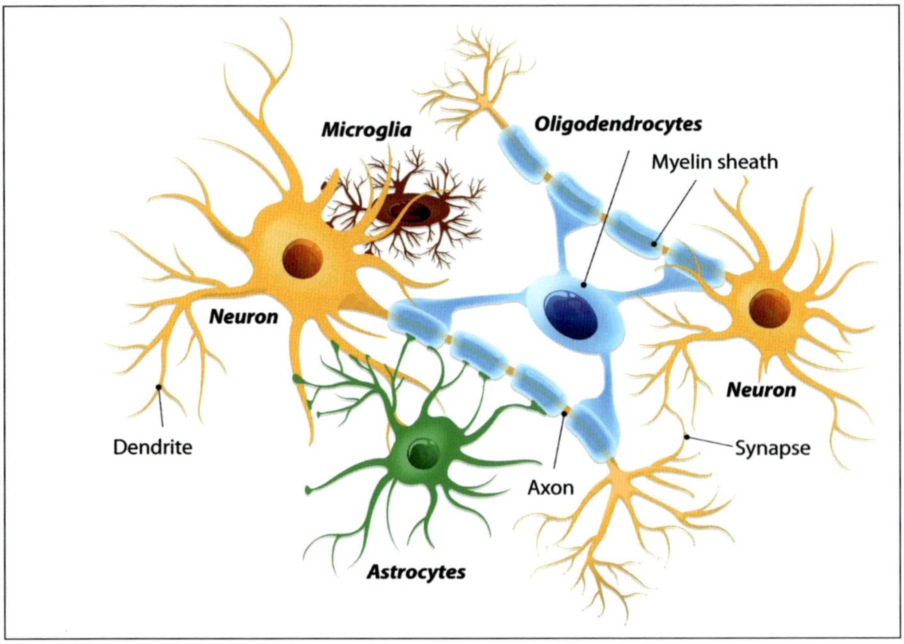

One more word about the myelin sheath: Oligodendrocytes myelinate brain cells, whereas Schwann cells myelinate cells in the body (PNS). Both add myelin layers to axons to increase the speed of neuronal communication. Myelin layers insulate nerve fibers (axons), which are essential for the normal transmission rates of electrical impulses (action potentials).

For example, many of the symptoms related to multiple sclerosis (MS) start with inflammation in the CNS. The disease disrupts normal nerve cell operation by compromising the function of oligodendrocytes.

At birth, the myelination process has just begun and so fewer layers mean slower transmission. That is why the PDR of a newborn infant is in the delta range (1–4 Hz). Delta is associated with sleep, and that's what infants do; they sleep much of the day and night. The developmental process promotes increased myelination; more wrappings mean faster neuronal communication: Delta no longer dominates. Eventually, by age 14, alpha becomes the dominant brain rhythm. The adult PDR is 10 Hz.

Sadly, the development process sometimes goes into reverse. Old age can be accompanied by a reduction to the myelin layers on axons; this results in slower mental processing or age-related cognitive decline. Some experience frequent senior moments or, worse, dementia. Of course not all seniors experience EEG slowing. Exercise, proper diet, and cognitive exercises can make a real difference. Furthermore, adults who have had mentally challenging careers often fare better in old age.

15

Brain Structures and Functions

THE STRUCTURAL BRAIN

Four outer brain lobes make up each hemisphere of the cerebral cortex. The brain is a highly complicated structure; countless connections beneath each lobe influence the operations of the lobe. To make matters more complex, each lobe can be divided into smaller functional units that sometimes lie on the border separating the lobes. Important regions include the right hemisphere (RH) and left hemisphere (LH), with four lobes in each. Sensor placement is often guided by our knowledge of brain lobes (Figure 15.1).

The LH is usually the dominant hemisphere. It is responsible for activities on the right side of the body. Most people are right handed. The LH keeps track of many details. If you were a forest ranger, the LH would examine individual trees and animals for defects, whereas the RH would take a much broader point of view: animal and tree health would be viewed as part of a larger system and not as individual, unrelated parts. The RH sees the forest as a complete unit. Some people are good at details; others are better at seeing the whole picture. The healthy brain can switch from LH to RH as needed. Alpha/theta training may promote interhemispheric switching.

The LH is good at logic, math, and analytical reasoning and academic performance. Verbal expression and understanding are linked to Broca's

Figure 15.1. Lateralization of Brain Functions

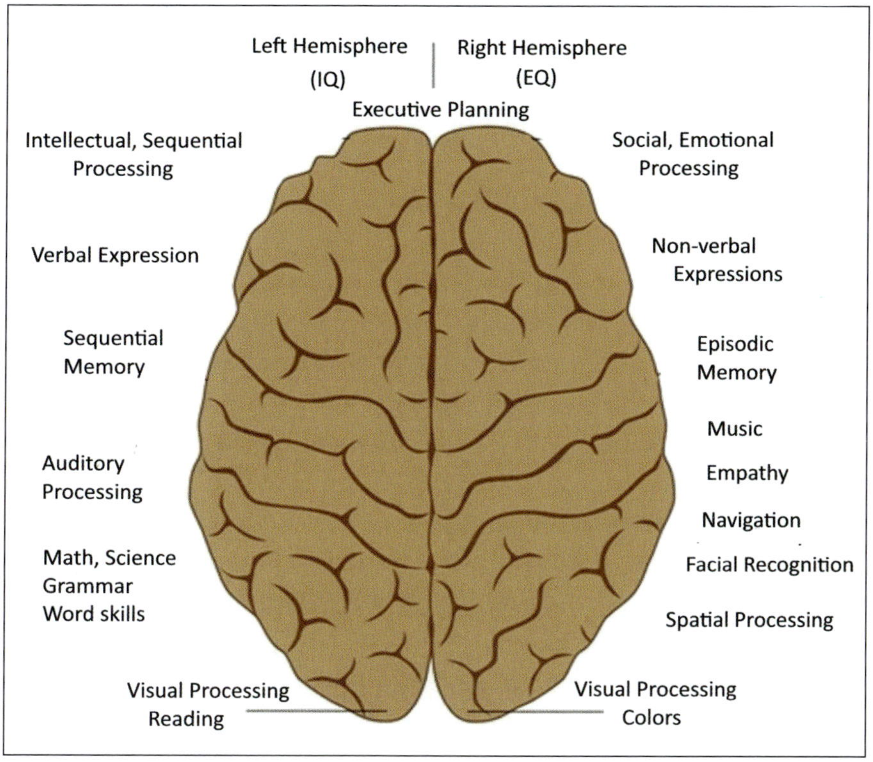

area and Wernicke's area of the LH. The LH is crucial to finding details during the research process; it governs grammatical principles and spelling. Verbal memories are stored in the LH.

The RH is usually the nondominant hemisphere. It is responsible for activities on the left side of the physical body because there is a reversal of communication in the spinal column. That means an RH stroke may cause paralysis in the left side of the body, and vice versa.

The RH governs emotions and music comprehension better than the LH. The sweet tones of singing and the bitter sounds of curse words all come from the RH. The RH knows why a joke is funny. Functions of the RH include creativity and perception, visual-spatial processing, not getting lost, and recognizing familiar places. My RH just knows where I am—without thinking about it. (Note that the brain's GPS, or navigational construct, is closely associated with the parahippocampus, a subcortical brain structure.) Logic may be on the left, but intuition and insight are on the right. Perhaps one of the most important features of the RH is its human qualities such as facial recognition, empathy, and early self-concept.

Problems result when there is no clear winner in the LH-RH competition. Two disorders that may reflect this struggle are dyslexia and stuttering. For example, in 70–80% of normal adults and children, the planum temporale (the center of Wernicke's speech area) is larger than the corresponding lateral RH location (Preis, Jancke, Schmitz-Hillebrecht, & Steinmetz, 1999). But such is not the case for dyslexics. Postmortem studies have indicated a symmetrical relationship—the right planum was similar in size to the left planum in dyslexics. In the case of stuttering, a functional difference has been observed in brain imaging studies. Normal reading and speech activate the left superior temporal gyrus, whereas stuttering activates the corresponding RH location (Springer & Deutsch, 1998, pp. 274–280). How does the LH-RH competition play out in the case of left-handers? Contrary to popular opinion, research has indicated that "only about 20 percent show right-brain dominance. Concurrently, left handed people also have a higher incidence of language impairment, stuttering, and dyslexia" (Ratey, 2001, p. 275).

Typically, women and men are not the same when it comes to LH-RH differences. "A woman's brain has a thicker corpus callosum [a major connection between the two hemispheres] than a man's, with women having up to 30 percent more connections between left and right" (Pease & Pease, 2000, p. 51). That means women have bigger and better connections between the emotional RH and the logical LH. This difference may contribute to a woman's ability to express and understand interpersonal emotions. Carter noted other functional differences between men and women:

> When they do complex mental tasks there is a tendency for women to bring both sides of the brain to bear on the problem, while men often use only the side most obviously suited to do it. This pattern of activity suggest that in some ways women take a broader view of life, bringing more aspects of the situation into play when making decisions, for example. Men, on the other hand, are more focused. (1998, p. 71)

When it comes to linguistic abilities, women also use more of the brain, on both sides, when compared to men; they usually speak at an earlier age than men (Pease & Pease, 2000, p. 70). Dual-hemispheric processing helps women to manage dyslexia better than men. However, men typically rely more heavily upon the LH for language processing. That is why a LH stroke will damage a man's language skills more than a woman's, because she has the RH edge (Ratey, 2001, p. 275). When it comes to emotion, men rely mostly on the RH, whereas women activate both sides of the brain (Pease & Pease, 2000, p. 134).

When it comes to spatial abilities, the tables are turned: men use more of their brain, on both sides, than women. They are better at left-right recognition, determining which way is north, reading maps, and playing three-dimensional games or puzzles. Most engineers, pilots, and air traffic controllers are men. Contrary to popular opinion, male and female occupational differences may not simply be a case of stereotyping or bias.

Generally, male and female brains are wired differently. This ought to be taken into consideration by EEG neurofeedback providers who are assessing for neurological deficits or recommending a change in family structure. For example, ask parents how much time their son is spending playing video games or how often their daughter is engaging in social networking. It must be noted that 10–20% of males and females may show cross-gender abilities, and individual differences abound.

How often does the LH dominate when men and women are grouped together? Ratey presented the following statistics: "Language resides predominantly in the left hemisphere in 90 percent of the population. About 5 percent have their main language areas in the right hemisphere, and another 5 percent split language fairly evenly between the hemispheres" (2001, p. 274). Electrical and metabolic differences between LH and RH are associated with disorders such as anxiety and depression. Davidson researched the relationship between cerebral cortex asymmetry and psychiatric disorders and proposed the following conclusion:

> We have hypothesized that the decrease in left prefrontal activation may be specific to depression, whereas the increase in right-sided prefrontal activation (as well as right parietal activation) may be specific to certain components of anxiety. . . . One common region we believe to be associated with both anxiety and depression is the amygdala. (1998, p. 321)

Davidson's research indicated that RH-LH asymmetries, especially in the prefrontal cortex, are traits that can be detected in infants and some animals. Protocols for EEG neurofeedback often target these asymmetries in an effort to stem the tide of anxiety and depression.

On the subject of TBI and stroke, Ayers reports the following LH and RH symptoms:

> Consistent with neurological findings generally, I have found that injuries on the right side often result in mood swings, personality change, problems with visuospatial organization, temper outbursts, impulsivity, and poor organization. Injuries on the left side often involve problems with language, such as lack of spontaneous speech, difficulty retrieving words, aphasia, paraphasia, agraphia or alexia, and/or problems with logic, math and judgment. (1999, p. 206)

Psychiatric interviewing and cognitive evaluation will likely identify if one hemisphere is over- or underactive. Thus, it may be possible to know which side of the brain is suspect even before EEG measurements are taken. Hemispheric asymmetry is only one of many possible problems; knowing the functions of each brain structure is another key to diagnostic and treatment success. The following section is designed to introduce the reader to various technical words and terminology employed by neurologists and found within anatomical textbooks.

TERMINOLOGY

Specific terms are employed to describe brain structures and anatomical features. Neurologists and those doing brain research typically refer to regions of interest (ROIs), including numbered Brodmann areas and named gyri and sulci; cortical and subcortical regions may also be defined by anatomical directional terms. Additionally, EEG neurofeedback practitioners utilize the Int'l 10–20 System, which assigns letters and numbers to 19 standardized scalp locations.

CORTICAL BOUNDARIES AND STRUCTURE

Fissures are the long deep grooves in the cerebral cortex that follow the boundaries between lobes. The wall or elevated ridge on each side of a deep groove is called a gyrus. For example, the surface of the deep groove that divides the LH and RH is called the cingulate gyrus. The cingulate gyrus is considered to be part of the limbic system (Pinel & Edwards, 1998, p. 118). A shorter groove or depression is called a sulcus.

In the inferior frontal lobes (prefrontal cortex), four ridges (two in the LH and two in the RH) make up the orbital gyrus; they are located just above the eye sockets. The angular gyrus forms part of the boundary separating the temporal and parietal lobes. The central fissure creates a dividing line between the somatosensory cortex and motor cortex that extends from the left lateral sulcus to the right lateral sulcus. The lateral sulcus forms part of the superior boundary of the temporal lobes (see Figure 15.2).

Figure 15.2. Cortical Divisions: Gyrus, Sulcus, Fissure, and Lobes

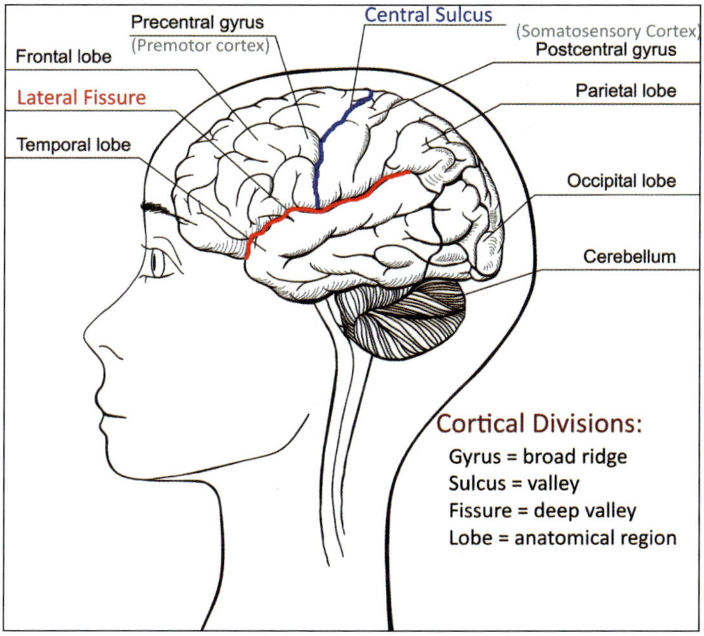

Lobe Specialization Areas and Functions

Much has been learned about lobe functions from the study of brain lesions (cuts in the cortex). Lesions may come from injuries, disease, or surgical interventions. Neurologists have observed that lesions occurring in specific regions of the brain produce specific symptoms. Conversely, specific symptoms relate to specific regions. It may be asserted that sensor placement is guided by matching specific brain functions with specific symptoms. Having the following information at hand will simplify the entire assessment and treatment process.

A few must-know regions (areas) and their assigned names (see Figure 15.3):

- Broca's area—LH, speech expression (F7/F3)
- Wernicke's area—LH, comprehension of written and spoken language, grammar (T5/P3)
- Auditory cortex—auditory processing, verbal skills (T3/C3)
- Angular gyrus—higher processing, academic skills, abstract thought (T5/P3)
- Primary visual cortex—visual processing and working memory, reading (O1, O2)
- Sensorimotor strip (or cortex)—divides frontal and parietal lobes and contributes to fine motor skills and sensory integration (C3, Cz, and C4) with two separate tracks:
    1. The somatosensory cortex is in the parietal lobe.
    2. The primary motor cortex is in the frontal lobe.

The LH Broca's, Wernicke's, and auditory cortex shown in Figure 15.3 have RH counterparts at homologous areas. The RH functions promote emotional and ambiguous speech processing for Broca's and Wernicke's

Figure 15.3. Essential Regions of Interest

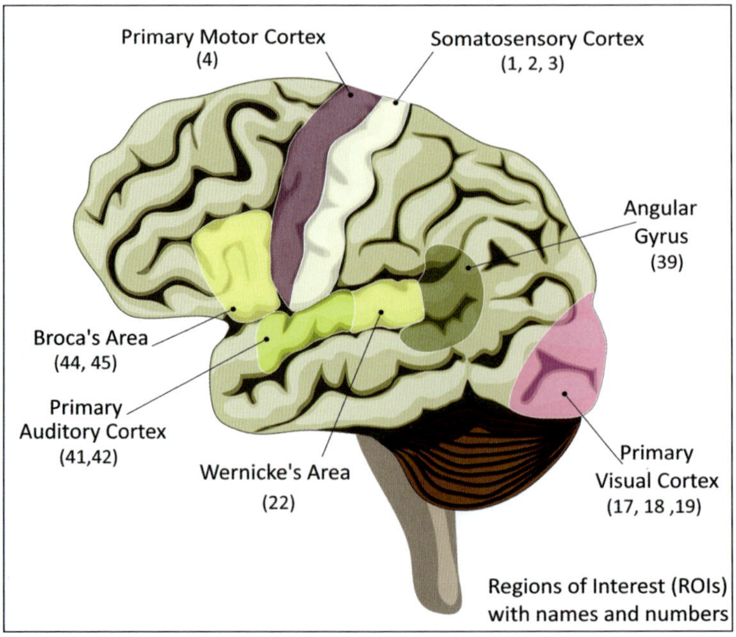

areas and music in the case of the auditory cortex; the angular gyrus conducts spatial calculations in the RH.

CORTICAL BRAIN LOBES (AND OTHER ANATOMICAL REGIONS)

There are four primary cortical brain lobes (Figure 15.4). Each one has a discrete set of functions as well as connections to other parts of the brain, both cortical and subcortical.

Figure 15.4. Four Primary Brain Lobes

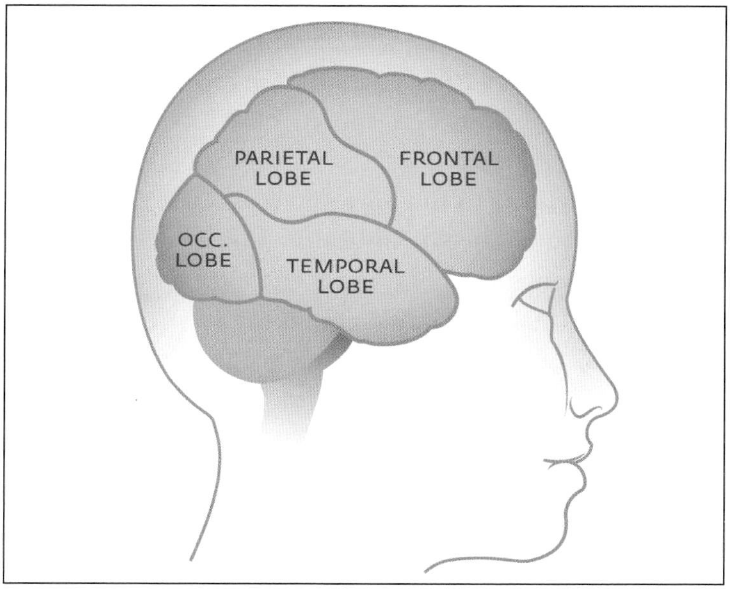

Frontal Lobes

Sites: Fp1 and Fp2 are called frontal poles. The prefrontal cortex is ventral: Fpz, Fp1, Fp2, F7, F8. The remainder of the frontal cortex is dorsal: Fz, F3, and F4.
Key functions: attention, memory, social awareness, character, motivation, and planning. Prefrontal lobes have connections (neuronal networks) leading to the amygdala (part of the limbic system).

Frontal lobes are responsible for immediate and sustained attention, social skills, emotions, empathy, time management, working memory, moral fiber or character, executive planning, and initiative. They identify problems and may send them to other brain regions for a solution.

One of the most famous cases of prefrontal lobe damage happened in 1848 in Vermont. Phineas Gage, a railroad foreman, was the victim of a fluke explosion that jettisoned a metal spike through the ventral medial portion of his brain, just dorsal lateral left of Fz. It did not damage Broca's area, so Gage was able to communicate with others. His vision—in his undamaged eye—was perfect; his motor skills were intact. What changed was his personality. His moral character was severely compromised. He was no longer the fine, upstanding member of the community he had been before the accident. His social skills and empathy for his fellow man had literally been destroyed (Damasio, 1994, pp. 4–33). The brain is not just a cognitive processing organism; it also is the seat of our conscience. Emotions, morals, and the social self cannot be isolated to frontal lobe activities; other, deeper structures are also involved. For example, Ratey clarified the relationship between the frontal lobes and the amygdala: "The frontal cortex, responsible for the brain's most complex processing, has the heaviest projections to the amygdala, and the two work together as part of the network that is the social brain" (2001, p. 312).

Training in EEG neurofeedback along the anterior dorsal (Fz) and ventral (Fpz) portions of the brain may have an impact on social behavior and moral fortitude. Weaknesses in this area are evident in oppositional-defiant and antisocial behaviors. This behavior may parallel excessive EEG slowing and inadequate cerebral blood flow (CBF) throughout other prefrontal areas as well, especially Fp1 and Fp2. Clients with excessive fear as a result of trauma, anxiety, and neglect may likely have an overactive amygdala. Neurofeedback training in the right prefrontal cortex may lead to "a reduction in fear as well as a sense of calm and well-being" (Fisher, 2004, p. 89).

Checking clients for frontal lobe problems often involves cognitive testing. Some clinical judgments can be made without testing. Do clients appear to be in a fog and unable to concentrate? Do they get into trouble with school or community authorities? Are they fearful? Are they ethical and moral? Do they care about other people? Do they have good social skills? Did it take them twice as long as usual to fill out the paperwork? Do they seem unmotivated and disconnected? Did they get lost or were they late on the way to the office? Negative, depressed, or anxious clients may have frontal lobe asymmetries.

Neurofeedback specialists have researched ADHD more than any other disorder. It is primarily a disorder of the frontal lobes. According to the Centers for Disease Control and Prevention, 6.4 million children from age 4-17 can be diagnosed with ADHD (Visser, 2014). This disorder can manifest with or without hyperactivity. Both adults and children can have ADHD. There is a genetic component, and it runs in families. Adults tend to lose the hyperactivity symptom but continue to struggle with inattention, disorganization, and impulsivity symptoms. Girls are often overlooked because they are less likely to be hyperactive—the squeaky wheel gets the grease.

Other disorders mimic ADHD, such as reactive attachment disorder, OCD, anxiety disorder, PTSD, mania, learning disorders, and others. Immature and spirited children are sometimes falsely given this label and inappropriately medicated.

It is reasonable to say that many potential clients will have ADHD as either a primary or a secondary disorder. Part VI reviews diagnostic approaches. But the task for the moment is to determine which brain structures are involved. Several different brain localities may be suspect when assessing ADHD. But the cingulate gyrus (Fz, Cz, and Pz) and the anterior ventral medial region (Fpz, Fp1, Fp2, F7, F8, and Fz) in the frontal lobes may be the first place to look.

Parietal Lobes

Sites: Pz, P3, P4.
Key functions: math, naming objects, complex grammar, spatial awareness.

Parietal lobes solve problems that have been conceptualized by the frontal lobes. They have been labeled the association cortex. Complex grammar, the naming of objects, sentence construction, and mathematical processing are traceable to the left parietal lobe. Acalculia or dyscalculia is a disturbance in the mental ability to calculate math problems. It should be noted that some forms of math involve spatial processing—for example, geometry—and so the right parietal lobe is also suspect. Basic math including addition, subtraction, and multiplication involves our working, or rote, memory, which occurs near the left anterior frontal lobes. However, deeper, more complex mathematical calculations engage the parietal lobes. Of course, if the frontal lobes fail to do their job, parietal lobe functioning may be compromised. Map orientation, knowing the difference between right and left, and spatial recognition are all functions of the right parietal lobe.

Specialization has its limits. For example, positron-emission tomography (PET) scans have shown that the naming of objects involves several brain regions, including the posterior frontal cortex, the inferior parietal cortex, and the superior temporal cortex. The sense of direction also encompasses the parahippocampal region as well as the RH parietal and temporal regions—elevated theta may also be a factor. Ratey commented on another symptom that may accompany posterior parietal lobe deficits:

> Damage to the posterior parietal cortex can cause a classic deficit called Balint's syndrome, in which patients are unable to attend to multiple objects simultaneously; they cannot see the forest for the trees. The damage limits a person's ability to shift attention from one location to another and perhaps from one sensory modality to another. (2001, p. 116)

Clients with parietal lobe problems may have more car accidents because they are not able to attend to both sides of the visual field. They might have trouble playing computer games like solitaire, which require scanning from left to right. If they draw pictures and the left half of the picture seems incomplete, this indicates a deficit in the right parietal lobe.

Commenting on the RH and the parietal lobe, Ratey also concluded:

> The right hemisphere, particularly the parietal lobe, is responsible for analyzing external space and the body's position in it. The parietal lobe is the "where" area of sensory perception. . . . Studies in lesions in the right parietal indicate that it is involved in attention, music, body image, body scheme, face recognition, and the physical act of dressing. Further the entire right hemisphere plays a role in the attentional system and in feeling and displaying emotion. (2001, p. 320)

Ask clients to write a few sentences, draw a simple picture, or play monkey see, monkey do. Have them do a few simple math (word) problems. How well did they perform? How accurate is their picture? How difficult was it for them to follow hand and body movements? Were the math problems answered with ease, with difficulty, or not at all?

Depressed clients may have increased alpha or theta in the LH parietal region, whereas anxious clients may have increased beta in the RH parietal region.

Temporal Lobes

Sites: T3, T4, T5, T6.
Key functions: LH, verbal memories, word recognition, reading, language, emotion; RH, music, facial recognition, social cues, object recognition, with proximity to the amygdala (emotion) and hippocampus (memory).

Luria (1973, pp. 135–143) indicated that lesions to the left midtemporal zone interfere with verbal memory making. Damage to this zone prevents the storage of longer passages of information, although short phrases may be retained. Consequently, it becomes difficult to keep up with a conversation because information is being lost. Lesions to the right temporal lobe often result in the inability to recognize intricate rhythmic melodies. Music appreciation may be lost.

The temporal lobe houses the auditory cortex in close proximity to the hippocampus. Consequently, it is critical to the memory-making process, especially verbal memories. Springer and Deutsch's (1998, pp. 207–211) review of the literature comparing CBF and memory explained that memory can be classified in three different categories: short-term, working, and long term. Each activity tends to activate different parts of the brain, as shown in PET scans. Short-term memory, which includes recalling a seven-digit number such as a telephone number, activates "Broca's area and the left inferior parietal cortex." If a short-term-memory task is visual or spatial in nature, then the RH is activated, including "right occipital, parietal, and prefrontal cortices." If a short-term memory task is phonetic, then suspect damage points to the left posterior or inferior parietal lobe. Phonological memory takes in the correct order and transmission of speech sounds; it contains the phonetic pattern of a language.

Long-term memory can be divided into two branches: semantic and episodic. Semantic memory includes the recall of objects and word understanding, especially in language, and is associated with left temporal lobe (Wernicke's area) problems. Episodic memory involves functional tasks such as remembering to pay the bills, to fill the gas tank, how to play baseball, where glasses and keys were placed, and so on. Deep lesions to the midtemporal extending into the hippocampal lobes result in a dysfunctional episodic memory. It may also be hypothesized that "left prefrontal cortical regions are more involved in retrieval of information from semantic memory and in simultaneously encoding novel aspects of the retrieved information into episodic memory. Right prefrontal cortical regions on the other hand, are involved in episodic memory retrieval" (Springer & Deutsch, 1998, pp. 215–216).

Working memory is an example of short-term plus long-term memory joined in a problem-solving task such as math or reading. Studies show an activation of the frontal lobes in the case of verbal or mental tasks (Springer & Deutsch, 1998, p. 206). When it comes to memory problems, it is not possible to isolate the problem to the temporal lobes. Another condition that may involve both the frontal cortex and temporal lobe is dyslexia. Wernicke's area (understanding) is located at the posterior superior temporal lobe, which is located at P3/T5. Broca's area (expression) is located at F7/T3. With reference to dyslexia, PET scans have revealed the following:

> Some types of dyslexia may be due to dissociation—a missing or inactive connection between two brain modules. A study in which PET scans were made of dyslexics' and non-dyslexics' brains while they attempted a complex reading task suggests that the two main language areas, Wernicke's and Broca's, do not work in concert in dyslexics. This appears to be because an important neural link in the vicinity of the Insula cortex is not activated during such tasks as it is in others. (Carter, 1998, p. 152)

Broca's area is activated when discriminating between two similar sounds, but so are the midtemporal lobe and Wernicke's area. All three areas must be suspected in cases of dyslexia (Springer & Deutsch, 1998, pp. 170–171).

Whereas the LH is associated with word recognition, the RH temporal lobe is associated with facial recognition:

> A deficit in the ability to recognize faces is called facial agnosia or prosopagnosia, derived from the Greek words for face (*prosopon*) and not knowing (*agnosia*). Prosopagnosia seems to be a result of impairment in the medial occipitotemporal cortex of the brain, due to stroke or brain damage. Although bilateral damage usually causes the full-fledged syndrome, damage to the right hemisphere alone is far more debilitating than damage to the left. (Ratey, 2001, p. 316)

Lesions to the temporal lobes may also contribute to the "auras of déjà vu, jamais vu, and formed visual hallucinations" (Rowan & Tolunsky, 2003, p. 47). Those terms are translated as "already viewed" and "never viewed," respectively. The temporal lobe is also near the amygdala, and so it may be another factor in angry or aggressive behavior in children. Amen commented on the change in his nephew Andrew's personality that came from a left temporal lobe tumor:

> But then his personality changed. He appeared depressed. He had serious aggressive outbursts and he complained to his mother of suicidal and homicidal thoughts (very abnormal for a nine-year-old). He drew pictures of himself hanging from a tree. He drew pictures of himself shooting other children. (1998, p. 11)

After Andrew's operation to remove his tumor, his condition improved, and he returned to his former likable self. His story is reminiscent of Phineas Gage's story because a personality change followed damage to a specialized brain region.

Slowing of the EEG in the temporal lobes is often seen following concussions, "since head injuries, regardless of the site of impact, often involve the scraping of the temporal lobes along the inner part of the sharp, bony middle fossa" (Hughes, 1994, p. 122). Actually, problems with temporal lobe slowing "are the most common kind of EEG abnormality in the majority of EEG laboratories. . . . The major pathological changes in aging, anoxic conditions, head injury and many other etiologies are found *in* the temporal lobe, especially within the depth of this lobe, the amygdala and hippocampus" (p. 120).

The anterior left temporal lobe, due to its proximity to the amygdala, may also be implicated in depression. Davidson, Abercrombie, Nitschke, and Putnam reported the following:

> Investigators found that blood flow in the left dorsolateral prefrontal cortex and the left anterior temporal cortex is negatively correlated with severity of negative symptoms, suggesting that these cortical zones play a role in generating positive affect, motivation and goal-setting, and that their inactivity leads to negative symptoms. (1999, p. 230)

Papp, Coplan, and Gorman's review of the literature also revealed a pattern of CBF change in the temporal lobes (especially the right temporal lobe) of subjects with anxiety disorder and panic disorder: "Mild anxiety increases CBF, whereas severe anxiety reduces CBF values and cerebral metabolism" (1992, pp. 314–316).

Temporal lobe functions affect us in various ways. Functions in the LH are associated with reading (word recognition), learning, memory, and a positive mood. Functions in the RH are associated with music, facial recognition, anxiety, and sense of direction. Comprehensive tests and questions are needed to isolate temporal lobe problems.

If a new client has trouble following the directions to my office, or reports a pattern of getting lost or getting turned around, or fails to recognize a simple tune or can't remember faces, then the right posterior temporal lobe may be suspect.

Training in the temporal lobes (especially with bipolar montages) has become a common practice among EEG neurofeedback providers for a number of conditions such as PTSD, anxiety, migraines, autistic spectrum disorders, and more.

Occipital Lobes

Sites: Oz, O1, O2
Key functions: visual field; helps to locate objects in the environment, see colors, recognize drawings, and correctly identify objects; reading, writing, and spelling depend upon an accurate visual field; some connections extend to the amygdala.

The occipital lobes are closely associated with the visual cortex. During the assessment phase, it is important to rule out vision problems before concluding that other lobes must be responsible for a learning disorder. For example, some children with ADHD who are challenged by reading tasks benefit from EEG neurofeedback training to help them focus, as well as vision therapy to help them process. Problems with the visual cortex, especially at O1, may result in visual inattention. The occipital lobe borders the parietal and temporal lobes. In posterior locations in those two lobes, EEG abnormalities often extend into occipital lobe regions. Visual memories and accurate reading require accurate vision. Furthermore, traumatic memories that accompany visual flashbacks are often processed in the occipital lobes. Two visual processing problems to look for are:

- Visual agnosia (inability to perceive and draw complete objects)
- Simultaneous agnosia (inability to see multiple objects at the same time)

Luria described simultaneous agnosia:

> They cannot place a dot in the centre of a circle or a cross, because they perceive only the circle (or the cross), or the pencil point at any one time;

> they cannot trace the outline of an object or join the strokes together during writing; if they see the pencil point they lose the line, or if they see the line they can no longer see the pencil point. (1973, p. 121)

Luria's description suggests a simple cognitive test. Sometimes conversations with parents reveal severe problems with writing, coloring, or other visual-spatial activities in their children. Posterior parietal lobes should also be suspect when considering visual-spatial activities. Adults also may have problems in the occipital lobes due to TBI or a stroke.

Davidson and Irwin reported a unique connection between the visual cortex and the amygdala (part of the limbic system):

> Moreover, the intensity of fear displayed in the faces was systematically related to increases in blood flow in the left amygdala. In a subsequent re-analysis of these data, Morris and colleagues found that increased blood flow in the amygdala predicted increased blood flow in extrastriate visual cortex during fear but not during happy presentations. These findings indicate functional connectivity between these regions is altered as a function of emotional expression condition. (1999, p. 15)

Neurofeedback interventions for PTSD, anxiety, addictions, personality disorders, type A personality, and mood disorders may include deep states training (alpha/theta training) with sensors placed on the visual cortex. The connections between the visual cortex and the amygdala can be enhanced with EEG neurofeedback. The rationale for this approach is in harmony with the above findings.

Sensory and Motor (Sensorimotor) Cortex

Sites: C3, C4, Cz

Note: The sensory and motor cortices run parallel to each other and are divided by the central sulcus. The two cortices combined are sometimes called the sensorimotor cortex. However, the sensory cortex alone may also be called the primary somatosensory cortex or just the somatosensory cortex. The primary motor cortex is associated with the motor cortex (see Figure 15.5).

Key functions of primary motor cortex: conscious control of all skeletal muscle movements.

Key functions of primary somatosensory cortex: spatial discrimination and the ability to identify where bodily sensations originate.

The sensorimotor cortex marks the division between the parietal lobes and the frontal lobes (Figure 15.5). The primary motor cortex is anterior and within the frontal lobes. The primary somatosensory cortex is posterior and within the parietal lobes. Together the sensory and motor cortices reach downward to both the left and right temporal lobes to the lateral sulcus. Considering the careful placement of these two adjacent structures lends support to the notion that they not only divide the anterior from the posterior but they also serve as a junction that coordinates movement that is, in part, guided by sensation. Much of what we do and who we are translates into moving our legs, hands, torso, or neck into action. "From the Greek root soma, for body, the somatosensory system is responsible for both the external senses of touch, temperature, pain, and the internal senses of joint position, visceral state, and pain" (Damasio, 1994, p. 65). Damage to the RH portion of the somatosensory cortex "compromises reasoning/decision making and emotion/feeling, and, in addition, disrupts the processes of basic body signaling" (p. 70).

The functions of the primary motor cortex have been associated with skillful movements and smooth, repetitive operations such as typ-

Figure 15.5. Primary Motor and Primary Somatosensory Cortices

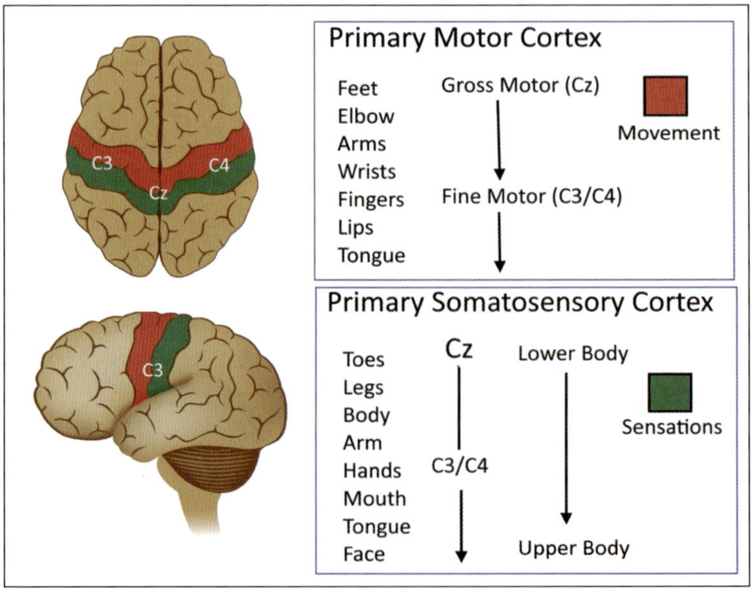

ing, playing musical instruments, handwriting, the operation of complex machinery, and fluid speaking. It is the hub and switching station between voluntary muscles of the body and the brain. Wilder Pennfield's (1961) research into the sensorimotor cortex led him to map out many of its functions. He found discrete locations that correspond to the movements of the hands, legs, mouth, jaw, and so on. Figure 15.5 shows that the top of the head (Cz) regulates the bottom of the body, such as the feet and trunk. Lower areas on the central sulcus, such as C3/C4, regulate upper parts of the body such as the hands and the face. Considering the far-reaching effects of this dual cortex, it is no wonder many pioneers in the field of neurotherapy started training along the sensorimotor cortex. One of the brain waves, sensorimotor rhythm (SMR), got its name from this cortex. Barry Sterman trained Margaret Fairbanks along the sensorimotor cortex to increase SMR. She was the first epilepsy sufferer to receive EEG neurofeedback training. In many ways, she was the first human neurofeedback success story.

Training along the sensorimotor cortex is implied for stroke, epilepsy, paralysis, ADHD, and disorders of sensorimotor integration. Training at C3 and C4 also improves handwriting. Keep in mind that the RH controls the left side of the body and vice versa. However, the sensorimotor cortex has other functions. Ratey explained that the motor cortex helps the cerebral cortex to encode both physical and cognitive tasks: "The brain circuits used to order, sequence, and time a *mental* act are the same ones used to order, sequence, and time a *physical* act" (2001, p. 149). That means that the somatosensory cortex shares in orchestrating both physical and mental processes. It governs more than just sensory and motor functions. Therefore, clients who have trouble seeing the logical sequence of cognitive tasks may benefit from EEG neurofeedback training along the LH sensorimotor cortex (C3). Note that depressed and anxious clients may respond to training at C3 (depression) and C4 (anxiety) because C3 and C4 are near the insular cortex (Brodmann Area 13) and not because C3 and C4 are in the sensorimotor cortex.

Sleep spindles, or SMR spindles, can be seen while we are sleeping. The sensorimotor cortex is the primary source of SMR waves. Consequently, training at C3 and C4 is often used to facilitate sleep. Furthermore, children with sensory defensiveness or dysregulation disorder are routinely trained in the RH of the sensorimotor cortex (C4) to reduce tactile sensitivity.

SUBCORTICAL AREAS WITH INT'L 10–20 REFERENCES

Cingulate Gyrus

Sites: Fpz, Fz, Cz, Pz (also called the cingulate or the z-line)
Note: The cingulate gyrus is a subcortical or subsurface ROI. Neurofeedback training with simple monopolar montages along the z-line may or may not have a direct impact on the cingulate gyrus—bipolar montages are often utilized, especially when inhibiting elevated beta. To train this area directly, use sLORETA.

For a cutaway view of the brain, see Figure 15.6. The cingulate gyrus is a deep brain structure that is generally considered to be part of the limbic system. Fz, Cz, and Pz are Int'l 10–20 scalp locations.

Figure 15.6. Cingulate Gyrus

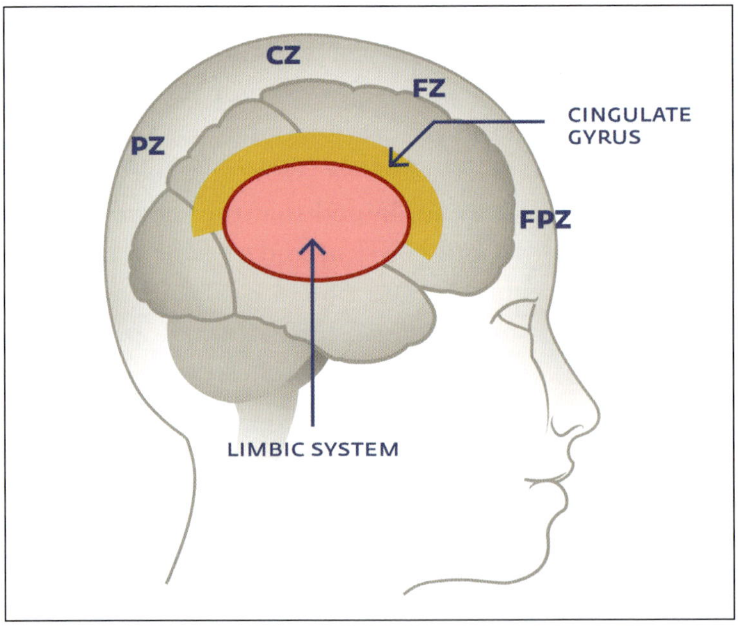

Key functions of anterior cingulate gyrus: contributes to mental flexibility, cooperation, and attention; helps the brain to shift gears and the young child to make transitions; helps the mind to let go of problems and concerns; helps the body to stop ritualistic movements and tics; contributes to the brain circuitry that oversees motivation, the social self, and our personality; is closely aligned with the amygdala.

Key functions of posterior cingulate gyrus: is closely aligned with parahippocampal cortices and shares in the memory-making process; provides orientation in space, as well as eye and sensory monitoring services (Vogt, Finch, & Olson, 1992, pp. 435–443). The division between anterior and posterior is generally considered to be at Cz.

In Figure 15.6, the entire cingulate gyrus (anterior plus posterior) divides the LH and RH. The anterior cingulate cortex is closely associated with the anterior ventral medial site that is central to the prefrontal cortex. The anterior cingulate is in the frontal lobes, and the posterior cingulate is in the parietal lobes. The cingulate gyrus intersects the central sulcus at the vertex. Hence, EEG neurofeedback training at the vertex (Cz) influences three cortices simultaneously: somatosensory, motor, and cingulate. The cingulate is called the cortical portion of the amygdala. Damasio summed up the operations of the cingulate in this way:

> I would like to propose that there is a particular region in the human brain where the systems concerned with emotion/feeling, attention, and working memory interact so intimately that they constitute the source for the energy of both external action (movement) and internal action (thought animation reasoning). This fountainhead region is the anterior cingulate cortex, another piece of the limbic puzzle. (1994, p. 71)

A hot cingulate means that it is overactive and causing problems. Several problems are closely related to imbalanced cingulate activity: anxiety, perfectionism, obsessions, worry, OCD, ADHD, and Tourette's syndrome.

Symptoms of OCD include obsessions and/or compulsions. It is accompanied by worrying, anxiety, and mental and physical tension. The mind, and sometimes the body, are stuck in ritualistic thoughts or behaviors. Telling the sufferer to lighten up will only make the condition worse. Schwartz specializes in the diagnosis and treatment of OCD using PET (Schwartz & Beyette, 1996). Hundreds of neuroimages have revealed an abnormal pattern of CBF unique to OCD. Schwartz developed a rigid four-step cognitive-behavioral program to counteract symptoms of OCD. PET scans taken before and after treatment have proven that positive changes in brain activity can be accomplished without the use of drugs. The mind can heal the brain. Clients with OCD should be encouraged to read *Brainlock: Free Yourself From Obsessive-Compulsive Behavior* (Schwartz & Beyette, 1996).

Do not confuse OCD with perfectionism, mental inflexibility, or obsessions. Although they may also be rooted in the anterior cingulate gyrus (especially elevated beta), these traits may not be OCD. For example, many survivors of sexual abuse often resort to obsessions to cope. So, before recommending Schwartz's book, make sure there is evidence of compulsions and not just obsessions.

Brain structures that contribute to OCD include the anterior cingulate gyrus, orbital gyrus (just above the eyes in the prefrontal cortex), and deeper structures such as the caudate nucleus. Evidently, the brain gets locked into obsessions or rituals in a closed-loop fashion.

> The anterior cingulate tells the orbitofrontal cortex what it should pay attention to, while the orbitofrontal cortex itself identifies what seems to be an error in behavior. It says, "Error, error, this action is a mistake." When the signals about attention and error conflict, motor programs get caught up in the turmoil. A panic message results, telling the brain to activate to get out of danger or to correct the problem by taking action, such as returning to the house, for the third time to turn off the stove that is already off. The typical OCDer is a perfectionist who is interminably searching for error. He or she explodes with worry and gets caught up in a never-ending do-loop of concern and rumination. (Ratey, 2001, p. 152)

Compulsivity is often reflected in the orbital gyri as hypercoherence springing from the frontal poles (Fp1 and Fp2). Obsessions are often reflected by elevated beta activity along posterior and anterior regions of the cingulate gyrus (Fz, Cz and Pz). The goal for the EEG neurofeedback provider is to find out what EEG abnormalities are negatively impacting key brain structures. Training, therefore, may include the anterior or posterior cingulate as well as the orbital gyri. Hammond (2003) conducted an extensive review of literature on OCD as well as an intensive EEG analysis of OCD subjects. Several OCD subtypes have been identified and differentiated according to specific EEG characteristics.

Unwanted verbal expressions and movements mark Tourette's syndrome—similar to OCD. The anterior cingulate cortex and the left dorsolateral prefrontal cortex (near F3/F7) are underactive in the brains of Tourette's syndrome sufferers. Deeper structures such as the left basal ganglia also contribute to the problem (Carter, 1998). If underactivity means EEG slowing, then EEG neurofeedback providers have the option of increasing regional cerebral blood flow (rCBF) with hemoencephalography (HEG) near infra-red (NIR) neurofeedback or decreasing frontal lobe hypercoherence with HEG passive infra-red (PIR) (see Part V). Clients with tics may also benefit from similar protocols.

The anterior cingulate cortex is known to monitor and control attention and impulse control; it keeps us motivated and on task. It is the home of the primary and secondary motor cortices, which control movement and activity. Some children with ADHD have difficulty understanding the consequences for their behavior. They may become hyperfocused, locked into a subject or activity for hours at a time. Getting mentally locked into something relates to the OCD loop. Cortical slowing along the anterior cingulate is often found to be the cause of this disorder.

Insular Cortex

Beneath the layers of the cerebral cortex lay key subcortical supporting structures. For example, the insular cortex (Brodmann area 13) exists within the folds of the cortex. It is cortical because it is part of the cortex, but because it is hidden below the layers of the cortex, it may also be considered subcortical. The insula is defined as a cortex or a lobe (see Figure 15.7).

Figure 15.7. Locating the Insular Cortex

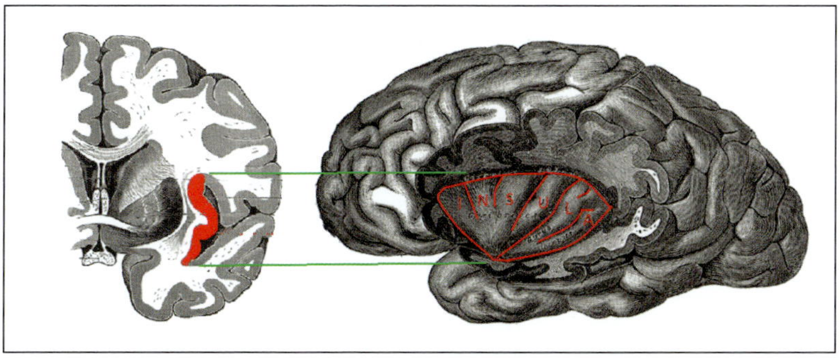

Image by Henry Vankyke Carter (1831-1897)

The functions of the insular cortex are nicely summed up by Menon and Uddin (2010):

- Control and suppression of natural urges.
- Subjective awareness of both positive and negative feelings,

including studies of anger, disgust, judgments of trustworthiness, and sexual arousal.

- High-level social cognitive processes.
- Anterior insula activation reflects emotional experience that may constitute the neural basis of empathy.
- Activated during pain perception.

Brodmann area 13 is the anterior (and larger) portion of the insula with many connections to the amygdala and is associated with depression, anxiety, and other emotional disorders. The posterior portion of the insula is more closely connected to the somatosensory cortex and is associated with pain and other bodily sensations. For a detailed review of brain lobe function, see Chart 15.1.

Chart 15.1. Brain Lobes: Functions and Symptoms

Regions	Sites	Functions	Symptoms
Parietal lobes	P3, P4, Pz	LH: Problem solving, math, complex grammar, attention, concept association, academia; RH: Spatial awareness, geometry, emotion	Learning disorders, poor spatial awareness and body image, poor abstract comprehension, anxiety, depression
Cingulate gyrus (subcortical)	Fpz, Fz, Cz, Pz	Mental flexibility, cooperation, attention, morals, and impulse control	Obsessions, worry, perfectionism, OCD, ADHD, anxiety, migraines, depression
Sensorimotor cortex	C3, C4, Cz	Calmness, fine motor skills, manual dexterity, sensory-motor integration, tactile sensitivity, and handwriting	Paralysis and stroke, seizure, poor handwriting, ADHD, anxiety (RH), depression (LH)
Frontal and prefrontal lobes	Fp1, Fp2, Fpz, Fz, F3, F4, F7, F8	Motivation (frontal poles), memory encoding, sustained attention, executive planning, attention, and judgment	Depression and anxiety, ADHD, poor executive planning, poor motivation, weak character, personality disorders, migraines, and OCD
Temporal lobes	T3, T4, T5, T6	Memory, object recognition, music, language, facial recognition, emotional stability, reading	Poor emotional control, rage, anger, learning disorders, poor memory, closed head injury, and amusia

Occipital lobes	O1, O2, Oz	Visual learning and working memory and attention, color processing, and eye contact	Learning disorders relating to visual processing such as reading and visual working memory
Broca's area	F7, F3, T3	Verbal expression	Poor verbalization, comprehension, and word recall
Wernicke's area	Parietotemporal junction	Verbal understanding	Dyslexia, poor spelling, writing, and verbal comprehension
Insular cortex	C3, F3 C4, F4		LH: depression; RH: anxiety, pain, PTSD, undue cravings
Left hemisphere	Odd-numbered sites	Logic sequencing, sequential memory, detail oriented, academic skills including learning, word retrieval, verbal fluency, reading, math, science, writing, problem solving	Depression, poor decision making, learning disorders, poor sequential processing and memory, and below-average IQ
Right hemisphere	Even-numbered sites	Episodic memory, social awareness, eye contact, music, artistic skills, humor, empathy, spatial orientation, insight, intuition, seeing the whole picture	Anxiety and phobia, weak empathy, codependent behavior, pain, and poor emotional processing, social skills, direction finding, and episodic memory, and below-average Emotional Quotient

Limbic System

- Amygdala (associated with deep emotions and fear)
- Subcallosal area (self-esteem and sadness processing)
- Hippocampus (crucial for memory storage and emotions)
- Parahippocampal gyrus (cognitive, visuospatial processing and episodic memory)
- Cingulate gyrus (influences emotion, memory, learning, mental flexibility)

The limbic system (Figure 15.8) is thought to be the seat of emotion even though the right cerebral hemisphere is also involved in processing emotions and feelings. Within the limbic system are two structures critical to memory development:

1. The hippocampus stores conscious memories; it orchestrates the process of making a memory permanent. Information that is combined with emotion may be stored faster because the hippocampus is contained within the limbic system. It is in proximity to the temporal lobes. The left temporal lobe seems to work closely with the hippocampus in the memory-making process. Victims of trauma with lifelong PTSD may have underdeveloped or smaller hippocampus structures.
2. The amygdala stores unconscious and non-verbal memories. Egregious memories stemming from early or preverbal child abuse experiences are likely stored via amygdala processes. Early childhood trauma may still govern adult behavior. Sharp negative reactions may follow a simple trigger in the environment, such as a particular smell, facial expression, hair color, or style of clothing. The reaction does not necessarily follow a clear memory of details; rather, it is an inward knowing. It is a memory that has been driven in by fear (van der Kolk, McFarlane, & Weisaeth, 1996, p. 230). The

Figure 15.8. Key Structures Within the Limbic System

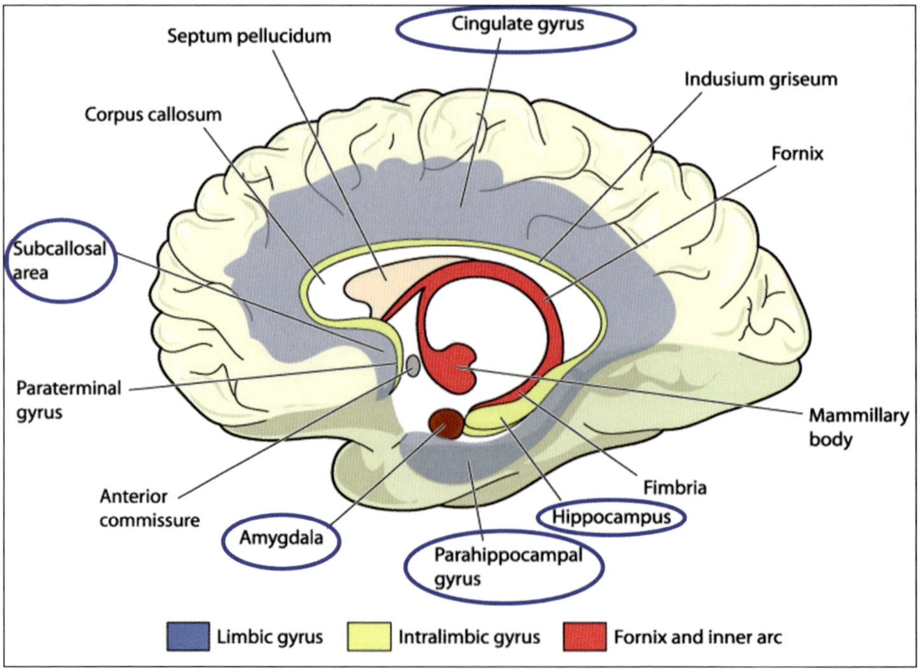

Subcortical regions that are detected by LORETA (circled)

> aggression of temporal lobe epilepsy may be partly driven by its proximity to the amygdala in the brain. There are many cerebral cortex connections to the amygdala, including the anterior ventral medial cortex, the visual cortex, and the temporal lobes. The emotion of the amygdala is not always dark; it is also involved in positive feelings and emotions. Regions circled in Figure 15.8 are critical when assessing.

Many other deeper brain structures are not detected by sLORETA. Nuclear imaging is required to track brain metabolism in these areas (Figure 15.9). It is important to understand the basic function of each of the following ROIs even though they are not targeted by sLORETA.

Figure 15.9. Median Section of the Brain

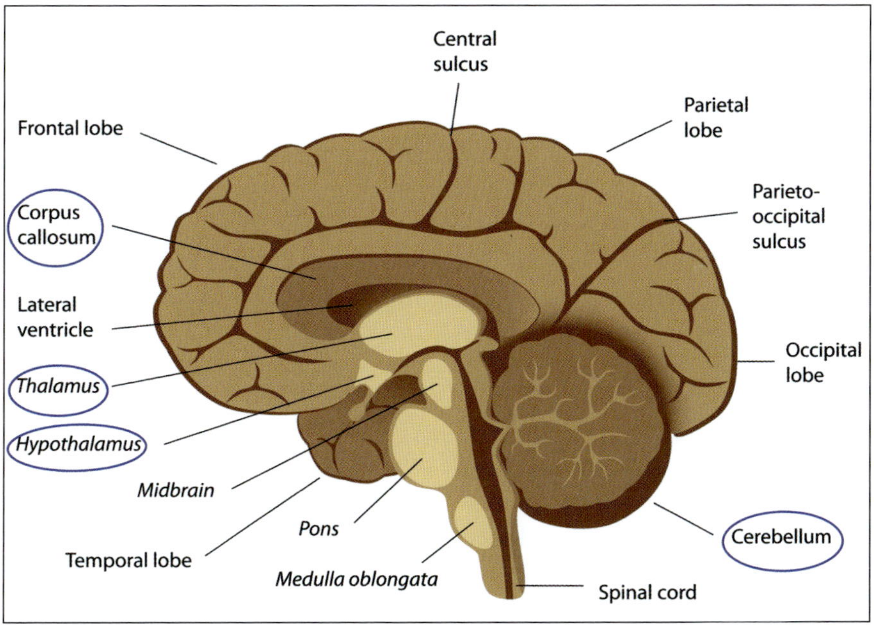

Key subcortical regions not detected by LORETA (circled)

Thalamus

The thalamus is an editor for sorting and directing sensory information and emotions. It moderates between sensory information and the cerebral cortex. Some consider it to be the Grand Central Station of the brain. Its influence over the cerebral cortex and the EEG were reported by Marieb:

> In addition to sensory inputs, virtually *all* inputs ascending to the cerebral cortex are funneled through the thalamic nuclei. . . . Thus the thalamus plays a key role in meditating sensation, motor activities, cortical arousal, and memory. It is truly the gateway to the cerebral cortex. (2015, pp. 393–395).

Thalamic nuclei also have a major role in orchestrating brain networks. Thalamic pacemakers in conjunction with the reticular formation, or brain stem, regulate the brain's 10 Hz dominant rhythm. Consequently, weak alpha (8–12 Hz) amplitudes may come from the thalamic-reticular connection. Together with the reticular formation in the brain stem, thalamic activity is the heart of EEG activity.

Hypothalamus

The hypothalamus is just below the thalamus. It is a key player in the control of the endocrine system and the ANS. It influences eating, body temperature, sleep, and emotional responses. It has the job of activating the fight-or-flight response. It arouses the sympathetic nervous system and the endocrine system, preparing the body to take action. It also is part of the chain of command that calms things down by activating the parasympathetic nervous system. The hypothalamus is part of the HPA axis, which responds to stress and secretes cortisol.

Corpus Callosum (Corpus Commissure)

The corpus callosum (CC) is the largest white matter structure in the brain. It consists of a bundle of nerve fibers that connect the right and left hemispheres and facilitates communication between the two hemispheres. In general, it is larger in females than males, which would suggest that women are more able to multitask than men. Younger children who take music lessons are likely promoting enhanced CC functioning. Imaging has indicated that those with dyslexia have a somewhat smaller CC. Learning to play a musical instrument enhances CC functioning and gives school-age children a scholastic advantage (Schlaug, Jäncke, Huang, Staiger, & Steinmetz, 1995).

Cerebellum

The word *cerebellum* literally means "little brain." It is beneath the occipital lobes and protrudes beyond them. It keeps us erect and governs posture. The lobes of the cerebellum work in conjunction with the cerebral cortex to carry out voluntary muscle movements. It processes information coming from proprioceptors (sensory receptors that respond to physical movements) throughout the body. It then becomes possible to direct and coordinate muscle movements smoothly and efficiently. For example, as a youngster I played ball in the city streets for hours every day after school. My ability to catch, throw, and do gymnastics was average to above average; I assume my cerebellum performance was enhanced by daily ball playing.

One of Margaret Ayers's last innovations was a protocol for urinary incontinence or a balance disorder due to a poorly functioning cerebellum. She selected two sites in the cerebellum region that were about half an inch below, or inferior to, O1 and O2 and about three-quarters of an inch farther apart (see Figure 15.10). Theta was inhibited and beta was rewarded simultaneously using a bipolar montage. Other clinicians in addition to Hammond and Ayers have had success with this protocol (Hammond, 2005). Note that Margaret Ayers only used bipolar montages.

Figure 15.10. Margaret Ayers's Cerebellum Protocol

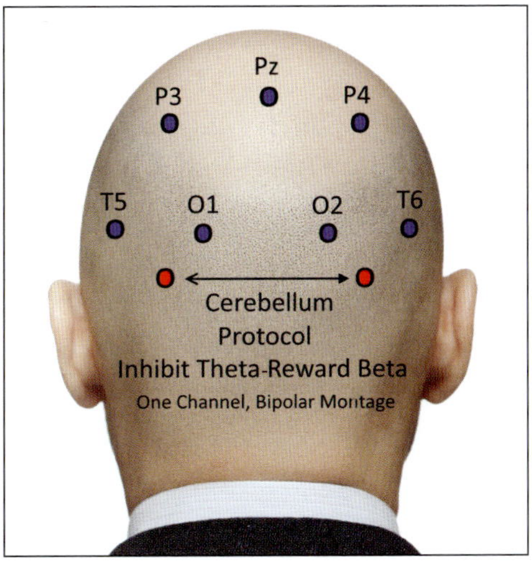

Note that difficulties with physical balance or dizziness may come from the cerebellum, a sinus infection, vertigo from an inner ear problem (Meniere's disease) or most dangerously from a blockage in the vertebral or carotid arteries that may soon result in a stroke. Older clients that present with dizziness should be made aware of the danger of stroke.

16

Regions of Interest: Cortical and Subcortical

TWO RESEARCHERS in Germany pioneered EEG graphics and functional brain dynamics. Their work stretches back to the early 20th century.

- Hans Berger (1873–1941). In the 1920s, Hans Berger discovered how to amplify the electrical activity of the brain (EEG) and project it upon a screen or shadow graph. He also recorded the raw EEG on paper; later he would identify two different filtered waves, alpha and beta. Ten Hz is known as the Berger rhythm (Budzynski, 1999, p. 65). Berger discovered that thinking and alertness accompany bursts in the beta frequency band, which ranges from 13 Hz to about 30 Hz. His landmark paper was published in 1929. He believed that abnormalities in EEG reflect clinical disorders (Criswell, 1995, p. 70; Cantor, 1999, p. 20). Many EEG neurofeedback providers design training protocols in harmony with Berger's assumptions. Training targets regions of the brain that are known to influence cognitive and behavioral performance.
- Korbinian Brodmann (1868–1918) was a German neurologist who studied the cellular structure of animal and human cerebrums. In 1909 his ground-breaking book *Comparative Localization Studies in the Brain Cortex: Its Fundamentals Represented on the Basis of Its Cellular*

> *Architecture* delineated 52 regions of the mammalian brain based on their unique "cytoarchitecture." Humans have 44 discrete areas in the LH that correspond to 44 in the RH. Each region was assigned a different number, but, more importantly, he asserted that each region had a unique function. Brodmann's research predated Berger's, but both agreed that the brain is a dynamic organism with unique functional characteristics.

Other researchers after Brodmann identified additional distinctive brain regions with unique functions; some newer regions are associated with gyri and others with sulci. All were assigned names rather than numbers. Some named regions are closely associated with Brodmann numbered regions. For example, Brodmann 39 is closely associated with the angular gyrus; 13 with the anterior insula cortex; 17 with the inferior occipital gyrus; 38 with the temporal poles, and so on. In turn, some of these areas are near Int'l 10–20 sites. For example, Brodmann areas 1, 2, 3, and 4 are represented by the pre- and postcentral gyrus and can be trained with montages at C3, C4, and Cz, according to the Int'l 10–20 System. This chapter includes an approximation conversion chart between location systems. Cortical ROIs may almost match some Int'l 10–20 System locations. Subcortical ROIs may relate somewhat to Int'l 10–20 System locations.

LORETA 3-D IMAGING (CURRENT SOURCE DENSITY)

The assumption that amplifiers detect only EEG data directly beneath the electrode can be challenged. For example, Nunez et al. (1994) wrote that only 50% of EEG amplified data are sourced directly beneath the electrode and that most of the remaining data are within a diameter of a quarter of an inch or 0.65 cm. But there's more to be considered than Nunez's research, because surface (cortical) measurements may have a deeper source. The data coming from subcortical regions create the inverse problem. It is a problem because the current source that appears beneath the electrode is not fully known.

LORETA software, was developed in 1994 by Pascual-Marqui, Michel, and Lehman, provides the inverse solution. The current source that is beneath each electrode is now traceable. LORETA measurements acquire data from a minimum of 19 of the Int'l 10–20 system locations. Data are transformed into thousands of small voxels, which are defined as small active "volumetric regions" of the brain (Hyde, Duffy, & Warfield, 2014).

Research and development have given birth to sLORETA and eLORETA: *s* for standardized and *e* for exact.

> Newer methods were developed by Pascual-Maqui in 2002 and it was named standardized LORETA or sLORETA (Pascual-Marqui, 2002). This new implementation had to its advantage the ability to localize test point sources with zero localization error in the absence of noise, which had not previously been accomplished. . . . The most recent release and development of this family of inverse solutions is Exact Low Resolution Brain Electromagnetic Tomography (eLORETA). eLORETA is not a linear imaging method but is a true inverse solution with exact and zero localization errors. (Sherlin, 2010)

Software for sLORETA produces over 6,000 voxels from amplified raw EEG data. Afterward, voxels are grouped or organized into cortical and subcortical named or numbered ROIs. Not all brain structures can be measured by sLORETA.

Theta-Band sLORETA Compared to Surface Int'l 10–20

Cortical sLORETA ROIs often correspond to the Int'l 10–20 sites. Figure 16.1 shows how similar sLORETA and surface Int'l 10–20 recordings can be at times. Cortical Brodmann areas (BAs) 22, 41, and 42 relate nicely to T5 of the Int'l 10–20 System.

However, subcortical sLORETA sites often generate the inverse problem (Figure 16.2). In the second example, notice the how subcortical parahippocampal areas influence LH temporal lobe Z-scores in the surface Int'l 10–20 head.

Parahippocampal gyrus (BA 27, 28, 34–36) theta Z-scores are likely increasing theta Z-scores at T3, T5 (surface or cortical sites). Tracing theta back to the subcortical current density source provides the inverse solution, whereas T6 likely reflects the activity in Brodmann 37.

Figure 16.1. LH Temporal Lobe to Brodmann 22, 41, and 42

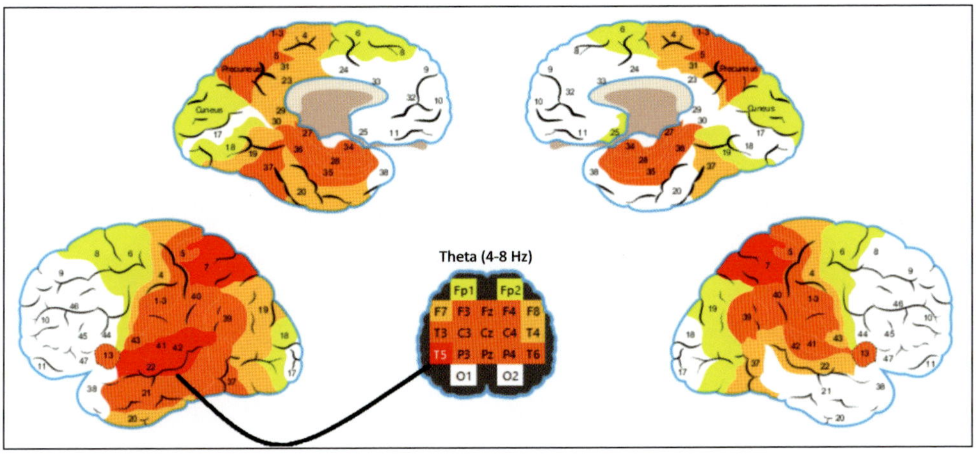

Brain maps adapted from Jewel database software

Figure 16.2. T3, T5 to Brodmann 27–28, 34–36, and T6 to Brodmann 37

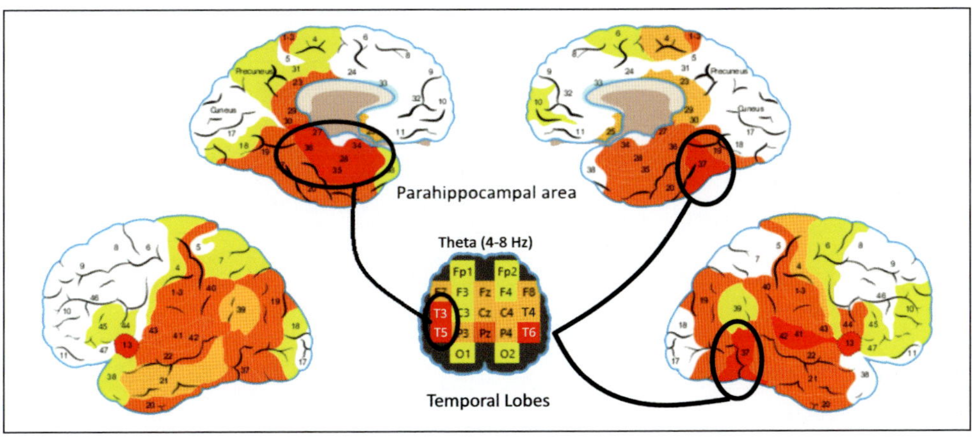

Brain maps adapted from Jewel database software

CORTICAL, SUBCORTICAL, AND SURFACE LOCATION COMPARISONS

Figure 16.3. Cortical Lobes to Brodmann ROIs

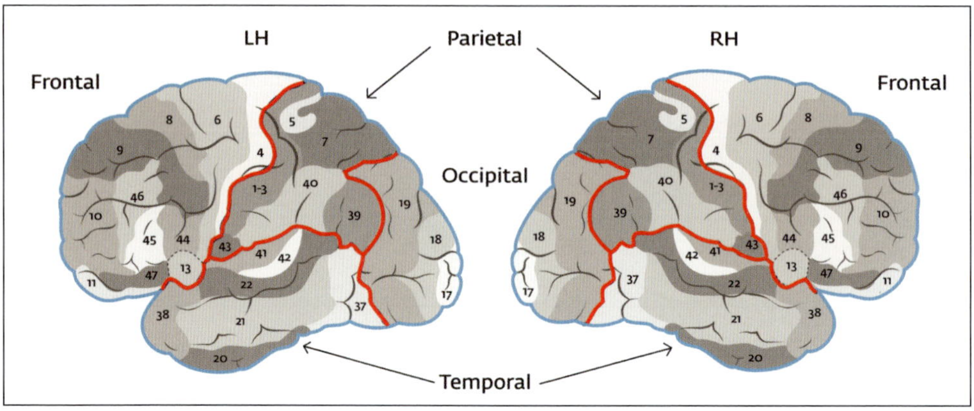

Cortical Heads adapted from Jewel database software

Chart 16.1

Lobe	Brodmann Nos.
Frontal	4, 6, 8, 9, 10, 11, 44, 45, 46, 47
Parietal	1, 2, 3, 5, 7, 39, 40, 43
Occipital	17, 18, 19
Temporal	20, 21, 22, 37, 38, 41, 42
Sensorimotor	1, 2, 3, 4
Insula	13

Figure 16.4. Subcortical Numbered to Named Regions

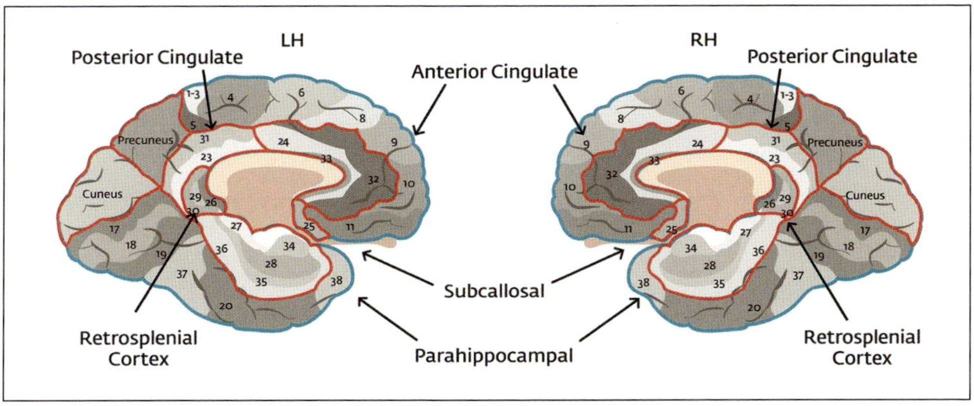

Sub-Cortical Heads adapted from Jewel database software

Chart 16.2

Region	Brodmann (BA) Nos.
Cingulate Gyrus	23, 24, 31, 32, 33
Retrosplenial Cortex	26, 29, 30
Parahippocampal	27, 28, 34, 35, 36
Subcallosal	25

Chart 16.3. Conversion (ROIs and Int'l 10–20 System)

ROI Numbers	ROI Names (abbreviations)	Location	Int'l 10–20
1, 2, 3	Postcentral G (PG)	Primary somatosensory cortex	C3, C4, Cz
4	Precentral G (PreCG)	Primary motor cortex	C3, C4, Cz
5, 7	Superior parietal lobule (SPL)	Somatosensory association	P3, P4
8	Frontal lobes	Frontal lobes/eye fields	F3, F4
9	Frontal lobes	Dorsolateral	F3, F4
10	Prefrontal lobes	Anterior prefrontal	Fp1/F7, Fp2/F8
11	Orbital G (OG)	Orbitofrontal	Fp1, Fp2

ROI Numbers	ROI Names (abbreviations)	Location	Int'l 10–20
13	Insula (INS)	Insular cortex	F3/C3, F4/C4
17	Inferior occipital G (IOG)	Primary visual (V1)	O1, O2
18	Middle occipital G (MOG)	Secondary visual (V2)	O1, O2
19	Superior occipital G (SOG)	Associative visual (V3–5)	O1, O2
20	Inferior temporal G (ITG)	Temporal lobes	T3, T4
21	Middle temporal G (MTG)	Temporal lobes	T3, T4
22	Superior temporal G (STG)	Part of Wernicke's area	T3-P3, T4-P4
23	Posterior cingulate (PCC)	Ventral posterior cingulate	Pz
24	Anterior cingulate (ACC)	Ventral anterior cingulate	Fpz/Fz
25	Subcallosal G (SubG)	Subgenual area	FpO1/FpO2
26	Retrosplenial cingulate	Ectosplenial	Pz
27	Parahippocampal G (PHG)	Piriform	
28	Parahippocampal G (PHG)	Ventral entorhinal	
29	Retrosplenial cingulate	NA	Pz
30	Retrosplenial cingulate	NA	Pz
31	Posterior cingulate (PCC)	Dorsal posterior cingulate	Pz
32	Anterior cingulate (ACC)	Dorsal anterior cingulate	Fpz/Fz
33	Anterior cingulate (ACC)	Anterior cingulate	Fpz/Fz
34	Parahippocampal G (PHG)	Dorsal entorhinal	
35	Parahippocampal G (PHG)	Perirhinal	
36	Parahippocampal G (PHG)	Ectorhinal	
37	Fusiform G (FFG)	Inferior posterior temporal lobes	T5, T6
38	Anterior temporal lobes	Temporal poles	T3/F7, T4/F8
39	Angular G (AG)	Part of Wernicke's area	T5/P3, T6/P4

ROI Numbers	ROI Names (abbreviations)	Location	Int'l 10–20
40	Supramarginal G (SMG)	Part of Wernicke's area	P3, P4
41, 42	Transverse temporal G (TTG)	Auditory cortex	T3/C3, T4/C4
43	Frontal lobes	Primary gustatory	T3, T4
44	Frontal lobes	Part of Broca's area	F7/C3, F8/C4
45	Prefrontal lobes	Part of Broca's area	F7/F3, F8/F4
46	Prefrontal lobes	Dorsolateral prefrontal	F7/F3, F8/F4
47	Prefrontal lobes	Pars orbitalis	F7, F8
	Lingual gyrus (LING)	Occipital lobes	O1, O2
38, 40	Inferior parietal lobule (IPL)	Parietal lobes	P3, P4
	Superior frontal G (SFG)	Frontal lobes	Fpz, Fz
	Rectal G (RG)	Limbic	
	Cuneus (CUN)	Occipital lobes	Oz
	Precuneus (PCUN)	Parietal lobes	Pz
	Paracentral lobule (PCL)	Includes superior sensorimotor	Cz
44, 45, 47	Inferior frontal G (IFG)	Frontal lobes	F7/F3, F8/F4
10, 45, 46	Middle frontal G (MFG)	Frontal lobes	Fpz
	Extranuclear (EN)	Limbic	
44, 45, 47	Medial frontal G (MedFG)	Frontal lobes	Fpz/Fz
	Subgyral	NA	
	Uncus	(Amygdala is beneath uncus)*	T3, T4
	Sublobar	NA	
23, 24, 26, 27, 28, 29, 30, 31, 32, 33, 34, 36	Limbic lobe* Measured by sLORETA	Anterior and posterior cingulate G, parahippocampal G, retrosplenial C, uncus, Extranuclear	T3, T4 or F7/T3, F8, T4
	Limbic lobe* Not measured by sLORETA	Hippocampus, hypothalamus, amygdala, thalamus	
8, 9, 10, 46	DLPFC	Dorsolateral prefrontal cortex	Fz, F3, F4

ROI Numbers	ROI Names (abbreviations)	Location	Int'l 10–20
10, 11, 13, 32	vmPFC	Ventral medial prefrontal cortex	Fpz, Fp1, Fp2, F7, F8
	Dorsal	Upper portion of the Int'l 10–20 System (including the vertex)	F3, F4, C3, C4, P3, P4, Fz, Cz, Pz
	Ventral	Lower perimeter of the Int'l 10–20 System	Fp1, Fp2, F7, F8, T3, T4, T5, T6, O1, O2
	Superior #	Toward the dorsal region, (upward)	↑ In an upward direction
	Inferior #	Toward the ventral region, (downward)	↓ In a downward direction

*Rajmohan & Mohandas (2007).
see Figure 4.3

Limbic Lobe-Associated Areas

Many emotional symptoms are driven by the limbic lobe; there is also a cluster of associated ROIs that work closely with the limbic system:

- Insular cortex (13)
- Temporal poles (38)
- Orbital gyrus (11)
- Subcallosal gyrus (25)
- Medial frontal cortex (44, 45, 47)
- Rectus gyrus
- Amygdala, "an almond-shaped structure deep *within the temporal lobe,* is a collection of nuclei lying beneath the Uncus" (Rajmohan & Mohandas, 2007)

RESEARCH INTO DISORDERS USING ROIS

The preceding information will be needed to understand research from peer-reviewed online journals common to the field of neurology, which often use ROI terminology and almost never use the Int'l 10–20 system. The following excerpts are from research articles from peer-reviewed online journals. The reader is provided with complete reference information.

ADHD, Combined Type (CT)

Silk et al. (2005). Fronto-parietal activation in attention-deficit hyperactivity disorder, combined type: Functional magnetic resonance imaging study. *British Journal of Psychiatry, 187*, 282–283.

The ADHD-CT group had:

> (a) decreased activation of the 'action-attentional' system (including Brodmann's areas (BA) 46, 39, 40) and the superior parietal (BA7) and middle frontal (BA10) areas and (b) increased activation of the posterior midline attentional system. These different neuroactivation patterns indicate widespread frontal, striatal and parietal dysfunction in adolescents with ADHD-CT.

Depression

Hamani et al. (2011). The subcallosal cingulate gyrus in the context of major depression. *Biological Psychiatry, 69*(4), 301–308.

> The subcallosal cingulate gyrus (SCG), including Brodmann area 25 and parts of 24 and 32, is the portion of the cingulum that lies ventral to the corpus callosum. It constitutes an important node in a network that includes cortical structures, the limbic system, thalamus, hypothalamus, and brainstem nuclei. Imaging studies have shown abnormal SCG metabolic activity in patients with depression, a pattern that is reversed by various antidepressant therapies.

Dyslexia

Shaywitz et al. (1998). Functional disruption in the organization of the brain for reading in dyslexia. *Proceedings of the National Academy of Sciences, U S A, 95*(5), 2636–2641.

> Significant reading group–task interactions were noted in four regions [posterior superior temporal gyrus (posterior STG, Wernicke's area), angular gyrus (BA 39), striate cortex (BA 17), and inferior frontal gyrus

> (IFG, Broca's area)] and marginally significant interactions were found in two additional regions [*ILES* cortex and anterior inferior frontal gyrus (BA 46/47/11)]. . . . It is important to recognize that we were looking for patterns of activation across tasks rather than differences on a single task; hence, our emphasis on task–reading group interactions.

Note that brain location abbreviations are usually defined in research articles. In the quote above, *ILES* stands for the inferior left extrastriate cortex, or, simply put, the LH inferior portion of BA 17.

Reaction to Sad Faces (Excerpt Does Not Include the Oxytocin Effect)

This fourth article contains a literature review that applies to several disorders. But learning about named and numbered ROIs promotes readability.

Labuschagne et al. (2012). Medial frontal hyperactivity to sad faces in generalized social anxiety disorder and modulation by oxytocin. *International Journal of Neuropsychopharmacology, 15*(7), 883–896.

> Functional imaging studies in mood and anxiety disorders have been mixed with regard to frontal cortical activation during processing of sad facial cues. For example, patients with generalized anxiety disorder (GAD) have been shown to have reduced PFC activation to sad (and fearful, angry and happy) facial expressions in regions of the ACC (BA 32) and medial orbitofrontal cortex (BA 10) (Palm *et al.* 2010). Similarly, patients with mania show reduced subgenual ACC (BA 25) activity to sad faces (Lennox *et al.* 2004). In contrast, enhanced activation in ventral mPFC (BA 11, 47) has been reported in autism spectrum disorders (Weng *et al.* 2011). Similarly, in major depressive disorder (MDD), studies have reported enhanced ACC activity (extending into the mPFC) (BA 24, 32) to sad words (Elliott *et al.* 2002), as well as enhanced capacity of activation in the ACC (BA 23, 24, 32) and reduced dynamic range (i.e. intensity load response) in the ACC (BA 24, 32) and mFPC (BA 8, 9) to sad faces (Fu *et al.* 2004). Overall these findings suggest that cortical regions, in particular, the mPFC and ACC are involved in processing of sad facial cues and activation is these regions may be abnormal in patients with mood and anxiety disorders.

FpO2 and Brodmann 25 (Subcallosal Gyrus)

Sebern Fisher first, for fear, and then Jonathan Walker for depression, have developed two protocols that have a scalp electrode at FpO2. It is possible that FpO2 training targets Brodmann area 25 (see Figure 16.5) and perhaps the amygdala.

Figure 16.5. FpO2 to Brodmann 25

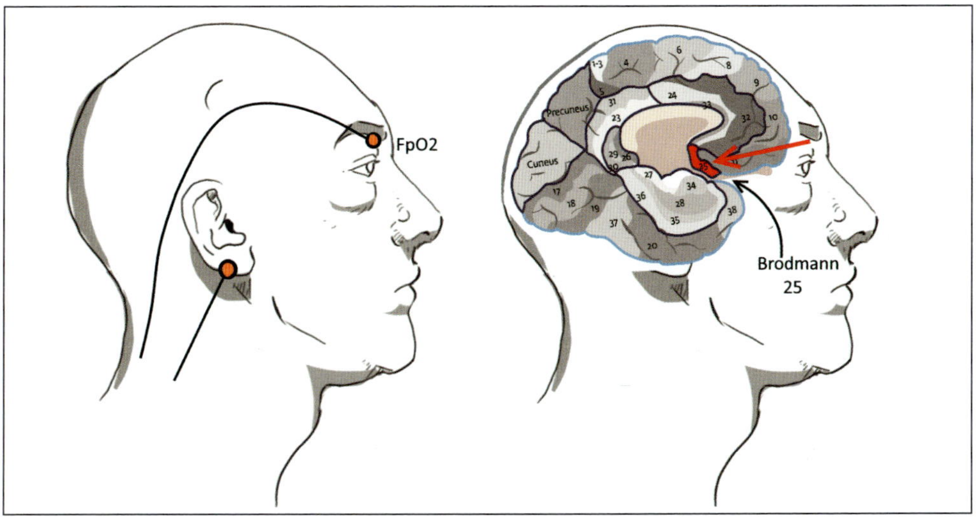

- Fisher, S. (2014). *Neurofeedback in the treatment of developmental trauma: Calming the fear-driven brain* (New York: Norton.
- Walker, J., & Lawson, R. (2013). FP02 beta training for drug-resistant depression—a new protocol that usually reduces depression and keeps it reduced. *Journal of Neurotherapy, 17,* 198–200.

> Mayberg (1997) delineated the circuitry of depression. She found that the subgenual cingulate region (Brodmann area 25; BA25) is metabolically overactive in treatment-resistant depression. . . . We chose to train at "FP02," a site used by Sebern Fisher to train patients with reactive attachment disorder and patients with chronic anxiety and fear related to physical and sexual abuse (Fisher, 2009). This site is located just medial to the right eyebrow beneath the ridge of the orbit, between the eyebrow and the bridge of the nose.

> [Fisher] found that a protocol designed *to inhibit 1–7 Hz and 21–30 Hz and to reward 5–9 Hz at FP02* ("FP02 alpha training") was found to reduce fear in these individuals, presumably via inhibitory effects on the right amygdala. . . .
>
> [*Walker*] One hundred eighty-three patients with drug resistant depression were trained with 6 sessions of neurofeedback to *reduce 2–7 Hz and increase 15–18 Hz at FP02* (the right fronto-polar orbital location). Remission or significant improvement (50%) occurred in 84% of subjects, as judged by the Rush Quick Self-Rated Depression Inventory. An additional 9% of patients experienced partial improvement. Improvement was maintained for 1 year or longer in all but 3 patients (1% of the entire group). These results indicate good efficacy in reducing drug-resistant depression and maintenance of the reductions in the majority of patients. (Walker & Lawson, 2013; brackets, italics, and underscoring added by author)

Fisher and Walker understood how subcortical areas of the brain could influence clinical symptoms. Experienced practitioners have a broad understanding of functional neurology and the power of operant conditioning.

If the above excerpts from peer-reviewed articles are starting to make sense, then Part IV has achieved its goal. The next step is to review research on brain networks that are easily trained and observed by LORETA 3-D imaging software.

17

Brain Networks

A BRAIN NETWORK is an organized group of connections between discrete ROIs (or voxel locations) designed to perform a task on its own or in concert with other networks. The network concept detracts from the notion of location, location, location. However, even power training with a single well-placed scalp-mounted electrode may well be targeting the weakest link of a given network. A chain is only as strong as its weakest link; therefore, repairing the weak link has value. The chain illustration implies linear thinking; brain networks, however, are multidirectional dynamic connections.

- Brain imaging techniques (functional magnetic resonance imaging [fMRI], EEG, etc.) are able to detect brain region synchronization during specific tasks. The synchronization must be goal directed. A single person can be on the dance floor and be in sync with the music but no network is implied, whereas when partners do the tango or the waltz they have created a mini network; they have a joint purpose. Interestingly, when the music stops, the couple are no longer under task. They are at rest, yet they continue as a network if they get to know each other better (Riedl et al., 2016; Bressler & Menon, 2010).

As the aforementioned example shows, when the couple stops dancing they are at rest, but the relationship continues. In brain network language, when the brain is in a resting state, a discrete network takes over; its purpose is to promote sense of self or an inner relationship. That brain network is the default mode network (DMN). Note that "intranetwork" means within a network, whereas "internetwork" refers to connections between other networks.

Communication within a network includes several brain regions with high and low degrees of intraconnectivity. Connector hubs bridge networks, creating interconnectivity between them. The links between each node are called edges; thicker edge lines reflect stronger connections. High-degree nodes with many branches are called hubs (see Figure 17.1).

What kind of links are there between nodes?

> Depictions of "edges" in a brain network, are defined by three types of connectivity: structural, functional, and effective. **Structural** connectivity refers to anatomical connections and (macroscopically) is usually estimated by fiber tractography from diffusion tensor MRI (DTI). . . . **Functional** and **effective** connectivity are generally inferred from the activity of remote nodes as measured by using BOLD-fMRI or EEG/MEG signals . . . defined by the correlation or coherence between nodes. (Park & Friston, 2013)

Figure 17.1. Brain Network Terminology

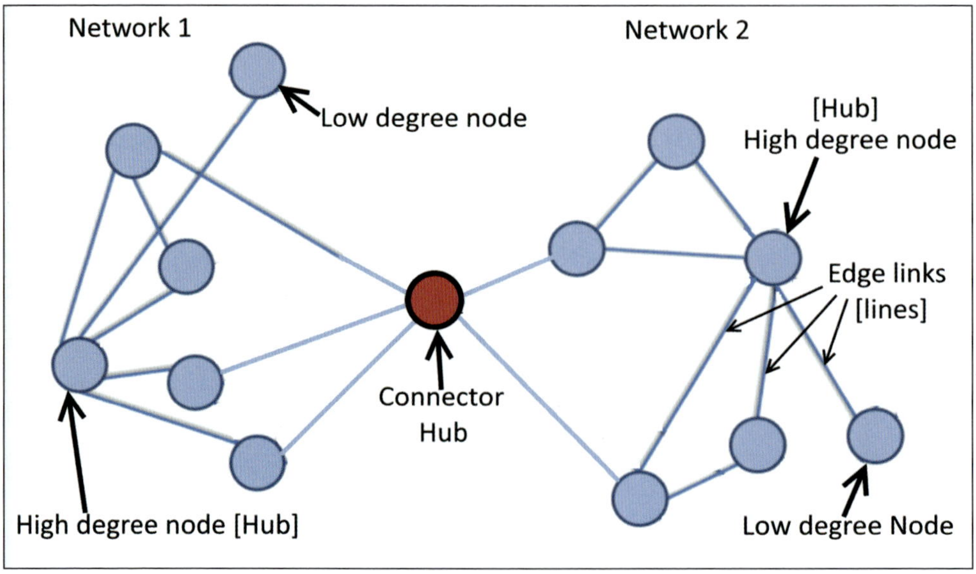

The structure is the hardwired pathway, but the communication between nodes is defined as coherence. While shared coherence between nodes can be calculated, effective coherence is directional rather than shared. Therefore, DTI imaging can differentiate between the sending and receiving nodes. What, though, is meant by a structural connection acquired by DTI?

> **Diffusion tensor imaging** (DTI) is an extension of diffusion weighted imaging (DWI) that allows data profiling based upon white matter tract orientation.
>
> DWI is based on the measurement of Brownian motion of water molecules. This motion is restricted by membranous boundaries. In white matter, diffusion follows the "pathway of least resistance" along the white matter tract; this direction of maximum diffusivity along the white-matter fibers is projected into the final image. (Smith & Bashir)

Diffusion tensor imaging follows the course of white matter tracts or white matter fibers by imaging the motion of water molecules within local tissue microstructures with weighted magnetic resonance imaging (MRI). Much more can be said about DTI, its potentials and limitations; it has broadened our understanding of brain networks that can be trained with EEG neurofeedback software. The discussion on specific networks will begin with the triple network.

TRIPLE NETWORK

- Default mode network (DMN)
- Salience network (SN)
- Central executive network (CEN)

The triple network is fundamental to most cognitive, emotional, and psychological brain function. The SN determines in what state the brain should abide. If there are external stimuli to manage, then the SN switches to the CEN; however, if there are internal issues to dwell on, the SN switches to the DMN. The CEN functions in the cognitive realm, aiding in executive planning, attention, and working memory. Of course, this masterful design works best when all three networks are functioning properly. The importance of each individual network and the interaction between them were explored by Wu:

> The triple network model consists of the central executive network (CEN), SN and DMN. These three networks are generally referred to as the core neurocognitive networks due to their involvement in an extremely wide range of cognitive tasks. . . . The triple network model suggests that the aberrant internal organization within each functional network and the interconnectivity among them are characteristic of many psychiatric and neurological disorders. Recently the triple network model has been widely applied to elucidate the dysfunction across multiple disorders, including schizophrenia, depression and dementia. (Wu, 2016)

The triple network (Chart 17.1) may be implicated in most symptoms. The SN has been implicated in ADHD and other cognitive deficits. Understanding the operation of each member of the triple network will help to explain why these three are so important.

Chart 17.1: The Triple Network

	ROI'S	FUNCTION	DISORDERS/ process
DEFAULT (DMN)	AG, ACC, IPL, MFG, MTG, PH, PCC, RG, PRECUN, SbG (25), SFG, STG, TTG	SENSE OF SELF, Reflections, dreams, goals, "internal" communication	Borderline PD, all PD's, Bipolar, ASD, schizophrenia, Codependency, Type A Personality, Alzheimer's, Etc.
SALIENCE (SN)	ACC, INS Brodmann: 6, 13, 24, 32, 33, 44, 45, 47	"External" communication, social behavior, and self-awareness Integration of sensory, emotional, & cognitive info	ADHD, "attention"
CENTRAL EXE (CEN)	IPL, SPL, SM, MFG Brodmann: 7, 8, 9, 46	High level cognitive functions such as planning, decision making, and the control of attention and working mem	Associated with Hi-IQ in adolescents. Help to suppress the DMN and allow for better exec-functions. Hence "control"

Balancing the Sense of Self While Meeting the Demands of the External World

The DMN is also associated with the theory of mind and considered to be one of the resting-state networks. The DMN activates when the brain stops task-oriented activities such as math, writing, driving, watching media, conversation, or any emotional, cognitive, social, extroverted actions. When at rest, specific regions of the DMN unite to moderate one's sense of self, including personal dreams, aspirations, and goals for the future, reflections of the past and one's place in society. The engaged DMN provides a glimpse of one's personal future. If that dream is strong enough, other networks of the brain align themselves in an attempt to make that dream come true. (Buckner, Andrews-Hanna, & Schacter, 2008; Spreng & Grady, 2010; Heine, 2012).

Disorders of the self are manifold, including all personality disorders (e.g., borderline personality disorder). Bipolar disorder, type A personality, autistic spectrum disorders, and psychosis are also disorders of the self. Furthermore, some cases of depression and anxiety relate to shattered personal dreams or lost visions; childhood sexual abuse is an attack on the DMN, a blow to the developing sense of self; PTSD and trauma compromise the normal functioning of the DMN.

The DMN plays a key role in EEG neurofeedback interventions designed to improve mental performance and alleviate distress. Additionally, the clinical issue may be with another triple network member. For example, what of the child or adult with ADHD who struggles with sustained focus or concentration because his or her mind wanders so easily? Is the problem with the DMN or is it the SN that fails to detect the need for external orientation or the CEN that aids in suppressing the DMN to complete a task? Maintaining the balance between the DMN (internal dreams) and the CEN (execution of those dreams) is the function of the SN (Figures 17.2 and 17.3).

Figure 17.2. The Salience Network Switches From Internal to External Focus

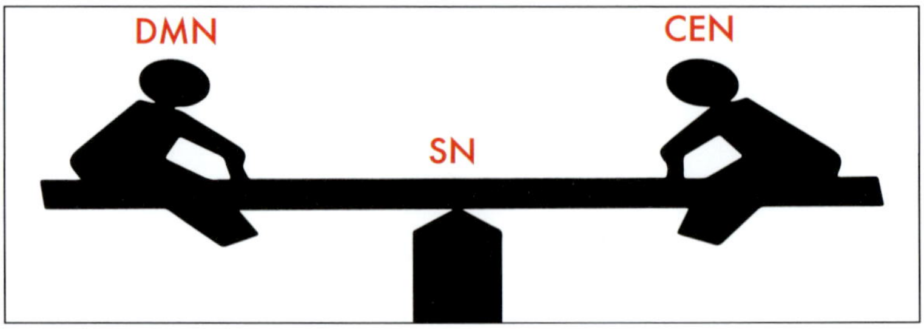

Figure 17.3. The Triple Network

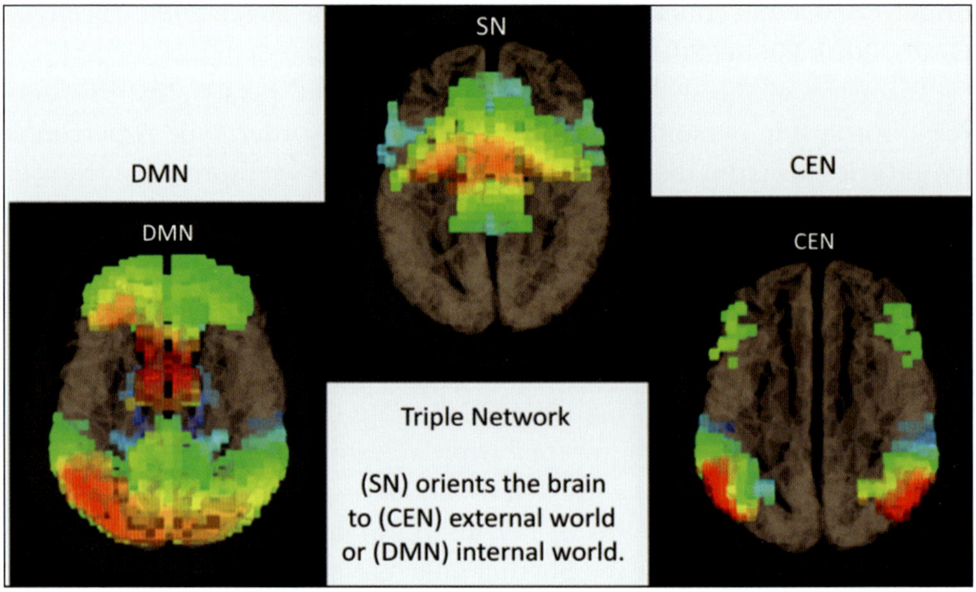

3D heads were created with BrainAvatar software by BrainMaster Technologies, Inc.
Figure 17.3 is displayed on the cover.

ATTENTION NETWORKS

The last two networks to be considered regulate attention:

1. Dorsal attention network (DAN)
2. Ventral attention network (VAN)

The dorsal and ventral attention networks (DAN and VAN) communicate with each other and other brain regions including those for vision, hearing, and sensation. The term "supramodal" has been applied to joint DAN and VAN functions because they allow for efficient attention to ever-changing external data coming from several sources. The concept is straightforward: the DAN activates during planned tasks while the VAN activates when unplanned changes occur in the environment that must be recognized. Efficient yet flexible control of moment-by-moment shifts of attention are critical to every task and learning challenge (Vossel et al., 2014).

- The DAN consists of the frontal eye fields and the temporoparietal junction: BA 6, 8, IPL, STG
- The VAN consists of the ventral frontal cortex and the intraparietal sulcus: BA 7, 40, 10, 11, 13, 32; BA 13 is larger than shown in Figure 17.4; it is hidden beneath the frontal lobes.

Figure 17.4. Dorsal and Ventral Attention Networks Connecting to Visual Cortex

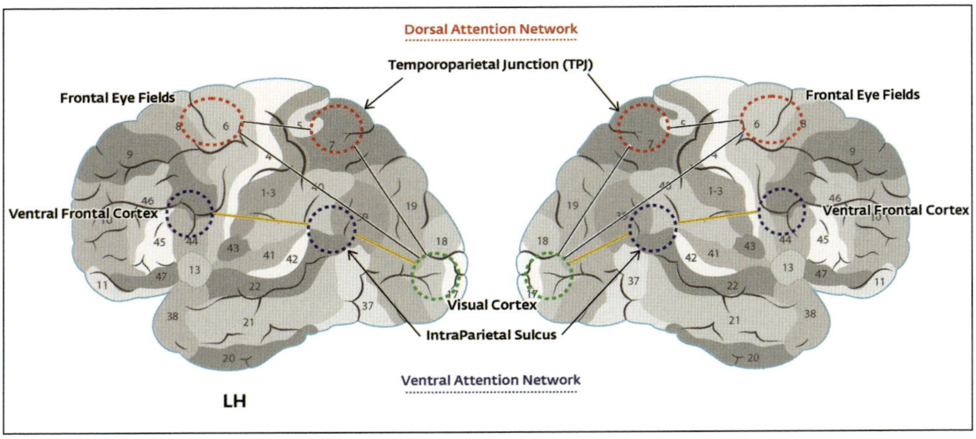

Drawing adapted from the Jewel database and report writing software

While Figure 17.4 emphasizes DAN and VAN communication to the visual cortex, similar lines of communication could be drawn between other ROIs that govern sentient, visual, and auditory awareness. DAN and VAN are heavily connected to multiple brain regions.

This part has been an introduction to brain structure and function. It provides a foundation for some of the intervention strategies in Part V.

Part V
Advanced Training and Protocol Generation

Chapters

18

Thresholds: Advanced Theory of Protocol Operation

THRESHOLDS ARE DESIGNED according to the principles of operant conditioning; they detect when the natural movements of the EEG have satisfied treatment goals. At the moment threshold requirements are met, feedback is triggered in the form of tones or graphics (tactile feedback is also possible). Since the EEG is rhythmic, feedback follows that rhythmicity, which is why the brain acknowledges and responds to threshold characteristics. Needless to say, there are many different threshold designs. Parts I and II laid the groundwork for threshold basics; please review if necessary before considering the information in this chapter.

FIXED THRESHOLDS FOR AMPLITUDE (POWER) TRAINING

Single-channel manual thresholds provide reward or inhibit reinforcement. Thresholds have microvolt values. They are set to ensure a steady flow of feedback. Reward thresholds are set just below the average amplitude of the wave. Inhibit thresholds are set just above the average amplitude of the wave. The trainee should always feel positive and never punished. Feedback tones or graphics should be flowing and not stilted. The training goal set by the threshold should be neither too difficult nor too easy.

AUTOMATIC THRESHOLDS FOR AMPLITUDE (POWER) TRAINING

Automatic thresholds facilitate:

- The use of multiple thresholds
- The use of multiple channels

Auto-thresholds are set in the following manner:

1. Determine the number of channels and thresholds per channel.
2. Adjust the percentages in the auto-threshold setting page.

In Figure 18.1, the Autoset Go's and Stops are 60%, 20%, and 10%. Those are the default settings; it may not be necessary to change them. It is a single-channel (C4) three-threshold design called SMR training because the electrode is on the sensorimotor strip at C4: theta and hi-beta are the Stops (inhibits) and lo-beta (SMR) is the Go's (reward).

Threshold values for all three conditions in Figure 18.1 adjust every 60 seconds, based on trainee performance. Only when all three conditions are met will the reinforcement tone or beep be triggered.

Figure 18.1. Protocol Creation by Bandwidths and Auto-thresholds

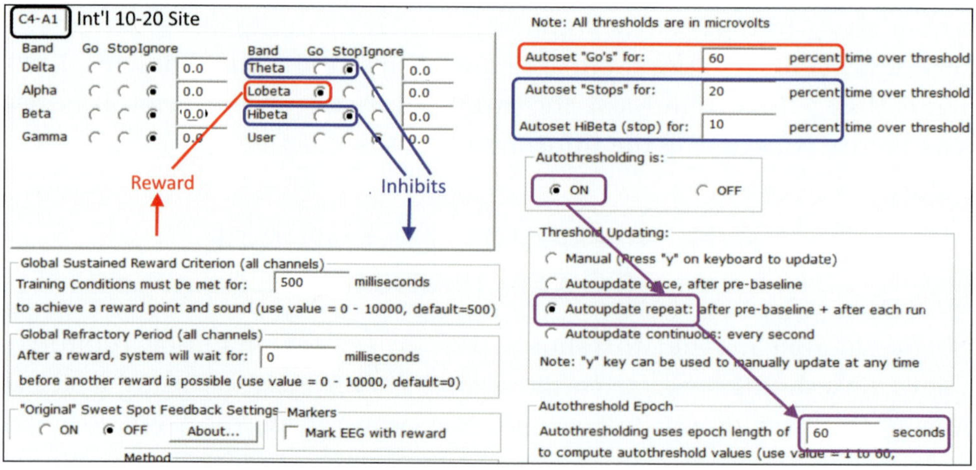

Adapted from BrainAvatar software by BrainMaster Technologies, Inc.

Autoset Percentage Adjustments

"Percent" means percentage time over threshold. The optimum percentage for each reward and inhibit is adjusted according to the total number of threshold conditions.

Percentage Suggestions

Threshold requirements depend on the number of conditions. The greater the number of threshold conditions the easier the threshold requirements. For example, if training was limited to just one reward or one inhibit then a 50% threshold challenge would likely work well. But what if there were 2, 3, or even 6 threshold conditions? Then the percentages would have to be modified, otherwise there would be no feedback because the increase of the number of threshold challenges would be too demanding. The following are typical guidelines when using multiple threshold challenges, or conditions.

One channel, one reward, and two inhibits (3 conditions):

- The reward, or "Go" percent for LoBeta (SMR) is 60%
- The inhibit, or "Stop" percent for Theta is 20%
- The inhibit, or "Stop" percent for HiBeta is 10%

Two channels, one reward, and two inhibits per channel (6 conditions):

- 75% "Go"
- 15% "Stop"
- 5% HiBeta "Stop"

How Autoset Thresholds Maintain Percentage Requirements

It is not necessary to change percentages when they are reasonable. Autothresholds maintain the percentages by moving the threshold bar up or down. If the reward is too hard, the threshold bar moves down. If the reward is too easy, the threshold bar moves up. Remember, the threshold bar is set by microvolts and is adjusted every minute to maintain the preset percentages. To illustrate:

- If hurdles are too high, the trainer will lower them so most of the runners will feel successful. Hurdles are like rewards or Go's.

- If the limbo bar is too low, the music director will raise the bar so that most of the dancers feel successful. Limbo bars are like inhibits or Stops.

The expressions "most of the runners" and "most of the dancers" refer to percentage success. The trainer and the director want most of the participants to be successful. So, they adjust the bar to make it so. The goal is to create a challenge that is not too easy or too hard.

Pitch-Variable Sounds and Thresholds

Pitch-variable sounds can also operate with or without a threshold. They are set to follow the trained EEG component. For example, if alpha amplitude increases, then the pitch increases; if alpha frequency increases, then the pitch increases; of course, if the trained component decreases, then the pitch decreases.

Frequency training is designed to increase the PDR. If a trainee has age-related cognitive decline, then the peak frequency may be 9.0 Hz or lower. Peak frequency training may promote faster processing. Note that sometimes peak frequency training results in the trainee feeling wired or on edge rather than more alert.

Ratio Thresholds

Single-channel ratio training compares the relationship between two different bandwidths. The most common form is theta/beta ratio training; elevated theta-to-beta ratios are common in children with ADHD (Rossiter, 2002). Feedback is triggered as the ratio decreases. Ratio training protocols often utilize pitch-variable sounds.

Sum Squash Threshold

There are times when more than one location has elevated amplitudes or power SDs. Inhibiting two channels simultaneously can be very effective. The protocol is very simple: if the amplitude of theta in two channels decreases at the same time, then feedback is triggered (Figure 18.2).

Figure 18.2. Two-Channel Sum Squash

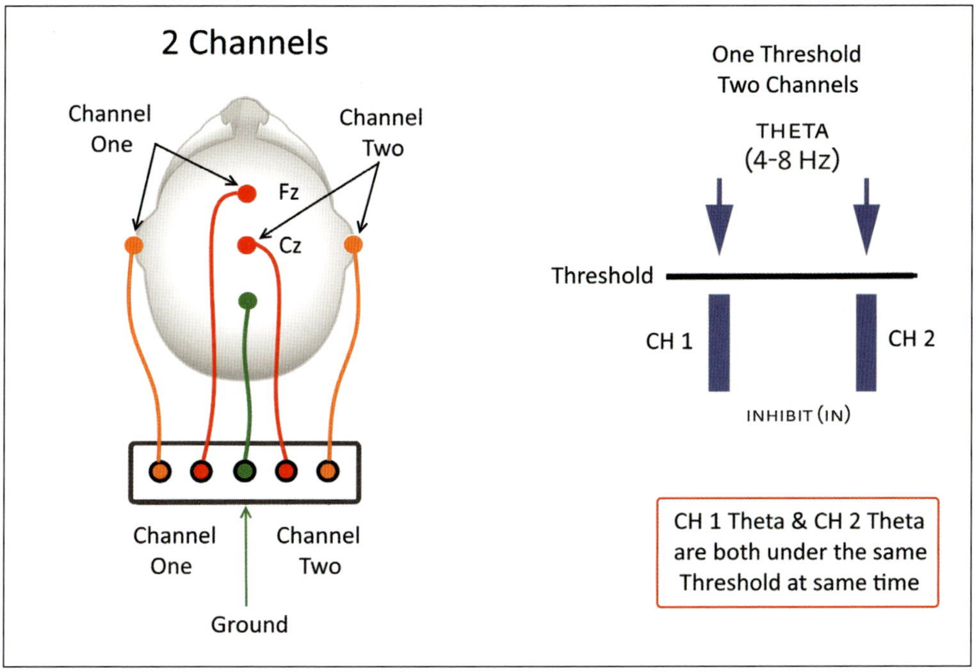

This method allows more coverage on the scalp and is a very powerful way to reduce amplitude. There are a number of sum squash variations with either monopolar or bipolar montages.

Alpha Synchrony Threshold

The alpha synchrony method is the exact opposite of a sum squash because feedback is triggered when the amplitude of alpha in channels 1 and 2 increases at the same time. Often O1 and O2 are the chosen locations because alpha amplitudes peak in the occipital lobes. Synchrony is promoted because the amplitudes rise and fall in sync. Technically, synchrony training is based on phase training. Fehmi and Robbins described the advantage of multiple-channel alpha phase-synchrony training: "Phase synchrony means not only that many parts of the brain are producing Alpha but that these waves are also rising and falling in unison. This means that a large number of cells are working together" (2007, p. 35).

Alpha Variability Threshold

The term "variability" refers to amount of fluctuation of a given bandwidth over a period of time. Variability is a measurement of the standard deviation of the wave to itself and not in comparison to other subjects in a normative database. The following example shows how to calculate alpha variability.

One minute of alpha may average 15 μVs, but during that same minute it may rise to 40 μVs and fall to 5 μVs. The amount of variation (peaks and valleys) can be calculated in SDs. If the average is 15 μVs, then one SD would normally be *approximately half of the mean* or 7.5 μVs. Therefore, if one SD is greater than 8.5 or 9 μVs, the variability is too high. If it is less than 8.5 μVs, the variability is not clinically interesting.

High alpha variability is an EEG marker or signature for migraine. Variability is reduced with a dynamic threshold. When the incoming alpha variability is less than the damped (historic) alpha variability, feedback is triggered. Training with a bipolar montage at C3-C4 is common. Alpha variability training reduces variability and amplitude. Therefore do not use this approach if alpha amplitudes are weak or have low SDs. There are other protocol options to treat migraine (see the end of Chapter 23).

Alpha/Theta Threshold

Alpha/theta training is unique because it employs two reward thresholds, alpha and theta, plus two inhibit thresholds, beta and delta. It is discussed in Chapter 21.

Dynamic Thresholds

Auto-thresholds average amplitudes every minute or so. Dynamic thresholds average amplitudes for shorter periods of time, for example, 10 or 15 seconds. The average is called a damped average. The incoming data are either above the damped average or below it. For example, if the goal is to increase alpha, feedback is triggered when the incoming data are above the damped average; if the goal is to decrease alpha, feedback is triggered when the incoming data are below the damped average. Therefore, whether the goal is to inhibit or to reward the trainee gets feedback about 50% of the time.

This principle works with any EEG component as well as Z-scores. A dynamic threshold is a simple comparison of the present with the immediate past: new incoming data are compared with old data.

Simple Z-Score Thresholds

Chart 18.1 highlights live Z-scores for alpha (2.5) and the alpha-to-beta ratio (2.0). Z-score training thresholds are designed to target problem areas; they are more like windows with upper and lower bounds than reward or inhibit thresholds. Z-score thresholds can also be compared to a corral that allows a horse space to move but not to run away. So the operative word is *boundary*: Z-score training boundaries have upper and lower limits. Feedback is triggered when incoming data are between boundaries.

Chart 18.1: Z-Scores (Power) For One Int'l 10-20 Location

Component	Delta Power	Theta Power	Alpha Power	Beta Power	Theta-to-Beta Ratio	Alpha-to-Beta Ratio
Ave Z-score	.75	.95	2.5	.5	.8	2.0

For example, the upper limit can be set to plus one Z-score and the lower limit can be set to minus one Z-score. Therefore, when the incoming data measure between plus or minus one (Z-scores), feedback is triggered.

As illustrated in Chart 18.1, when alpha and the alpha-to-beta ratio fall between plus or minus one Z-score then feedback occurs. The rest of the Z-scores are not trained (theoretically).

Percentage of Success

If there were only a single channel with just a few components, then upper and lower limits would be sufficient. But Z-score training can include up to 19 channels of surface data and 82 ROIs of sLORETA data. Picture the rising and falling of hundreds, perhaps thousands, of Z-score metrics. A simple fixed boundary with upper and lower limits would be too rigid. How could all of those components be within an upper and lower boundary at the same exact moment in time?

When training with a fixed boundary the percentage of success is important. It reveals the difficulty of the training. The clinician wants to know how often the EEG components are corralled, or within set limits.

Simple live Z-score training can be explained this way: When a desirable percentage of all EEG components falls within plus or minus one (Z-scores), feedback occurs. Of course, if plus or minus one is too hard, the clinician needs to widen the boundary to plus or minus two or three in order to keep a desirable percentage of EEG components in the corral and to generate adequate feedback tones.

Consequently, simple Z-score training requires threshold boundary adjustments to ensure a desirable percentage of success.

Simple Z-score training has two factors:

1. Movable boundaries
2. Percentage of success

Dynamic Z-Score Training Thresholds

Dynamic Z-score training has three factors:

1. Movable boundaries
2. Percentage of success
3. Dynamic thresholds that yield feedback about 50% of the time

Dynamic live Z-score training can make use of pitch-variable sounds, monotone sounds, and bonus sounds during prolonged success (see footnote in Chapter 6, page 50). Once a boundary has been set, further adjustments may not be needed.

Watch for artifacts! Never train an artifact!

All too often, training sessions are sabotaged because of:

- sEMG (muscle tension, especially at ventral sites)
- EOA (excessive eye blinks or movement)
- Noise (poor electrical contact)
- Defective electrodes

When artifacts flood the recording, only artifacts are trained—with no benefit. To prevent this problem:

1. Observe the raw EEG at each training site.
2. Observe live Z-scores.
3. Attempt to make trainees aware of the problem. Are legs tightly

crossed? Is clothing tight and restrictive? Have trainees seen how the raw EEG looks when they clench their jaws or blink? Is the problem coming from dry eyes due to contact lenses?

4. Increase training comfort. Is the chair suitable, with adequate neck support? Does it limit movement for younger children—is it time to purchase a footstool for short legs?
5. Try training with eyes closed.
6. Move electrodes away from artifact-ridden locations.
7. Remove components from training list if they are artifact ridden.
8. If steps 1–7 fail, then Z-score training may be contraindicated, and other training modalities with monopolar or bipolar montages may provide a real training experience.

19

Z-Score Training Concepts and Concerns

NEW CLINICIANS ENTERING the field appreciate the simplicity of Z-score training. It can be quickly learned and applied to many clinical disorders. Several training concepts or approaches have emerged.

1. *Train to the brain map.* Training sites are selected based on high or low SDs. It is assumed that the trainee's distress will diminish as Z-scores move toward the mean of the database. Anywhere from two to eight channels are trained.
2. *Balance the brain.* Strategic training sites are selected. For example, each brain quadrant is represented by F3, F4, P3, and P4 (sometimes called the box); balancing those four locations with Z-scores promotes cognitive regulation and mood stability. Each of those four locations falls within essential ROIs.

Figure 19.1 shows the box (F3, F4, P3, and P4). Power Z-scores include *Abs* (absolute power), *Rel* (relative power), and *Rat/* (power ratio). Connectivity Z-scores include *ASY* (asymmetry), *COH* (coherence), and *PHA* (phase). In this example, there are elevated absolute (Abs) power Z-scores at F3 theta, P3 delta and alpha 2, F4 theta, and P4 delta and gamma.

Another balancing area is C3, C4, T3, and T4; balancing those four locations promotes emotional regulation. C3 and C4 are near the insular

Figure 19.1. The Box: F3, F4, P3, and P4 Z-Score Training

SITES: F3 P3 (EO)	Abs	Rel	Rat/T	Rat/A	Rat/B	Rat/G
F3						
Delta (1.0-3.0)	-0.7	-1.0	0.0	0.0	0.0	0.0
Theta (4.0-8.0)	1.7	3.2		0.0	0.0	0.0
Alpha (8.0-12.0)	0.8	1.5			0.0	0.0
Lobeta (12.0-15.0)	-0.6	-0.4				0.0
Beta (15.0-20.0)	-0.3	-0.4				
Hibeta (20.0-30.0)	0.3	0.7				
Gamma (38.0-42.0)	-0.2	-2.0				
Alpha1 (8.0-10.0)	0.9	1.5				
Alpha2 (10.0-12.0)	-0.0	0.3				
P3						
Delta (1.0-3.0)	2.2	0.8	-0.0	0.0	0.0	0.0
Theta (4.0-8.0)	1.1	1.0		-0.0	0.0	0.0
Alpha (8.0-12.0)	1.4	1.8			0.0	0.0
Lobeta (12.0-15.0)	1.1	0.5				0.0
Beta (15.0-20.0)	-0.1	-1.2				
Hibeta (20.0-30.0)	0.2	-0.5				
Gamma (38.0-42.0)	-0.3	-2.8				
Alpha1 (8.0-10.0)	0.7	0.5				
Alpha2 (10.0-12.0)	2.0	2.9				

SITES: F4 P4 (EO)	Abs	Rel	Rat/T	Rat/A	Rat/B	Rat/G
F4						
Delta (1.0-3.0)	-1.3	-2.2	0.0	0.0	0.0	0.0
Theta (4.0-8.0)	1.9	3.6		0.0	0.0	0.0
Alpha (8.0-12.0)	0.1	0.6			0.0	0.0
Lobeta (12.0-15.0)	-1.1	-1.3				0.0
Beta (15.0-20.0)	-0.5	-0.7				
Hibeta (20.0-30.0)	0.5	0.7				
Gamma (38.0-42.0)	0.2	-1.6				
Alpha1 (8.0-10.0)	-0.2	-0.2				
Alpha2 (10.0-12.0)	-0.2	0.1				
P4						
Delta (1.0-3.0)	1.8	0.9	0.0	0.0	0.0	0.0
Theta (4.0-8.0)	1.3	1.7		-0.0	0.0	0.0
Alpha (8.0-12.0)	0.8	0.9			0.0	0.0
Lobeta (12.0-15.0)	0.3	-0.3				0.0
Beta (15.0-20.0)	0.2	-0.3				
Hibeta (20.0-30.0)	1.1	0.6				
Gamma (38.0-42.0)	1.7	-1.1				
Alpha1 (8.0-10.0)	-0.3	-0.8				
Alpha2 (10.0-12.0)	1.5	2.0				

	F3-P3:			F3-F4:			F3-P4:			P3-F4:			P3-P4:			F4-P4:		
	ASY	COH	PHA	ASY	COH	PHA	ASY	COH	PHA	ASY	COH	PHA	ASY	COH	PHA	ASY	COH	PHA
D (1.0-3.0)	-2:9	3.0	-0.9	0.8	-0.3	0.6	-2.5	2.6	-0.8	3.4	2.5	-1.4	0.9	2.1	-0.4	-3.1	1.1	-0.3
T (4.0-8.0)	0.1	2.3	-1.8	-1.0	-0.8	0.4	-0.3	1.6	-1.2	-0.4	3.3	-2.5	-1.1	-0.6	-0.1	0.1	2.0	-1.4
A (8.0-12.0)	-1.2	1.8	-1.5	4.1	1.8	-0.5	-0.2	1.8	-1.3	1.4	2.0	-2.5	2.4	2.5	-0.8	-0.9	1.2	-0.9
L (12.0-15.0)	-2.7	0.9	-0.5	1.4	0.2	0.4	-0.9	1.6	-1.3	2.7	1.3	-0.0	3.2	1.2	-0.5	-1.5	0.8	0.7
B (15.0-20.0)	-0.1	2.0	-1.2	0.7	2.3	-1.0	-0.3	1.7	-1.8	0.4	2.4	-2.7	-0.8	2.4	-1.3	-0.6	1.7	-1.5
H (20.0-30.0)	0.1	2.4	-2.3	-0.3	2.3	-1.5	-0.7	2.4	-3.2	-0.4	1.5	-1.9	-2.2	0.4	-0.6	-0.4	1.7	-2.0
G (38.0-42.0)	-0.1	0.9	-1.$	-0.7	2.0	-1.$	-1.8	1.8	-1.$	-0.5	1.2	-1.$	-3.6	-0.9	-1.$	-1.2	2.5	-1.$
A1 (8.0-10.0)	0.1	2.7	-2.0	>6.0	1.8	1.2	1.8	3.2	-1.7	1.2	3.5	-2.3	3.9	0.5	0.8	0.3	2.6	-0.8
A2 (10.0-12.0)	-2.7	2.9	-2.0	0.7	2.5	-0.8	-2.2	3.3	-3.0	1.9	2.6	-2.8	2.0	4.1	-1.6	-2.0	2.6	-2.3

Figure 19.1 adapted from BrainAvatar software by BrainMaster Technologies, Inc.
Z-Scores derived from qEEG-Pro database

cortex and sensorimotor strip. The amygdala is embedded within the temporal lobes.

On the one hand, if the client presents with cognitive issues, anxiety, or depression, then train with the box: F3, F4, P3, and P4. On the other hand, if the client presents with emotional instability or sensory imbalance, then train at C3, C4, T3, and T4 (four-channel training models).

3. *Site selection based on symptom-to-location matching.* Several symptom-to-location combinations are reviewed here:

- T5 and P3 are near the angular gyrus and Wernicke's area, both of which are critical to writing, grammar, and advanced math.
- T3 and T4 are near the hippocampus, which assists in memory processing.
- C3 and C4 are in the sensorimotor strip, which regulates sensory integration and sleep regulation (SMR relates to sleep spindles). Fine motor skills are regulated at C3 and C4.
- C3 and C4 are also in proximity to the insula, which helps to regulate mood, pain, and social well-being (anxiety, RH; depression, LH).

- Fz, Cz, and Pz are above the anterior and posterior cingulate gyrus, which regulates flexibility that is often lacking in cases of impulsivity, obsession, worry, attention, and anxiety.
- Pz is above the precuneus, the posterior hub of the DMN, which is often trained for cases of anxiety, PTSD, and personality disorders.
- Fp1 and F7 in the left prefrontal cortex are needed for sequential processing and attention.
- Fp2 and F8 in the right prefrontal cortex are needed for sustained attention and attachment.
- Fp1, Fp2, F7, and F8 are near the orbital gyrus, which assists in error detection, often exaggerated in OCD.

The site-to-symptom match list is lengthy. Training with four channels makes sense when the presenting symptom is reflected by four or less locations. If the presenting symptom(s) is reflected by more than four locations then additional 4-channel training montages may need to be included during a training session. However, if possible, it may be more advantageous to train with six, eight or ten channels.

Location is critical to this method. The EEG neurofeedback practitioner checks all Z-score components including power, coherence, asymmetry, and power ratio when making the match between symptom and location. A brain map derived from clean EEG data is essential.

Neurofeedback practitioners focus on emotional, cognitive, and psychological issues—not medical issues, unless they are within the practitioner's scope of practice and if there is research to support the training intervention.

Chapter 20 explores the use of symptom checklists when creating training protocols that employ surface Int'l 10–20 sites or ROI training (sLORETA); also see the introduction.

4. *Train all locations: (1) 19-channel Z-score training or (2) sLORETA Z-score training of all ROIs.* Training all 19 Int'l 10–20 locations with Z-scores would seem to cover all clinical issues. All electrodes are placed on the scalp. Sometimes Fp1 and Fp2 are omitted when there is undue eye blinking. Some clinics train all ROIs with or without 19 surface locations. Of course, sLORETA Z-score training needs all 19 electrodes connected to locate all ROIs.

This method depends on clean EEG data being acquired and trained for each of the 19 sites; if not, Z-score training will focus on artifacts. Before attempting this method, consider the following:

- The cap must be mounted in a timely fashion with low impedance.
- The clinic needs space and water to clean and dry out EEG caps.
- The clinic must purchase enough caps.
- Quick-insert electrodes must be handy when an electrode fails.
- Young and old alike must tolerate a training cap.
- Adults with migraines or pain are sensitive to head pressure.
- Some adult trainees need to go work after training (electrode gels can disturb a hairdo).

In the future, more and more manufacturers will create dry EEG sensor caps that do not need gels and can be mounted in minutes. Currently, dry sensor caps are expensive and may have limitations. Some recording caps use saline solutions instead of gels (see, e.g., Neurofeedback Partner, www.neurofeedback-partner.de).

5. *Combine 19-channel surface Z-score training with 3-D sLORETA power training.* Some practitioners add sLORETA power training with 19-channel Z-score training. For example, trainees with anxiety disorders or PTSD may benefit if alpha is rewarded in the precuneus, the posterior hub of the DMN. Trainees with attention issues may benefit from inhibiting theta in the anterior cingulate to reduce distractibility. Inhibiting alpha in the subcallosal gyrus may help with depression. Of course, the brain map must be consulted first before targeting any bandwidth in a given location. How many feedback sounds are needed? There could be one tone when all Z-score components are in tolerance or two tones, one for surface and the other for sLORETA. Or graphics could be driven by Z-score success while a tone is used for sLORETA feedback, and so on.

20

Automated Site or Network Selection and Training by Symptom With Jewel

Z-SCORE TRAINING with Int'l 10–20 locations, 3-D sLORETA networks, and ROIs have added many dimensions and choices to consider during the protocol development stage. For example, 19 channels of Z-score training compute absolute power, relative power, power ratio, asymmetry, coherence, and phase across 10 separate bandwidths: there are hundreds of trained components. Also, sLORETA Z-score training has about 82 LH and 82 RH ROIs, for a total of 164 power training and 164 coherence combinations possible between them across 10 bandwidths. If both Z-score methods are considered, thousands of trained combinations are possible.

Manifold choices suggest the need for automated software that can process and generate training protocols, brain maps, and treatment plans in minutes. The entire process of creating complex protocols has been simplified and expedited. The following case study demonstrates the process. The subject is a 14-year-old with reading deficits. The step-by-step process shows how the training protocol was created. Individual ROIs and surface locations were inputted automatically.

1. Figure 20.1 shows the surface brain map.
2. Figure 20.2 matches symptom with corresponding power and coherence locations at surface Int'l 10–20 sites.

Figure 20.1. Brain Map of 14-Year-Old With a Learning Disorder

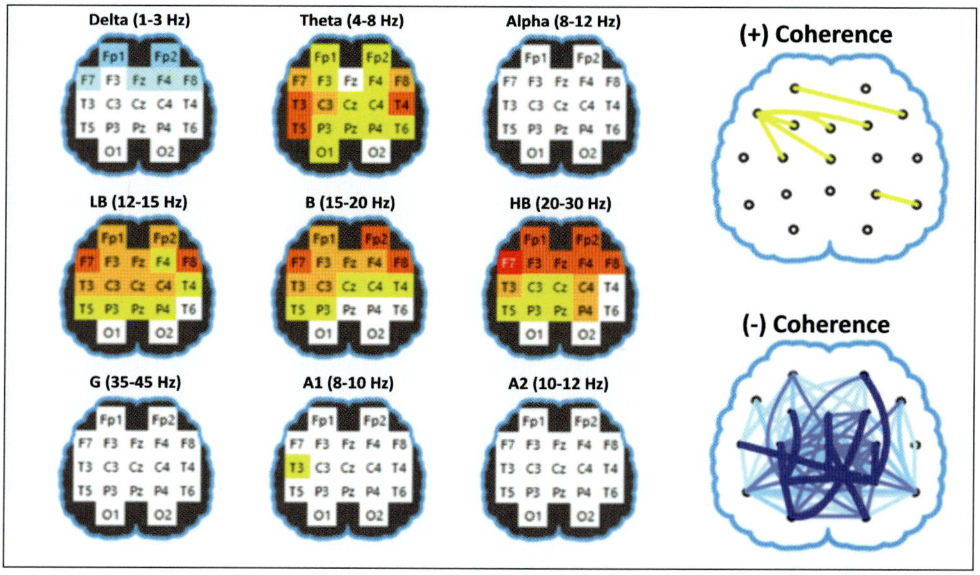

Adapted from Jewel database software

Figure 20.2. Jewel Protocol Generator Selects Training Sites

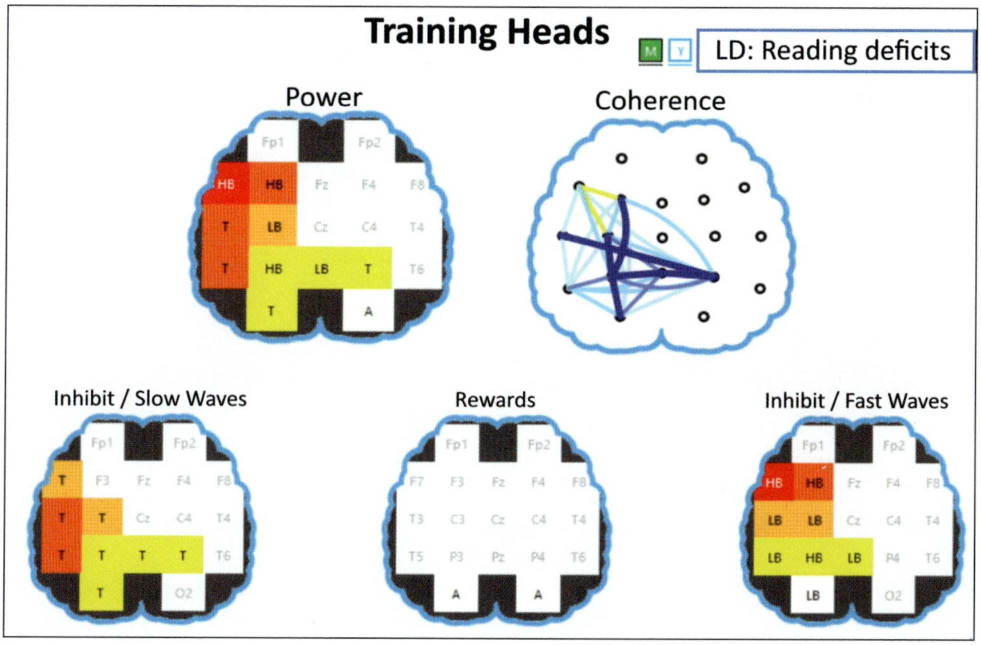

Adapted from Jewel database software

3. Figure 20.3 matches sLORETA ROIs with the symptom (protocol is created).
4. Figure 20.4 traces the protocol uploading method.
5. Figure 20.5 shows ROI Z-scores.
6. Figure 20.6 shows +/– 1.0 Z-score boundary for training.

The Jewel surface protocol generator selected sites appropriate to the selected symptom. There is a drop-down symptom list. Once a symptom is highlighted, the training heads are filled in with sites that correspond to the subject's brain map—sLORETA is next.

The Jewel protocol generator allows the clinician to limit the number of ROIs being trained. In Figure 20.3, the number of ROIs being trained was limited to 21% of all matching channels. The percentage was manually decreased to target ROIs with the highest Z-scores that corresponded to the symptom. Lower percentage selections result in fewer sites being trained with Z-scores that are further from the mean (red, orange, or blue).

Figure 20.3. Jewel Protocol Generator–Selected sLORETA ROIs to Train

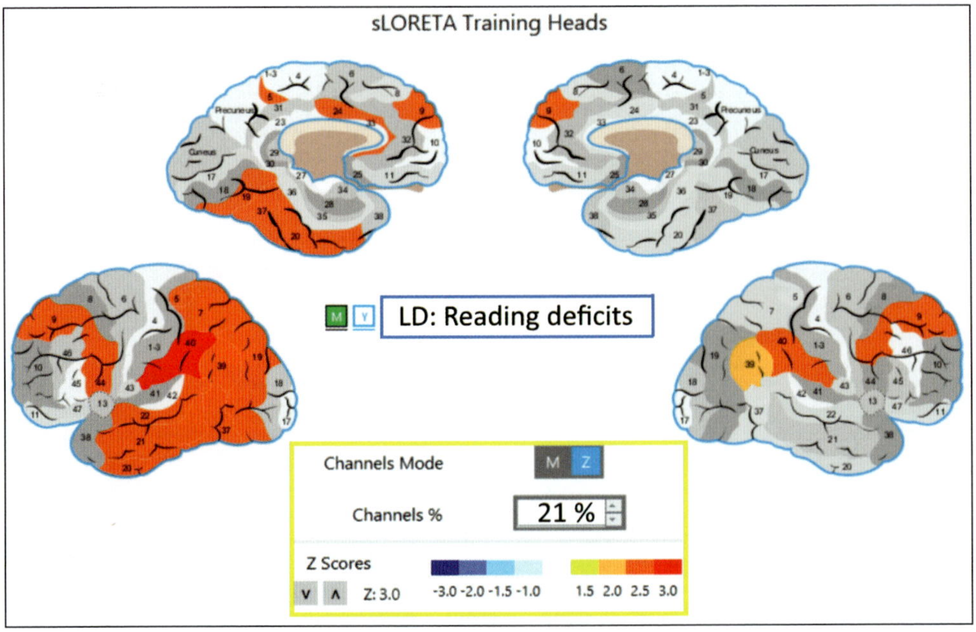

Adapted from Jewel database software

But there's more: Jewel outputs protocol selections that can be read into BrainAvatar training protocol files. The user sets up a file with the subject's name and age, and Jewel fills in all the blanks (i.e., sites and bandwidths that correspond to the selected symptom). Protocol is auto-generated by Jewel, placed in the client folder, and then uploaded into BrainAvatar, as shown in Figure 20.4.

Figure 20.4. BrainAvatar Protocol Selection Procedure

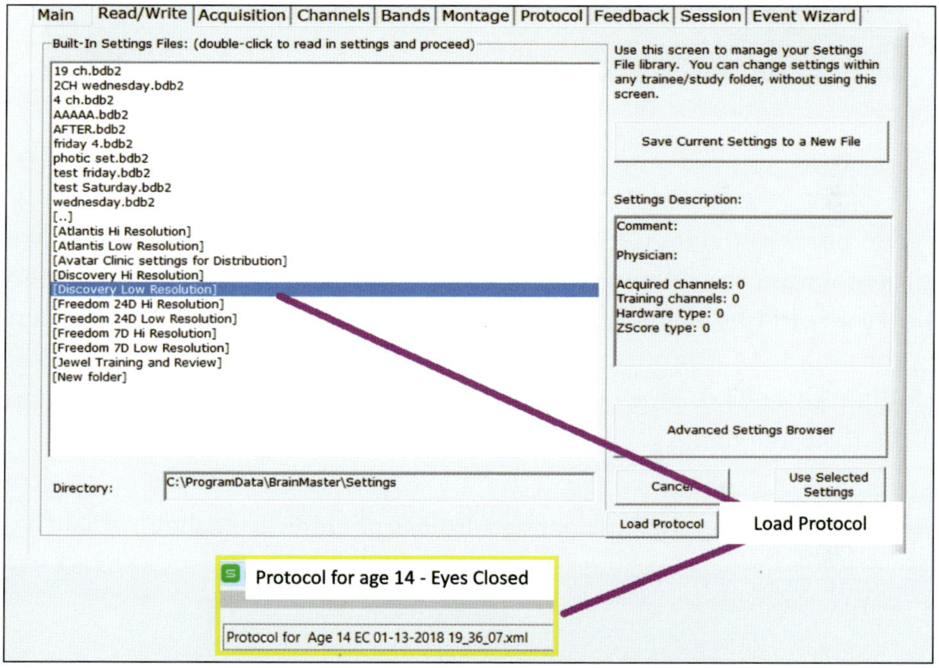

Adapted from BrainAvatar software by BrainMaster Technologies, Inc.

In Figure 20.4, the clinician blue-highlighted "Discovery Low Resolution" and the protocol for age 14 eyes closed trainee was inputted (from the subject's qEEG folder) into a standard BrainAvatar training template.

Figure 20.5 shows the sLORETA ROIs that would be trained once the protocol was automatically uploaded from the Jewel protocol generator to a BrainAvatar template.

Figure 20.5. BrainAvatar Z-Score Training: Selections Input by Jewel

	Left Delta	Left Theta	Left Alpha	Left Lobeta	Left Beta	Left Hibeta	Left Gamma	Left Alpha1	Left Alpha2
Angular Gyrus	3.09	2.83	1.04	1.54	2.03	2.42	2.96	1.45	1.02
Fusiform Gyrus	2.43	1.74	0.42	1.01	1.02	0.65	1.41	0.78	0.63
Inferior Parietal Lobule	3.45	2.93	0.94	1.64	1.98	2.21	3.09	1.35	0.92
Inferior Temporal Gyrus	1.62	1.91	0.58	1.32	0.78	0.22	0.85	0.94	0.81
Insula	1.69	1.55	0.10	1.39	0.69	0.18	1.14	0.43	0.39
Middle Temporal Gyrus	2.06	2.19	0.73	1.41	1.05	0.61	1.20	1.05	1.01
Parahippocampal Gyrus	1.31	0.80	-0.31	0.56	0.60	0.22	1.30	0.08	-0.13
Postcentral Gyrus	3.38	2.55	0.87	1.93	1.62	1.66	3.25	1.29	0.79
Subcallosal Gyrus	-1.00	-0.07	-0.08	1.20	0.76	-0.14	0.69	-0.07	0.64
Superior Temporal Gyrus	1.50	1.89	0.53	1.43	0.87	0.34	0.97	0.76	0.94
Supramarginal Gyrus	3.40	2.83	0.93	1.53	2.02	2.03	2.65	1.31	1.01
Transverse Temporal Gyrus	2.16	2.12	0.14	1.22	0.70	0.33	0.93	0.50	0.35

Adapted from BrainAvatar software by BrainMaster Technologies, Inc.
Z-Scores derived from qEEG-Pro database

The processed data were loaded into Jewel, a symptom was chosen, and a protocol was created and then uploaded so that training could start and feedback could be triggered. Loading the data into Jewel and commencing training took minutes. In Figure 20.6, the upper and lower thresholds defaulted to +/– 1.0. However, the clinician was free to adjust these scores on the fly as needed.

Figure 20.6. Z-Score Performance Training Screen (Threshold: +/–1.0)

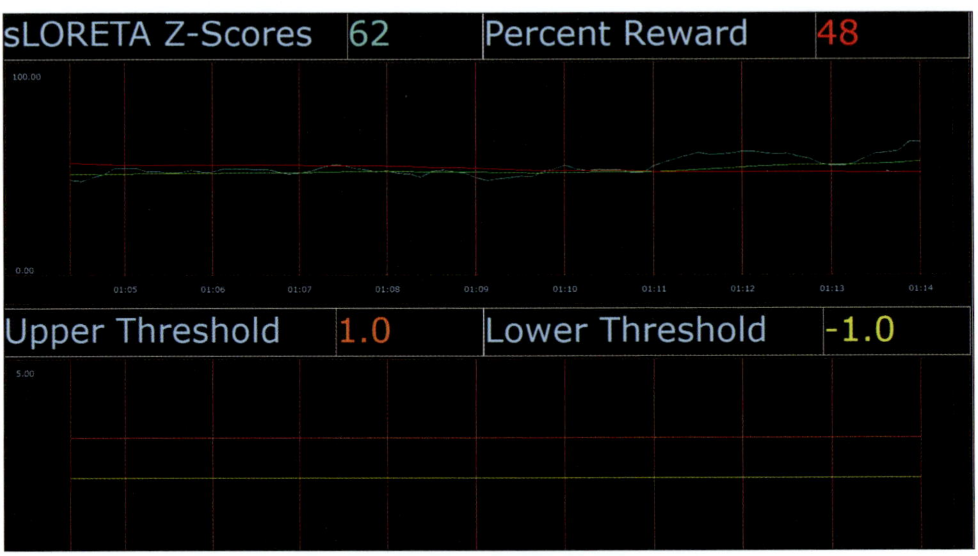

Adapted from BrainAvatar software by BrainMaster Technologies, Inc.
Z-Scores derived from qEEG-Pro database

21

Deep States Training and Protocol Suggestions for PTSD and Addictions

ALPHA WAS THE FIRST brain wave to be named and trained and the first to be explored. Alpha states are often associated with meditation or a deep sense of inner calm. Herbert Benson studied the body's response to deep relaxation and learned that "Alpha waves increase in amplitude and regularity during meditation" (1975, p. 58).

Neurofeedback training can lead to an increase in alpha amplitudes and robust alpha synchrony. The relaxation response and mindfulness meditation effects can be acquired in a relatively short period of time. Alpha/theta (A/T) training, alpha enhancement training, and alpha synchrony training also have many nonclinical applications, such as peak performance training to improve cognitive flexibility, creativity, athletic control, hemispheric synchrony, and inner awareness (Mason & Brownback, 2001).

Alpha/theta training holds out the promise of resolving past issues while the client remains in a fairly relaxed condition (Robbins, 2000, pp. 158–192). It has been known to bring the client into a witness state in the quest to build a bridge to the true self. It can cool down the limbic system, allowing the trainee to process trauma with the frontal lobes. It is an effective tool for the resolution of trauma and the building up of the human spirit (White, 1999, 341–367).

HISTORY

Early trainers facilitated twilight states of healing. Kamiya, Green, Budzynski, and others, using standalone EEG neurofeedback equipment, rewarded alpha, theta, or both. It worked; emotional issues were resolved while the client entered the depths of the psyche in a relaxed state. Later, Peniston and Kulkosky (1991, 1999) applied A/T training to two separate disorders: PTSD and alcoholism. They used two small populations of Vietnam War veterans. Both experiments were done in an institution. Building upon their success, Scott, Brod, Siderof, Kaiser, and Sagan (2002) demonstrated the efficacy of their model with much larger numbers of volunteers: 121 court-mandated poly-substance abusers participated. Scott and colleagues had the support of a major institution. A/T training was proven to be superior to talk therapy when it came to resolution of long-entrenched trauma and recovery from substance abuse. This study, unlike the Peniston and Kulkosky studies, assessed the EEG prior to training and subsequently trained with two different protocols: (1) alpha suppression, and (2) alpha enhancement (Budzynski, 1999; Robbins, 2000; Scott et al., 2002; White, 1999).

Nearly half of those who participate in a rigorous 30–40-session A/T training program will experience the Peniston effect, which is an allergic reaction to alcohol or other psychoactive substances that comes with intensive A/T training (Peniston & Kulkosky, 1999). Participants in A/T training programs are informed of the possibility of losing drug-related effects and becoming allergic to the substance they have been abusing. It is a major issue; clients must sign a release stating their knowledge of the Peniston effect. Note that I have not as yet seen the Peniston effect with trainees who trained once or twice per week. Nonetheless, everyone fills out the form.

However, the success of A/T training programs is not related to an allergic side effect. Peniston and Kulkosky described the following benefits related to their program:

> This procedure can produce profound increases in Alpha and Theta brain rhythms . . . prevent an elevation of serum Beta endorphin levels during the course of treatment of alcoholism, and produce decreases in self-assessed depression and other fundamental changes in personality variables. The personality changes reported correspond to being more

> warmhearted, more intelligent, more emotionally stable, more socially bold, more relaxed and more satisfied. (1999, p. 172)

Traditional addiction treatment programs tend to raise cortisol levels (measured by taking blood samples). Consequently, participants become more anxious and have more cravings. A/T training programs seldom add to the anxiety that comes with being in treatment. They often result in reduced cravings. Intensive programs are best managed on an institutional level. Neurofeedback training for addictions is likely to include two training sessions each day—14 sessions per week. A/T training programs have also been adapted to smaller private practices (White, 1999). There is a place for alpha enhancement training in most EEG neurofeedback practices. A/T training is a valuable tool for the treatment of several clinical disorders.

WHAT MAKES DEEP STATES SO DEEP?

A/T training opens the door to healing and the reclamation of repressed feelings and memories. The healing activity takes place during the so-called twilight states that are a natural part of the sleep-wake cycle. Our wakeful hours are accompanied by a great deal of beta activity. Beta helps us to stay focused and on task during the day. Then day eventually turns into night and the EEG shows increases in theta and decreases in alpha (Rowan & Tolunsky, 2003, p. 29). Sleep is associated with higher amplitudes of delta. Our interest is in the transition from alpha to theta to delta as we go to sleep and then back again as we wake up. Imagery that comes while we are waking up is called hypnopompic. Hypnagogic imagery occurs while we are going to sleep. The transition into sleep creates a state of mind that mixes reality with subconscious images. White (1999) described the role of alpha and theta in the healing process:

> With a predominance of Theta waves (4–8 Hz) focus is on the internal world, a world of hypnogogic imagery where an "inner healer" is often said to be encountered. Alpha brain waves (8–13 Hz) may be considered a bridge from the external world to the internal world and vice versa. (p. 344)

A/T training promotes twilight states that may evoke hypnagogic imagery. Some clients report striking imagery and/or deep insights about their life. Traumatic events may be safely reexperienced. Working through requires less assistance from the therapist. Others gain a broader perspective on life. Rigid character traits soften up, and life takes on a new dimension. Thus, A/T training is more than a trauma resolution technique. The release of traumas and personal growth happen side by side. A/T training is empowering because the client is doing the work. The therapist serves as the empathic facilitator. Termination issues are reduced because the client is more self-sufficient and less therapist dependent.

Note that A/T training is not just another protocol. The trainee must have a good relationship with a trauma-educated practitioner who understands the concept of readiness.

A/T training is primarily the process of rewarding both alpha and theta. Other bandwidths may be rewarded or inhibited. Alpha reinforcement ranges from 50% to 70%, whereas theta reinforcement ranges from 20% to 50%. Some clients go into a deeper state of consciousness with ease. The training graph shows a definite trend. Alpha amplitudes begin to decrease while theta amplitudes remain constant or begin to rise. When theta amplitudes exceed alpha amplitudes, it is called a crossover. Clients who take the plunge into theta often report striking images of the past or the reclamation of repressed feelings or emotions. Not all agree with this concept: one study questioned the need for the theta reward. It clearly demonstrated that imagery can take place without having a crossover or a theta reward (Moore et al., 2000). However, imagery is not the sole component of the healing process. If imagery were the only goal, then the theta component might have little value.

Memories are stored in four different planes: behavior, affect, sensation, and knowledge, known as the BASK model (Braun, 1988). For example: ask the client, "Do you remember when you last had ice cream? If so, please visualize it."

- B, behavior: I can see myself licking the ice-cream cone.
- A, affect: Vanilla is my favorite flavor and I was so happy to be with friends.
- S, sensation: The ice cream was cold on that hot summer day.
- K, knowledge: It was July 5th. I had a day off from work, and there were four friends in the car. We traveled for about an hour before we reached the ice-cream stand. I know the names of my friends and the kind of clothing we were wearing that day.

Thus, visualization opens up the memory, but much more than knowledge is needed. I have treated many a trauma survivor who remembered the K events but continued to suffer from the symptoms of PTSD because affects and sensations were repressed.

The goal of treatment is healing. The therapist must create a protocol that fits each client. For some of my clients, theta reward was too much; it revivified the trauma. For others, training with just alpha reward did not bring them to a state of healing and recovery. It is appropriate to question the value of efficacy of either alpha or theta reward. For example, Scott and colleagues (2002) indicated that substance abusers had either too much or too little alpha. Protocols were adjusted according to the EEG data. The study concluded that "there was no significant difference in abstinence rates between the Alpha augmentation and Alpha suppression groups." Consequently, the decision to reward, inhibit, or remove either alpha or theta from the treatment protocol is determined by the assessment process and client's response to the treatment protocols.

Other clients benefit in a more informal way. They come once a week and train for about 20 to 25 minutes. The training begins after about 10 to 15 minutes of counseling and debriefing. During training, they often experience personal insights or reclaim repressed memories. Between sessions, clients spend time reflecting and journaling. These clients have a secure base, steady employment, and a good support system. They are not at risk for suicide, nor will they decompensate in the office or at home. In this way, A/T training becomes an adjunct to talk therapy. Some weeks you may skip training to talk through issues. Informal A/T training will likely reduce the total number of psychotherapy sessions.

ASSESSMENT AND PROTOCOL SELECTION

Most forms of slow-wave enhancement are typically done with eyes closed in a quiet room and in a reclined position. The number of training sessions needed to bring relief varies from client to client. Slow-wave enhancement may be contraindicated in some cases. For example, clients with widespread EEG slowing may not be good candidates for this protocol until they have learned to regulate theta, which accompanies foggy thinking and dissociation. Survivors may be prone to drift into a theta state as a coping mechanism. When interviewing clients with dissociative disorders, it is common to see them zone out for brief periods of time; they lose eye contact and begin to stare aimlessly into space. This retreat into theta is a form of self-hypnosis that prevents the survivor from squarely dealing with life. Before beginning A/T training, theta regulation is needed. Theta can be inhibited with eyes open at Fz or Cz. Other protocols include beta/SMR and theta/beta ratio training. As part of the talk therapy process, the client needs to learn basic grounding skills (Herman, 1992, 2015). I encourage trauma survivors to "hold on to your keys and stay in the present."

WHAT IS INVOLVED IN A/T TRAINING?

The client must be emotionally ready and living in a supportive environment. Trauma survivors may need skills: communication skills, cognitive therapy skills, assertiveness training, and general coping skills such as grounding, journaling, and exercise. It may take a few sessions or many sessions of coaching before the client is ready to proceed. Skin temperature training and diaphragmatic breathing are part of the original Peniston and Kulkosky A/T protocol. Qualified trainees can raise their skin temperature to 93–95°F and hold it for 15 to 20 minutes. Daily practice is required for at least one week prior to the first A/T training session. I seldom begin A/T training unless the client can demonstrate both diaphragmatic breathing and the ability to raise hand temperature. Note that daily HRV training for two weeks can be substituted.

The client must be mentally and physically prepared for each A/T training session. The client arrives early enough to unwind, breathe, and release muscle tension. Electronic communication devices are turned off. A few minutes later, training begins. While the sensors are being mounted, it's time to review briefly the previous session and bring up any pertinent issues. After the client assumes a comfortable position in a reclining chair, the clinician mounts the sensors and does an impedance test. The room temperature is made comfortable, noise level is at a minimum, and lights are turned off when ready. Many clients feel chilly or cold during deep-states training. Therefore, it is wise to have a light blanket available.

Before training, the trainee does a 2-to-5-minute constructed visualization. This visualization may take several forms. It may be an image of the ideal self. It may contain scenarios of the client entering a potentially troublesome conflict. In the imagery, the client handles the problem with nondefensive language or assertiveness. Or the client imagines being in a temptation scene where substances may be present, and the client walks away without using or purchasing. The therapist facilitates the process of choosing a constructed visualization. In most cases, the client repeats one or more visualizations over and over again for the 3 to 8 minutes. In a few cases, the therapist does a form of guided imagery and walks the client through the process (Scott, 2000). Do not minimize the power of this technique. I have assigned it as homework for talk therapy clients. It helps them build sense of self.

Once the visualization process ends, EEG training can begin. The trainee is instructed to "let go." I add a few gentle reminders to make sure clients understand what is expected of them: "Imagine you are getting a massage. What would you be thinking about? Remember that your problems will be there at the end of the session. If worry really helps, then why are there so many problems? Focus on your breathing. Imagine a safe place. Repeat supportive statements." The next step is to start the training. Alpha (8–12 Hz) is rewarded 50–70% of the time and theta (5–8 Hz) is rewarded 20–50% of the time. When the feedback consists of two separate soothing tones, the higher pitch is used for alpha and the lower pitch for theta. Inhibits may be added to the protocol. For example, inhibit 15–30 Hz if the client is struggling to relax. On the other hand, inhibit 2–5 Hz if the client is at risk for powerful traumatic images or sensations (Scott, 2000).

In some cases, it is better to leave the room and allow the client to be alone. If it seems best to leave the room, keep track of the training with a baby monitor or some other method. Other clients request the therapist's presence. Trauma survivors often need it. Sometimes, just reminding clients to breathe slowly prevents relaxation-induced anxiety. It goes without saying that A/T training requires a good therapeutic relationship. In a clinic environment, make sure that all clients with emotional issues, regardless of the EEG neurofeedback training modality, have the same therapist each week. Healing takes place within the therapeutic bond amid an arena of trust (Bowlby, 1988).

A/T training sounds promote success. Make sure the sounds are the correct volume and degree of pleasantness to suit the client's taste. In some cases headphones may be able to block outside noise. If the room is relatively quiet, the regular speakers are fine. Do not train in high-traffic or noisy areas.

FIVE RESPONSES TO A/T TRAINING

Not all respond to A/T training in the same way. One of the chief problems related to A/T training is the presence of busy thoughts that won't stop. When that happens, there are several techniques that will help. For example, the client can repeat the same word or words over and over again internally or name several objects in the room over and over again—"bore it to death" (Scott, 2000). Other clients find that repeating self-supportive statements over and over again helps. Imagining a waterfall or some other pleasant and safe scene may help. Above all, diaphragmatic breathing must be maintained.

In time the trainee falls into one of five patterns:

1. The client with negative experiences, such as painful imagery or body sensations.
2. The client with frustrations, who remarks, "I just can't get deep."
3. The client who goes to sleep.
4. The client who reports no experiences but a state of deep relaxation.
5. The client with excellent experiences, such as insight and the unlocking of repressed memories.

The next five paragraphs expand on these five types.

1. Once a client begins to reexperience painful trauma in a painful way, it will become harder to make progress. Many therapists inhibit 2–5 Hz to minimize pain (Scott, 2000). A/T training is supposed to minimize painful revivifications. However, teary eyes and deep sighs are common signals of relief. But sharp pains must be prevented. There are several ways to keep ahead of this problem. Watch the progress of the EEG and compare it to the client's body language. Sharp changes in delta or high beta may signal a change. Peripheral biofeedback equipment may also be helpful. Checking the client's pulse rate and/or breathing rate is very important; I have seen clients double their breathing rate. Catch it before that happens and slow it down to within normal limits. If the above measures fail to work, turn off all theta feedback—leaving only alpha feedback—and gently talk to the client, to make your presence known. Don't leave the room. Be ready to shut off the equipment. Don't let the client go into a painful abreaction.

2. Some clients can stop the busy thoughts by boring them to death, imagining a colorful waterfall, repeating self-supportive statements, or just concentrating on their breathing. For clients who do not see in colors, the goal is to see jet black. Seeing pure black is evidence of deep relaxation unless the client sees in color. Watch the training graph, it's easy to spot clients with busy thoughts; they are the ones with increasing beta and alpha that never dares to drop below theta. A/T training protocols also inhibit 2–5 Hz as well as 15–30 Hz (Scott, 2000). Clients who are anxious will have great difficulty doing A/T training unless they master the art of diaphragmatic breathing. Classes may be available locally that will help them learn stretching or movement therapy. The goal is to prevent feelings of frustration or failure. Carefully screen clients before the process begins.
3. Some clients go directly into sleep when they begin to relax. They have not mastered the ability to relax during wakeful states. This condition may be a defense mechanism to prevent working through issues. Regardless, watch the delta carefully. Remind the client to keep track of breathing. Ultimately, it is the client's responsibility to stay awake, not the therapist's. A/T training may be contraindicated.
4. Some clients report, after training for 30 minutes, "I felt relaxed. It was okay." The trainee's nonchalant way of describing A/T training suggests that it was the kind of relaxation that resembles lounging by the pool or the beach on a sunny day. Examine the EEG and look for evidence. Positive changes include decreases in beta or hi-beta and gradual alpha attenuation during periods of deep relaxation that may or may not accompany increased theta. If the EEG stays about the same, it is unlikely that the client went deep. Watch out for clients who open their eyes the instant the session is over. If they were truly deep, it would take a little time to reenter the real world.
5. The client who is truly benefiting from the training often has much to say. It is the therapist's job to limit comments to open-ended questions such as:

- What was your experience like?
- Did you have any bodily sensations (floating, dizziness, hand tingling, or myoclonic jerks)?
- Did you see any colors?
- What was happening in your mind?

Notice that the client is not asked about imagery, memories, or trauma. Clients who are asked about imagery after each session may come to believe that success depends upon seeing images. Allow clients to express themselves. Facilitate the process. If a significant realization is uttered, gently help them to work through it. Training logs or journal entries are made for each session. Some clients receive insights when journaling at home later that day. Others experience vivid dreams that will enrich the therapy process. But do not assume that rich personal expressions are vital to the process. One former male trainee tells people in the community that his life was transformed by A/T training, even though he shared little with me during his training experience.

If the client reveals a traumatic memory, act as a facilitator and have the client do as much of his or her own work as possible. Consider the following questions: "If you could be there at the very moment the incident began, what would you do? What would you say to those present? What would you say to yourself? What words of comfort do you have for the part of you that survived the trauma? What does that part want from you now? Does that part feel safe now?" Remember that your gentle debriefing is not trying to dig up something new. However, it may be an opportunity to facilitate insight, self-esteem, and self-empathy and tear down the shackles of shame and toxic guilt. When all goes well, the relaxed client works through the deepest, darkest moments of his or her life. The symptoms of PTSD—flashbacks, startle response, paranoia, low self-esteem, fearfulness, depression and anxiety—will begin to fade as the number of sessions builds. After the program ends, the client continues to get stronger. Most clients can complete the training in 30 sessions; sometimes more sessions are required. A/T training is a learning experience that is not limited to trauma resolution and recovery. It promotes inner growth, enhanced cognitive flexibility, and other intrinsic benefits.

After each session, make sure that the client is completely grounded. Some clients require theta inhibition at Cz or Fz for 5–10 minutes to restore a state of alertness. Other clients will feel more alert after the session than when they came in. Check out clients' condition before they leave. Make sure they are okay to drive. Sometimes clients will call on the phone, complaining that they are still foggy. I direct them to listen to or sing with upbeat rock-and-roll music. After 20–30 minutes, fogginess usually fades because the music entrained a beta state.

CASE STUDIES: ALPHA ENHANCEMENT TRAINING FOR ANXIETY AND DEPRESSION

Jack

Jack, a 38-year-old adult, was demeaned for most of his life by family and relatives. He had a poor sense of self and responded slowly to psychotherapy. His was diagnosed with depression, generalized anxiety disorder, and compulsions.

Figure 21.1 is a review graph that reflects deep relaxation. Although only alpha was rewarded, it's helpful to see the course of both alpha (8–12 Hz) and theta (4–7 Hz). At first, alpha was rising and theta remained steady. After peaking, alpha began to plummet and theta began to rise. Toward the end of the session, the amplitude of theta exceeded the amplitude of alpha. This phenomenon is called a crossover. It is normal for alpha to decrease and theta to increase in amplitude during periods of drowsiness or deep relaxation.

Figure 21.1. Crossover: Theta (Dark Blue) > Alpha (Light Blue)

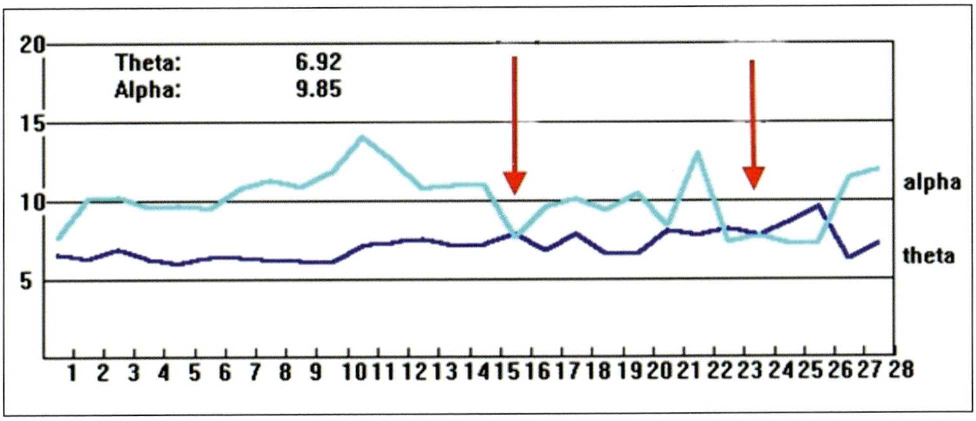

Adapted from BrainMaster Technologies, Inc. software

Figure 21.1 shows that the dark blue theta amplitude is greater than light blue alpha; this crossover is unusual because when eyes are closed, the alpha band is almost always the highest of all bandwidth amplitudes in adults. However, it is not so during a crossover, which may well reflect the beginning of a reverie state, which is a place of deep inner healing and peace.

A crossover happens when:

- Theta amplitude exceeds alpha.
- Delta amplitude does not significantly increase.
- Beta amplitude does not significantly increase.

If delta has a marked increase, it may signal the onset of sleep. If beta increases, it may signal tension, worry, or anxiety. In either case, the trainee may be headed for deep sleep or an unwanted abreaction or flashback: If either trend continues, stop training.

Alice

Alice was a young single mother and a survivor of abuse. Her apartment was disorganized, messy, and unclean. Daily functioning was difficult. Treatment began with teaching her coping skills. The initial goal of EEG neurofeedback was theta reduction to keep her grounded. Cz/SMR training rewarded 13–15 Hz, whereas theta and hi-beta were inhibited. Each session was divided between counseling and neurotherapy. Twenty-four sessions later, therapy ended. Her house was clean and organized. She was not overwhelmed by child care. She was able to return to college despite the fact that she had flunked out. The flashbacks had stopped. She stopped zoning out. A/T training was not begun.

Betty

Betty was a single young adult. After two years of talk therapy, she still suffered from panic attacks, flashbacks, and occasional depression. Talk therapy was ended. Two years later she returned for neurotherapy. Training started with 15 sessions of Cz/SMR. Next came twice-weekly sessions of A/T training with Pz sensor placement, for a total of 30 sessions. Betty experienced BASK for the first time in treatment. She worked through repressed memories and reclaimed more and more of her emotional self. Panic attacks and flashbacks were greatly diminished.

Cindy

Cindy was a married adult with adequate social and spousal support. She was an adult survivor of alcohol abuse, negative labeling, and toxic parenting. Her symptoms were depression, anxiety, codependency, passivity, and low self-esteem. The first session trained her to do diaphragmatic breathing. When she returned the next week, her level of anxiety had dropped 50%. Weekly sessions for several months were used to teach her assertiveness, cognitive, interpersonal, coping, and relaxation skills. Talk therapy was needed. Issues arose each week. Eventually, Cindy felt safe enough outside and inside the therapeutic arena to commence neurotherapy. After 10 sessions of Cz/SMR training, we began informal A/T training with Pz sensor placement. A pattern of healing was noted in most 30-minute sessions. After about 10 minutes, her alpha dropped so low that no alpha feedback could be heard. For the next 5–10 minutes, only theta feedback could be heard. Then, as she moved out of the depth state, both alpha and theta tones could be heard. Painful issues were discussed at each session without Cindy becoming overwhelmed. Issues came up that had not been addressed in talk therapy. She squarely faced both the cognitive and emotional reality of her upbringing. Training of this nature proceeded for about 15 to 20 sessions. At that point, A/T training stopped. Cindy's reason for coming into treatment had been addressed. Therapy was terminated.

Dorothy

Dorothy was a married adult with good social and family support. She was diagnosed with dissociative identity disorder. She specifically came to my office looking for neurotherapy. Talk therapy had not helped; she could not trust a therapist with her stuff. It was difficult to know what was happening inside because she made few self-disclosures to me. Weekly training started along the sensorimotor strip: 10 minutes of C3/beta was followed by 20 minutes of C4/SMR. While training in the RH (C4), she reexperienced repressed memories but shared little with me. I was not sure if the treatment was working until I received reports from the family that indicated major changes were happening. Dorothy stopped training after 30 sessions. She returned a year later. This time I suggested A/T training. More traumas were worked through, but this time she shared them with me. Dorothy developed more friends outside of therapy. Flashbacks stopped and she reported an end of depression. Training stopped after 15 sessions.

Neurofeedback has long been used to treat PTSD. Potential trainees learn grounding skills, diaphragmatic breathing, and basic coping skills.

Theta reduction is a key to prevent zoning out. Rewarding SMR in the RH may lead to emotional releases. Deep-states training can have many variations in the diverse world of trauma and recovery. The key to success is prior assessment. Scott and colleagues (2002) were successful because they altered the Peniston and Kulkosky model to fit two different EEG patterns found in the experimental group. Some needed alpha suppression, whereas others needed alpha enhancement: one size does not fit all.

PRETRAINING REQUIREMENTS FOR ADDICTION OR TRAUMA

Do not begin unless the following has been established:

- Strong therapeutic relationship.
- Social support system (friends).
- Grounding skills training and assess for dissociation.
- Journaling and diaphragmatic breathing (begin 1–2 weeks before training starts).
- Temperature training: the ability to hold a hand temperature of 93–95 degrees for at least 20 minutes four or five separate times in as many days. Chapter 24 thoroughly explains skin temperature or hand warming methods. Protect your trainee against relaxation-induced anxiety (RIA).
- Personal and family safety.
- To-do list implementation for emotional crisis.
- Have an antianxiety agent available. Do not take daily; take as needed (PRN).
- Permission to treat form: make sure the client knows that A/T training may bring to light repressed memories and is also known to increase medication sensitivity or physiological reactions to addictive substances.
- Teach client what it means to let go, because that is what is needed during A/T.

JOURNALING SUGGESTIONS

1. Find a quiet time and place where there are few distractions.
2. Take a few minutes to think about how your traumatic event or addiction has impacted you and your life.

3. Begin writing about your deepest thoughts and feelings regarding the traumatic event you experienced.
4. Once you have finished writing, read over what you wrote and pay attention to how you feel. Notice any changes in your thoughts or feelings as a rcsult of writing.
5. Although long-term benefits of writing have been found, writing about your traumatic event will naturally initially bring up some distressing thoughts and feelings. Therefore, make sure you have a plan for how to manage this distress.
6. When writing, don't worry about spelling or grammar. Focus simply on getting all of your thoughts and feelings down.
7. Try to be as descriptive as possible in your writing. For example, when describing your feelings (for example, sadness or anxiety), write about the thoughts connected to those feelings and how those emotions felt in your body (for example, "my heart was racing" or "my muscles were very tense"). This will help increase your awareness and the clarity of your emotions and thoughts.
8. You may find it helpful to keep what you write so that you can see how your thoughts and feelings change over the course of using this coping strategy. However, if you are concerned about others finding them, you should find a safe and secure way of disposing of your writings.
9. It may be important to first set aside some time every day to write. However, you can also use expressive writing whenever something stressful happens. It can be a good coping strategy to add to your healthy coping repertoire.

CONDUCTING A SESSION

Just before the session begins:

- Mount sensors for monopolar montage (Pz or P4, T6, O2 or O1.
- Have client sit in a reclining chair in a darkened room (Figure 21.2).

Each session starts with the client visualizing two or three changes in his or her life. (Most clients do this silently for 2–5 minutes.) Some write out the visualizations and read them or request that the therapist read them. Others ask for assistance and have the therapist work with them to create a positive visualization. Clients need help to create a

Figure 21.2. Alpha/Theta Training

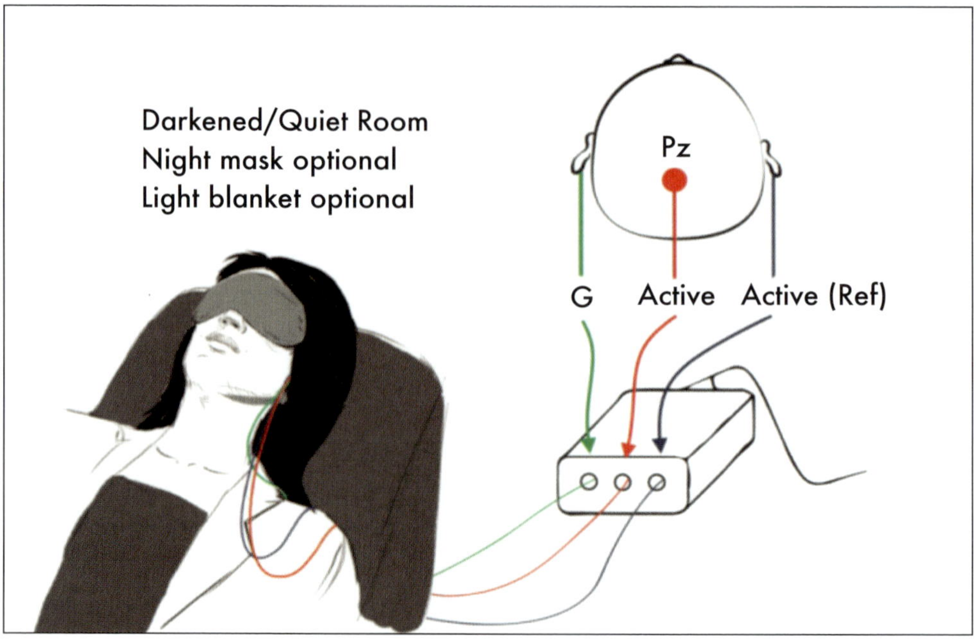

positive visualization. It's not enough to say "I want to be happy"; it's necessary to dissect the steps that need to be taken to arrive at happiness. Stop visualizing before feedback tones begin!

Chose one of the following visualization techniques:

1. Reaction change: Visualize a situation in which you might act in an inappropriate manner, but this time you see yourself handling it better. It might involve refusing to drink or take drugs, or it might be an interpersonal situation that in the past has caused problems for you.
2. New behavior: Visualize a new positive behavior.
3. New self: Visualize yourself (after treatment is over)—how you want to act and look and what you want to do. (This is about changing you, not about changing other people.)

As the training progresses, watch for anxiety or sleep:

1. Increases in delta (sleep or possible abreaction trauma).
2. Increases in beta (anxiety or possible abreaction).
3. Decreases in hand temperature—use digital thermometer probe.

Postsession Debriefing

Each session ends with the same licensed therapist debriefing the client. The client shares any sensory experiences he or she would like to talk about. Some clients may have come to certain realizations about their life or their future. Others may want to talk about the past and how abuse may have hurt them. It must be understood that an A/T reverie state is akin to but not the same as hypnosis. Therefore, when debriefing:

- Ask open-ended questions!
- Do not ask leading questions!
- Be conscious of false memory syndrome risks.
- Inquire about physical sensations such as tingling and floating.
- Ask about colors seen during the training process.
- Encourage the client to practice journaling after each session.
- Clients who are survivors of abuse and trauma may reexperience body memories and images from the past. It is important to remind them that nothing is actually happening in the training room, regardless of the images they may be seeing. If they can stay in a witness state, that is, keep a mental distance from the images or see them as if they are on a movie screen, it may help to do abdominal breathing.

OTHER A/T CONSIDERATIONS

Before deciding to do A/T training, there are several considerations:

1. Is there a low-traffic, low-noise area in your office?
2. Are you prepared to debrief clients in the case of trauma?
3. If alcoholism is the issue, do you have training in addictions counseling?
4. If peak performance is the goal, obtain computer-driven performance test to measure progress. How will the trainee know that progress has been made?
5. Have you trained your clients to manage relaxation (not merely discussed it)? That is, can they do diaphragmatic breathing? Or do they practice some other form of relaxation therapy? Have you taken steps to prevent RIA?

CLIENT READINESS FOR ADDICTION AND TRAUMA RECOVERY WITH A/T TRAINING

- Clients who are struggling with addictions need to be highly motivated.
- Drinking or drug abuse will most likely sabotage the training because they artificially raise the level of alpha. Also, roughly 40–50% of completed A/T trainees will have adverse reactions to future alcohol consumption. A similar number of drug users will not be able to experience the same high that they did before training started (including those who are daily users of benzodiazepines).
- Consequently, it would be unwise to start training unless you are completely committed and determined to stop substance abuse. Alpha/theta training is designed to help you make your own alpha without the assistance of drugs or alcohol. When successful, it can lead to feeling good in the absence of these substances.

THERAPIST READINESS FOR ADDICTIONS AND TRAUMA THERAPY WITH A/T TRAINING

- Experienced A/T training
- Had mentoring or training in A/T
- Education in trauma
- Experience with trauma and recovery
    - Debriefing
    - Grounding and coping skills
    - Decompensation

COMMENTS FROM THE EXPERTS

Nancy White: “Alpha-Theta Neurotherapy seems to enhance the ability of the brain to shift state. By encouraging the brain to move toward the lower end of the arousal continuum, the protocol may access Theta state-dependent memories of early traumas, which when retrieved, can be altered in a positive way, with accompanying positive changes in neurochemistry” (White, 1999).

Richard Soutar on crossovers: "Recent research on this topic indicates that there is not a direct correlation between crossovers and these (healing*) images. However if you include spontaneous visualizations, then there is an increased correlation. . . . It may be dangerous to conclude that individuals are repressing material merely because they are not demonstrating crossovers" (Soutar & Longo, 2011).

COMMENTS ON A/T TRAINING FOR TRAUMA AND PTSD

The goal is to provide the trauma survivor with the best treatment available. I have trained a number of clients with A/T protocols in both formal and informal ways. In many cases it worked very well. The treatment for PTSD may require 50 sessions or more, that is, 20 sessions to reduce the EEG abnormalities and 30 sessions of A/T training. Neurotherapy is an excellent way to resolve trauma. I have seen it repeatedly open up repressed memories and issues; I have no doubt of its power.

In the 1990s when this technique became widely known and used, it was viewed as a cure for alcoholism and PTSD. But A/T training in private offices proved to be less effective than Peniston's model for these reasons:

- Trainees were not insulated from the stress of the world.
- Daily training for a month proved to be impractical in most cases.
- Unwanted abreactions accompanied some sessions.
- Some offices were too noisy to create a setting for deep states.
- Some clients with elevated beta simply could not let go and enter into a reverie state needed for healing.

CURRENT APPLICATIONS FOR A/T TRAINING

Alpha/theta training may be combined with HRV training and is most often used in offices for the following:

- Peak performance training
- Addictions
- Personality disorders
- Type A personality
- Deep relaxation/anxiety disorders

OTHER PROTOCOLS FOR PTSD AND TRAUMA RESOLUTION

A/T training is not for all trauma survivors or for all clinics. Other successful protocols can be employed. Neurofeedback interventions for PTSD in addition to A/T training have expanded to include:

1. LORETA Z-score training: Foster, D.S. and Thatcher, R.W. (2015) considered a comprehensive approach to the treatment of PTSD and mild traumatic brain injury. Sub-cortical LORETA neurofeedback targets sub-cortical ROIs including the limbic system and the amygdalae, which are embedded within the medial temporal lobes.
2. Surface Z-score training for stabilization (F3, F4, P3 & P4) and (C3, C4, T3 & T4).
3. Training protocols that target the insula cortex, which is thought to be the cortical repository of PTSD symptoms.
4. Alpha reward training at the precuneus (sLORETA power reward) with 19-channel surface Z-score training.
5. Theta reduction training along the cingulate (Fz, Cz, Pz) to limit dissociation and promote grounding. (Teaching grounding and coping skills are an integral part of all psychotherapy interventions for PTSD).
6. Monopolar montages at FpO2 for fear reduction, innovated by S. Fisher (2004), see the close of Chapter 16.
7. See Appendix 2 for comments on Low Frequency training.
8. Research by Bessel A. van der Kolk and associates (2016) also showed promise for the treatment of PTSD. The single channel bipolar montage with a 3 threshold design has the following features:
    - Montage: T4-P4 (bipolar montage)
    - *Starting* reward range: 10-13 Hz: 65% threshold

- 9-12 Hz for over aroused trainees
- 10.5-13.5 Hz for under aroused trainees
    - Inhibit: 2-6 Hz: 35% threshold
    - Inhibit: 22-36 Hz: 25% threshold
    - Number of Sessions: 24
    - Length of session: start at 12 minutes increase by 3 minute increments if positive results are achieved, maximum time is 30 minutes

- Eyes-open training while watching graphics (simple media - not movies) and reinforcement tones
- Subjects who completed study: 22 for Neurofeedback (NF) training and 22 in waitlist group. Members in both groups were selected randomly

Results:

Twenty four sessions of NF produced significant improvements in PTSD symptomatology in multiple traumatized individuals with PTSD who had not responded to at least 6 months of trauma focused psychotherapy, compared to a waitlist control group that continued to receive treatment as usual . . . *In this study 72.7% of the NF sample no longer met criteria for PTSD* . . . Only one participant in the active treatment condition (4%) reported significant side effects, an increase in flashbacks.

The NF subjects also had statistically significant improvements in measures of affect regulation, identity impairment, abandonment concerns, and tension reduction activities. In contrast with most evidence based therapies for PTSD, which focus on processing memories of traumatic events, the target of NF is neural regulation and stabilization. Since lack of self-regulation has been identified as a principal cause of failure of exposure-based treatments, NF may be particularly helpful for traumatized individuals who are too anxious, dissociated or dysregulated to tolerate exposure based treatments . . . Van der Kolk, B et.al., (2016).

Van der Kolk's single channel bipolar montage protocol is of interest because it

- Does not require eyes-closed training which can easily trigger flashbacks
- Can be mounted in minutes (right side of Figure 21.3)
- Requires less clinical finesse than A/T training
- Provides an exact protocol that has statistical weight. While Alpha/Theta training has value in the treatment of trauma it is no longer viewed as the primary treatment for PTSD.

Reports from the field indicate that those being trained with the Van der Kolk protocol achieve stability—even if they were unable to tolerate other forms of EEG Neurofeedback, including Z-score training (with link ears).

9. The last protocol recommendation is the (eyes open) Dual Bipolar Montage (DBM). Based on a clinical review study by the author: see the left side of figure 21.3.

Approximately 10 years ago the author created a limited adult bipolar montage database. One set of montages included T3-Pz and T4-Pz, which seemed to be an ideal montage for PTSD and other disorders related to sense of self because it spans key areas of the default mode network (DMN). Training with the DBM protocol has yielded positive outcomes in dozens of cases of PTSD, some cases of bipolar disorder, several older teens with conduct disorder and a few cases of tinnitus. No unwanted abreactions have been reported. Some clinicians start with 10 minutes of 4-channel Z-score training at T3, Fz, T4, Pz and then end with the 10-minute DBM protocol.

The DBM is a eyes-open live database driven protocol that has been derived from the author's (bipolar montage) clinical database of 20 healthy adults. Do not use on subjects less than 17 years old! It has two types of

Figure 21.3 PTSD Protocols

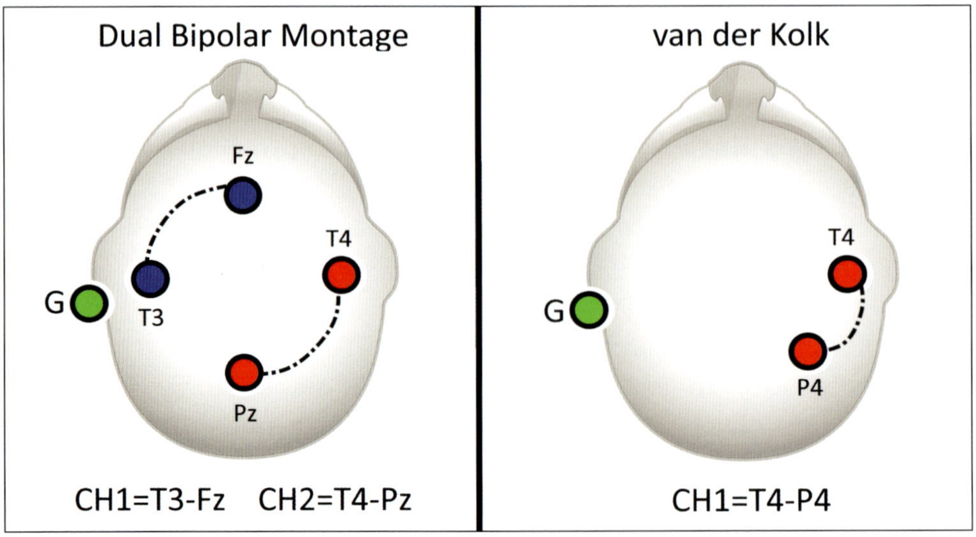

feedback: one tone for increased Alpha synchrony between channels 1 and 2 and a second tone for database training. Each channel has 8 bandwidths for a total of 16 database conditions. The live database threshold is adjusted by a vertical slide thermometer bar (Figure 21.4).

The goal of training is to maintain feedback 50-65% of the time. Recently, the DBM was used with a client diagnosed with bipolar disorder who later said after the standard 10-minute training session:

"I feel very relaxed, my mind is clear; it feels like a positive flow of energy rather than a manic one. That night I slept well and woke up the next morning feeling rested and refreshed."

Over 20 clinics have used this database driven protocol with success. The protocol is definitely ready to be tested with a larger research group.

Figure 21.4. Dual Bipolar Montage for PTSD/DMN

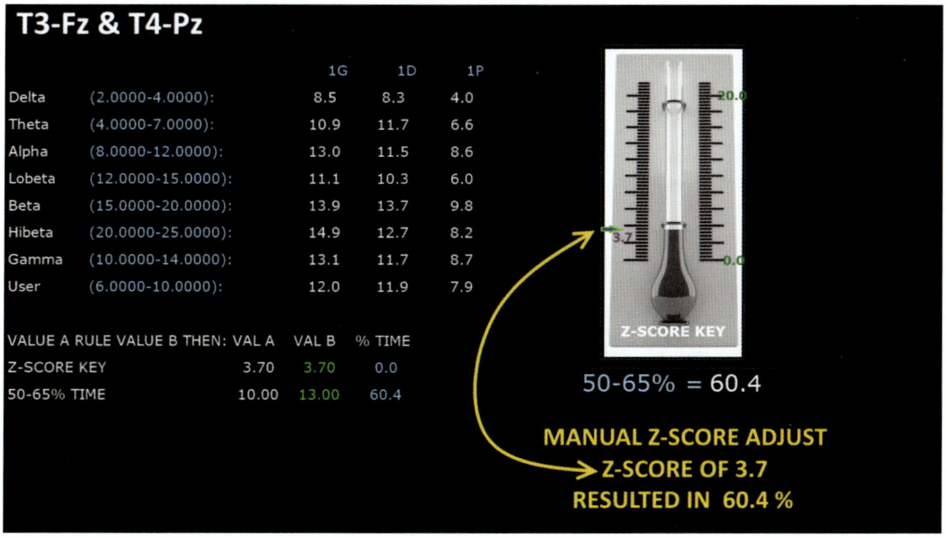

Training screen adapted from BrainAvatar software by BrainMaster Technologies, Inc.

22

Photic Stimulation: Gamma and Cross-Frequency Coupling

BRAIN WAVE ENTRAINMENT (BWE) is induced by photic and audio stimulation. The literature refers to this modality in several other ways, including light and sound (L&S) and audiovisual stimulation (AVS). Photic stimulation entrains synchronous brain wave activity. It is a gateway to gamma training. It serves as an excellent homework assignment, especially for clients who train once per week or who simply cannot afford EEG neurofeedback. It is very helpful with age-related cognitive decline (Budzynski, 1999) and ADHD. Neurofeedback practitioners use BWE to augment training or for slow or nonresponders.

HOW DOES BRAIN WAVE ENTRAINMENT WORK?

Photic stimulation is the process of emitting pulsating light at a specific frequency. The pulses come from light-emitting diodes (LEDs) mounted inside the lenses of darkened eyeglasses. LEDs come in different colors, such as blue and white. Some entrainment systems require users to keep their eyes closed to prevent damage to the retina. The intensity of the pulsating light is adjusted for individual comfort.

Photic stimulation generates repetitive flashes that reach the cortex via the optic nerve. Brain cells respond to visual and auditory stimuli by discharging electrical impulses known as evoked potentials. Visual and auditory evoked potentials can be measured by placing electrodes on the scalp at various locations. How long does it take the visual cortex to respond to a flash of light?

> When the stimulation is repetitive in nature, each stimulus follows the previous one by a short period of time (less than 500 milliseconds) and the successive evoked responses in the brain are found to overlap in time, so that the trailing end of one response is superimposed upon the beginning of the next. . . . In general, a repetitive flash produces an EEG response at the same frequency as the stimulation. (Collura, 2002, p. 49)

Consequently, the repetitive flashes of photic stimulation are programmed to pulsate within frequency ranges that are common to EEG neurofeedback. For example, 10-Hz photic stimulation is in the alpha frequency bandwidth. Alpha bandwidth cannot be entrained from 8 to 10 Hz, but it can be entrained one step at a time (for example start at 8 Hz then increase by 1 Hz increments: 9,10,11,12 Hz). Finer steps are also possible, such as 10.0, 10.1, 10.2, 10.3, and so on. BWE programs may have a series of changing frequencies. The total length of BWE programs varies, but most programs last at least 15 minutes and others go as long as 60 minutes. The combinations are endless. Sophisticated BWE machines can also vary the way the sound is output, which is a study all by itself. Neurofeedback and photic stimulation have much in common. However, operant conditioning terms such as *reward* and *inhibit* do not apply to BWE.

BWE CAUTIONS

Brain wave entrainment poses danger to clients who have had or are at risk for seizure disorders. Ruuskanen-Uoti and Salmi examined a patient with a photoparoxysmal response (seizure) induced by photic stimulation. They came to the following conclusions:

> Intermittent red light has reported to be particularly provocative, although green may be more so. The most common frequencies causing a photoparoxysmal response in photosensitive patients are between 15 and 20 Hz. The prevalence of photosensitive epilepsy is about one in 4,000 children and young adults, lesser in older adults, and higher in females. (1994, p. 181)

Clients who buy, rent, or borrow BWE equipment should have their first experience in the clinician's office and not at home alone. They should be made aware of the dangers. Never use BWE when there is a risk or history of seizure disorder. I have introduced dozens of clients to photic stimulation without a serious incident. However, a few adult clients were too light sensitive for photic stimulation. When one younger (anxious) client became jumpy within the first few seconds of stimulation, entrainment was immediately stopped and no serious incident precipitated.

Brain Wave Entrainment (BWE) or Photic-Stimulation Protocols and Concepts

Contingency Programs

BWE devices are programmed according to frequency and time. For example, a custom program for ADHD can pulse at 10 Hz for 2 minutes, then 18 Hz for 2 minutes, and finally 12 Hz for 2 minutes—the cycle can be repeated over and over again. Why are those three frequencies helpful with ADHD?

David Siever's (2003, 2004) observation and research indicates that photic pulses between 10 and 20 Hz have both a stimulating and an inhibiting effect. For example, 14 Hz pulsing increases 14 Hz while decreasing 7 Hz. The entrainment effect is temporary, but it may provide an essential boost to EEG neurofeedback training. More (SMR) 14 Hz and less (theta) 7 Hz benefits about half of the children with ADHD. Figure 22.1 provides the stimulation to inhibit rule.

Figure 22.1. 14-Hz Pulsing Inhibits 7-Hz EEG (Theta) (2:1 Ratio)

2:1 Ratio from 10-20 Hz
20 Hz pulse inhibits 10 Hz
10 Hz pulse inhibits 5 Hz

Creating photic stimulation programs that are contingent on the cycling of EEG bandwidths augments neurofeedback training. For example, if a client had elevated 7 Hz (in the theta range), then every time 7 Hz or theta went up, it would activate 14-Hz photic stimulation. Hence, the 14-Hz stimulation emission would be contingent on the rise and fall of brain waves, which would make, in this case, photic stimulation an auxiliary part of the operant conditioning cycle (Collura, 2002). In addition to 14 Hz, consider contingent gamma pulsing programs. An effective photic stimulation contingency program emits frequencies in response to EEG rhythmicity; it has the potential of becoming an extension of operant conditioning.

Hemi-Fields and Gamma Photic Stimulation

BWE affects the brain globally; it is not site specific. The regions of the brain that process light or sound are likely the ones that receive the most stimulation. The dorsal and ventral attention networks both tap into the visual cortex, and the dorsal attention network taps into the frontal eye fields. The flashing lights in photic stimulation glasses are organized for independent pulsing because only one frequency can be entrained at any given moment for each eye field. Images presented to the right visual hemi-field are processed in the LH and images presented to the left visual hemi-field are processed in the RH (see Figure 22.2). Photic stimulation glasses are built to pulse in concert with RH and LH visual eye fields or hemi-fields. They have independent programmable right-field and left-field LED lights.

One pulsing protocol that makes use of this phenomenon (shifting from right to left) was originally conceived by Jeffery Tarrant to emulate eye movement desensitization and reprocessing (EMDR) therapy for BrainMaster's low-intensity pulsing electromagnetic field (pEMF). I adapted his program to photic stimulation: the program shifts from left hemi-field to right hemi-field every second. The pulse rate is 40 Hz, a key part of the overall gamma frequency range (28–80 Hz). Most subjects with mTBI and other cognitive deficits report a marked improvement in mental clarity and calmness in 5 to 10 minutes; subjects with no history of cognitive impairment or mTBI report no change. The training screen is shown in Figure 22.3.

Figure 22.2. Left and Right Visual Fields

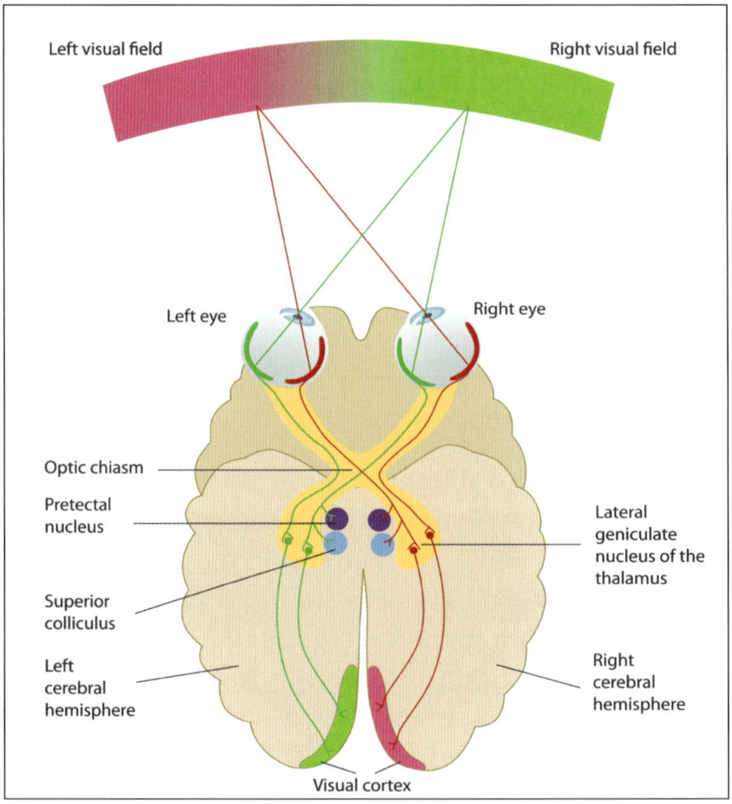

Figure 22.3. Pulsing Gamma Between Left and Right Hemi-fields

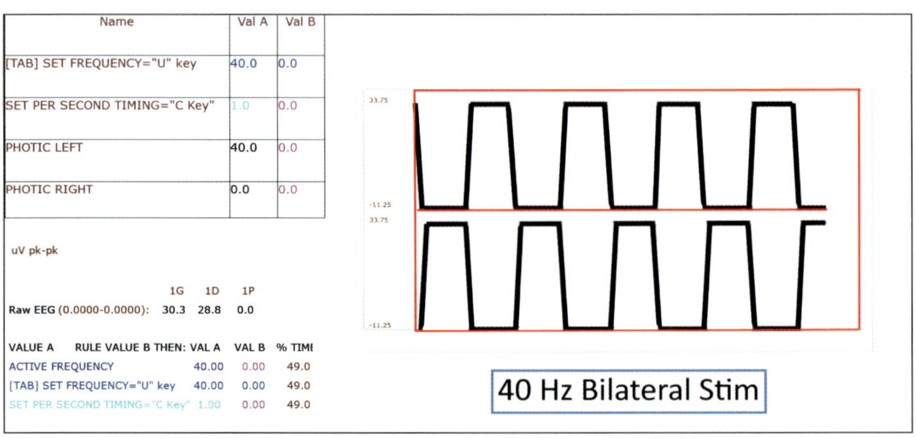

Adapted from BrainAvatar software by BrainMaster Technologies, Inc.

CROSS-FREQUENCY COUPLING

EEG comparisons between two locations within the same frequency range include coherence or asymmetry. EEG frequency comparisons at one location include ratios, such as a theta-to-beta ratio. Other comparisons are possible, including theta-to-gamma cross-frequency coupling (CFC), which is the relationship between the oscillations of gamma and theta when the brain is under task:

> Gamma power in the hippocampus is modulated by the phase of Theta oscillations during working memory retention, and the strength of this cross-frequency coupling predicts individual working memory performance. . . . For instance, a change in cross-frequency coupling could be explained either by a change in the number of gamma cycles per Theta cycle (the duty cycle) or by a change in gamma amplitude with a constant number of gamma cycles per Theta cycle. (Lisman & Jensen, 2013)

Koster and associates (2014) wrote of the importance of the "Theta/ Gamma coupling in the entorhinal–hippocampal system." Other articles have stressed the importance of theta/gamma CFC across brain network information sharing and other brain tasks including learning, computation, memory, short-term and retrieval memory, sensory and visuomotor memory as well as visual perception. It is also possible that alcohol consumption interferes with CFC functioning (see also Perfetti et al., 2011; Zhang, Kendrick, Zhou, Zhan, and Feng, 2007).

Figure 22.4. Cross-Frequency Coupling (Theta to Gamma)

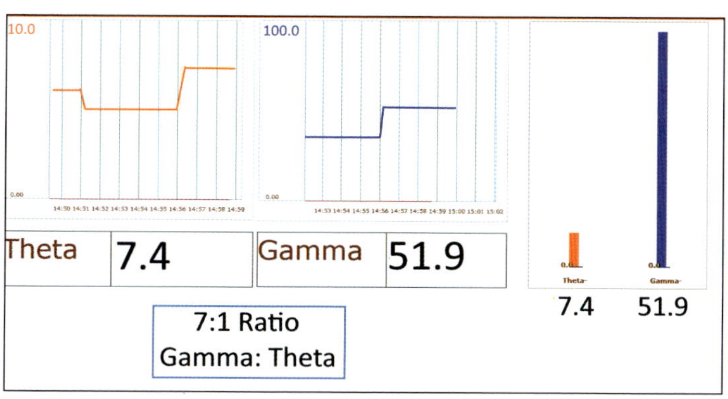

Adapted from BrainAvatar software by BrainMaster Technologies, Inc.

Photic stimulation can be programmed to make use of the known ratio between theta and gamma oscillations: 7:1. That is, for every seven oscillations of gamma there is one oscillation of theta. For example, if theta was pulsed at (left field) 4 Hz, then gamma would be pulsed at (right field) 32 Hz. In the program shown in Figure 22.4 the frequency numbers are randomly generated, but the 7:1 theta/gamma CFC is maintained.

RANDOM FREQUENCY GENERATION WITH PHOTIC STIMULATION

Photic stimulation can also be programmed to generate random frequencies for the purpose of lessening the effect of entrenched brain wave patterns. For example, some clients have diffuse theta or beta that responds slowly to EEG neurofeedback interventions. In effect, the brain has developed a habit that is difficult to break. Random frequency generators can be programmed to change pulsing every few seconds. The following photic stimulation program changes frequency every 5 seconds with upper and lower frequency limit.

The thermometer bars are movable (Figure 22.5). For example, they can be set at 0–50 Hz (wide range), 8–12 Hz (alpha range), 12–16 Hz (SMR range), 15–20 Hz (beta range), 35–45 Hz (gamma range), and so on. Random frequency generation for a short range can serve to stimulate

Figure 22.5. Photic Random Frequency Generator Program

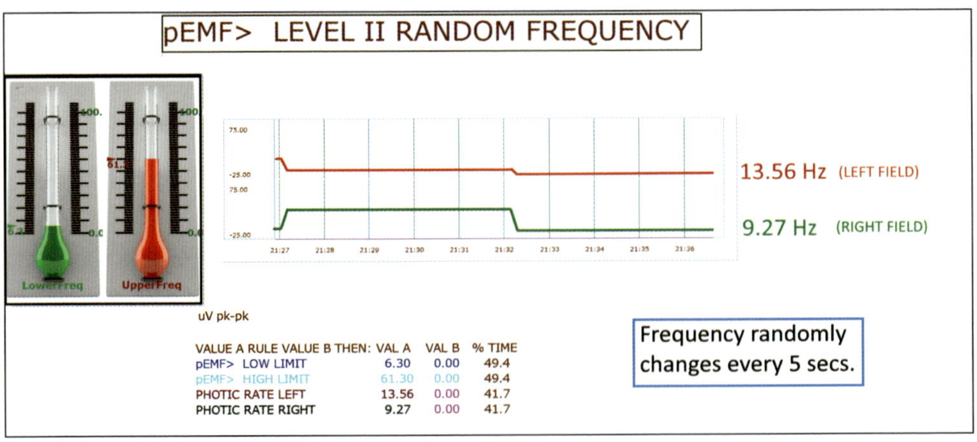

Adapted from BrainAvatar software by BrainMaster Technologies, Inc.

or increase bandwidth power, whereas random frequencies over a wide range serve to break up unwanted, entrenched EEG patterns. Note that the 2:1 rule applies when the stimulation range is 10–20 Hz, which suppresses amplitudes of 5–10 Hz.

TWO CASE STUDIES

The first client was diagnosed with ADHD, and though he improved with neurofeedback training, it had to be cut short because he was off to college. While away, he used a BWE program that cycled between 10, 12, and 18 Hz at 2-minute intervals. He reported that photic stimulation kept his distractibility in check. I encouraged him to drink coffee so that the caffeine could help reduce theta. He maintained a high GPA.

The second client presented with historic childhood family issues. He could not afford a brain map or EEG neurofeedback training and relied heavily on insurance. When counseling started, he freely talked about his family issues from the past, but after a few sessions he was stuck in mundane issues relating to the here and now: psychodynamic psychotherapy had, in effect, stopped. To overcome this problem, I introduced a photic stimulation program that started at beta (16 Hz) then gradually stepped down one Hertz at a time and finally dwelled in theta (4–6 Hz). The program ended by gradually stepping up and returning to 16-Hz beta. After each photic stimulation session, talk therapy resumed; we continued to have talk sessions until another photic stimulation session was needed. The photic stimulation program acted as a modified A/T neurofeedback session.

CONCLUSION

Photic stimulation programs are worth considering because they are likely the least expensive brain-based non-neurofeedback intervention. Most practices can afford this technology for the office and possibly for homework assignments. For information about stand-alone home trainers, go to Mind Alive (https://mindalive.com).

Other pulsing therapies not covered in this edition include:

- Low-intensity pEMF (Demos, 2014)
- VieLight therapy (Naeser, 2014)

Pulsing therapies share the same protocols. But their effect on the EEG is different. For example, photic stimulation is an entrainment therapy, whereas pEMF works somewhat differently. For example, the 2:1 rule does not apply to pEMF—and there are other differences. The same is true of Vielight therapy, which may use the same protocols as photic stimulation but does not necessarily follow the same principles.

23

Hemoencephalography Neurofeedback

THE BRAIN'S BLOOD SUPPLY

Neurofeedback training is most often identified with the electrical activity of the brain. However, the brain's blood supply or regional cerebral blood flow (rCBF) activity is also of great interest because hemoencephalography (HEG) neurofeedback equipment can teach trainees to improve cerebral blood flow in key areas of the brain. In some cases, HEG EEG neurofeedback is more efficient than EEG neurofeedback. Understanding the relationship between rCBF and the EEG is essential.

No brain wave activity occurs unless the brain is supplied with enough oxygen and glucose. Cerebral blood flow carries these needed elements to various brain structures in order to prevent brain damage:

> The adult brain requires 750 milliliters (almost a quart) of oxygenated blood every minute to maintain normal activities. Of the total amount of oxygen delivered to the body tissues by arteries, 20 percent is consumed by the brain alone. Under normal conditions cessation of blood flow to the brain for 5 to 10 seconds is sufficient to cause temporary changes in neuronal activity. Interruption of flow for 5 to 10 minutes can produce irreversible neuronal damage. Delivery of blood to the brain is accomplished by two pairs of arteries. (Diamond, Scheibel, & Elson, 1985)

Figure 23.1. Ischemic and Hemorrhagic Stroke

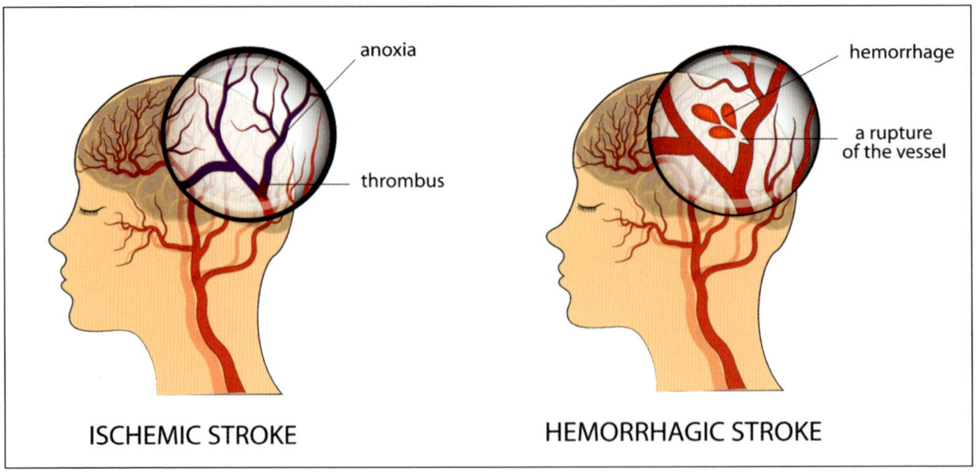

Stroke relates to a disruption of the brain's blood supply. Figure 23.1 shows an ischemic stroke, which happens when the brain suffers from an interrupted supply of oxygen and nutrients; arteries are blocked or blood clots form. A transient ischemic attack (TIA) is a temporary blockage sometimes called a mini stroke. Hemorrhagic stroke refers to a brain aneurysm, or a rupture of a blood vessel.

NUCLEAR IMAGING

On the cortical level, rCBF can be recorded by brain imaging techniques such as PET and single-positron-emission computerized tomography (SPECT). Both PET and SPECT scans measure brain metabolism. Underactive regions of the brain may have an inadequate supply of oxygenated blood leading to poor cognitive functioning. For example, OCD, ADHD and other disorders have an abnormal cerebral metabolic rate.

The working brain requires more oxygenated blood in specified regions related to the task at hand. Improving the quality of blood flow in the brain translates to enhanced mental capacity. Research by Lubar and colleagues showed the relationship among EEG, HEG, and cortical slowing:

> Cerebral blood flow (CBF) measures, like PET and fMRI, support the association of slow-wave EEG with brain deactivation. Cognitive neuroimaging studies using CBF measures have shown increases in cerebral metabolism

> at brain areas responsible for different reading modalities. . . . Increases in cerebral metabolism have been correlated with increases in *fast* frequency EEG amplitude; and decreases in cerebral metabolism have been correlated with increases in *slow* frequency EEG amplitude. (2001, p. 8)

In Figure 23.2 brain regions highlighted in red indicate increased brain metabolism or increased rCBF because those areas of the brain are activated. Areas in blue indicate just the opposite: inactive areas. The normal subject on the left shows DMN activation or a normal metabolic rate. The brain of the Alzheimer's subject on the right shows DMN deactivation or hypo-metabolism. Key areas of the DMN are circled in white.

Figure 23.2. PET Scans and Brain Metabolism

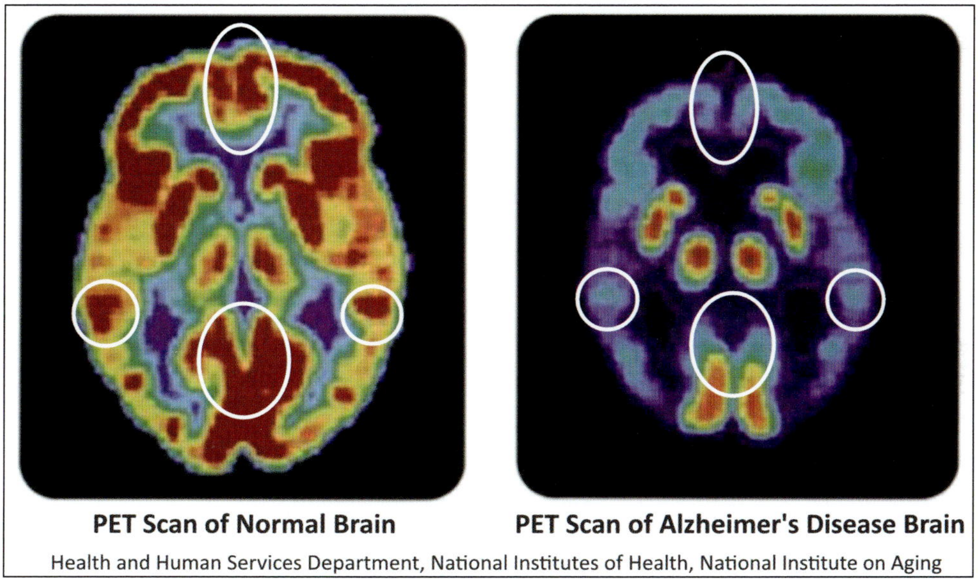

Circled areas reflect Brain Metabolism in DMN

TRAINING WITH HEG

Hemoencephalography does not measure the brain's electrical activity and therefore is mostly immune to muscle (sEMG) and eye movement (EOA) artifacts. It requires no gel or scalp abrading. Infrared sensors can be mounted in less than a minute (Figure 23.3). Before investing in HEG equipment, it is essential to know the difference between passive infrared (PIR) and near infrared (NIR).

Figure 23.3. Two Different HEG Sensor Configurations

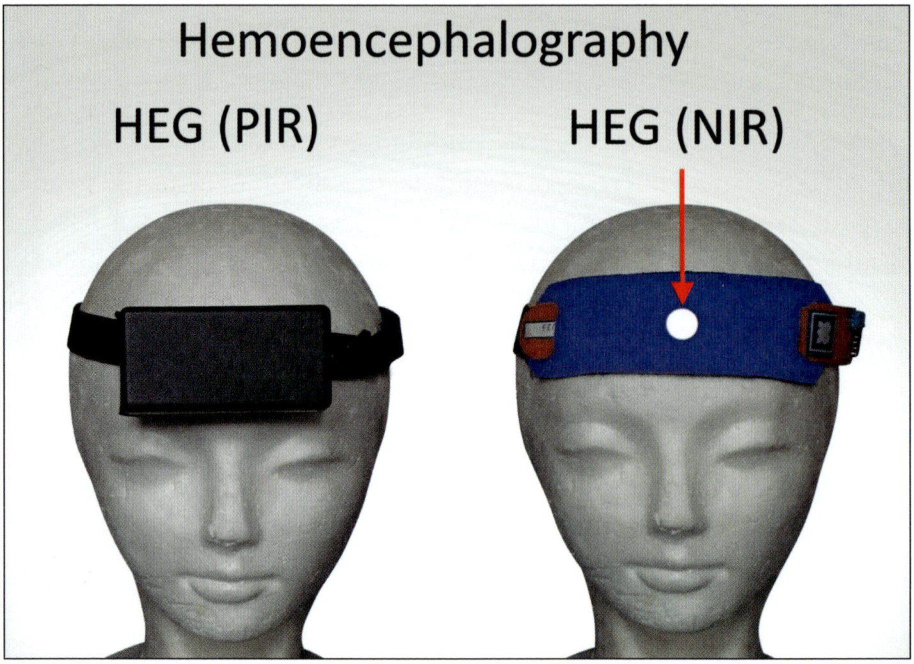

TYPE 1: NEAR-INFRARED HEMOENCEPHALOGRAPHY NEUROFEEDBACK

Neurofeedback includes more than just the electrical activity of the brain. The metabolic rate of the brain can also be measured and trained. When the brain lacks sufficient blood supply to perform a specific task, it is called hypoperfusion. In general, hypoperfusion corresponds to elevated theta-to-beta ratios or slower metabolism. On the other hand, hyperperfusion relates to more beta or faster metabolism. Many mental tasks require adequate oxygenated blood in the prefrontal cortex.

Note that HEG protocols vary. Effective HEG-NIR training is dependent on the following concepts:

1. Train under task: Play Tetris or use an interactive software such as the "robot program" that depicts a robot going up the slide when the metabolic rate increases and down the slide when it decreases. Regardless of the task, the trainee must be mentally engaged.
2. Training with movies will likely result in failure because the trainee may be mesmerized by the movie rather than mentally challenged.

HEG-NIR targets the frontal lobes while watching movies seldom engages frontal lobe activation.

3. Train with pitch-variable sounds that have bonus sounds at peaks in oxygenated blood flow and not with repetitive monotone sounds. One program uses graphics alone and no audible feedback; for this program to work the trainee must stay on task.

Frontal lobe oxygenated blood increases when under task. The most effective sounds provide stunning bonus tones during peaks. The change in alertness happens within minutes; it is not subtle. Trainees with elevated frontal lobe theta get the best results from HEG-NIR (see Figure 23.4).

Figure 23.4. Ideal Ratios for HEG-NIR

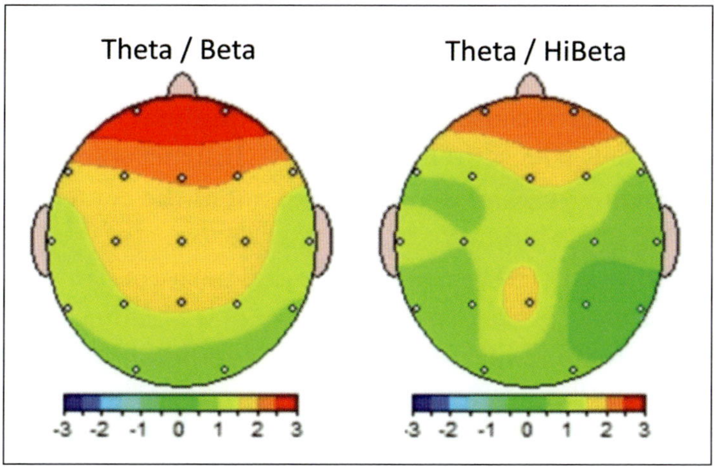

Figure by NeuroGuide Lifespan database

Hemoencephalography neurofeedback has sensors that measure frontal lobe metabolism, information about frontal lobe oxygenated blood, and feedback to the trainee. One definition of this treatment is as follows:

> Hemoencephalography (HEG) is cortical circulatory biofeedback using refracted light tuned to oxygenated hemoglobin, emitted into the skull and detected at the scalp using a photoelectric cell. Red light at 660 nm is used as the probe, with changes in the returning refracted light representing changes in cortical circulation. (Mize, 2004)

The HEG neurofeedback provider focuses training in the prefrontal cortex; the Velcro headband needs to be swiveled. The late Hershel Toomim recommended the following training:

1. 10 minutes at Fpz
2. 10 minutes at Fp2
3. 10 minutes at Fp1

Two sensors are used to measure the quality of the circulating blood in HEG Neurofeedback: one projects the infrared light inward while the other catches the returning rays. In this way, it is possible to determine the color of the blood in the tissue. Red tissue is oxygen rich whereas blue tissue is oxygen depleted. Sensors are mounted on an elastic band that wraps around the head and fastens together with Velcro. No special paste or preparation is needed. I clean the forehead of trainees with alcohol to prevent an oily buildup on my sensors. Most of the training will take place along the forehead, especially at the orbital gyrus, ventral medial cortex, or ventral lateral prefrontal lobes (Fp1, Fp2, Fpz, F7, or F8). The band is moved from one location to another. The hookup is less than 1 minute for each site along the forehead. Minor muscle movements of the forehead, eye blinks, and other facial movements have minimal effects on infrared lights (Toomim & Carmen, 1999, pp. 10–14). Instruct younger trainees to limit facial movements. Note that the white dot in the center of the Velcro headband is the site location for training.

Trainees are instructed to concentrate and perform a task that directly relates to the region of the brain being trained. Trainees may read, do math problems or homework, study, or play a computer game such as solitaire, FreeCell, or Tetris. Training in the LH is enhanced by cognitive challenges. Successful trainees notice that they become better at winning games, reading, or doing math problems. If trainees start to zone out, change the task to prevent boredom.

Poor functioning at frontal pole sites is associated with many disorders, such as schizophrenia, autism, learning disorders, and ADHD. It is important to remember that HEG hypoperfusion relates to EEG hypoactivation (EEG slowing). It happens when specific areas of the brain are lacking in oxygen-rich blood. In EEG slowing, slow waves have amplitudes that are much greater than fast waves. For example, slow-wave dominance is indicated when theta (4–8 Hz) amplitudes are at least 2.5 times greater than beta (13–21 Hz) amplitudes at Fpz (normal theta/beta ratios are higher with children and lower with adults). Training clients with fast-wave dominance is usually contraindicated; it may cause them to feel wired or on edge.

HEG neurofeedback is ideal for the child with facial tics plus anterior EEG slowing. Such a child can train at the frontal poles with eyes open and under task. HEG neurofeedback may require fewer training sessions than EEG neurofeedback to improve executive functioning (Toomim, 2002). Among the symptoms of poor executive functioning in the prefrontal lobes are inattention, poor planning or judgment, slow reaction time, lack of social awareness, and poor impulse control.

HEG neurofeedback training is a simple, straightforward way to manage prefrontal slowing. It is minimally affected by muscle artifact and has already proved itself to be an effective form of neurofeedback. However, when it comes to sites located within the hairy regions of the scalp, problems with specific frequencies, fast-wave dominance, coherence, and asymmetry, as well as the need for deep relaxation, require EEG, not HEG, neurofeedback.

Just one cautionary note: If any client is at risk for cerebral aneurysm or hemorrhaging, consult his or her neurologist before commencing HEG neurotherapy.

The following is a modified list of symptoms that respond to NIR-HEG neurofeedback training. (see Biofeedback Institute of Los Angeles, https://www.biocompresearch.org):

- Attention deficits, cognitive enhancement and faster mental processing
- Hyperactivity, agresssion and impulsivity
- Attachment disorder and developmental delays
- Autism, improved memory
- Brain injury
- OCD

TYPE 2: PASSIVE INFRARED HEMOENCEPHALOGRAPHY NEUROFEEDBACK

A second type of HEG was developed by Jeffrey Carmen (see Stop My Migraine!, https://www.stopmymigraine.com), primarily for migraine headaches. PIR-HEG neurofeedback (not to be confused with NIR-HEG) measures frontal lobe brain activity as it relates to blood flow dynamics. Passive infrared measures brain metabolism heat in the infrared band, and the infrared sensor looks like a coal miner's hat.

Jeffrey Carmen (2004) explains, "Infrared light is not heat. It represents light waves that have been generated from an object. All objects that have temperatures above absolute zero generate infrared light. The intensity and frequency of the IR output represent a calculable variable from which assumptions can be made about the thermal output of the object from which the IR light is emitted. PIR-HEG training teaches prefrontal lobe brain efficiency and regulation." Carmen also said the following:

> When the PIR assembly was placed at Fpz and the training process was directed towards increasing prefrontal cortical activity, the effects were direct and positive on both migraine prophylaxis and actual abortion of migraine headaches. This effect on migraine activity may have more to do with training control over the inhibitory effects of the prefrontal cortex than training direct vascular control. (Carmen, 2004)

Applications for HEG-PIR:

- Migraines (primary application)
- Depression
- ADHD

One last reminder: effective HEG-NIR and HEG-PIR neurofeedback training requires specialized software that is in harmony with the principles set forth by the late Hershel Toomim (for theta reduction) and Jeffrey Carmen (for migraines).

Other protocols for migraines:

- Migraines with auras may be rooted in the occipital lobes (visual cortex). Z-score training that includes the visual network makes sense if there are elevated Z-scores (power or coherence) at O1, O2, T5, T6, P3, P4, and Pz. (Also pay special attention to C3, C4, F3, and F4 because they are associated with saccadic eye movements.) This approach is qEEG-guided; that is, the brain map must be consulted.
- Inhibit elevated alpha variability (see Chapter 18).
- Weak alpha combined with strong beta presentations with migraine may respond to C3-C4 or P3-P4 bipolar montage with three thresholds: one reward (8–11 Hz) and two inhibits (20–32 Hz and 4–8 Hz). Weak alpha and strong beta are often easy to see in the raw EEG.
- The last protocol was developed by Jonathan E. Walker (2011).
    - All qEEG results indicated an excess of high-frequency beta activ-

ity (21-30 Hz) in 1-4 cortical areas. Forty-six . . . selected neurofeedback training . . . Neurofeedback protocols consisted of reducing 21-30 Hz activity and increasing 10 Hz activity (5 sessions for each affected site). All the patients were classified as migraine without aura. *For the neurofeedback group the majority (54%) experienced complete cessation of their migraines,* and many others (39%) experienced a reduction in migraine frequency of greater than 50%. Four percent experienced a decrease in headache frequency of < 50%. Only one patient did not experience a reduction in headache frequency.

- Protocol review: Inhibit 21-30 Hz and reward 10 Hz (author comment: consider 8-11 Hz): Locations "most commonly Parietal, Central or Frontal Areas (P3, P4, Pz & C3, C4, Cz & F7, F8, F3, F4, Fz). Thirty minutes of training was typical.
- Note: *qEEG guided treatment* targeted from 1-4 different Int'l 10-20 locations. It was for aura-free migraine suffers. 54% complete recovery, 39 % significant improvement.
- Author comment: Walker utilized monopolar montages whereas I have been using bipolar. But the same frequency range was inhibited based on a QEEG map. Also, in addition to HiBeta (20-32 Hz) please consider Alpha 2 (10-12 Hz) suppression as needed.

Resolution of migraines is enhanced by the holistic approach. Check for food allergies and intolerance; encourage the client to make the needed adjustments. Diaphragmatic breathing or HRV training is essential (see Chapter 24).

Part VI
EEG Neurofeedback in Clinical Practice

Chapters

24

Treating the Whole Person

NEUROFEEDBACK IS AN EFFECTIVE TREATMENT, especially when the whole person is taken into account. Our clients exist in an environment that provides their daily needs and at times reinforces or even creates clinical problems. The evaluation process, at its best, determines the likely source of symptoms or distress. Brain maps may not reveal or reflect what's behind the problem. Before acquiring qEEG data, it is necessary to find out how the client's lifestyle or habits may be contributing to symptoms or how family dynamics may be reinforcing a behavior problem at school. It is no secret that Western society is plagued with metabolic issues such as diabetes, hypertension, and obesity. Pollution, pesticides, junk food, and heavy metal toxins have taken their toll. While the scope of practice for most mental health practitioners does not include functional medicine, it does include the practice of spreading common sense.

There is a difference between diagnosing and treating organic issues and making our clients aware of the connection between lifestyle and clinical symptoms. The following subheadings are a brief review of environmental, family, and organic problems that are implicated in mental health issues.

ORGANIC PROBLEMS

Candidiasis *(Candida albicans)*

A male carpenter in his 30s presenting with mental fog and disorganization was forced to reduce his work schedule to 15 hours per week. At first glance it looked like ADHD. But the lifestyle interview helped him appreciate that he was at risk for candidiasis or yeast overgrowth. Several factors led to this conclusion: overuse of prescribed antibiotics, mental fog, fatigue, thrush, athlete's foot, and a diet that was high in white flour products and carbohydrates. To make matters worse, antibiotic treatments were never followed up by probiotic treatments. While I screen for candida, I am not authorized to diagnose or treat it. However, I do suggest books to read or a referral to a doctor of functional medicine (or any licensed practitioner who is trained in functional medicine). Needless to say, the man and his wife read about candidiasis and made immediate changes to their diet. The result: after 5 weeks, the issues of mental fog and disorganization were greatly reduced. He resumed his normal work schedule and regained his ability to calculate staircase rises. Neurofeedback was not started because the brain was not the underlying cause of the symptom (Severance et al., 2016; Johns Hopkins Medicine, 2016).

Migraine, ADHD, and Allergies

There are several effective ways for the migraine sufferer to enhance neurofeedback training. Research from the Menninger clinic revealed the value of skin temperature biofeedback in the treatment of migraines (Drury, 1979). Diaphragmatic breathing is a technique that promotes skin temperature (ST) biofeedback, which is also called hand warming.

Children diagnosed with ADHD may have allergies that worsen symptoms; checking them out will improve overall treatment outcomes. Tests that may identify food allergies or intolerances include the radioallergosorbent test, ImmunoCAP test, and the ELISA test. One simple technique that can be done at home is Dr. Coca's pulse test: check your resting pulse rate, eat a food in question, and check again after 20 minutes. If your pulse goes up 15–20 points, then that food is suspect. Many online sources and YouTube videos explain in detail this simple and free technique. Research supports the importance of allergy testing and ST training for migraines and ADHD (Mitchell et al., 2011; Stokes & Lappin, 2010; Suwan, Akaramethathip, & Noipayak, 2011; Coca, 1994).

Thyroid

Thyroid malfunction, Hashimoto's thyroiditis, may present as a mental health issue with symptoms of depression, mood swings, fatigue, and memory issues. It is an autoimmune disease that may include physical problems of hair loss, dry hair and skin, weight gain, constipation, and cold sensitivity. A complete thyroid panel test is needed; otherwise Hashimoto's may be missed. Nutritional supplements are also part of the treatment. Consult the award-winning website Hypothyroid Mom (https://hypothyroidmom.com/; see Liontiris & Mazokopakis, 2017; An et al., 2016).

Lyme Disease

I am a former Lyme sufferer: my Lyme was diagnosed 10 days after the classic bull's-eye signature appeared on my shoulder and was identified at a conventional medical clinic. I was given the standard treatment. After 28 days of antibiotics, the fever and muscle aches were gone, as well as most of the fatigue, but I still had some mental fog and partial zone-outs. A local alternative health clinic prescribed a one-month supply of Japanese knotweed and cat's claw herbal remedy. My mental fog, fatigue, and momentary zone-outs lessened, but it still felt like my mental sharpness was not fully restored. After further research, I added Boswellia Extract, N-A-G Jarrow Formulas (N-acetyl glucosamine), New Chapter Zyflamend (tumeric and ginger with other herbs), coenzyme Q10, and vitamin D3 plus resveratrol, and ate wild-caught fish as a source of omega 3. I am my old self again. Note that research on using N-acetyl glucosamine for Lyme is not conclusive.

Dr. Kim Lewis leads the Lyme disease research team at Northeastern University. Singer (2016) reported on his efforts to find effective Lyme treatments:

> So it's no surprise that when Northeastern researchers reported last May how the bacterium that causes the disease evades antibiotics, suggesting new treatments, the media and the general public took notice . . .
>
> Doxycycline may be standard first-line treatment for Lyme, but, says

> Lewis, it doesn't even kill *B. burgdorferi,* it just suppresses its growth, leaving the rest of the work to the immune system. "We simply asked the question: 'Is it possible to combine existing antibiotics to treat not only chronic Lyme but any stage of Lyme if the diagnosis is unambiguous? (News@ Northeastern)

Doxycycline is the standard of care, but many medical researchers know it is not enough; conventional medical clinics do not have the complete solution at this time. Therefore additional treatments are needed including supplements and/or brain based treatments such as photic stimulation and pulsed Electromagnetic Field therapy (pEMF).

The Importance of Fats and Oils in the Diet

Recent studies at Johns Hopkins University have shown the importance of including dietary fats when treating subjects at risk for seizure disorder who have not responded to traditional drug management therapy (Freeman, 2013). For example, spike and wave activity was observed with one child who was raised on a low-fat diet. The family physician recommended introducing fats into the diet. Unfortunately, some health conscious parents equate a healthy diet with a low-fat diet. Before training children or adults at risk for seizure disorder make inquiries concerning fat intake.

Cognitive Decline

When seniors come for help with age-related cognitive decline, it is essential to review their lifestyle, which may be exacerbating poor cerebral functioning. It is not enough to do EEG neurofeedback training with photic stimulation (Budzynski, 1996); lifestyle changes are needed. Consider the following program, which was successful with a small group of Alzheimer patients (Wheeler, 2014):

- Eliminating all simple carbohydrates, gluten, and processed food from their diet, and eating more vegetables, fruits, and nonfarmed fish
- Meditating twice a day and beginning yoga to reduce stress
- Sleeping 7–8 hours per night (up from 4 to 5)

- Taking melatonin, methylcobalamin, vitamin D3, fish oil, and coenzyme Q10 each day
- Optimizing oral hygiene using an electric flosser and electric toothbrush
- Reinstating hormone replacement therapy, which had previously been discontinued
- Fasting for a minimum of 12 hours between dinner and breakfast, and for a minimum of 3 hours between dinner and bedtime
- Exercising for a minimum of 30 minutes, 4–6 days per week

To recap, when presented with issues of age-related cognitive decline, dietary and lifestyle changes are an integral part of successful outcomes. Make sure those changes are in place before beginning treatment. Exercise brings needed oxygen to memory-making regions of the brain, including the hippocampal region.

It is essential to be familiar with complementary and alternative medicine; workshops are available. Please do not conclude that alternative health is simply a matter of taking more supplements. Experts in functional medicine start with a customized test battery, thereafter a program of dietary and lifestyle changes will begin. Locate health care professionals who understand and have learned the practice of functional medicine (see American Board of Functional Medicine, https://www.dabfm.org; and Institute for Functional Medicine, https://www.ifm.org/find-a-practitioner). If possible, determine how they are rated by consumers.

FAMILY PROBLEMS

A teenage boy came to my office with his mother, who reported behavioral problems in school. The clinical interview revealed the following about the family dynamics:

- Teenager was not assigned chores and did not have to clean his room.
- The family did not sit together for at least one meal per day.
- No bedtime hour was enforced, and he stayed up very late.
- Family did not engage in group activities or go to religious services.
- Family discussions were few and far between.
- No family vacations were planned.
- The father had little or no time for his son.

- The teenager's diet seemed to revolve around soda, pizza, and macaroni and cheese.
- Entitlement was an issue.

The parents wanted their son's behavior problems to go away. But, in fact, they were the ones in need of therapy. Neurofeedback could not fix this family; therefore, it was never started. Family therapy or coaching was a necessary first step. However, the father had no interest in spending time with his son. His main interest was golf.

One of the core principles of child training is mastery before pleasure. For example, no media or social networking until homework is complete. Neurofeedback does not create family structure; parents create structure, plan family activities, and assign chores. It is evidence of love for their offspring and prepares children for the real world. As EEG Neurofeedback providers, we cannot sidestep family dynamics, especially since many of our trainees are children.

Note that you cannot force teenagers to train for their own good. They must see the need for change and be willing to put forth the effort. A conduct disorder is very difficult to treat because success depends on family cooperation and diligent follow through, which is often lacking. On the other hand, do not confuse conduct disorder with hyperactivity or impulsivity related to ADHD, both of which are very treatable but still require a structured family system. Make sure family structure is in place before commencing brain wave treatment.

HOMEWORK ASSIGNMENTS

Neurofeedback "is orchestrated by the therapist and played out by the client" (Demos, 2005). Trainees can become partners to a successful treatment program. The practitioner's job is to show the trainee how to continue the training process at home: homework.

Breathing Therapies and HRV

The brain needs oxygen and glucose to survive; impress upon potential trainees the need to do effective breath work, a key to successful biofeedback treatment. Diaphragmatic breathing is taught in conjunction with most other biofeedback modalities. In most cases, it can be mastered without equipment. Breath work is a fundamental homework assignment for those who suffer from anxiety, tension, and stress.

Normal ventilation depends upon the movement of the diaphragm and intercostal muscles; the lungs have no muscle system. The diaphragm is like two double sheets of muscles that extend up toward the chest beneath the lungs. It contracts during inspiration and rests during expiration. Normal breath rates are 12–15 breaths per minute (Schwartz, 1995). However, training lower breath rates (4–8 breaths per minute) will likely lower levels of tension and anxiety.

Clients with anxiety often have higher breath rates and forced inspiration that result in an exaggerated expansion of the upper chest (thoracic cavity). Rapid breathing (tachypnea) can lead to hyperventilation, which causes carbon dioxide to be exhaled faster than it can be produced. Alveolar hyperventilation causes an excessive loss of carbon dioxide from the blood, which contributes to respiratory alkalosis, or increased blood pH (Marieb, 1995).

Blood alkalosis causes arteries to constrict and inhibits the flow of blood to the brain. Consequently, the brain receives a reduced supply of oxygen. Dizziness and symptoms of anxiety emerge. The heart begins to pound; panic takes over. It feels like suffocation and, in a desperate attempt to survive, inhalation becomes deeper, which causes a further carbon dioxide imbalance and more anxiety. Breathing into a paper bag increases carbon dioxide. In some cases it can limit the symptoms of a panic attack.

I demonstrate proper breathing to almost all of my new clients, including children. Train yourself to do diaphragmatic breathing before you train someone else. Here's how: Put on a top that shows your profile without being uncomfortably tight. Get a watch with a second hand. Count the number of complete breaths you take (that is, both inhale and exhale) in 1 minute. The optimum rate is 4 to 8 breaths per minute while relaxed. Breath rates of 15 to 25 are too fast. Next, observe the way your lungs fill with air: stand sideways in front of a mirror and take a deep breath. What moved? Your chest, your abdomen, or a combination of the two? If your chest moved the most, then you are a reverse breather—sometimes known as a shallow breather. There are two factors in correct breathing: breath rate and method of breathing. Learning to slow down your breath rate goes hand in hand with abdominal, or diaphragmatic, breathing. Fill the abdomen first and foremost, rather than the chest cavity. If you have no medical restrictions, do the following:

- Exhale while pushing in your stomach with both hands.
- Try to talk. If you can still talk, then air remains in your lungs.
- Evacuate the air until you can no longer talk.
- Inhale. You should observe that only your stomach is moving.
- Your chest should not be moving.
- Repeat.

If you are having trouble mastering this skill, get a partner. Ask your partner to apply light pressure to your back and stomach simultaneously (like playing the accordion) when you are exhaling. Release the hand pressure when inhaling. Repeat out loud: "Belly in, belly out." Have your partner work with you until you have mastered the technique. Sometimes it's helpful to lie on your back and put a large book on your stomach. Watch the book go up and down while your chest remains still. Once this skill has been mastered, work on adjusting your breath rate to 4–8 breaths per minute. Learning and teaching this technique is an excellent way to begin a treatment program. Some anxious clients resist the idea of taking time off to relax during the day. They want to practice at bedtime, when they are already feeling more relaxed. Practicing diaphragmatic breathing for 15 minutes each day during the daylight hours, however, works best. There are home training devices that promote corrective breathing: RESPeRATE (FDA-cleared device for hypertension) and Heart Rate Variability (HeartMath). "Inner Balance" is an HRV training app for android and iphones.

The variability between heartbeats is measured by HRV (this definition does not do justice to the complexities of HRV measurement and training). HRV training is an integral part of many practices. Abundant research supports its application to an array of disorders. Also, there are several cell phone apps that teach slow breathing: 5.5 breaths per minute for clinical treatment. The connection between breathing and HRV has been studied (Lin, Tai, & Fan, 2014; Gevirtz, 2013).

Simplified Skin Temperature Training (Thermal Biofeedback)

Skin temperature (ST) training, or the practice of hand warming, improves circulation in the extremities, which often reflects a decrease in stress essential for anxious clients; it is augmented by diaphragmatic breathing. It is also used as a treatment for hypertension, migraines, and Raynaud's disease. The temperature of our skin relates to the alternating activities of the sympathetic and parasympathetic nervous systems. It is an indirect measurement of peripheral vasoconstriction (the constriction of blood vessels). Skin temperature changes when the body undergoes a stress response. This causes blood to flow toward key areas of the body, such as the brain, spinal cord, and muscles, and away from the extremities such as the hands and feet. The sympathetic nervous system sends out signals in order to contract smooth muscles of blood vessels, resulting in a decrease of ST. The stress response is reversed when the peripheral nervous system (PNS) sends out signals to cause vascular dilation. Consequently, hand or fingertip temperature may be as low as 80°F (27°C) or less. All this happens unconsciously in the autonomic nervous system (ANS). ST training promotes conscious control of the ANS (Criswell, 1995, pp. 112–123).

Many practitioners employ ST training because it is the fastest and least expensive way to introduce a new client to neuroregulation skills. I instruct clients as follows:

- Purchase a digital thermometer with finger probe (see Figure 24.1).
- Tape the probe to the midsection of the middle finger from either hand (palms up).
- Begin diaphragmatic breathing at 5.5 breaths per minute to activate the PNS.
- Raise your finger temperature to 93–95°F and hold it for 15–20 minutes.
- Practice ST training daily until it becomes a natural way to destress.

Figure 24.1. Thermal Biofeedback With Thermometer

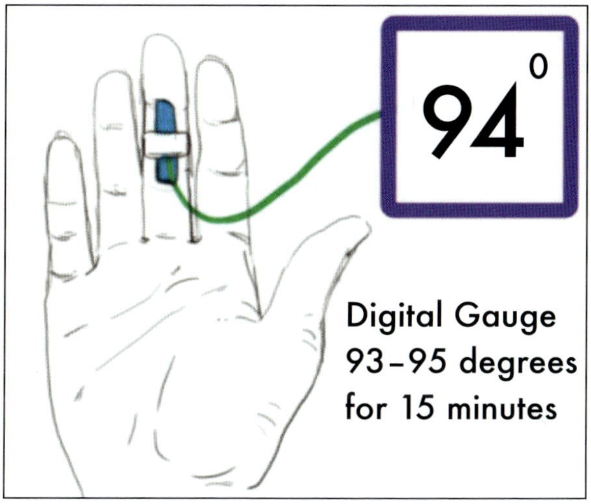

Learning to do ST training involves the process of letting go. What does letting go mean? It means replacing worry thoughts or ruminations with self-supporting thoughts or relaxing thoughts. Sometimes the temperature decreases because trainees are trying to force relaxation or diaphragmatic breathing while they are trying to let go. I tell them that this is a time for feeling, not thinking. I also say, "Imagine you are getting a massage. What would you be thinking about? Your bills? The argument you had with your spouse? Problems with the family? No, rather, it would be time out from your problems."

Fortunately, the majority of adults and children are capable of learning this technique. However, not everyone is a good candidate for this treatment; some have very warm hands to begin with and will benefit more from other relaxation techniques. It may be necessary to refer the highly anxious client to an alternative health care provider for bodywork.

During EEG neurofeedback, one of the goals is for the trainee to remain alert without becoming tense. It's important to be engaged with the process without developing performance anxiety or zoning out. A state of passive awareness is needed. ST training teaches passive awareness and is especially useful for clients who suffer from anxiety. It prepares the client for neurotherapy. It is used in the first stage of deep states (EEG neurofeedback) training.

Hand temperature can be checked quickly without equipment. Even an anxious person usually has a warm cheek. Put your fingers on your cheek to find out if they are cold or warm. In this way, changes in hand temperature can be readily detected. Before assigning someone to do ST training, master the skill yourself. With practice, you will be able to raise your hand temperature in the presence of clients.

Homework Assignments by Symptom

Each week before training begins, homework assignments can be briefly reviewed. Written exercises can be reviewed in less than 10 minutes. Do not give the impression that homework is optional. Note that many psychotherapists have difficulty setting boundaries and creating structure when setting up training programs. Remember, when treatment fails, the practitioner or the clinic will be blamed even when clients fails to do their homework. In some cases, it's best to forgo treatment until the client takes responsibility for his or her part of the treatment plan. The following are suggested assignments for various presenting disorders:

Anxiety Disorders

- HRV home training, teach diaphragmatic breathing.
- Limit or eliminate caffeine consumption; emphasize need for daily relaxation exercises.
- Cognitive Behavior Therapy (CBT) exercises that include assertiveness training with very brief written assignments that can be reviewed before training session begins.

OCD

OCD clients ought to do exercises in *Brain Lock* (Schwartz & Beyette, 1996) if they have compulsions. This book is not meant for clients struggling mainly with obsessions.

PTSD

- Prevent relaxation-induced anxiety (RIA). Before doing EEG Neurofeedback for relaxation it is essential that clients learn to relax the body, with breathing or other exercises in order to prevent a sharp backlash that can occur when relaxation comes during training (Kerson, 2002).
- Bibliotherapy can help clients to adopt coping skills. The following books are suggested:
    - A.L. & Kim L. Gratz K.L. (2011) *The Dialectical Behavior Therapy Skills Workbook for Anxiety: Breaking Free from Worry, Panic, PTSD, and Other Anxiety Symptoms* (A New Harbinger Self-Help Workbook).
    - Boon, S., Steele, K., van der Hart, O. (2011) *Coping with Trauma-Related Dissociation: Skills Training for Patients and Therapists* (Norton Series on Interpersonal Neurobiology) 1st Edition.

Depression, Dysthymia, Unipolar Depression

- Aerobic exercise for endorphins, resistance or strength training (Gordon, 2018).

- Implement dietary changes when candidiasis is present or suspected.
- Socialize to the cognitive model to limit automatic negative thoughts (catastrophizing) and assign book or workbook with cognitive exercises to promote healthy thinking.
- Do not assign homework if the client has been diagnosed with major depression with psychotic symptoms as it may be overwhelming.

ADHD, Learning Disorders

- Children with ADHD often need daily aerobic exercises and a nutritious diet while omitting junk food.
- Check for food allergies: Dr. Coca's pulse test.
- Parents must create structure in the home with a set time for homework, bedtime, meal time, etc.
- Books for parents to read:
    - *The Survival Guide for Kids With ADHD* (Taylor, 2014).
    - *Teaching Life Skills to Children and Teens With ADHD: A Guide for Parents and Counselors* (Monastra, 2015).
- When school is out for the summer, make sure the child is being tutored in math or reading for learning disabilities.
- Assign activities with same-sex parent (or a big brother) for conduct disorder.
- If adult with learning disorder, assign skills training workbook.

Hormone Imbalance Bibliotherapy, books for clients to read:

- On the importance of natural progesterone cream (paraben free):
    - *What Your Doctor May Not Tell You About(TM): Menopause: The Breakthrough Book on Natural Progesterone* (Lee, 2004).
    - *The Estrogen Alternative: Natural Hormone Therapy with Botanical Progesterone (*Martin, 1998).
- On the importance of Vitex (herb) for reproductive disorders and premenstrual syndrome:
    - *Vitex agnus-castus extracts for female reproductive disorders: a systematic review of clinical trials.* (van Die, 2013)

Migraines, Headaches, Pain

- Check for allergies (Dr. Coca's pulse test).
- Check for hormone imbalance (Lee and Hopkins, 2004).
- Supplements: coenzyme Q10, malic acid, B12, magnesium.
- Possibly engage the services of an MD board certified in functional medicine to guide alternative therapy treatment.
- Train diaphragmatic breathing with thermal biofeedback (hand warming).

Age-Related Cognitive Decline

- Brain-enrichment mental exercises including the card game Concentration.
- Aerobic exercises to improve oxygen flow to brain.
- Increase intake of Omega 3 EFAs (Alaskan wild-caught salmon)

Schizophrenia (and Other Disorders)

- Clients should be introduced to the question "how do I know that's true?" Thereafter, written homework should help them question their belief system. Beliefs should be backed up by evidence.
- Eliminating gluten from diet often limits paranoid thinking.

Subjective Trainee Progress Sheet

Learning through EEG neurofeedback training is gradual. When clients train once per week, they are subject to mini relapses before their next appointment until biofeedback learning has been solidified. When clients or parents return for the next training session, they are prone to forget how they felt or how their child behaved in the first few days following training. We want them to keep track, day by day. They need to understand that learning at first will not last; they need to expect it and not be surprised by setbacks. Clients need to keep a daily tracking sheet.

Chart 24.1 can easily be modified to fit the child or client in training. It also serves as a reminder of current progress compared to earlier weeks. Each trainee should be handed a Symptom Tracking Chart: it takes just a few minutes to create the chart with the help of the trainee or the parents or guardians.

Chart 24.1: Symptom Tracking Chart: Daily Ratings

Symptoms [Rate 1-10]	Mon	Tues	Weds	Thur	Fri	Sat	Sun
Week of xx / xx / 20xx							
Completes homework							
Helps with household chores							
Gets along with siblings							
Wakes up in timely fashion							
Listens to instructions							
Less fidgety							
Waits for turn to speak							
Puts away toys							
Brings home school assignments							
Refrains from fights at school							
Brings home books for homework							

Photic Stimulation

There is much we can do to engage our trainees at home. Also, consider adding audiovisual entrainment training as appropriate. When lending this equipment to trainees, charge a reasonable weekly fee, as well as obtaining a security deposit to cover damage or loss. Have trainees do their first audiovisual entrainment session in the office, if possible with electrodes still on after training. In that way, the EEG can be reviewed for spike and wave formations.

25

Evaluation: Contraindications, Readministering Baseline Tests, and Termination

CONTRAINDICATIONS

Not every individual or family is ready for EEG neurofeedback training. It may be contraindicated due to the nature of the disorder or the limits of the treatment facility. During the initial interview (before qEEG analysis), it is essential to continue to assess clients' readiness to undergo the training process. They must have the time and the finances to complete the training process. Also, it is essential to determine if the clients have Axis II disorders. If the initial interview has revealed a pattern of interpersonal problems, biofeedback training may be contraindicated. Dialectical behavior therapy may be the first place to start treatment (Linehan, 1993). Neurofeedback training will not magically undo the covert nature of transference, countertransference, splitting, or distrust (Demos, 1995). Neither will the risk of suicidality, self-harm, or explosive anger melt away with biofeedback training. The cycle of overvaluation and devaluation may find its way into the training arena. The best time to start EEG biofeedback may be after the behavior therapy program has been completed.

Cautionary remarks may also be made about clients with dissociative identity disorder, who are prone to switch from one alter personality to another. Scores of 25% or greater on the Dissociative Experiences

Scale (DES; Putnam, 1989) are often found in survivors of psychological trauma. Correcting EEG abnormalities may not be the best place to start. The experienced practitioner who has received appropriate training in both dynamic psychotherapy and EEG neurofeedback may well be in a position to treat dissociative disorders (consider van der Kolk's (2016) protocol for PTSD).

What about clients with borderline personality disorder who have been in psychotherapy treatment with you for a number of years? Likely, the transference is so potent for them that only a minority of your clients will be able to make the transition from psychotherapy to biofeedback. Also, it may be unwise to switch if the client is doing well with talk therapy. Sometimes the old adage applies: "Don't switch horses in midstream." On the other hand, some may well respond to site-specific training or deep states training (A/T training). Others may do well training in the DMN, especially the precuneus.

Behavior problems cannot be simply labeled ADHD until the problem is seen in context. Biofeedback will not fix a family problem; it is not a silver bullet. In order for the treatment to be successful, the family must be ready to participate in the program. Building family structure includes changes in nutrition, better control over TV and video game usage, curfews, boundary setting, improved sleep patterns, and sometimes family therapy. Many families need coaching to make these changes. It may take several sessions before parents or guardians can combine their efforts to make it work. Families who are unable to make crucial changes may not be ready to participate in a training program. The following issues usually need to be resolved before commencing training: child custody problems, family arguments and screaming, an impending divorce, inadequate family structure, excessive strife associated with a newly combined family, bullying at school, daily interpersonal struggles, and so on. The life of our adult and child clients must have a measure of stability.

Preadolescent children often accept the authority of adults. In just a few short developmental years, however, that acceptance may fade. Adolescents who view EEG biofeedback as mind control are unlikely candidates for training. Parents who view training as a way to stop conduct disorder will likely be disappointed. Teenagers who succeed in training are most likely motivated from within. They have parents who are a steady source of support. Teenagers who fail in training have one or more of the following symptoms: sleep deprivation, poor lifestyle habits, poor choice of associates, permissive parenting, lack of attention from one or both parents, or a pattern of defiant or criminal activity. You cannot force teenagers to train for their own good. They must see the need for change and be willing to put forth the effort. On the other hand, do not confuse conduct disorder with hyperactivity, impulsivity, and developmental delays. When communicating with parents, help them to understand the limitations of EEG neurofeedback. Make sure they have come to you with realistic goals in mind.

Neurofeedback training may be contraindicated for those with severe learning disorders, psychotic behaviors, or mental deficits. The appropriate candidate must be able to learn a new skill in a relatively healthy and supportive environment. If you are a new provider, some problems will be over your head. Consult with your supervisor (mentor) and jointly determine if you are ready to take on a new challenge.

At the close of your initial interview, consider the following questions: Do I feel capable of working with this client? Is it possible to set a few simple goals? Are there too many presenting problems? Does the client expect me to fix his or her life? Is this client truly motivated for training and willing to make lifestyle changes? Is he or she both willing and able to come to my office once, twice, or three times per week? Does this case require a more experienced practitioner? Would supervision help? And finally, is there evidence that EEG neurofeedback can really help such a person (Hammond, 2001)? Invite the client to review Hammond's *Comprehensive Neurofeedback Bibliography* online (International Society for Neurofeedback and Research, https://www.isnr.org). There are many situations that could rule out operant conditioning training; the sooner this is determined, the better. It's better for the reputation of the clinical practice because it will reduce treatment failures, and it's better for the prospective trainees because they will waste neither time nor money in their search for wellness.

CAUTIONS

Interpersonal Cautions

Some individuals are not ready for operant conditioning training, and it is clearly not in the best interest of either the client or the clinician to move forward with treatment. In some cases certain types of treatment are contraindicated. Forewarned is forearmed, as the saying goes. Consider the following contraindications:

- The client wishes to have a peer relationship with the clinician. He or she makes neurofeedback recommendations and wishes to engage in scientific discussions.
- The client has just begun a new medication or has had electroshock therapy and wants to try neurofeedback immediately. The client also wants you to invest time in exploring other interventions.
- The client has been to other neurofeedback clinics and now believes that you are the only one who can offer help—even though he or she just met you (possible symptom of a severe personality disorder).
- Client has no intention of doing homework and believes that neurofeedback should fix the problem, or, in the case of a teenager, stays up all night and eats junk food.
- The client makes demands and applies pressure that makes the staff nervous.
- The prospective client wants an extended free phone call consultation at no charge.

Intervention Cautions

- On the one hand, practicing qEEG data acquisition on friends and family carries little or no risk. On the other hand, avoid doing neurofeedback training experiments with family or friends, which can easily backfire. See the next bullet point for more information.
- Relaxation-induced anxiety (Kerson, 2002) comes when the trainee is not ready for the sudden relaxation response that comes with neurofeedback training. If the trainee is a survivor of trauma, RIA can lead to decompensation. Training with eyes closed exacerbates the backlash that is experienced. Never do relaxation training with anyone with a history of trauma, panic, or wide mood swings. On the other hand, if a survivor of trauma (PTSD) has been prepared, it may go well. Preparation can include one to two weeks of successful HRV training or diaphragmatic breathing. Afterward, when EEG neurofeedback treatment starts, train with eyes open with Z-scores or other less arousing interventions.
- Another type of backlash comes when training children or adults who have been diagnosed with an autistic spectrum disorder or Asperger's syndrome. This time clients need preparation for an

emotional backlash. Training on the posterior RH can trigger an emotional response. If the trainee is not prepared, treatment may be terminated. Train in both hemispheres at first to limit an emotional backlash.

- Avoid doing alpha/theta (AT) training when there is a risk for seizure or if spike-and-wave morphology is observed in the raw EEG. Margaret Ayers was known to suppress theta with clients at risk for seizure. But rewarding theta (e.g., AT training) may trigger a seizure.
- Avoid rewarding (amplitude/power training) alpha or theta in the frontal lobes. Be very cautious about rewarding alpha in the left hemisphere (with the possible exception of O1). Never reward delta anywhere. If delta is weak, then resolve the issue safely with Z-score training.
- If you are new to EEG neurofeedback, do not train children with conduct disorder or oppositional defiant disorder. Training cannot overcome dysfunctional family dynamics.
- Do not train clients with PTSD until coping skills are mastered.
- If the prescribing physician frequently changes medication type and dosage, it will likely sabotage training. Once a new medication has been started, it takes 3–6 weeks to become fully active. If EEG neurofeedback is started immediately, the results are questionable. What is causing changes for the better or worse? Is it the medication? Is it the training? Or is it a combination of the two?
- Never train an artifact: An entire training session can be in vain if muscle tension or eye movements are skewing the EEG. Z-score training targets can shift from normalizing real EEG component Z-scores to artifact reduction. Excessive artifacts often have the highest power Z-scores, and sEMG often lowers Z-score coherence—be watchful of electrodes near the temporomandibular region (T3, T4, F7, and F8). The raw EEG must be reviewed before training begins. Note that some artifact is normal—perfection is not possible.
- Never train unless the impedance is acceptable. Weak connections result in electrode pop and sometimes reduced amplitudes. Sometimes the problem stems from a bad electrode.
- Never leave children in a room alone to train. Their performance improves with the presence of an adult. Also make sure they are not eating or chewing gum.

- Any type of cell phone activation can compromise a session. Set out the rules in the evaluation session; do not wait for it to happen.
- Consult with the client's neurologist before beginning any brain-based treatment plan with someone who is at risk for a brain aneurism or has had a serious brain injury or EEG abnormality.
- Prevent iatrogenesis or problems created by single-region training. While consulting on a specific case, I observed the baseline brain map and compared it to the current brain map. Initially there were elevated posterior SDs. After 20 training sessions, posterior SDs were much closer to the mean, but anterior SDs were elevated. Lesson learned: after 10 or more sessions of single-region training, consider widening out. For example, train the four-channel Z-score box (F3, F4, P3, P4) for at least 10 minutes for each session.

EVALUATION: HELPING THE CLIENT UNDERSTAND HOW NEUROFEEDBACK WORKS

Prospective trainees need to have a general understanding of operant conditioning training. Neuroplasticity means that the brain can change and EEG neurofeedback or instrument-guided learning can help them to make the needed changes. The following is a simple explanation.

Brain waves rise and fall in rhythmic and arrhythmic patterns. EEG neurofeedback thresholds are set to reinforce the wave at just the right time in the natural cycle. For example, if a beep sounds every time your pattern of brain waves moves into an alert state, then focusing is enhanced. This concept can be demonstrated as follows: I hold my left arm out as if it were a limbo bar while I move my right hand in a waveform pattern. I say out loud, "Beep, beep, beep" as long as my right hand remains below the limbo bar. I stop saying "beep" when it rises above the bar. As soon as my hand goes below the bar again, the beeping resumes. I repeat this action a few times. The brain is a marvelous organ; it pairs the beeping with the change in brain wave patterns. The brain knows you want to hear the beep, so the brain cooperates and works with the training—it's as simple as that. This explanation may work for some, whereas for others it's simpler to say, "Healthy brain wave patterns are reinforced by biofeedback training—frequent training will likely increase your ability to stay focused without equipment."

Neurofeedback training can be compared to other training modalities. For example, physical fitness experts recommend that you exercise at least two or three times per week. It's also important to eat the right foods and to keep reasonably active, even on nontraining days. Training may also be compared to learning to play a musical instrument. The student practices several times per week to prepare for the next lesson. Discipline is an integral part of most training programs. In the same way, EEG neurofeedback training is often done two to three times per week. Trainees keep their brain active on nontraining days with activities such as reading, studying, or relaxation exercises. Adequate sleep and good nutrition also boost training results. Children with ADHD may need more structure in the home. Neurofeedback training can become an adjunct to supervision in the home, but never a replacement.

Neurofeedback training is all about learning. Each person's rate of learning is unique; some respond more quickly than others. The total number of sessions may vary anywhere from 15 to 60, or more, depending on the severity of the disorder.

BASELINE MEASUREMENTS: BEST PRACTICE, STANDARD OF CARE

Neurofeedback is a brain-based scientific treatment. Baseline tests are periodically readministered to ensure progress. For example, I was asked to consult on a case of depression. The clinician said that his trainee, a female, was not responding to training. I asked for the baseline Beck Depression Inventory (BDI) score. He replied, "I didn't take a baseline measurement." To which I replied, "Then how will we know if the treatment is working?"

Needless to say, the first step in this case would be to administer the BDI. The standard of care in EEG neurofeedback is a program that includes baseline measurements that can be readministered to confirm progress or lack thereof.

Symptoms that cannot be tracked likely should not be trained. Each new client is assessed with at least one clinical test as well as the baseline qEEG. What if a child cannot sit for a qEEG, or what if the artifact is so great that qEEG data cannot be processed? Then acquire EEG data from the box (F3, F4, P3, P4), or just C3 and C4 with Z-scores to establish a baseline and to differentiate between overaroused and underaroused subjects. How is this done? Set up for standard Z-score training at box sites or C3 and C4, then run the program without sound for 2–5 minutes. It can be replayed or reviewed afterward. What if no specific diagnosis can be assigned to the young child? Then create a symptom checklist with ratings from 1 to 10 that can be tracked from week to week. Always be ready to support the rationale for initiating and continuing treatment.

For example, the child or adolescent with Asperger's syndrome may have difficulty with cognitive flexibility, interpersonal connections, and normal emotional displays. These characteristics can be transformed into a daily behavioral checklist:

1. How many times did he make eye contact?
2. When giving hugs, how stiff was his body, on a scale of 1 to 10?
3. How many times did he mention the name of a friend?
4. How much time was spent in repetitive activities?
5. How many times did he offer to help without being asked?
6. How much interest does he have regarding other family members, on a scale of 1 to 10?
7. How many times did you observe him in nail-biting behavior?

Customized questionnaires can be typed out, copied, and filled out each week. They can be used to chart progress in a way that is similar to baseline comparisons.

THE RATIONALE TO CONTINUE TRAINING

My daughter, who was living on the West Coast, told her work supervisor that I had just completed the first edition of *Getting Started With Neurofeedback*. Her supervisor retorted, "Well, neurofeedback does not work. My son with ADHD had 35 sessions, and there is *no* change." Wow! That means after training for 10–15 sessions, training was continued, even though there was no rationale to continue. Likely, the standard of care lacked continuous performance tests (CPTs) and weekly symptom checklists. Was my daughter's supervisor given the impression that training sometimes takes many sessions to kick in? On the contrary, progress in operant conditioning is realized incrementally.

The following statement is taken from the Biofeedback Certification International Alliance (BCIA) *Professional Standards and Ethical Principles of Biofeedback* (A4): "BCIA professionals should only continue biofeedback services as long as their clients benefit from training." (www.bcia.org)

In summary, take baseline measurements, then readminister them after 10–15 sessions. If there is no rationale to continue treatment, terminate and refer to another, more qualified, practitioner or at the very least obtain corrective supervision. While clients are not abandoned, neither should they be given (expensive) false hopes.

Richard Soutar's (2004) five-session rule is also very helpful. That is, if there is no progress after five sessions, then consider changing treatment strategy. Einstein (or maybe someone else) said it best: Insanity is doing the same thing over and over again and expecting different results.

ESTABLISHING THE CLINICAL BASELINE

Computerized Assessment Tests and Continuous Performance Tests

Some children have been given a battery of tests by the school or private psychologists. It's no wonder that many parents balk at the idea of more testing. I try to explain that one of the purposes of testing is to establish a clinical baseline that we can use to monitor progress. If parents complain, saying that the school has already tested their child, I counter that the school will not reevaluate after every 10 or 15 training sessions. Furthermore, they rarely administer CPTs that provide precise measurements of attention and reaction time.

The most affordable CPT is the Test of Variables of Attention (T.O.V.A.) by the TOVA Company. Other CPTs include the Intermediate Visual Auditory (IVA) by BrainTrain and Conners CPT by MHS Assessments. Continuous performance tests report on errors of omission (distractibility) and errors of commission (impulsivity). Results are rendered in histograms. Pre- and posttraining results are easy to compare. The following is a review of IVA.

The IVA is a continuous performance test that helps identify problems of attention, hyperactivity, and impulsivity. Written in a Microsoft Windows format, it is a tool to evaluate executive functioning. The test taker is instructed to click the mouse every time the number 1 is seen on the computer screen or heard through the speakers. Reaction time, accuracy, and consistency are all important components of the test. The IVA identifies most children and adults who have trouble sustaining attention. Some individuals with ADHD, however, achieve an average to above average score. Distraction and inattention in life are not the same as test taking. Test taking can be stimulating and challenging. Coping skills can be powerful enough to last for 15–20 minutes of testing. The entire computerized test including warm-up and cool-down cycles takes about 20 minutes. The results are ready for printing and reviewing with the client immediately after the test ends. Scores are evaluated according to a normative database. After seeing the standard IVA printed report, I often hear a parent say something like this: "How could a 15-minute test describe my child so well?" Often that same caring parent had already spent large sums of money on psychological testing.

Note: I don't show poor results to children. If a child is on stimulant medication, there are different test-taking strategies. Some clinicians obtain all IVA baselines when the daily dose of medication has not been taken. Other clinicians, however, use the on-medication IVA score as a goal. Neurofeedback training continues until off-medication IVA scores equal on-medication scores.

Administer Paper Test Instruments with Computerized Objective Tests:

Paper test instruments are easy to readminister. In my practice, new adult clients fill out the BDI and Burns Anxiety Inventory along with standard paperwork and releases before starting treatment. In addition to paper tests, there are computer and online administered tests:

- ADHD: ADHD Test, Psych Central (https://psychcentral.com/quizzes/adhd-quiz)
- Beck Depression Inventory (BDI, Psychological Corporation)
- Burns Anxiety Inventory (Burns, 1999)
- Dissociative Experiences Scale (Bernstein & Putnam, 1986) (PTSD and trauma)
- Personality inventories (e.g., Millon, MMPI)
- SCL-90-R (Pearson Education) (dyslexia, mania, eating disorder, and addiction scales)
- Continuous performance test: TOVA, IVA, or Conners CPT (ADHD, hyperactivity, impulsivity)
- The MicroCog or PsyTest Assessment Management System (memory, and brain function, suitable for mTBI)
- Comprehensive test batteries: CNS Vital Signs (http://www.cnsvitalsigns.com) is an online source that keeps track of client records and offers numerous test battery options. Separate CPT software tests are still needed.

FAMILY AND PERSONAL HISTORY

In addition to paper instruments (symptom evaluations) and computer-generated tests, a psychosocial interview or assessment can be valuable. There are many online sources if you need a template.

Some of the key topics I ask about during the initial interview include the following:

Prescribed medications
Over-the-counter medications
Alcohol consumption
Head injuries (ask several times)
Seizure disorder
Stroke
Learning disorders
Developmental disorders
Memory deficits
Attention deficits
Cognitive functioning
Hearing problems (headphones needed during training?)
Dissociative disorders, PTSD, Axis II disorders
Severe psychiatric or neurological disorders
Bipolar disorder
Mood or anxiety disorders
Divorce
Custody issues
Moving (how often, etc.)
Education goals or accomplishments
Employment issues
Upcoming nodal events in family or personal life
SAD (seasonal affective disorder)—mood drops in winter?

Functional or Dysfunctional Family

Describe a typical day in family.
What daily and weekly chores have been assigned to children?
Do issues of entitlement, obedience, or respect come up each day?
Do the parents or guardians understand they are in charge of the family, or have they abdicated that role?

Does the family eat at least one meal together each day?
For teens, have you discussed career goals?
For tweens, have you discussed sexuality?
For children, have you prepared them to say no to sexual abuse?
Do your children have trouble-making friends, or are they unduly influenced by friends?
What provisions are there for family vacations?
What is the typical bedtime hour?
Is arising in the morning for school difficult? Is breakfast eaten?
Troubling reports from school system, or are teacher relationships problematic?
Describe interaction with siblings.
Homework completion issues: Is mastery before pleasure the family standard? For example, after supper, does homework completion take priority over electronic game playing or social networking?
Attention from same-sex parent? Activities with same-sex parent or guardian?
How much time spent each day on cell phone or video games?
Does the family have a game night?
If conduct problems: what sort of ongoing religious or ethical training is in place?

Questions for Practitioners

Does the family reinforce the problem?
Are family structural changes needed before biofeedback can commence?
Is the child a symptom of dysfunctional family dynamics?
Does the family want us to fix their child?
Have the parents set unreasonable scholastic goals?
Are they aware that plumbers often make more money than university-trained professionals? Is the school program challenging enough for the bright student? Is the problem inattention or simply boredom because the school curriculum is targeting the average student (e.g., Thomas Edison was labeled "addled" by teachers)?

TERMINATION

Termination is discussed during the evaluation phase. Questions to be asked include: How will you know when you are better? What changes to your child's behavior and attention do you expect when treatment is completed? The prospective trainee also needs to know that no clinic on earth has a 100% success rate. That is why baseline cognitive and behavioral measurements are readministered; they are the touchstone that limits fiscal loss for the client and provides evidence for the efficacy of interventions. The trainee should be disappointed, not shocked, if treatment fails. And the practitioner, if possible, should have referral suggestions.

INSURANCE COMPANIES

In the past, only a few health insurance companies or policies covered neurofeedback even though there are billing codes for training (90901, 90875, and 90876) and for EEG data acquisition and processing (95816, 95957, and 99090). Policy coverage and insurance company standards dictate reimbursement. Client progress notes are always a must with insurance companies. Providing and charging for noncovered services may lead to ejection from an insurance panel. Imagine an insurance company demanding the return of all reimbursement money. The largest for-profit neurofeedback clinics in the United States are cash only.

26

Objective Treatment Plans and Comparison Reports

OBJECTIVE DATA ARE THE BACKBONE of treatment plans. Brain maps highlight specific neurological regions corresponding to the presenting symptoms. Computer-driven tests or paper test instruments confirm qEEG results. Treatment plans require a great deal of forethought and exploration; they are the net result of testing, interviewing, and EEG data acquisition and processing. They give clients concrete evidence that there is a plan of action. No treatment plan can take into account all the variables that will arise during the training process. Certain decisions are made while the client is training. Those decisions are seldom outside the parameters set forth in a good treatment plan. Treatment goals govern the flow of each training session.

Subjective data are also of great value; they enhance the quality of each training session. Subjective units of distress (SUDS) or scaling (from 1 to 10) are an integral part of every training session, before and after (e.g., "On a scale of 1 to 10, how would you rate your anxiety, with 10 being high and 1 being low?"). Scores do not change overall treatment goals, but they might help practitioners tweak or make alterations in starting protocols. Communication during the treatment process is augmented by subjective data.

Treatment plans are designed to clarify therapeutic goals and mutual responsibilities. Jewel database and report-writing software was designed to generate a basic client report and treatment plan in minutes. After qEEG data are acquired and edited, BrainAvatar or BrainAnalysis software processes the EEG, edits, and then outputs an XML file that can be read into Jewel. Figure 26.1 shows how BrainMaster processes EDF files with BrainAnalysis. (EDF, European Data Format, is a standard for EEG recordings used in commercial equipment; it was developed by European medical engineers. It is one of several formats used to define EEG data.)

Figure 26.1 shows BrainAnalysis at work after the EDF file has been edited. Upon clicking Run Analysis, an XML file is generated and loaded into the client file. The XML file contains the results of the edited data selections.

Figure 26.2 shows Jewel being opened and the test subject's edited data being loaded. With one click, the data are processed with Jewel's clinical database as well as qEEG-Pro's Z-scores for observation and comparison. Users who possess the BrainDx database can process results through Jewel. Three separate database results can be viewed in Jewel.

Figure 26.1. Analyzing an Edited EDF File

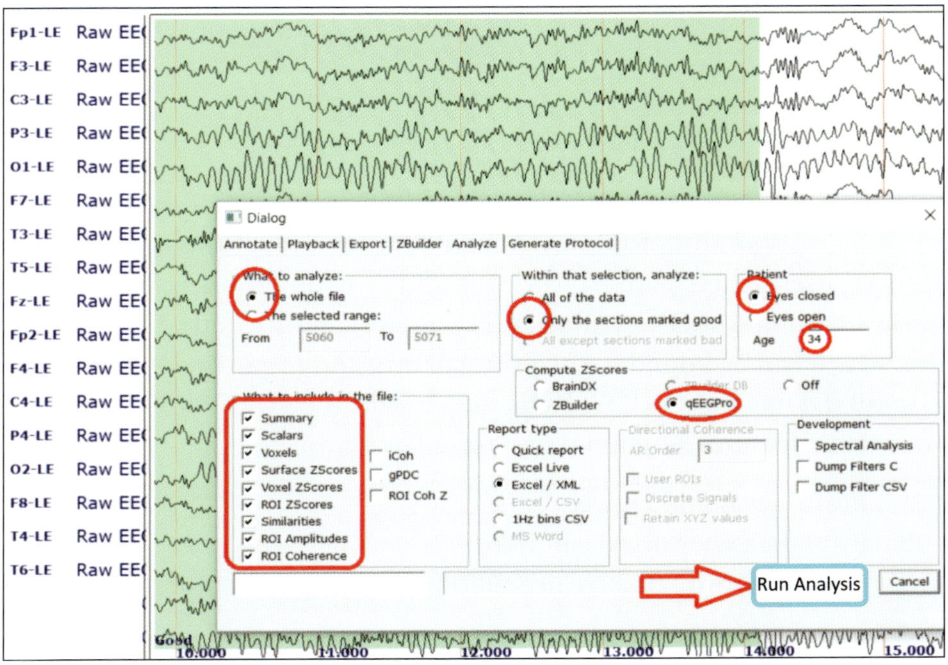

Adapted from BrainAvatar software by BrainMaster Technologies, Inc.

Figure 26.2. Open Jewel: Read in Analyzed File

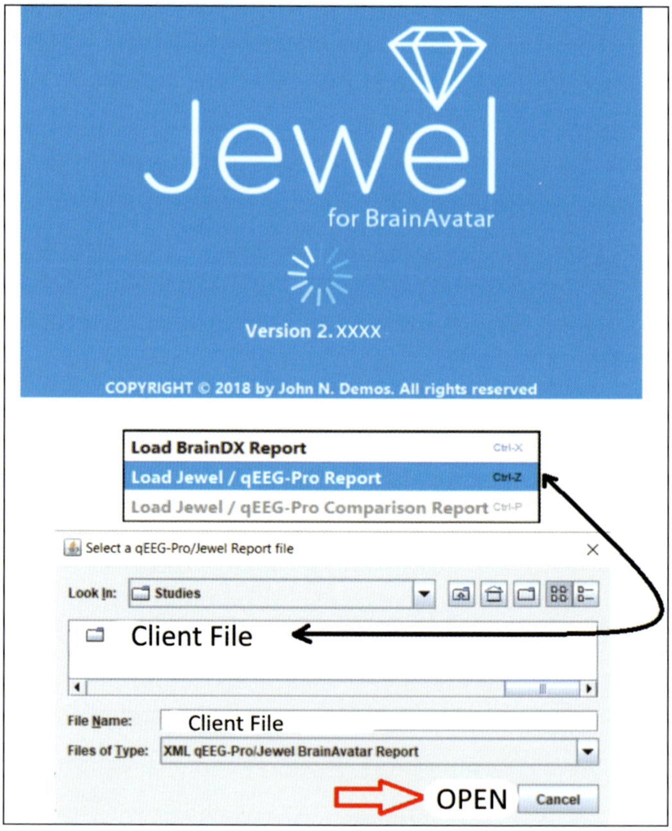

Adapted from Jewel database software

Figure 26.3 shows Jewel database sLORETA images. A symptom is chosen and corresponding ROIs are selected for training. When generating a protocol, users can isolate bandwidths and sync up numbered Brodmann areas with named sLORETA ROIs. The newest feature is sLORETA coherence, which can be added to the protocol mix and organized by symptoms.

Jewel database sLORETA ROIs match selected symptoms. Figure 26.4 shows three features of Jewel database software:

1. Brain maps and charts
2. Protocol generator dashboard
3. The beginning of a treatment plan based on symptoms

Some clients find a printed treatment plan evidence of professionalism. Most medical clinics provide a report with test results and recommen-

Figure 26.3. sLORETA Training Heads Output by Jewel

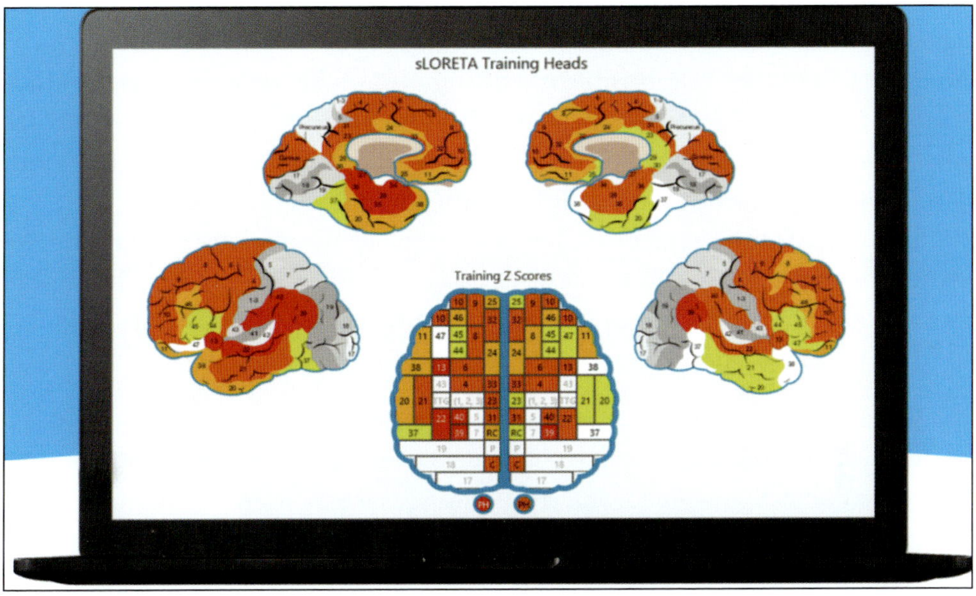

Adapted from Jewel database software

Figure 26.4. Generating a Client Report and Protocols

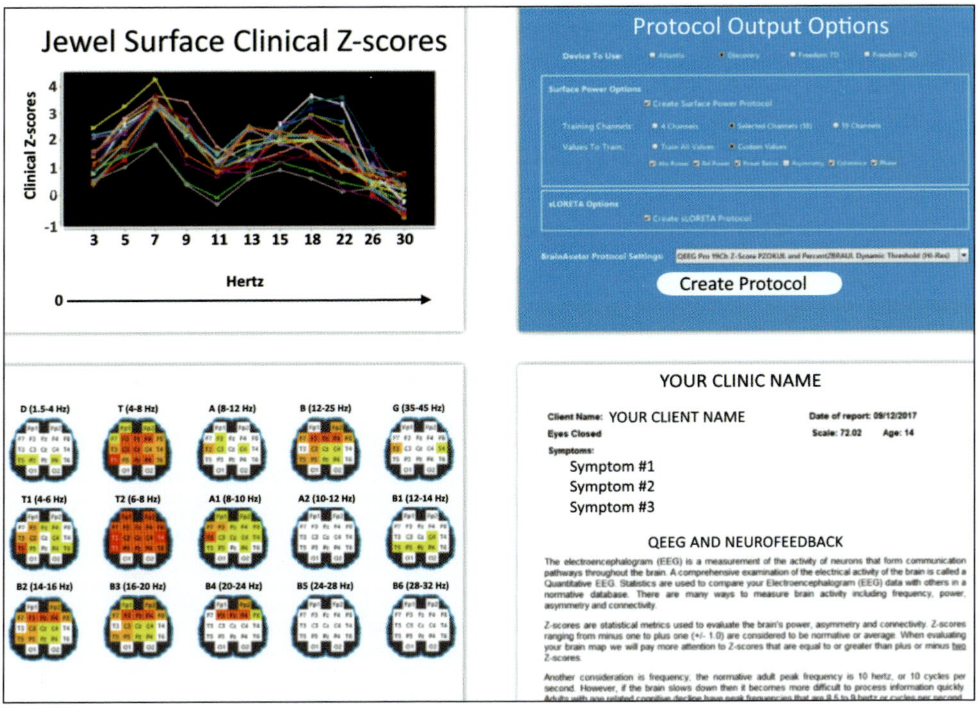

Adapted from Jewel report-writing software

dations. Treatment plans need to be discussed thoroughly with clients. They can be viewed as mini contracts between two parties that are in full agreement. Training twice per week should result in measurable gains in 5 weeks. Clients are responsible for filling out weekly progress sheets; clinicians are responsible for readministering baseline tests after 10–15 training sessions. Together the rationale to continue treatment will be fortified. The motivated trainee will want to reach well-defined goals.

Figure 26.5 shows part of a Jewel written summary, which includes the symptom description and homework assignment for the client. The report can be edited. Additional information can be typed or pasted in.

The Jewel treatment plan ends with the following words:

> We invite you to share in our training program. Neurofeedback training will be customized to fit your particular needs. Participating in home relaxation assignments or life style changes such as exercise and dietary changes will enhance your success. Please use "Weekly Symptom Tracker" forms to measure progress. After 10–12 sessions are completed we will consider the benefits of continued training.

Figure 26.5. Sample Portion of Client Report

WRITTEN SUMMARY:

Introduction

Our clinic has completed its evaluation. Goals have been set-forth and unwanted symptoms have been identified. Additionally, cortical functions have been evaluated with statistics and brain Maps have been created. They assist in the evaluation of the following 3 components:

1. Cortical areas of interest that are of statistical significance
2. Cortical functions in those same areas of interest
3. Client symptoms that are reflected in those same areas of interest

Neurofeedback training will take place in corresponding areas of interest. A further explanation of symptoms or client goals is listed below:

- **ADHD [EEG Slowing]**

- Definition: Attention deficit hyperactivity disorder or attention deficit disorder may include symptoms such as hyperactivity, inattention, distractibility, disorganization and over focus. If impulse control is the primary issue, please select INHIBITION [IMPULSE CONTROL].
- Neurology: Frontal lobes and the Cingulate gyrus govern attention.
- Neurofeedback interventions: Our QEEG analysis has identified at least one brain wave pattern known to accompany ADHD. We often find elevated Theta or Alpha with reduced Beta in the executive circuit of the brain. When anxiety or agitation is present there may be excessive Beta in the central region of the brain. Neurofeedback training can target executive networks and reduce symptoms. This may include Z-score training, HEG neurofeedback or simple suppression treatments.
- Additional treatments & homework: Even loving homes need assistance to create a highly structured household for a child with ADHD. While children need parental management, adults may benefit from life coaching. Dietary changes have shown to improve outcomes when food allergies are a factor and aerobic exercise is very helpful; lifestyle changes to build structure.

Adapted from Jewel report-writing software

PRE- AND POSTTRAINING BRAIN MAP COMPARISONS DEMONSTRATE PROGRESS

In addition to readministering baseline clinical tests, EEG results should also be reviewed. The original (baseline) qEEG can be compared to current measures. Original and posttraining qEEG acquisitions are done at the same time of day. Figure 26.6 is an example of an automated pre/post-training brain map report output by Jewel database software. Ten training sessions demonstrate progress for this trainee.

Comparing the before-and-after brain maps with Jewel software demonstrates learning, because the posttraining Z-scores are closer to the mean of the database than the baseline Z-scores. Pre- and post- clinical and qEEG baseline measures demonstrate progress, provide a rationale, and motivate clients to continue training until treatment goals are met.

Figure 26.6 . Jewel Comparison (Before and After Training)

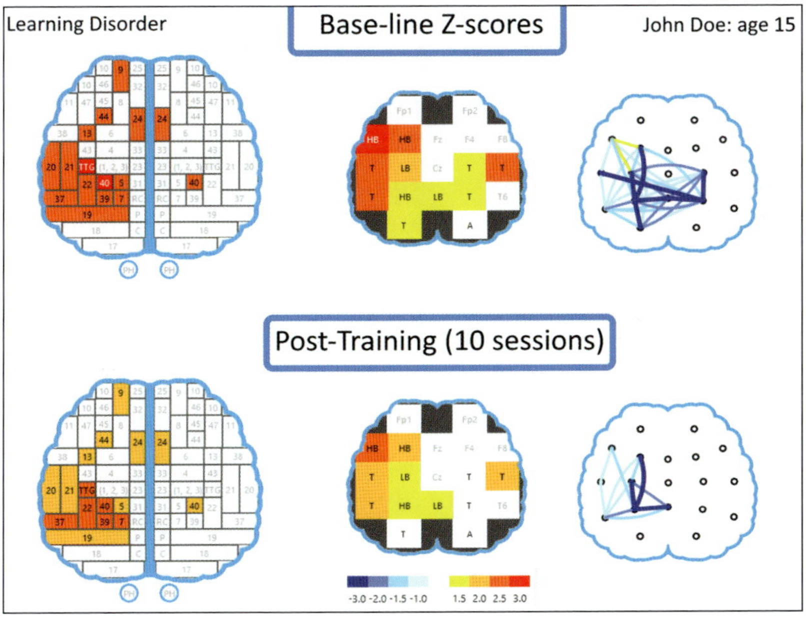

Adapted from Jewel report-writing software

27

Maintaining Professionalism

THE PRACTICE OF EEG neurofeedback is relegated to the realm of licensed health care providers. The FDA limits the sale of medical equipment to licensed practitioners. Unfortunately, there are some unaccredited trainers who invite one and all to attend and even sell them equipment. It is unethical to buy equipment and set up shop without the proper credentials and training. Why? Neurofeedback facilitates changes in the brain—each person's central processing unit. Health professionals who have a broad understanding of topics such as mental health, suicide risks, cognitive performance, and family dynamics best supervise its application. Furthermore, they screen for individuals who need talk therapy more than operant conditioning training.

Most independent EEG neurofeedback practitioners already possess credentials in the health care system. Credentials are granted by duly authorized authorities—usually the state, regional, or national government. For example, I am licensed by the state of Vermont as a clinical mental health counselor. Licensing requires a minimum of a master's degree, 3,000 hours of supervised practice, and a passing grade on two separate clinical tests. Forty continuing education units are required every two years. Other examples of independent state-credentialed practitioners include licensed social workers, counselors, psychologists, marriage and family therapists, doctors, chiropractors, medical doctors, psychiatrists, neurologists, and registered nurses (especially psychiatric nurses). Occupational and physical therapists also have taken up the practice of EEG neurofeedback.

I encourage health care professionals and their staff members to become certified by the Biofeedback Certification International Alliance (BCIA). Note that certification is not a license to practice, and it requires the same steps as most states' licensing requirements. Staff members can aid in electrode placement for training and qEEG data acquisition; they can run training programs and review the results. However, a licensed practitioner is always on the floor, so to speak, ready to jump into action as needed. It is the licensed practitioner that reviews test results, creates the diagnosis, and forms a treatment plan. The (ethical) practice of EEG neurofeedback is in the purview of the licensed practitioner and is not left in the hands of unlicensed staff members.

Neurofeedback is a credible treatment because outcome studies and research trials have demonstrated its effectiveness. BCIA is considered by many in the field to be the primary certification organization. It has also certified individuals in areas outside the United States, including Canada, Mexico, Europe, the United Kingdom, South America, Central America, Africa, Asia, Australia, and many island nations.

BCIA is a certifying organization rather than a membership organization. Requirements include having credentials in the health care system, special education, supervision (mentoring), clinical practice hours, and passing a test. Continuing education units are required after certification has been awarded. The units acquired may be acceptable to both the state and BCIA. For example, I seek out biofeedback training that is approved by the American Psychological Association, National Board of Certified Counselors, Association of Social Work Boards, and BCIA. Check the BCIA website for the most up-to-date requirements and recommended training programs (http://www.bcia.org). Their curriculum changes every few years to keep up with advances in the field. Examples of other professional organizations that promote professionalism in neurofeedback include the International Society for Neurofeedback and Research (https://www.isnr.org), Association for Applied Psychophysiology and Biofeedback (https://www.aapb.org), and Biofeedback Federation of Europe (https://bfe.org).

Prepare for your first workshop by reading this book and others by authors including (but not limited to) Collura, Soutar and Longo, Swingle, Chapin, Fisher, Thatcher and Lubar, and Sterman and Thompson. Join ISNR and read their journals. Get an overview of the history of neurofeedback by reading *A Symphony in the Brain* (Robbins, 2000).

After attending an official BCIA blueprint program with 36 hours of instruction, BCIA recommends at least 25 hours of mentoring. Certification candidates should also train themselves; experiential learning is so important. Additional workshops and keeping up with peer-reviewed journals are needed to keep the newly certified practitioner up to date. Research in neurology and neurofeedback is ever expanding—don't fall behind.

PURCHASING EQUIPMENT

Those who enter the field of neurofeedback are expected to purchase expensive equipment before they have gained any practical experience. Educated decisions require advanced reading and surfing the internet. Every equipment manufacturer will tell you they have the best equipment. Asking questions of those already in the field will help. Talk to more than one practitioner if possible. If none can be found in your area, consult BCIA for certified practitioners. Checking out websites of practitioners may help provide you with a vision of what you want. This book has emphasized the need to do a brain map based on qEEG data for each and every prospective trainee. Doing so provides a guide to treatment and a concrete way to check training progress. Equipment to do qEEG acquisitions must have at least 19 channels. As of 2018, expect to pay $5,000 to $6,000 just for qEEG hardware. Software costs vary based on options, pay anywhere from $3,500 to $6,000 for training software. Don't forget to also factor in the cost of the workshop; expect to pay over $1,000, not including accommodations if it is an on-site workshop. (I do live online webcasts, four days of training in four weeks, Fridays only.) The following are some purchasing suggestions.

Equipment Requirements

- The equipment is used at BCIA-accredited training workshops.
- BCIA-accredited mentoring is available after the workshop on purchased equipment.
- It comes with a warranty and can be repaired and returned to you within a few days or a week at most.
- It can run qEEG acquisition software and Z-score training software and do power/amplitude training. Do not limit your future in neu-

rofeedback by buying equipment that is limited to just one modality or style of training.

- It is supported by a team of technicians who are familiar with training and acquisition software.
- It has attained an FDA 510(k) (or has been cleared by the Food and Drug Administration as a medical device) or has a long-standing reputation as a quality commercial amplifier.

Other Suggestions

- Do not purchase more than you need: purchase what you need to get started.
- Make no additional purchases until your practice has grown.
- Always have a backup unit. For example, in addition to a qEEG acquisition/training amplifier, it makes sense to have a two- or four-channel training unit that will take up the slack if the main amplifier needs repair or if two clients need to be trained at the same time.
- Purchase a high-quality PC gaming computer with a minimum of 16 GB of RAM and a 4 GB NVIDA dedicated graphics card. Expect to pay at least $1,100 for a 15-inch laptop. I prefer a minimum 256 GB solid-state drive. Do not skimp on the specs. Training/assessment computers are not family computers.
- Sooner or later, an impedance meter will be needed. Many qEEG amplifiers come with a built-in impedance meter. Otherwise, purchase a stand-alone unit.
- Purchase a nonrocking recliner chair for qEEG that does not have a built-in head rest. A very small movable neck support is ideal.

OFFICE REQUIREMENTS

- Make sure you have easy access to hot water in order to clean and dry out qEEG recording caps and electrodes.
- Find a way to hang up electrodes to prevent tangles.
- Make sure the wiring is properly grounded.
- Make sure you have a good internet connection for mentoring and streaming movies to reinforce training.

- Meet your neighbors and check out the noise level.
- Find an office that gives your business exposure and has easy access.
- Avoid excessive electromagnetic field (EMF) and radio frequency interference:
    - Elevator shafts
    - Pool motors
    - Transformer stations
    - Radio stations
    - Office neighbors that have commercial motorized equipment
    - A Gauss meter may be needed to check for EMFs. Obtain an inexpensive three-pronged hardware device (with LED lights) for grounding verification.

TRAINING SCREENS AND GAMES

- Many practitioners train with streaming movies.
- Others purchase third-party games: ZUKOR Interactive has the best online support.
- Training while under task may be necessary at times: Tetris, FreeCell, Concentration, Microsoft Paint (for young children), or just reading an age-appropriate book.
- Training with eyes closed may be indicated by the brain map. Note: show caution with survivors of trauma or those at risk for panic attacks.
- Purchase a large flat-screen monitor to show graphics while you observe statistics and the raw EEG. Find out how to extend a screen from your PC to an external monitor (HDMI cable needed).
- Rule: The client must never be bored! A trainee who is bored will zone out and sabotage the training.
- Rule amendment: Trauma survivors often do better with low-arousal training screens that most children would find boring.

Practice, Practice, Practice

Practice placing sensors on family members. Take measurements and readings. Determine the theta-to-beta ratio at various positions on the scalp.

Practice doing qEEG acquisitions on volunteers before attempting to do qEEGs and train in the clinical arena. (Note: avoid training experiments.)

CREATE A NEW PRACTICE WITH STYLE

Obtain a mentor who can help you to grow in your understanding of EEG neurofeedback. There is no one right method of doing neurofeedback. There is no ultimate intervention style. I have consulted with clinics for well over a decade; they all have different styles or ways of approaching neurofeedback training, and yet most have met with success. Mentors should not box you into a single method. Do not be afraid to try new modalities or go to different workshops or read articles and books about other modalities. Yes, this book is *Getting Started With EEG Neurofeedback*, but the title is in no way meant to rule out other modalities such as Multivariate Coherence training (Coben, 2014). It simply reflects my personal experience as a practitioner and consultant.

I have been in practice for a number of years. My mental health practice was at one time devoted solely to psychotherapy for individuals and couples. I gradually transitioned to a full-time neurofeedback practice that includes some mental health counseling. The name of my business is Neurofeedback of Southern Vermont, LLC. I am not shy about declaring my specialty. Others have realized a vision different than mine. They do not see their professional life consumed with neurofeedback. For example, a group practice may choose to offer neurofeedback as one of many therapies at their clinic. An independent therapist may envision neurofeedback as an adjunct that is applied to specific clinical disorders.

Advertisement is critical. One practitioner who took my workshop was unable to develop a practice because almost no one knew she offered neurofeedback. This is the advice I always offer:

> If I put the words *neurofeedback practitioners in Cleveland* into my Google search engine, then all neurofeedback providers come up in that area. What about you? Will your name or practice come up in a web search? It's relatively easy to set up or design a website without hiring an expensive professional web designer (try Weebly or HostMonster). Get ideas for web designs from neurofeedback providers who already have an online presence. Some practitioners start by advertising through *Psychology Today*

or network with other professionals, such as pediatricians. Seek out PTA members and join the chamber of commerce. How about writing articles for the local shopper or newspaper? Purchase brochures (ISNR's online store sells them) or create one on your PC and then hand them out. Of course, the best advertisement is the satisfied parent who tells all her friends about your practice and how it helped her child.

SEEKING OUT CLINICAL POPULATIONS

Begin the practice of neurofeedback with the treatment of symptoms that are known to respond to training. Start training new clients with symptoms of depression, anxiety, ADHD, learning disorders, and migraines. School-age children make up the bulk of many neurofeedback clinics. Parents bring children with autistic spectrum disorders and OCD, and many adopted children face reactive attachment disorder and PTSD. Do not fill up your new practice with children diagnosed with conduct disorder or oppositional defiant disorder. Be careful of dysfunctional family dynamics.

If your practice includes ADHD and learning disorders, a CPT will be needed. TOVA is the most affordable. Be ready to assist parents in setting up family structure and help them to become aware of allergies and food sensitivities. Consider purchasing HEG neurofeedback equipment as well as photic stimulation. Homework can include HRV training and audiovisual entrainment equipment. A number of practices include remote training, which requires parents to train their children at home in addition to office training. Effective remote training can be added after you have become an experienced provider.

If your practice brings in clients with TBI, consider purchasing pEMF coils or Vielight therapy. Photic stimulation training with CFC is also very effective. In other words, clients with more egregious problems may need ancillary treatments. A fundamental knowledge of nutrition, exercise, and healthy lifestyles is needed.

Post-traumatic stress disorder, exposure to combat, or childhood trauma requires additional clinical expertise such as EMDR, internal family systems, and guided imagery interventions. More is required than simply putting electrodes on the scalp and training. The same can be said about personality disorders and addictions, which may be rooted in childhood trauma. Sessions likely include more interaction with trained professionals who can debrief as needed. Training rooms need to offer safety and seclusion, with closed doors and few distractions.

There has been a growing trend of holistic health care providers, including but not limited to chiropractors and doctors of functional medicine who have a metabolic approach. New clients are tested for organic problems and treated before or during neurofeedback training. This is a comprehensive approach that offers much to the clinical population. Other practitioners make referrals to holistic practitioners if and only if they agree to return the favor.

Peak performance for executives and others can take on many forms. There are several approaches to peak performance or cognitive enhancement. It often includes training for enhanced attention as well as alpha/theta training and HRV. Gamma training with Z-score sLORETA and pulsing therapies may also be part of this program. What makes this approach unique is its emphasis on positive growth and personal development rather than on symptom reduction and clinical disorders. Consequently, the client presents challenges and goals, whereas symptom reduction and diagnosis are not emphasized or even mentioned unless absolutely necessary. For more information on alpha synchrony training and peak performance training, see McKnight and Fehmi (2001), Norris and Currieri (1999), and Mason and Brownback (2001). Further information can be found in *Biofeedback*, volume 29, number 1 (2001). This issue heralds the theme: "The Pursuit of Optimal Functioning."

CONCLUSION

Getting Started With EEG Neurofeedback emphasizes the need for assessment before training commences. No comprehensive list of canned protocols is provided for the reader because of the diversity and complexity of the cerebral cortex: One size does not fit all. The same clinical disorder may have many neurological faces. The application of any protocol without prior assessment may well result in poor treatment outcomes. The rationale for any treatment plan must be founded upon a clinical diagnosis, a careful analysis of the EEG, and a working knowledge of neurology. Treatment protocol decisions, clinical methods, and theory vary from practitioner to practitioner. However, the proof is in the pudding. Exit questionnaires and before-and-after baselines demonstrate practice efficacy.

Finally, there is no single way, no one approach that surpasses all others. Keep an open mind and be ready to learn, grow, and adapt—actually, that is the way of the professional neurofeedback practitioner. After finishing this book, read "Assessing the Effectiveness of Neurofeedback Training in the Context of Clinical and Social Neuroscience" (Orndorff-Plunkett, Singh, Aragón, & Pineda, 2017).

Appendix 1: Relative Power

Appendix Figure 1.1. Absolute Power Compared to Relative Power

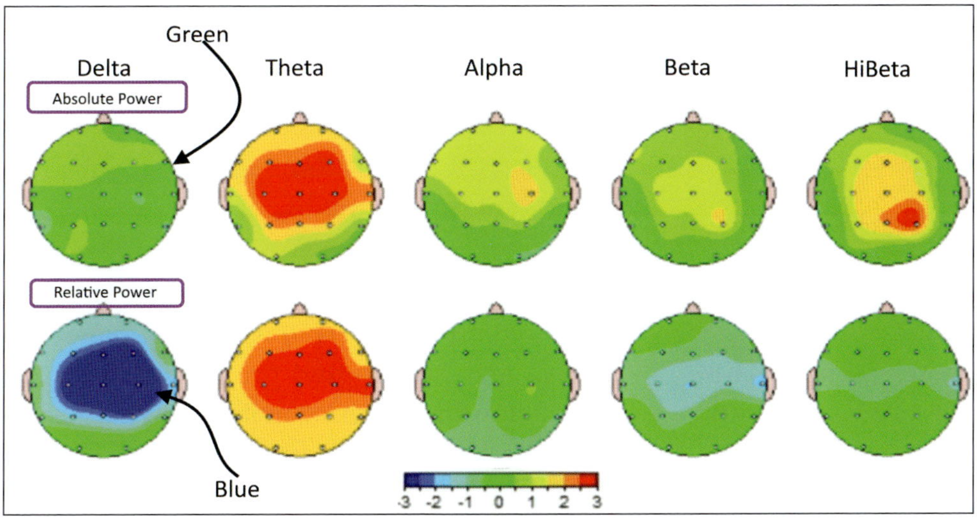

Brain maps were created by NeuroGuide LifeSpan database

Relative power SDs come from comparisons or relationships among bandwidths. Therefore, since the absolute power SD of theta is very high and hi-beta is somewhat high, it will tend to make another bandwidth appear low, in this case delta. To illustrate: If a first grade student was 6 feet tall (2 meters), all of his fellow classmates would appear relatively short. However, from an absolute point of view, the first grade class has just one statistical outlier, the 6-foot student.

In Appendix Figure 1.1, absolute delta SDs are near the mean and green, whereas relative delta SDs are low or negative and dark blue. Theta SDs are elevated and red in both relative and absolute power heads.

Relative maps have a seesaw effect (Appendix Figure 1.2). If the amplitude at one site is abnormally high, then other amplitudes will be evaluated as low; or, when sEMG or EOA is significantly high, relative maps can be misleading. Absolute maps must be consulted to determine value of relative maps.

Appendix Figure 1.2. Seesaw Effects With Relative Power

Relative power may or may not be helpful when matching symptoms to sites. Some maps have low absolute power SDs in almost all bands. In those cases, a relative power map may help to find proportionately high SDs. Last, relative power Z-score training often contributes to successful outcomes because it likely helps to restore bandwidth balance.

Appendix 2: Infra-slow Oscillation Training

Infra-slow oscillation (ISO) training has also been called infra-slow fluctuation (ISF) training or infra-low-frequency (ILF) training. The training frequencies are lower than 1/10 of 1 Hz (.1 Hz). What is being trained? There is no simple answer. It may be glial cell (astrocyte) activity, or it may be the interaction between glial cells and neurons, or it may be associated with thalamic relay nuclei and possibly resting-state brain networks, or training may influence gamma output. Training may be accompanied by physiological responses. ISO methodology, hardware, and programs differ; whereas training locations are somewhat similar (Smith, Collura, Ferrera, & de Vries, 2014; Othmer, 2017).

TESTING ISO TRAINING IN THE FIELD

BrainAvatar training protocols were created by the author to test the potential of low-frequency training. The goal was to independently assess response to training without using already existing protocols. Several clinicians were introduced to two ISO training concepts: (1) appropriate training site selection, and (2) careful attention to the trainee's subjective response to training. Clinicians who were the most comfortable making on-the-fly changes found the greatest success. Clinicians who were the least comfortable making changes on the fly stopped using ISO training.

Most of the following outcomes come from the psychologist Katie A. Cate in my home state of Vermont. She employed two ISO programs to track detectable bursts of low frequencies in these ranges:

A. Starting at 0-.016 Hz with a possible low range of 0-.002 Hz.
B. Starting at 0-.0010 Hz with a possible low range of 0-.0001 Hz

In general, Program A was applied to personality disorders, sense of self, and headaches. Program B was applied to clients with a history of trauma and emotional dysregulation.Training was started with Program A at 0–.016 Hz. Often, T3-T4 was chosen for stability during the first training session. Other montages could be selected in future sessions. The trained frequency was tweaked according to (1) the trainee's subjective response, and (2) the clinician's intuition (Appendix Figure 2.1). Z-score training or power training often followed ISO training.

Appendix Figure 2.1. ISO Training: Tweaking on the Fly

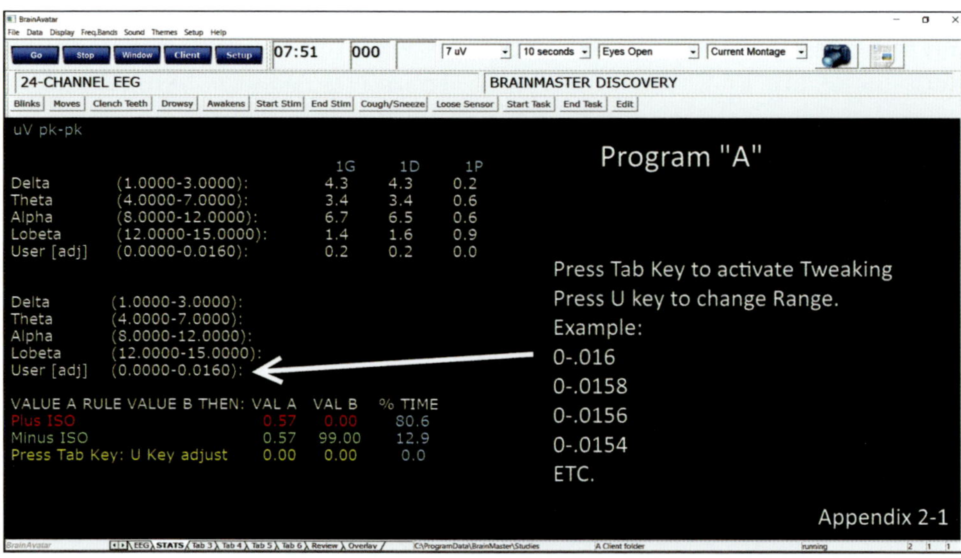

Training screen adapted from BrainAvatar software by BrainMaster Technologies, Inc.

The client's physiological response can be monitored during the frequency selection process to insure progress. There are several ways to monitor the training, including (1) skin temperature, (2) heart rate variability, and (3) perspiration (electrodermal response measured on a finger or the palm). For example, hand temperatures may rise to 90°F (32°C) or higher as the trainees relax. However, hand temperatures may fall when the response to training is negative. Decreased hand temperatures signal that it is time to tweak the training range or change the montage. Frequency ranges are *tweaked slowly* as the clinician discerns the response to training.

Programs A and B have no specific threshold challenge; the concepts of inhibit or reward reinforcement do not apply; feedback follows or tracks amplitude bursts within the tweaked range. Likely, A and B programs promote awareness of optimal subconscious brain states; on-the-fly adjustments (tweaking) were made as the training progressed. They were guided by the trainee's subjective response and supported by physiological data. For example, training-Program A starts at the high range of 0-.016 Hz and then is tweaked downward towards the low range of 0-.002 Hz as needed. Program B starts at the high range of 0-.0010 Hz and then is tweaked downward towards the low range of 0-.0001 Hz. Tweaking follows the trainee's subjective units of distress or SUDS. The first case study on pain, below, explains the tweaking process.

The process of finding the ideal training range requires clinical skills and intuition. It is not simply a matter of setting up and running a program. Protocol montages (Appendix Figure 2.2) were selected based upon the recommendations found in the *Protocol Guide for Neurofeedback Clinicians* (Othmer, 2017). Only bipolar montages were used. ISO training requires the use of high-quality sintered silver/silver chloride electrodes (Ag/AgCl): mastoid montages were used instead of ear clips. BrainAvatar software was the operating system and Discovery was the amplifier.
The following is a sample of the results.

Appendix Figure 2.2. Primary Bipolar Montages for Low Frequency Training

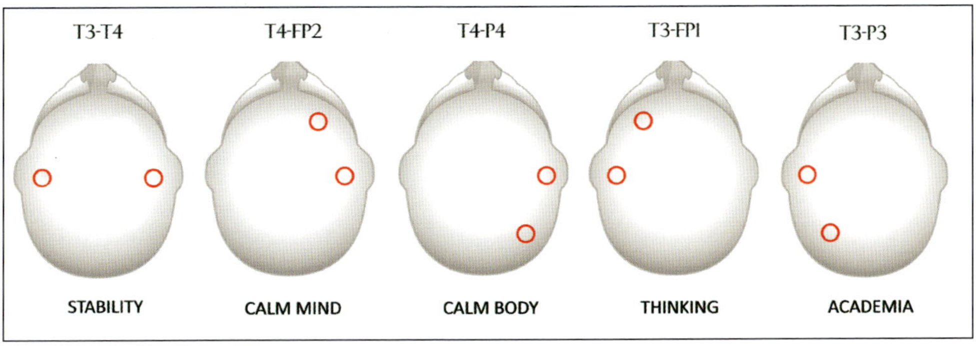

Montage locations derived from 2017 Protocol Guide for Neurofeedback Clinicians
by Susan F. Othmer-EEG Institute (Author)

T4-P4 (Program B) for Pain

Client comes in with significant pain and stiffness in hands and feet due to osteoarthritis. During a 20-minute session, the ISO range is tweaked from 0-.0010 down to 0–.0004 Hz. Client reports hands and feet are pain free at end of session, but stiffness remains. Client calls the next day to report that she is pain free and now the stiffness is gone.

Comment on the tweaking process (on-the-fly adjustments): The trainee's pain lessened as we tweaked down the frequency, but when we hit 0–.0003 Hz she began to have shooting pain in hands and feet; consequently, the frequency range was raised to 0–.0004 Hz, which stopped the pain, and we recognized it to be her sweet spot. This illustrates the importance of having a precise setting range and the power of the entire process to promote change. Unfortunately, the client's pain was the result of a chronic back injury. Training did not heal the injury; however, it could relieve the pain for several days.

T4-FP2 (Program A) for Mood

A client was diagnosed with developmental trauma and depression: the decision was made to train for 15 minutes of T4-FP2 (Program A) at 0–.016 Hz. The client left treatment with no reported improvement. However, 10 minutes later, when she arrived home, she said that her depression seemed to have lifted and she felt "so much better." Results held for 3 days after her first session and until we had our next appointment.

T3-T4 (Program B) for Emotional Regulation

A client was diagnosed with PTSD and emotional dysregulation; in the morning before coming to treatment she had multiple panic attacks accompanied with weeping. After 20 minutes of T3-T4 training at 0–.0001 Hz, she began to emotionally regulate. By end of session she reported feeling "calm and centered."

Note that some survivors of abuse are unable to report on their subjective state. In those cases, the van der Kolk protocol (T4-P4) presented at the end of Chapter 21 may be the first intervention of choice.

T3-T4 (Program A) for Migraine

A client came into session with a migraine headache. The training range was tweaked down from 0–.016 Hz to 0–.006 Hz, which stopped the headache.

T3-T4 (Program A) for Sense of Self

A survivor of egregious child abuse manifested a poor sense of self and lacked an internal secure base (Bowlby, 1988). This client reported a greater sense of inner direction and calm after two training sessions at 0–.016 Hz for 15 minutes each.

Recap of ISO Training With Bipolar Montages

Training with bipolar montages can be very powerful. It should not be delegated to EEG techs, but remains in the purview of the licensed clinician who can think on his or her feet and act with intuition when it comes to frequency range selections.

RELEVANT RESEARCH

> Low-frequency training regimens have been used for more than a decade to address issues related to post-traumatic stress disorder, attentional problems, and anxiety disorders [67]. Even complex issues that remain largely under-investigated such as attachment resolution, complex PTSD, and behaviors associated with personality disorders have been addressed [68]. While the overall working mechanisms of ILF and SCP training are not fully understood, including the implications of how such training may influence metabolic or endocrine function, or potentially even transcriptional regulation at the receptor level, their apparent success and widespread use in the clinical community require further study. (Orndorff-Plunkett et al., 2017)
>
> We show that the *default network* is characterized by significant *high-gamma-band* (65–110 Hz) coherence at infra-slow (<0.1 Hz) frequencies. This coherence occurs over a narrow frequency range, centered at *0.015*

> *Hz*, commensurate with the frequency of BOLD signal fluctuations seen by fMRI, suggesting that quasi-periodic, infra-slow changes in local cortical activity form the neurophysiological basis for this network. (Ko, Darvas, Poliakov, Ojemann, & Sorensen, 2011)
>
> In recent years there has been an increasing interest in brain activities that take place on a much slower timescale than is generally recognised in traditional EEG bands; those which occur at <0.1 Hz and which are usually referred to as very slow or infra-slow oscillations (ISOs). . . . *These fluctuations identify functional anatomical networks, termed resting state networks (RSNs),* which are conserved across subjects (Hughes, Lorincz, Parri, & Crunelli, 2011)

Note that the DMN is a key resting-state network.

> The time scales of these fluctuations form a continuum from seconds to tens and hundreds of seconds corresponding to slow (0.1–1 Hz), *infra-slow* (0.01–0.1 Hz), and "*ultradian*" (<0.01 Hz) frequency bands, respectively. . . . We conclude that ISFs in electrophysiological recordings, BOLD signals, neuronal activity levels, and behavioral time series are likely to reflect the same underlying phenomenon; a superstructure of interacting and transiently oscillatory ISFs that regulate both the integration within and decoupling between concurrently active neuronal communities. . . . Converging evidence shows that ISFs reflect quasi-periodic excitability fluctuations in cortical and subcortical networks. We suggest that the infra-slow regulation of local excitability and inter-areal communication in functionally specialized *brain networks* determines the brain-state dynamics that underlie the clustering of *behavioral performance in cognitive tasks.* (Palva & Palva, 2012, italics added)

It is possible that Program A tracks infra-slow fluctuations, whereas Program B tracks ultradian rhythms.

CONCLUSION

ISO, ILF and ISF training are promising modalities, especially when they are combined with other modalities including Z-score training and power training. Clinicians who are comfortable with making changes on the fly and who attend formal workshops will likely find lower frequency interventions to be of value along with other EEG neurofeedback interventions.

The importance of this modality was made clear to me after a clinic dedicated to ILF training requested my help. They wanted to add power training to their clinical population—mostly sports-related brain injuries. The marriage of ILF training and qEEG-guided power training has proved very fruitful. Consequently, I decided to add case studies to this edition that would show the potential of ISO training. For some already doing EEG neurofeedback, it may lead to further study and workshops. To those just getting started, the introduction to this modality is often part of module IX in the BCIA didactic curriculum Current Trends in Neurofeedback.

Appendix 3: The EEG and Phase

Phase is a complex mathematical calculation. It is "usually computed at the same time as EEG coherence" (Thatcher, 1999). Phase comparisons between two EEG waves are computed in angles. Each complete wave cycle is 360 degrees. When two waves of the same frequency begin at the same moment in time they are *in phase* and have a phase angle of zero. Graphically, they rise and fall simultaneously in the same pathway. When two waves of the same frequency begin at different times, they are *out of phase* and have a phase angle that is greater than zero. Phase angles are seen graphically as phase shifts (Appendix Figure 3.1).

Appendix Figure 3.1. Sine Waves Out of Phase

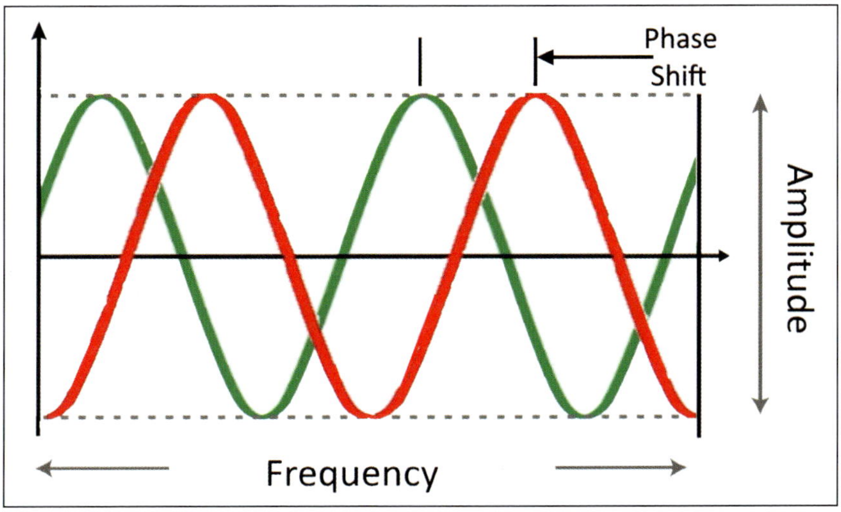

When reading a book, the eyes look from right to left, which may result in a phase reversal, best seen between F7 and F8 (Appendix Figure 3.2).

Appendix Figure 3.2. Phase Reversal F7/F8 caused by lateral eye movements

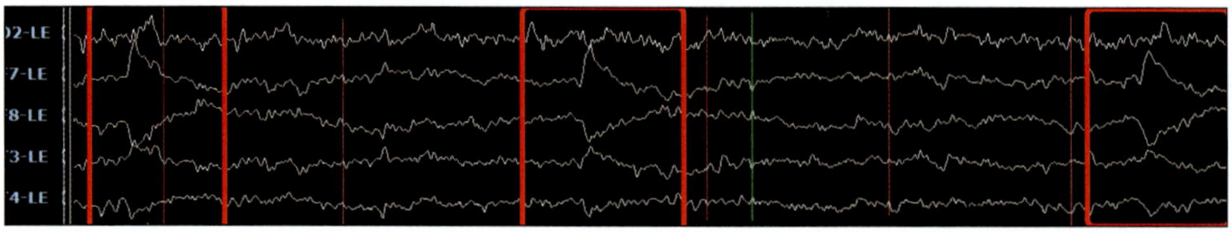

Caption: EEG adapted from BrainMaster Technologies, Inc. Software

PHASE TRAINING WITH ALPHA WAVES

Phase training can be accomplished in several ways. One example is the dual bipolar montage protocol (end of Chapter 21) which does synchrony or phase training between Fz-T3 and Pz-T4 by comparing phase angles. Feedback is a reflection of the phase angle; when the phase angle between channels approaches zero the trainee receives feedback. Hence, the two channels are more in sync because alpha waves rise and fall in unison. Another example of phase training was a method developed by Tom Collura. Rather than measuring phase angles, it tracks the rise and fall of amplitudes through complex equations. The author automated the program, removing the need for manual adjustments. The training screen is shown in Appendix Figure 3.3. The review screen shows a sharp increase in alpha amplitude, especially at P3 and P4; other protocols were not as successful.

Some practitioners use alpha phase training to enhance Z-score training. It is an essential part of many peak performance programs and promotes healthy cortical activity in a number of ways. Phase is a reflection of "underlying cortical connectivity" which relates to the rate of speed of communication between two brain locations (Thatcher, 1999, page 52). Research indicates the value of alpha phase in brain dynamics and intelligence (Thatcher et al., 2005). Also, there is a connection between alpha band oscillations and "attentional, executive and contex-

Appendix Figure 3.3. 4 Channel Alpha Phase Training

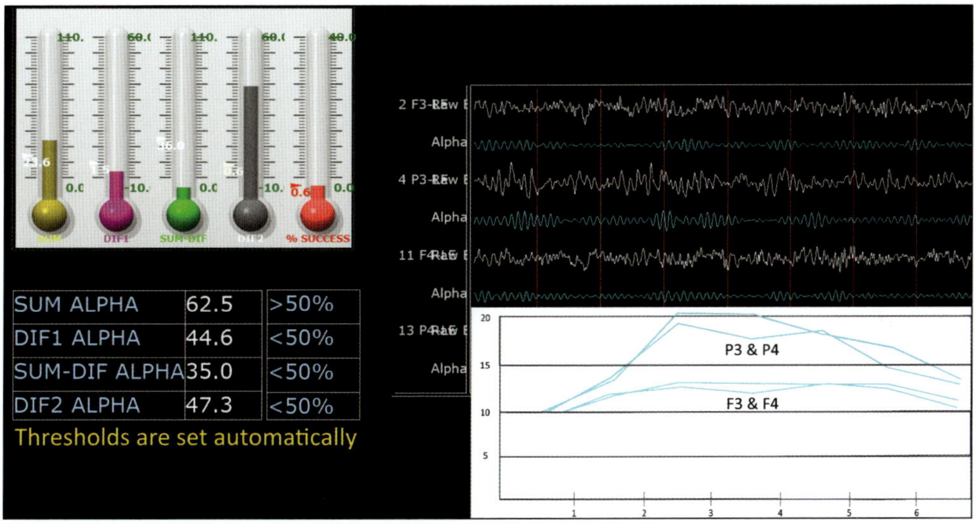

Training Screen adapted from BrainMaster Technologies, Inc. software

tual functions." Alpha phase promotes timely "neuronal responses and stimulus perception." Visual processing speed performance is reflection of alpha phase and, as expected, the thalamus is a key player in production of normal alpha phase connectivity throughout the cortex (Palva & Palva, 2011).

References

Amen, D. (1998). *Change your brain, change your life.* New York: Three Rivers.

American Medical Association. (1998). *Current procedural terminology: CPT 1999.* Chicago: Author.

An, J. H., Kim, Y. J., Kim, K. J., Kim, S. H., Kim, N. H., Kim, H. Y., . . . Kim S. G. (2016). L-carnitine supplementation for the management of fatigue in patients with hypothyroidism on levothyroxine treatment: A randomized, double-blind, placebo-controlled trial. *Endocrine Journal, 63*(10), 885–895.

Arns, M., Swatzyna, R. J., Gunkelman, J., & Olbrich, S. (2015). Sleep maintenance, spindling excessive beta and impulse control: An RDoC arousal and regulatory systems approach? *Neuropsychiatric Electrophysiology, 1,* 5.

Ayers, M. (1999). Assessing and treating open head trauma, coma, and stroke using real-time digital EEG neurofeedback. In J. R. Evans & A. Arbarbanel (Eds.), *Introduction to quantitative EEG and neurofeedback* (pp. 203–222). San Diego, CA: Academic Press.

Baehr, E., Rosenfeld, P. J., Baehr, R., & Earnest, C. (1999). Clinical use of an alpha asymmetry neurofeedback protocol in the treatment of mood disorders. In J. R. Evans & A. Arbarbanel (Eds.), *Introduction to quantitative EEG and Neurofeedback* (pp. 181–201). San Diego, CA: Academic Press.

Berger, H. (1929). U¨ ber das Elektrenkephalogramm des Menschen (On the human electroencephalogram). Archiv f. Psychiatrie u. Nervenkrankheiten 87:527–70.

Benson, H. (1975). *The relaxation response.* New York: William Morrow.

Bernstein, E., & Putnam, F. W. (1986). Development, reliability, and validity of a dissociation scale. *Journal of Nervous and Mental Disease, 174,* 727–735.

Biofeedback Certification International Alliance (date unknown). *Professional Standards and Ethical Principles of Biofeedback*, www.bcia.org.

Blume, W. T., & Kaibara, M. (1995). *Atlas of adult electroencephalography.* New York: Raven Press.

Boon, S., Steele, K., & van der Hart, O. (2011). *Coping with trauma-related dissociation: Skills training for patients and therapists.* Norton Series on Interpersonal Neurobiology. New York: Norton.

Boutros, N., Galderisi, S., Pogarell, O., & Riggio, S. (2011). *Standard electroencephalography in clinical psychiatry: A practical handbook.* New York: Wiley-Blackwell.

Bowlby, J. (1988). *A secure base: Parent-child attachment and healthy human development.* New York: Basic Books.

Braun, B. G. (1988). The BASK model of dissociation: Clinical applications. *Dissociation, 1*(2), 16–23.

Bressler, S. L., & Menon, V. (2010). Large scale brain networks in cognition: Emerging methods and principles. *Trends in Cognitive Sciences, 14*(6), 277–290.

Brodmann, K. (1909). Comparative localization studies in the brain cortex, its fundamentals represented on the basis of its cellular architecture.

Buckner, R. L., Andrews-Hanna, J. R., & Schacter, D. L. (2008). The brain's default network: Anatomy, function, and relevance to disease. *Annals of the New York Academy of Sciences, 1124*, 1–38.

Budzynski, T. H. (1996). Brain brightening: Can neurofeedback improve cognitive process? *Biofeedback, 24*(2), 14–17.

Budzynski, T. H. (1999). From EEG to neurofeedback. In J. R. Evans & A. Arbarbanel (Eds.), *Introduction to quantitative EEG and neurofeedback* (pp. 65–79). San Diego, CA: Academic Press.

Burns, D. D. (1999). *The Feeling Good Handbook.* New York: Plume.

Cantor, D. S. (1999). An overview of quantitative EEG and its applications to neurofeedback. In J. R. Evans & A. Arbarbanel (Eds.), *Introduction to quantitative EEG and neurofeedback* (pp. 3–27). San Diego, CA: Academic Press.

Carmen, J. (2004). Passive infrared hemoencephalography: Four years and 100 migraines. *Journal of Neurotherapy, 8*(3), 25.

Carmody, D. P., Radvanski, D. C., Wadhwani, S., Sabo, M. J., & Vergara, L. (2001). EEG biofeedback training and attention-deficit/hyperactivity disorder in an elementary school setting. *Journal of Neurotherapy, 4*(3), 5–27.

Carter, R. (1998). *Mapping the mind.* Los Angeles: University of California Press.

Chapman, A. L., Gratz, K. L., & Tull, M. T. (2011). *The dialectical behavior therapy skills workbook for anxiety: Breaking free from worry, panic, PTSD, and other anxiety symptoms.* Oakland, CA: New Harbinger.

Coben, R., (2014). *Four Channel Multivariate Coherence Training: A New Form of Neurofeedback.* Presented at the 2014 ISNR conference in San Diego, CA on 10/18/2014.

Coca, A. F. (1994). *The pulse test: The secret of building your basic health* (rev. ed.). Fort Lee, NJ: Barricade.

Collura, T. (2002). Application of repetitive visual stimulation to EEG neurofeedback protocols. *Journal of Neurotherapy, 6*(2), 47–70.

Collura, T. (2017). *Technical foundations of neurofeedback, First Edition.* New York: Routledge.

Congedo, M., & Lubar, J. F. (2003). Parametric and non-parametric analysis of QEEG: Normative database comparisons in electroencephalography, a simulation study on accuracy. *Journal of Neurotherapy, 7*(3–4), 1–29.

Crane, A. (1998, October). *Modules A and B biofeedback training.* Ossining, NY: American Biotech Corp.

Criswell, E. (1995). *Biofeedback and somatics.* Novato, CA: Freeperson.

Crook, W. G. (1986). *The yeast connection.* Jackson, TN: Professional Books.

Damasio, A. A. (1994). *Descartes' error: Emotion, reason, and the human brain.* New York: Quill.

Davidson, R. J. (1998). Affective style and affective disorders: Perspectives from affective neuroscience. *Cognition and Emotion, 12*(3), 307–330.

Davidson, R. J., Abercrombie, H., Nitschke, J. B., & Putnam, K. (1999). Regional brain function, emotion and disorders of emotion. *Current Opinion in Neurobiology, 9,* 228–234.

Davidson, R. J., & Irwin, W. (1999). The functional neuroanatomy of emotion and affective style. *Trends in Cognitive Sciences, 3*(1), 11–21.

Demos, J. N. (1995). Creating resonance within the therapeutic bond: Empathy and transference as covert transmissions. *Voices, 31*(1), 90–98.

Demos, J. N. (2005). *Getting started with neurofeedback.* New York: Norton.

Demos, J. N. (2014, winter). Getting started with pulsed electromagnetic field (pEMF) therapy. *NeuroConnections.*

Diamond, M. C., Scheibel, A. B., & Elson, L. M. (1985). *The human brain coloring book.* New York: HarperPerennial.

Drury, R. L., DeRisi, W. J., Liberman, R. P., (1979). Temperature Biofeedback Treatment for Migraine Headache: A Controlled Multiple Baseline Study. *Headache, 19*(5), 278-84.

Edmonds, H. (2015). Central nervous system monitoring. Retrieved from https://clinicalgate.com/central-nervous-system-monitoring-2/

Enoch, M. A., Schuckit, M. A., Johnson, B. A., & Goldman, D. (2003). Genetics of alcoholism using intermediate phenotypes. *Alcoholism Clinical and Experimental Research, 27*(2), 169–176.

Fehmi, L., & Robbins, J. (2007). *The open-focus brain: Harnessing the power of attention to heal mind and body.* Boston: Trumpeter.

Fields, D. (2009). *The other brain.* New York: Simon and Schuster.

Fisher, S. (2004). Fear and FPO2: The implications of a new protocol. *Journal of Neurotherapy, 8*(1), 88–89.

Fisher, S. (2014). *Neurofeedback in the treatment of developmental trauma: Calming the fear-driven brain.* New York: Norton.

Foster, D. S., & Thatcher, R. W. (2015). Surface and LORETA neurofeedback in the treatment of post-traumatic stress disorder and mild traumatic brain injury. In R. W. Thatcher & J. F. Lubar (Eds.), *Z score neurofeedback: Clinical applications.* San Diego, CA: Academic Press.

Frederick, J. A., Lubar, J. F., Rasey, H. W., Brim, S. A., & Blackburn, J. (1999). Effect of 18.5 Hz auditory and visual stimulation on EEG amplitude at the vertex. *Journal of Neurotherapy, 3*(3–4), 23–28.

Freeman, J. M., (2013). Epilepsy's Big Fat Answer. *Cerebrum,* Mar-Apr; 2013: 3.

Gevirtz, R. (2013). The promise of heart rate variability biofeedback: Evidence-based applications. *Biofeedback, 41*(3), 110–120.

Gordon, B. R., McDowell, C. P., Hallgren, M., et al. Association of Efficacy of Resistance Exercise Training With Depressive SymptomsMeta-analysis and Meta-regression Analysis of Randomized Clinical Trials. *JAMA Psychiatry.* jamapsychiatry.2018.0572

Gunkelman, J. (2006). Transcend the DSM using phenotypes. *Biofeedback, 34*(3), 95–98.

Gurnee, R. (2002). *QEEG subtypes of major depressive disorder and implications for treatment.* Workshop at the conference of the Society for Neuronal Regulation, Scottsdale, AZ.

Gurnee, R. (2003). *Central 12–15 Hz activity in ADHD.* Paper presented at the conference of the International Society for Neuronal Regulation, Houston,TX.

Gurnee, R. (2013). *Beta Waves.* Retrieved from http://scottsdaleneurofeedback.com.

Hamani C., Mayberg, H., Stone, S., Laxton, A., Haber, S., & Lozano, A. M. (2011). The subcallosal cingulate gyrus in the context of major depression. *Biological Psychiatry, 69*(4), 301–308.

Hammond, D. C. (1999). Roshi compared with the Rosenfeld depression protocol: A case report. *Journal of Neurotherapy, 3*(3–4), 63.

Hammond, D. C. (2000). The role of 40 Hz activity and training (question 1). *Journal of Neurotherapy, 4*(2), 95–100.

Hammond, D. C. (2001). Comprehensive neurofeedback bibliography. *Journal of Neurotherapy, 5*(1–2), 113–128.

Hammond, D. C. (2003). QEEG-guided neurofeedback in the treatment of obsessive compulsive disorder. *Journal of Neurotherapy, 7*(2), 25–52.

Hammond, D. C. (2005). Neurofeedback to improve physical balance, incontinence, and swallowing. *Journal of Neurotherapy, 9*(1).

Heine, L. (2012). Resting state networks and consciousness: Alterations of multiple resting state network connectivity in physiological, pharmacological, and pathological consciousness states. *Frontiers in Psychology, 3*, 295.

Herman, J. L. (1992). *Trauma and recovery: The aftermath of violence - from domestic abuse to political terror.* New York, NY: Basic Books.

Herman, J. L. (2015). *Trauma and recovery: The aftermath of violence - from domestic abuse to political terror.* 1R edition, New York, NY: Basic Books.

Hughes, J. R. (1994). *EEG in clinical practice* (2nd ed.). Boston: Butterworth-Heinemann.

Hughes, S. W., Lorincz, M. L., Parri, H. R., & Crunelli, V. (2011). Infra-slow (<0.1 Hz) oscillations in thalamic relay nuclei: Basic mechanisms and significance to health and disease states. *Progress in Brain Research, 193*, 145–162.

Hyde, D. E., Duffy, F. H., & Warfield, S. K. (2014). Voxel-based dipole orientation constraints for distributed current estimation. *IEEE Transactions on Biomedical Engineering, 61*(7).

Johns Hopkins Medicine. (2016, May 4). Yeast infection linked to mental illness: Candida infections also more common among those with memory loss. *ScienceDaily*.

Johnstone, J., & Gunkelman, J. (2003). Use of databases in QEEG evaluation. *Journal of Neurotherapy, 7*(3–4), 31–52.

Johnstone, J., Gunkelman, J., & Lunt, J. (2005). Clinical database development: Characterization of EEG phenotypes. *Clinical EEG and Neuroscience, 36*(2), 99–107.

Kaiser, D. A. (2008). Functional connectivity and aging: Comodulation and coherence differences. *Journal of Neurotherapy, 12*(2–3).

Kerson, C. (2002). *The benefits of measuring basal skin response during neurofeedback training.* Paper presented at the conference of the International Society for Neuronal Regulation, Scottsdale, AZ.

Ko, A. L., Darvas, F., Poliakov, A., Ojemann, J., & Sorensen, L. B. (2011). Quasi-periodic fluctuations in default mode network electrophysiology. *Journal of Neuroscience, 31*(32), 11728–11732.

Köster, M., Friese, U., Schöne, B., Trujillo-Barreto, N., & Gruber, T. (2014). Theta-gamma coupling during episodic retrieval in the human EEG. *Brain Research, 1577*, 57–68.

Labuschagne, I., Phan, K. L., Wood, A., Angstadt, M., Chua, P., Heinrichs, M., Stout, J. C., & Nathan, P. J. (2012). Medial frontal hyperactivity to sad faces in generalized social anxiety disorder and modulation by oxytocin. *International Journal of Neuropsychopharmacology, 15*(7), 883–896.

Lee, J. R., and Hopkins, V. (2004). *What your doctor may not tell you about™ menopause: The breakthrough book on natural progesterone* (rev. ed.). New York: Warner.

Leuchter, A. F., Cook, I. A., Hunter, A. M., Cai, C., & Horvath, S. (2012). Resting-state quantitative electroencephalography reveals increased neurophysiologic connectivity in depression. *PLoS ONE 7*(2), e32508.

Lin, I. M., Tai, L. Y., & Fan, S. Y. (2014). Breathing at a rate of 5.5 breaths per minute with equal inhalation-to-exhalation ratio increases heart rate variability. *International Journal of Psychophysiology, 91*(3), 206–211.

Linehan, M. M. (1993). *Skills training manual for treating borderline personality disorder.* New York: Guilford.

Liontiris, M. I., & Mazokopakis, E. E. (2017). A concise review of Hashimoto thyroiditis (HT) and the importance of iodine, selenium, vitamin D and gluten on the autoimmunity and dietary management of HT patients. *Hellenic Journal of Nuclear Medicine, 20*(1), 51–56. doi:10.1967/s002449910507

Lisman, J. E., & Jensen, O. (2013). The theta-gamma neural code. *Neuron, 77*(6), 1002–1016.

Lubar, J. F. (1995). Neurofeedback for the management of attention-deficit/hyperactivity disorders. In M. S. Schwartz (Ed.), *Biofeedback: A practitioner's guide* (2nd ed., pp. 493–523). New York: Guilford.

Lubar, J. F. (2001). Rationale for choosing bipolar versus referential training. *Journal of Neurotherapy, 4*(3), 94–97.

Lubar, J. F., Angelakis, E., Frederick, J., & Stathopoulou, S. (2001). The role of slow-wave electroencephalographic activity in reading. *Journal of Neurotherapy, 5*(3), 5–25.

Lubar, J. F., & Lubar, J. O. (1999). Neurofeedback assessment and treatment for attention deficit/hyperactivity disorders. In J. R. Evans & A. Arbarbanel (Eds.), *Introduction to quantitative EEG and neurofeedback* (pp. 103–143). San Diego, CA: Academic Press.

Lubar, J. F., & Lubar, J. O. (2002, February). Workshop at the meeting of the Future Health Winter Brain Conference, Miami, FL.

Luria, A. R. (1973). *The working brain: An introduction to neuropsychology* (B. Haigh, Trans.). New York: Basic Books.

Lutz, A., Lawrence, L., Greischar, N. B., Rawlings, M. R., & Davidson, R. J. (2004). Long-term meditators self-induce high-amplitude gamma synchrony during mental practice. *PNAS, 101*(46), 16369–16373.

Marieb, E. N. (1995). *Human anatomy and physiology* (3rd ed.). London: Pearson.

Marieb, E. N. (2015). *Human anatomy and physiology* (10th ed.). London: Pearson.

Martin, R., & Gerstung, D. C. (1998). *The estrogen alternative.* Rochester, VT: Healing Arts.

Mason, L. A., & Brownback, T. S. (2001). Optimal functioning training with EEG biofeedback for clinical populations: A case study. *Journal of Neurotherapy, 5*(1–2), 33–43.

Maynard, S., & Hughes, J. (1984). A distinctive electrographic entity: Burst of rhythmic temporal theta. *Clinical Electroencephalography, 15*(3).

McKnight, J. T., & Fehmi, L. G. (2001). Attention and neurofeedback synchrony training: Clinical results and their significance. *Journal of Neurotherapy, 5*(1–2), 45–61.

Menon, V., & Uddin, L. (2010). Saliency, switching, attention and control: A network model of insula function. *Brain Structure and Function, 214*(5–6), 655–667.

Miltner, W. H. R., Braun, C., Arnold, M., Witte, H., & Taub, E. (1999). Coherence of gamma-band EEG activity as a basis for associative learning. *Nature, 397,* 434–436.

Mitchell, N., Hewitt, C. E., Jayakody, S., Islam, M., Adamson, J., Watt, I., & Torgerson, D. J. (2011). Randomised controlled trial of food elimination diet based on IgG antibodies for the prevention of migraine like headaches. *Nutrition Journal, 10,* 85.

Mize, W. (2004). Hemoencephalography—a new therapy for attention deficit hyperactivity (ADHD): Case report. *Journal of Neurotherapy, 8*(3), 77.

Monastra, V. (2015). *Teaching life skills to children and teens with ADHD: A guide for parents and counselors.* American Psychological Association (APA).

Moore, J. P., Trudeau, D. L., Thuras, P. D., Rubin, Y., Stockley, H., and Diamond, T. (2000), Comparison of alpha-theta, alpha and EMG neurofeedback in the production of alpha-theta crossover and the occurrence of visualizations. *Journal of Neurotherapy, 4*(1), 29-42.

Naeser, M. A. (2014). Significant improvements in cognitive performance post-transcranial, red/near-infrared light-emitting diode treatments in chronic, mild traumatic brain injury: Open-protocol study. *Journal of Neurotrauma, 31*(11), 1008.

Nir, Y. (2017). Quality sleep is primary to mental and physical health: What happens when it is lacking? *Nature Medicine, 23,* 1474–1480.

Nishida, M., & Walker, M., (2007). Daytime naps, motor memory consolidation and regionally specific sleep spindles. *PLoS One, 2*(4), e341.

Norris, S. L., & Currieri, M. (1999). Performance enhancement training through neuro-feedback. In J. R. Evans & A. Arbarbanel (Eds.), *Introduction to quantitative EEG and neurofeedback* (pp. 223–240). San Diego, CA: Academic Press.

Nunez, P. L., Silberstein, R. B., Cadusch, P. J., Wijesinghe, R. S., Westdorp, A. F., & Srinivasan, R. (1994). A theoretical and experimental study of high resolution EEG based on surface Laplacians and cortical imaging. *Electroencephalography and Clinical Neurophysiology, 90*(1), 40–57.

Orndorff-Plunkett, F., Singh, F., Aragón, O. R., & Pineda, J. A. (2017). Assessing the effectiveness of neurofeedback training in the context of clinical and social neuroscience. *Brain Science, 7*(8), 95.

Othmer, S. (2017, July 1). *Protocol guide for neurofeedback clinicians.* EEG Institute.

Palva, S. and Palva, J. M. (2011). Functional roles of alpha-band phase synchronization in local and large-scale cortical networks. *Frontiers in Psychology, 2,* 204.

Palva, J. P., & Palva, S. (2012). Infra-slow fluctuations in electrophysiological recordings, blood-oxygenation-level-dependent signals, and psychophysical time series. *NeuroImage, 62*(4), 2201–2211.

Papp, L. A., Coplan, J., & Gorman, J. M. (1992). Neurobiology of anxiety. *Review of Psychiatry, 11*, 307–322.

Park, H. J., & Friston, K. (2013). *Structural and functional brain networks: From connections to cognition. Science 342*, 1238–1411.

Pascual-Marqui, R. D. (2002). Standardized low-resolution brain electromagnetic tomography (sLORETA): Technical details. *Methods and Findings in Experimental and Clinical Pharmacology, 24*(Suppl. D), 5–12.

Pease, B., & Pease, A. (2000). *Why men don't listen and women can't read maps.* New York: Broadway.

Pennfield, W. (1961). *Activation of the Record of Human Experience.* Ann R Coll Surg Engl. *29*(2): 77–84.

Peniston, E. G., & Kulkosky, P. J. (1991). Alpha-theta brainwave neurofeedback for Vietnam veterans with combat-related post-traumatic stress disorder. *Medical Psychotherapy, 4*, 1–14.

Peniston, E. G., & Kulkosky, P. J. (1999). Neurofeedback in the treatment of addictive disorders. In J. R. Evans & A. Arbarbanel (Eds.), *Introduction to quantitative EEG and neurofeedback* (pp. 157–179). San Diego, CA: Academic Press.

Perfetti, B., Moisello, C., Landsness, E. C., Kvint, S., Lanzafame, S., Onofrj, M., . . . Ghilardi, M. F. (2011). Modulation of gamma and theta spectral amplitude and phase synchronization is associated with the development of visuo-motor learning. *Journal of Neuroscience, 31*(41), 14810–14819.

Pert, C. B. (1997). *Molecules of emotion: The science behind mind-body medicine.* New York: Simon and Schuster.

Pinel, J. P. J., & Edwards, M. (1998). *A colorful introduction to the anatomy of the brain.* Needham Heights, MA: Allyn and Bacon.

Preis, S., Jancke, L., Schmitz-Hillebrecht, J., & Steinmetz, H. (1999). Child age and planum temporale asymmetry. *Brain and Cognition, 40*, 441–452.

Putnam, F. W. (1989). *Diagnosis and treatment of multiple personality disorder.* New York: Guilford.

Rajmohan, V., & Mohandas, E. (2007). The limbic system. *Indian Journal of Psychiatry, 49*(2), 132–139.

Ratey, J. J. (2001). *A user's guide to the brain: Perception, attention and the four theaters of the brain.* New York: Vintage.

Riedl, V., Utz, L., Castrillón, G., Grimmer, T., Rauschecker, J. P., Ploner, M., . . . Sorg, C. (2016). Metabolic connectivity mapping reveals effective connectivity in the resting human brain. *PNAS, 113*(2), 428–433.

Robbins, J. (2000. *A symphony in the brain.* New York: Atlantic Monthly Press.

Rossiter, T. (2002). Neurofeedback for AD/HD: A ratio feedback case study and tutorial. *Journal of Neurotherapy, 6*(3), 9–35.

Rowan, A. J., & Tolunsky, E. (2003). *Primer of EEG with a mini-atlas.* Boston: Butterworth-Heinemann.

Ruuskanen-Uoti, H., & Salmi, T. (1994). Epileptic seizure induced by a product marketed as a "brainwave synchronizer." *Neurology, 44,* 181.

Schlaug, G., Jäncke, L., Huang, Y., Staiger, J. F., & Steinmetz, H. (1995). Increased corpus callosum size in musicians. *Neuropsychologia, 33*(8), 1047–1055.

Schwartz, J., & Beyette, B. (1996). *Brain lock: Free yourself from obsessive-compulsive behavior.* New York: Regan.

Schwartz, M. S. (1995). Breathing therapies. In M. S. Schwartz (Ed.), *Biofeedback: A practitioner's guide* (2nd ed., pp. 525–559). New York: Guilford.

Scott, W. (2000, June). *Alpha/theta training.* Presented at EEG-Spectrum, Philadelphia.

Scott, W., Brod, T. M., Siderof, S., Kaiser, D., & Sagan, M. (2002, May). *Type specific EEG biofeedback improves residential substance abuse treatment.* Poster presentation at the meeting of the American Psychiatric Association, Philadelphia.

Severance, E. G., Gressitt, K. L., Stallings, C. R., Katsafanas, E., Schweinfurth, L. A., Savage, C. L., . . . Yolken, R. H. (2016). *Candida albicans* exposures, sex specificity and cognitive deficits in schizophrenia and bipolar disorder. *NPJ Schizophrenia, 2,* 16018.

Shaywitz, S. E., Shaywitz, B. A., Pugh, K. R., Fulbright, R. K., Constable, R. T., Mencl, W. E., . . . Gore, J. C. (1998). Functional disruption in the organization of the brain for reading in dyslexia. *Proceedings of the National Academy of Science USA, 95*(5), 2636–2641.

Sherlin, L. (2010, Winter). A historical introduction to LORETA. *NeuroConnections.*

Siever, D. (2003). Audio-visual entrainment: I. History and physiological mechanisms. *Biofeedback, 31*(2), 21–27.

Siever, D. (2004). Applying audio-visual entrainment technology for attention and learning, part III. *Biofeedback, 31*(4), 24–29.

Silk, T., Vance, A., Rinehart, N., Egan, G., O'Boyle, M., Bradshaw, J. L., & Cunnington, R. (2005). Fronto-parietal activation in attention-deficit hyperactivity disorder, combined type: Functional magnetic resonance imaging study. *British Journal of Psychiatry, 187,* 282–283.

Sills, F. (2001). *Craniosacral biodynamics: The breath of life, biodynamics, and fundamental skills.* Berkeley, CA: North Atlantic.

Simon, M., Schmidt, E. A., Kincses, W. E., Fritzsche, M., Bruns, A., Aufmuth, C., . . . Schrauf, M. (2011). EEG alpha spindle measures as indicators of driver fatigue under real traffic conditions. *Clinical Neurophysiology, 122*(6), 1168–1178.

Singer, T. (2016, March 29). Researchers investigate four promising new treatments for Lyme disease. *News@Northeastern.* Retrieved from https://news.northeastern.edu/2016/03/29/researchers-investigate-four-promising-new-treatments-for-lyme-disease/

Smith, D., & Bashir, U. et al. *Diffusion tensor imaging.* radiopaedia.org.

Smith, M. L., Collura, T. F., Ferrera, J., & de Vries, J. (2014). Infra-slow fluctuation training in clinical practice: A technical history. *NeuroRegulation, 1*(2), 187–207.

Soutar, R. (2004). *Linking the EEG of the anxious mind to behavior.* Workshop presented at the International Society for Neuronal Regulation, Ft. Lauderdale, FL.

Soutar, R., & Longo, R. (2011). *Doing neurofeedback: An introduction.* Miami: ISNR Research Foundation.

Spreng, R. N., & Grady, C. L. (2010). Patterns of brain activity supporting autobiographical memory, prospection, and theory of mind, and their relationship to the default mode network. *Journal of Cognitive Neuroscience, 22*(6), 1112–1123.

Springer, S. P., & Deutsch, G. (1998). *Left brain, right brain: Perspectives from cognitive neuroscience* (5th ed.). New York: W. H. Freeman.

Stampi, C., Stone, P., & Michirnori, A. (1995). A new quantitative method for assessing sleepiness: The alpha attenuation test. *Work Stress, 9,* 368–376.

Stokes, D. A., & Lappin, M. S. (2010). Neurofeedback and biofeedback with 37 migraineurs: A clinical outcome study. *Behavior and Brain Function, 6,* 9.

Striefel, S. (1999). Ethical, legal, and professional pitfalls associated with neurofeedback services. In J. R. Evans & A. Arbarbanel (Eds.), *Introduction to quantitative EEG and neurofeedback* (pp. 371–399). San Diego, CA: Academic Press.

Suwan, P., Akaramethathip, D., & Noipayak, P. (2011). Association between allergic sensitization and attention deficit hyperactivity disorder (ADHD). *Asian Pacific Journal of Allergy and Immunology, 29*(1), 57–65.

Taylor, J. F. (2014). *The survival guide for kids with ADHD.* Minneapolis: Free Spirit.

Thatcher, R.W., Northa, D., Bivera, C. (2005). EEG and intelligence: Relations between EEG coherence, EEG phase delay and power. *Clinical Neurophysiology, 116,* 2129–2141

Thatcher, R. W. (1999). EEG database-guided neurotherapy. In J. R. Evans & A. Arbarbanel (Eds.), *Introduction to quantitative EEG and neurofeedback* (pp. 29–64). San Diego, CA: Academic Press.

Toomim, H. (2002). Neurofeedback with hemoencephalography (HEG). *Explore!, 11*(1), 19–21.

Toomim, H., & Carmen, J. (1999). Hemoencephalography (HEG). *Biofeedback, 27*(4), 10–14.

Urdan, T. (2010). *Statistics in Plain English, Third Edition.* New York: Routledge.

U.S. Food and Drug Administration. (1994, August). Biofeedback devices—draft guidance for 510(k) content. www.fda.gov/cdrh/ode/143.html

van der Kolk, B. A., Hodgdon, H., Gapen, M., Musicaro, R., Suvak, M. K., Hamlin, Ed., & Spinazzola, J. (2016). A randomized controlled study of neurofeedback for chronic PTSD. *PLoS One.* https://doi.org/10.1371/journal.pone.0166752

van der Kolk, B. A., McFarlane, A. C., & Weisaeth, L. (1996). *Traumatic stress: The effects of overwhelming experience on mind, body, and society.* New York: Guilford.

Van Die, M. D., Burger, H. G., Teede, H. J., & Bone, K. M. (2013). Vitex agnus-castus extracts for female reproductive disorders: A systematic review of clinical trials. *Planta Medica, 79*(7), 562–575.

Visser, S.N., Danielson, M. L., Bitsko, R.H., Holbrook, J.R.,Kogan, M.D., Ghandour, R.M., Perou, R., Blumberg, S.J. (2014). Trends in the Parent-Report of Health Care Provider-Diagnosed and Medicated Attention-Deficit/Hyperactivity Disorder: United States, 2003–2011. *Journal of the American Academy of Child & Adolescent Psychiatry, 53*(1) p. 34-46.e2

Vogt, B. A., Finch, D. M., & Olson, C. R. (1992). Functional heterogeneity in cingulate cortex: The anterior executive and posterior evaluative regions. *Cerebral Cortex, 2*(6), 435–443.

Vossel, S., Geng, J. J., & Fink, G. R. (2014). Dorsal and ventral attention systems: Distinct neural circuits but collaborative roles. *Neuroscientist, 20*(2), 150–159.

Walker, J. E. (2011). QEEG-guided neurofeedback for recurrent migraine headaches. *Clinical EEG and NeuroScience, 42*(1).

Walker, J. E., & Lawson, R. (2013). FP02 beta training for drug-resistant depression—a new protocol that usually reduces depression and keeps it reduced. *Journal of Neurotherapy, 17,* 198–200.

Walker, J. E., Norman, C. A., & Weber, R. K. (2002). Impact of qEEG-guided coherence training for patients with mild closed head injury. *Journal of Neurotherapy, 6*(2), 31–43.

Walton, A. G. (2016, December 9). 7 ways sleep affects the brain (and what happens if it doesn't get enough). *Forbes.*

Wheeler, M. (2014, October 2). Memory loss associated with Alzheimer's reversed for first time. UCLA Newsroom. Retrieved from http://newsroom.ucla.edu/releases/memory-loss-associated-with-alzheimers-reversed-for-first-time

White, N. E. (1999). Theories of the effectiveness of alpha-theta training for multiple disorders. In J. R. Evans & A. Arbarbanel (Eds.), *Introduction to quantitative EEG and neurofeedback* (pp. 341–367). San Diego, CA: Academic Press.

Wolters, C., & Munck, J. C. (2007). Volume conduction. *Scholarpedia, 2*(3), 1738.

Wu, X. (2016). A triple network connectivity study of large-scale brain systems in cognitively normal APOE4 carriers. *Frontiers in Aging Neuroscience, 8,* 231.

Zhang, X., Kendrick, K. M., Zhou, H., Zhan, Y., & Feng, J. (2012, June 21). A computational study on altered theta-gamma coupling during learning and phase coding. *PLoS One.*

Index